THE
LIFE AND GLORIES
OF
ST. JOSEPH

THE
LIFE AND GLORIES
OF
ST. JOSEPH

HUSBAND OF MARY, FOSTER-FATHER OF JESUS, AND
PATRON OF THE UNIVERSAL CHURCH

GROUNDED ON THE DISSERTATIONS OF CANON ANTONIO VITALI,
FATHER JOSÉ MORENO, AND OTHER WRITERS

By

EDWARD HEALY THOMPSON, M.A.

Can we find such another man, that is full of the
spirit of God? . . . can I find one wiser and one like
unto thee? Thou shall be over my house and at the
commandment of thy mouth all the people shall obey.
—Gen. 41:38-40

TAN Books
An Imprint of Saint Benedict Press, LLC
Charlotte, North Carolina

"Spend your life in honouring St. Joseph, and your love and homage will never equal the love and homage paid to him by Mary; it will approach never so distantly to the obedience, the love, the homage paid to him for thirty years on earth by the Son of God. But in proportion as your heart grows towards him in the reverence and unbounded confidence of a son will you trace in your soul a more faithful copy of the Incarnate Word."—*Letter on Devotion to St. Joseph,* by Herbert, Bishop of Salford, 1877.

Originally published in 1888 by Burns & Oates, Limited, London, and M. H. Gill & Sons, Dublin. Republished by arrangement with Burns & Oates, Ltd.

Library of Congress Catalog Card Number: 80-53744

ISBN: 978-0-89555-161-0

Printed and bound in the United States of America

TAN Books
An Imprint of Saint Benedict Press, LLC
Charlotte, North Carolina
2013

Preface

THIS is a composite work, constructed with materials gathered from various quarters, principally from the dissertation of Don Antonio Vitali, Canon of the Basilica of San Lorenzo in Damaso at Rome, entitled *Vita e Glorie del Gran Patriarca S. Giuseppe, Sposo Purissimo di Maria, Padre Putativo di Gesù, e Patrono Potentissimo della Cattolica Chiesa*, 1883. To him, therefore, special acknowledgments are due, not only for the valuable contributions to the present work which his volume has supplied, but for the permission to make free use of the product of his labors. The early chapters, extending to the birth of Joseph, are, indeed, almost a literal translation of his work. Subsequently, his materials have been largely used, sometimes verbally, at other times only substantially, but with frequent omissions and retrenchments.

Much use has also been made of a Spanish work by P. Joséf Moreno, of the Minor Clergy of the House of the Holy Spirit at Seville, entitled *Discursos sobre las Virtudes y Privilegios de S. Joséf,* 1788. It professes to be taken from the French; but, if the idea or the groundwork of the compilation be as represented, its genius and spirit are indubitably Spanish; being characterized throughout by that gravity, solidity, and depth which so especially distinguishes the theologians of Spain. To this work, which is both highly instructive and eminently suggestive, the present writer is indebted, not only for large portions of several chapters of the book, but for eight of the more important among them, including those

v

on the Subjection of Jesus, the Paternity and Offices of Joseph, his Interior Life, and the Glory of his Soul and Body in Heaven; all which are especially calculated to deepen our conceptions of the dignity and sanctity of the great Patriarch. But here, as generally throughout the volume, he has not always adopted the author's language or the form in which he expresses himself, but has rather digested and developed the truths he has propounded.

Occasional recourse has likewise been had to the *Vita di S. Giuseppe* by the Rev. Vincenzo de Vit, 1868, which is valuable for the general justness and discrimination of its views.

Passages from the visions and revelations of saints and holy contemplatives—St. Bridget, Sister Maria de Agreda, and others—have been interwoven with the narrative, simply in the way of illustration, and not as being invested with authority, except in the sense in which, after due examination, they have been favored with ecclesiastical approval: namely, as containing nothing contrary to faith and morals, and affording pious and profitable helps to meditation.

Finally, observations and reflections have been introduced as occasion offered which were suggested by various authors whose works have been consulted, or which occurred to the writer's own mind from consideration of the materials before him.

It is no uncommon idea, even among Catholics, that the devotion paid to St. Joseph and the lofty estimate of his prerogatives now prevailing in the Church are innovations of comparatively modern date, and that they have no precedent or sanction in antiquity. But this is far from being the case. In the writings of the ancient Fathers are to be found, not only what may be called prolific germs, but also positive and explicit statements of doctrine, which sufficiently show how deep in the consciousness of the Church lay the belief of Joseph's exalted dignity and sanctity, and how definite a shape it had

assumed even in the early ages. The devotion paid to
him has, it is true, been much more distinctly formulated in later centuries, when his place in the celestial
hierarchy came to be more fully recognized; but from
the first this great Saint had a peculiar attraction for
many holy and gifted souls, who regarded him with singular veneration and affection, as the citations given
abundantly testify.

The Church brings out of her treasury things both
old and new, according as the exigencies of the time
require; and this is especially true of the devotions which
have arisen from age to age and have received her ready
sanction, or, rather, have been joyfully welcomed and
embraced as the fulfillment of her heart's desire. Thus,
the devotion to Our Blessed Lady, though dating from
Apostolic times, received a powerful impulse at the Council of Ephesus, where the dogma of the Divine Maternity was proclaimed in opposition to the heresy of
Nestorius; and, among other instances, may be mentioned the ardent devotion to the Holy Places, which
resulted in the Crusades; the public and solemn adoration of the Blessed Sacrament, which found its satisfaction in the Feast of Corpus Christi and the Rite of
Benediction; and, at later epochs, the devotion to the
Sacred Heart and to the several mysteries of the Passion in all their pathetic details: the Five Wounds, the
Precious Blood, etc.; and, in our own days, renewed devotion to the Adorable Face of Our Lord. But what is most
remarkable about the devotion to St. Joseph is that,
after centuries of obscurity and apparent oblivion, it
received a sudden and mighty impulse, which carried
it, as it were, at a bound into the hearts of the Christian populations and disseminated and planted it in
every clime. Or, rather, we may say that the breath of
God's Holy Spirit quickened into life and energy the
devotion which lay, as it were, dormant and passive in
the hearts of the faithful, and rapidly stirred the smol-
dering fire into a blaze. Some account of this extraordinary movement and expansion is given in the

concluding chapters of the work.

If to some it may be matter of surprise that saints and doctors should have written and discoursed so largely and so eloquently respecting one of whom it might appear scant notice is taken in the Gospels, and of whom no single word spoken by him has been recorded; that a voluminous theology should have grouped itself around him; and that he should have been proposed by the Holy See to the veneration and devotion of the faithful as Patron and Guardian of the Universal Church—this can only be because they have never sufficiently considered what was Joseph's position in the economy of redemption; and it may safely be affirmed that the more they realize that position, and the more they study him in his several aspects, as presented in Holy Writ, the more will his grandeurs open upon them and the deeper and the higher will be their thoughts about him. For who, in fact, was St. Joseph? And what were the offices he filled, and the privileges he enjoyed? He was predestined to be the virgin spouse of the Virgin Mother of the Son of God, and to be His and her guardian and protector; he was the chosen minister of the counsels of the Most High in the mystery of the Incarnation; he was for years the habitual companion both of Mary and of Jesus; he bore the Divine Child constantly in his arms, lovingly caressed Him, and received His caresses in return; to him, as to His Blessed Mother, Jesus was subject in the house and workshop of Nazareth; he was as a father and a tutor to Him; he was the daily witness of His hidden life, and heard the sacred words that fell from His lips, all through His boyhood, youth, and early manhood; and he had the unspeakable blessedness of dying in His embrace. But further: with this sublime vocation and these incomparable privileges the graces and virtues of Joseph fully corresponded; his merits were commensurate with his dignity; and therefore it is that he ranks next to Mary in the Court of Heaven and is seated in glory so nigh unto the throne of the Incarnate Word.

But again: there is another and a fundamental Christian doctrine, the disregard or imperfect recognition of which lies at the root of the difficulty entertained respecting the position and power of Joseph in Heaven, as also respecting that of his Immaculate Spouse. It is this— that Our Blessed Lord is as truly Man now that He is seated in Heaven at the right hand of the Father as He was when He trod the streets of Jerusalem and the ways of Galilee. The Incarnate God, enthroned in His majesty on high, is still our Brother-Man. Nothing, indeed, is more remarkable than Our Lord's solicitude (so to say) after He had risen from the dead, not only to prove His identity to His disciples, but to convince them of His possession of the full attributes of man. "See My hands and feet," He said, "that it is I Myself"; nay more: "handle and see; for a spirit hath not flesh and bones, as you see Me to have"; and then He took and ate before them. (*Luke* 24:39, 42, 43). But not only so: it seemed as though He wished to impress upon them the fact that the relationship which He had assumed with men remained, not merely unbroken, but, as it were, sealed and enhanced, now that He was about to ascend into the Heaven of Heavens. The words He spoke to St. Mary Magdalen immediately after His Resurrection: "Go to My *brethren,* and say to them, I ascend to My Father and to your Father, to My God and your God" (*John* 20:17)—words differing in their solemn emphasis and expression from any which He had heretofore used—seem to have been uttered to this end. Thus, being ever perfect Man as well as perfect God, as He had a mother and a foster-father on earth, so now in Heaven Mary is still His mother and Joseph retains the honored name of father. The ties of their human relationship still endure, and will endure forever. Hence the dignity of Joseph and the power of his intercession. His Foster-Child is the Almighty and Adorable God.

Many books of devotion to St. Joseph have been written in many languages; indeed, the literature dedicated to him may be said to form a library of itself. The object of the present work is, not only to increase and stimulate that devotion, but to exhibit the theological basis on which it rests, and to show how great is the amount of authority and how strong are the intrinsic reasons for holding that a profound and solid reality of heavenly origin underlies the dignity and office to which the husband of Mary and foster-father of Jesus was elected. The chapters on the Paternity and Offices of Joseph, which are drawn (as has been said) from P. Moreno's work, may be particularly mentioned as having been composed with this intention.

And now, humbly kneeling at the feet of this great Patriarch and most powerful Saint, solitary in his grandeur as in his endowments, the writer implores his blessing on a work devoted to his honor; not only for the exaltation of that honor among men, but for the glory of his Immaculate Spouse, and, supremely, for the glory of Him the companion and guardian of whose Childhood he was ordained to be, and to whom, indeed, he owes his incomparable dignity and his very being— the Eternal Son of the Eternal Father made Man for us and for our salvation.

For the satisfaction of the reader it is desirable to state that the work has been carefully revised by a most competent theologian in its progress through the press.

CHELTENHAM,
Feast of the Patronage of St. Joseph, 1888

Contents

Chapter IV.

JOSEPH PREFIGURED IN HIS VIRTUES, AND FORESHADOWED IN VARIOUS OTHER WAYS.

Chapter V.

JOSEPH OF A MOST NOBLE AND ROYAL LINEAGE.

Chapter VI.

JOSEPH THE SON OF JACOB AND THE SON OF HELI.

Chapter VII.

JOSEPH SANCTIFIED BEFORE HIS BIRTH.

Chapter XXXI.

THE ADORATION OF THE SHEPHERDS. THE CIRCUMCISION.

Chapter XXXII.

THE ADORATION OF THE MAGI.

Chapter XXXIII.

PURIFICATION OF THE BLESSED VIRGIN AND PRESENTATION OF JESUS IN THE TEMPLE.

Chapter XLII.
JOSEPH'S INTERIOR LIFE OF PRAYER AND CONTEMPLATION.

Chapter XLIII.
JOSEPH'S SINGULAR FAITH AND SUPERNATURAL WISDOM.

Chapter XLIV.
JOSEPH'S LOVE AND LIFE OF BLISS.

Chapter I

Joseph Included in the
Decree of the Incarnation.

T O DESCRIBE the life and the glories of Joseph
is to describe at the same time the life of Jesus
and the glories of Mary; for Jesus, Mary, and
Joseph are so intimately united, that it is impossible
to speak of one without treating of the others. These
three dear names—Jesus, Mary, Joseph—form that
triple heavenly alliance which can never be broken. He,
therefore, who undertakes to narrate the life of Joseph
is under the happy necessity of narrating at the same
time, in large measure, the life of Jesus and Mary. The
reader will never object to this, since, after God, Jesus,
Mary, and Joseph are the sweetest and sublimest objects
with which our minds and hearts can be filled; they
are the three powerful advocates of our cause, the three
guiding stars of our salvation. But, in order clearly to
understand the greatness of Joseph, we must look very
far back; for his greatness did not begin with his birth,
neither did it begin with his espousals to Mary. Its origin is far more remote, and must be sought, not in time,
but in eternity; it began with his predestination.

Predestination, according to St. Thomas Aquinas, is
the divine preordination from eternity of those things
which, by divine grace, are to be accomplished in time.[1]
Now, the most compassionate Lord God had, in the
admirable dispositions of His Providence, from all eter-

---

1. P. iii. q. xxiv. a. 1.

nity, preordained the ineffable mystery of the Divine Incarnation to repair the fall of Adam and save his descendants from eternal ruin. This mystery "hidden from ages," as the Apostle says (*Col.* 1:26), was to be revealed in the fullness of time. The Eternal Word was to assume human flesh, and, after a life full of sufferings, was to offer Himself as a voluntary victim to die upon a cross, in order, as an innocent Lamb, to expiate the sins of all mankind. This mystery, then, was to be accomplished in Jesus; and, therefore, Jesus, the Saviour of all, was, according to the Apostle Paul, "predestinated the Son of God in power" (*Rom.* 1:4); and, as St. Augustine explains, it was predestined that Jesus, who according to the flesh was the Son of David, was in truth to be the Son of God, seeing that it was preordained that human nature was one day to subsist in the Eternal Person of the Word along with the Divine Nature, in order that the sufferings of Jesus might have an infinite value to satisfy worthily the Divine Justice. And this is what is called the eternal decree of the Divine Incarnation.

Now, in this decree is comprehended, not only the mystery itself of the Divine Incarnation, but also the mode and order in which this mystery was to be accomplished, and, consequently, those persons who were principally and more immediately to have a part in it; for, according to the doctrine of the Angelic Doctor, the eternal predestination includes, not only what is to be accomplished in time, but likewise the mode and order according to which it is to be so accomplished.[2] And the mode and order predestined by God in the Incarnation of His Divine Son was this: that the Most Sacred Humanity of Jesus Christ was to be taken, but without sin, from that same human nature which had sinned in Adam: that It was to descend from the blood of Abraham, to be of the tribe of Juda and the race of David, and that the Body of Jesus was to be formed by the

---

2. *Summa,* p. iii. q. xxiv. a. 4.

power of the Holy Ghost in the pure womb of an immaculate virgin. This elect virgin is Mary; and therefore Mary, after Jesus, was immediately comprised in the decree of the Divine Incarnation, and from eternity predestined to be the most august Mother of the Son of God. "The Virgin," says the great doctor Suarez, "could not be disjoined from her Son in the Divine election." The Church herself puts into the mouth of the Virgin these words of the Divine Wisdom: "I was preordained from eternity." (*Prov.* 8:23). Mary was truly a predetermined end of the eternal counsel, and St. Augustine calls her "the work of eternal counsel."

But, in order to conceal this mystery of love from the world until the appointed time had come, and to safeguard at the same time the reputation of the Virgin Mother and the honor of the Divine Son, God willed that Mary by a marriage altogether heavenly should be espoused to the humblest, the purest, and the holiest of the royal race of David, one therefore expressly predestined for this end; a virgin spouse for the Virgin Mother, who at the same time should be in the place of a father to the Divine Son. In the Divine mind Joseph was the one chosen from amongst all others. Joseph held the first place. Joseph was predestined to this office. True, from the tribe of Juda, from the family of David, great patriarchs were to arise, famous leaders of the people, most noble kings; but God did not choose any of these. He chose Joseph alone. Joseph was the beloved one. Joseph was specially preordained to become one day the happy spouse of Mary and the foster-father of Jesus. "As Mary," says Echius, the famous opponent of Luther, "was from eternity predestined to be the mother of the Son of God; so also was Joseph elected to be the guardian and protector of Jesus and of Mary."[3]

Thus Joseph was, after Mary, comprehended in the very decree of the Incarnation, and, after Mary, was called to have an integral part, as it were, in this inef-

---

3. *Sermo de S. Joseph.*

fable mystery. It is easy to perceive how much honor hence redounds to Joseph; for if, next to the mystery of the Most Holy Trinity, the mystery of the Divine Incarnation is the essential foundation of the Christian Faith, who can fail to see that to be included in the eternal decree of so admirable a mystery, into which the angels themselves "desire to look" (*1 Ptr.* 1:12), is an incomparable glory to this great saint? We must always, therefore, bear well in mind this singular destination of Joseph, because this is truly the ground of all his greatness. This is the basis upon which all his glories are raised. Whoever thoroughly realizes the fact of this preordination will no longer marvel at God's predilection for Joseph, and at seeing him so highly privileged and exalted to be the guardian and patron of the Universal Church.

Chapter II

Joseph Included in the Order of the Hypostatic Union.

WHATEVER God disposes is disposed in a marvellous and perfect order. Wherefore the Church which Jesus came to found on earth imitates the Heavenly Sion. As in Heaven there are angelical hierarchies, and in these hierarchies there are divers orders, so also on earth there is a hierarchy of grace, and in that hierarchy are included various orders, or ministries, which, according to the Angelic Doctor, St. Thomas, excel each other in proportion to their approximation to God.[1] The highest of all these orders, whether angelic or human, is the order of the Hypostatic Union, in which is Christ Jesus, God and Man. By the Hypostatic Union is meant that the Eternal Son of God, in His Incarnation, assumed human nature, and united it to Himself in Personal unity; in other words, that in the one Divine Person of Jesus Christ, the two Natures, the Divine Nature and the Human Nature, ever distinct in themselves, became inseparably and eternally united. If a wonderful order is displayed in all the works of nature, an order supremely perfect is displayed in all the works of grace, especially in the great work of the Incarnation. Among these orders of grace some precede the mystery of the Incarnation, others follow it. Among those which precede it the most remote is the order of the Patriarchs,

1. *Summa,* p. i. q. cvii. a. 6.

5

chosen to prepare the progenitors of Jesus down to St.
Joachim and St. Anne. To some of these, as to Abraham and to David, it was expressly revealed that of
their blood and of their family the Saviour of men should
be born into the world. The next is the Levitical and
sacerdotal order, which was preordained by God to figure in all its rites the Priesthood of Jesus, His Church,
His Sacraments, the Bloody Sacrifice of the Cross, and
the Unbloody Sacrifice of the Altar. The third is that
of the Prophets, destined to foretell and announce to
the world, so many centuries before the coming of Jesus,
His Birth of a Virgin, His country, the place of His
Nativity, His flight into Egypt, His Apostles, His preaching, His miracles, His Passion, His death, His Resurrection, His glorious Ascension into Heaven. Greater
than all these Prophets was John the Baptist, because
destined and preordained to be the immediate Precursor of Christ, and to point to Him as being actually
present on the earth; whence Jesus Himself affirmed
that among those who were born of woman there was
not a greater prophet than John the Baptist. (*Luke*
7:28). These are the orders which under the Old Law
preceded Jesus.

Others succeeded Him; and these are the various
orders or ministries of Holy Church, which form the
ecclesiastical hierarchy, beginning with the Apostles.
The Apostles were to render to the whole earth and
to all ages their solemn testimony to the Divinity of
Jesus Christ; they were to announce to all His doctrine, His Law, His Sacraments; they were to found
and to spread His Church throughout the world, so
that all might attain to salvation. And, as the Apostolic order was nearer than any other to Jesus, even
so, says the Angelic Doctor, did the Apostles receive
greater grace than any saints in the other orders[2] of
the Church. Of the inferior orders we need not here
speak. Now, above all these orders rises supreme the

---

2. *In Epistolam ad Ephes.* i. 8.

order of the Hypostatic Union. All the other orders, comprising even the angelic, are subordinate and subject to it; for this reason, that Jesus is the beginning, the author, and the head of this order, and on Jesus, as Sovereign Prince, depends every hierarchy, every sacred princedom in Heaven and on earth, since Jesus, as the Apostle says, is the end of the whole law. (*Rom.* 10:4). Jesus is the chief cornerstone (*Eph.* 2:20) upon which rests the whole sacred edifice of the Church. Jesus, according to the Prophet Isaias, is set up as an ensign to the people (*Is.* 11:10, 12), the desire of all nations, the centre of universal hope. Jesus is the sole and true source of salvation to all men. By faith in Him who was to come all were saved who lived justly from Adam until His day; and all those who have lived and shall live justly since His coming have been and shall be saved by Him alone. In Him alone, from Him alone, and through Him alone, is truth, salvation, and life; so that, even as the planets in the firmament revolve round the sun, receiving from it light, heat, and power, so also around Jesus, the Eternal Sun of Justice, all the various orders of grace circle, from Him alone receiving light, virtue, and power to fulfill faithfully the holy offices to which they are ordained; and so much the greater or the less grace and dignity do they receive as they are more or less approximated in their ministry to Jesus, the author of grace, just as one who is nearer to the fire participates more largely in its heat. It is clear, then, that the order of the Hypostatic Union transcends and surpasses the other subaltern orders, even as the sun transcends the inferior stars.

Now, Joseph by divine predestination was placed in this sovereign order. Three only composed it—Jesus, Mary, Joseph. Jesus is true God and true Man; Mary is true mother of God and mother of men; Joseph is true spouse of Mary and putative father of Jesus. Jesus is the principal subject of the Incarnation, and the author of the Redemption of the world; Mary is the immediate co-operatrix and, so to say, the executrix of the

Incarnation itself; Joseph, the faithful depositary of these two most precious pledges, was to provide that this sublime mystery of the Incarnation and Redemption should be brought about with the greatest possible congruity, so that the honor of the mother and of the God-Man, her Son, should remain intact.

That Joseph should be comprised in this supreme order is not a mere devout opinion or the fruit of pious meditation; it is a sure decision of the soundest theology. Suarez, that eminent theologian, after having spoken of the order of the Apostles, upon which he said the greatest grace was conferred, goes on to say: "There are other ministries appertaining to the order of the Hypostatic Union, which in its kind is more perfect, as we affirmed of the dignity of the Mother of God, and in this order is constituted the ministry of St. Joseph; and, although it be in the lowest grade of it, nevertheless, in this respect, it surpasses all others, because it exists in a superior order."[1] Thus spoke Suarez, the learned theologian of Granada, about three hundred years ago, when the opinion of the faithful respecting St. Joseph and the devotion due to him had not been so openly and generally displayed.

But the doctors who followed spoke still more clearly. Giovanni di Cartagena, contemporary of Bellarmine and Baronius, and very dear to Pope Pius V for his piety and science, out of the numerous learned homilies which he wrote, devoted thirteen to the praises of Joseph. After having spoken of the Apostolic order, he passes on to treat of the order of the Hypostatic Union, and says that in its kind it is more perfect than the other, and that in this order the first place is held by the Humanity of Christ, which is immediately united to the Person of the Word; the second place is held by the Blessed Virgin, who conceived and brought forth the Incarnate Word; the third place is held by St. Joseph, to whom was committed by God the special care, never

---

3. Tom. ii. disp. viii. sec. 1.

given to any other, of feeding, nursing, educating, and protecting a God-made-man![4] After Cartagena comes P. Giuseppe Antonio Patrignani, highly praised also by Benedict XIV, who, almost two centuries ago, wrote thus of St. Joseph: "He, as constituted head of the Family immediately belonging to the service of a God-Man, transcends in dignity all the other saints; wherefore he is happily established in an order which is superior to all the other orders in the Church."[5]

We might adduce other Doctors of high authority, but we will proceed to consider some of the legitimate consequences which flow from this doctrine.

1. It is an exceeding honor to Joseph to be comprised in the same order wherein are Jesus Himself, the Son of God, the King of kings, and Mary, Mother of God and Queen of the universe, to be united with them in the closest relations, and enjoy their most entire confidence. The nobles of the earth deem themselves to be highly honored in being brought into near association with monarchs of renown, holding the foremost places in their courts, and being the most trusted in their councils. What, then, shall we say of Joseph, who, placed in the order of the Hypostatic Union, was destined by God, not only to be the first in His court and the closest in His confidence, but even to be the reputed father of the King of kings; to be, not only the confidential friend, but the very spouse of the most exalted of all the empresses in the universe? Next to the Divine Maternity, no honor in the world is comparable with this.

2. To be comprised in the order of the Hypostatic Union implies being, after Jesus and Mary, superior to all the other Saints, both of the Old and the New Testament; and the reason is clear: for, this order being superior to all the other orders in the Church, it follows that whosoever has a place in this order, albeit in its lowest grade, as Joseph has, ranks before all who are even in the highest grade of a lower order, such as that

---

4. Lib. iv. Hom. viii.
5. *Il Divoto di S. Giuseppe,* Novena, Gior. vi.

of the Apostles, which is the most eminent among them.

3. It follows that Joseph is superior, not in nature, but in dignity, to the angels themselves, since the orders of angels are subject to the order of the Hypostatic Union, subject to Jesus, their King and their Head, subject to Mary, their Queen; hence, as the Apostle declares, when the Eternal Father sent His Divine Son upon earth He commanded all the angels to adore Him. (*Heb.* 1:6). And on account of Jesus the angels became subject also to Mary and to Joseph: thus we find them hastening gladly to serve them, to warn them, to console them; and were they not sent expressly from Heaven to act as attendants on Joseph, at one time to assure him that his Spouse has conceived the Son of God Himself; at another to make known to him the plot of Herod, so that he might place the Virgin and her Divine Son in safety by flying into Egypt; and, again, to announce to him that now he may joyfully return into the land of Israel? (*Matt.* 1:20, 21; 2:13, 19, 20).

4. We conclude that Joseph was comprehended in this order because he was truly the head and guardian of this Divine Family. To rule and govern this august family belonged of right to Jesus, who was God. Mary and Joseph, exalted as they were in dignity, were, nevertheless, only creatures; but Jesus willed to give an example of the most perfect humility. It was His Will to magnify our saint, and to concede to him this high glory, making him the head and guardian of His family; so that Joseph had rule and authority over the Son of God Himself and over the very Mother of the Son of God. And Joseph, being thus destined to be the head and guardian of Jesus, the head and guardian of Mary, became at the same time the patron and guardian of the Church, which is the spouse of Jesus and, in a manner, the daughter of Mary. Whence Pius IX, of blessed memory, in proclaiming Joseph Patron of the Church, did not so much confer a new title of honor upon him as affirm and declare this his most ancient prerogative, which had not before been so expressly promulgated by Holy Church.

5. It follows that Joseph was comprised in that order and in that family by the highest representation which it is possible to conceive, inasmuch as he was made the very representative of the Divine Father, who alone has the right to call Jesus His Son, having begotten Him from all eternity; and yet that same God, who by the mouth of Isaias (*Is.* 42:8) protested that He would never give His glory to another, that God who, in communicating to the Word and to the Holy Spirit His Divine essence, does not in any wise communicate to them His Divine paternity, was so generous to Joseph as to concede to him His glory, and communicate to him His name and His paternity; not actually, for that was impossible, but so that he should be in His place and stead, and should be called the father of Him who was the Divine Word, and that the Word Himself should call Joseph by the sweet name of father, so that he might with true joy appropriate to himself that passage in Holy Scripture: "I will be to Him a father and He shall be to me a son." (*Heb.* 1:5). Herein we see manifested the great love of the Three Persons of the Blessed Trinity for our saint and the confidence They reposed in him; for the Eternal Father committed wholly into his charge His well-beloved Son; the Divine Son delivered Himself entirely to his care and to his will; the Holy Spirit consigned and committed to him His most immaculate Spouse; so that this Holy Family, of which Joseph became the head, was another Triad on earth, a resplendent image of the Most Holy Triad in Heaven, the Ever-Blessed Trinity: Joseph representing the Eternal Father, Jesus representing and being in very truth the Eternal Word, and Mary representing the Eternal Love, the Holy Spirit. This thought is borrowed from the new Doctor of the Church, St. Francis de Sales. "We may say"—these are his words—"that the Holy Family was a Trinity on Earth, which in a certain way represented the Heavenly Trinity Itself."[6]

---

7. *Entretien,* xix.

6. Finally, it follows that Joseph, in that he was comprised in that sublime order, superior to that of all the other saints, must as a natural consequence have been predestined to receive greater gifts and graces than all the other saints, that he might be made worthy to be so near to Jesus and Mary, and fitted to discharge most faithfully those high ministries to which he was elected. Hence the pious Bernardine de Bustis makes this bold assertion: "Since Joseph was to be the guardian, companion, and ruler of the Most Blessed Virgin and of the Child Jesus, is it possible to conceive that God could have made a mistake in the choice of him? Or that He could have permitted him to be deficient in any respect? Or could have failed to make him most perfect? The very idea would be the grossest of errors. When God selects any one to perform some great work He bestows upon him every virtue needful for its accomplishment."[7]

Let us rejoice, then, with our most loving Patriarch that he has been exalted to so sublime an order, and has obtained such grace, power, and dignity as none other, after Jesus and Mary, has ever received, to the glory of God, who made him so great, and for our profit and that of the whole Church.

---

7. *Mariale,* Sermo xii.

Chapter III

Joseph Prefigured in Holy Scripture as to His Name,
His Life and His Glory.

WE HAVE undertaken to speak, not only of the
life, but of the glories of St. Joseph; it behooves
us, therefore, to exhibit the glory that accrued
to him in having been prefigured in Holy Scripture.
Nor is this a most signal glory only; it is also a manifest sign of that great love and especial regard which
God had for him from all eternity. They are greatly
mistaken who suppose, and indeed complain, that, considering how great a personage Joseph was, so little is
said of him in Holy Writ. For, even in the literal and
historical sense, there is sufficient mention of him in
the Holy Gospels to make us apprehend his exalted
dignity; while, prophetically speaking, he is so clearly
foreshadowed in the Old Testament as to make it abundantly evident that it pleased God to present him to
the world many centuries before he was born.

In the first place, there can be no manner of doubt
that God designed to give an exact and elaborate figure of our saint in the person of the ancient patriarch
Joseph, the son of Jacob. Nor let it be objected that,
according to the Fathers, that ancient patriarch was a
true type and figure of our Divine Redeemer, and therefore that he cannot be at the same time a type and figure of our saint; for in Holy Scripture, dictated as it
was by the infinite wisdom of God and containing man-
ifold meanings, it often happens that one and the same

13

thing or person is a type or figure of several things or
persons; or the same individual may, under one aspect
or in one action, represent one person, and, under
another aspect and in another action, represent a different person; or, again, under the one literal sense of
a passage are often contained various mystical and spiritual senses: thus, for instance, Jerusalem in the literal sense is the capital city of the Hebrew people,
where was the Holy Temple; allegorically it is the Holy
Catholic Church; in a tropological and moral sense it
is the soul of the Christian; in an anagogical sense it
is Paradise. So it is very true that the ancient Joseph
was in many events of his life a type and figure of
Jesus, especially when he was sent by his father in
search of his brethren, and they plotted his death; when
he was sold for a sum of money to a band of barbar-
ians; when he was falsely accused and made no defense,
but suffered the punishment due to the accuser; when
he was kept in bonds between two criminals, and foretold death to the one and glory to the other; when he
supplied food to those who had sought to compass his
death; and, finally, when he received the name of "saviour of the world." (*Gen.* 41:45). But it is also true that
in other points this ancient patriarch most clearly prefigured our saint.

For this opinion we have the express authority of
St. John Chrysostom, St. Ambrose, St. Augustine,
St. Bernard, St. Bonaventura, St. Bernardine of Siena,
and, to descend to more recent times, that of the two
new Doctors of the Church, St. Francis de Sales and
St. Alphonsus Liguori; and, again, of the solemn decree
of the Holy See wherein Joseph was declared Patron
of the Universal Church.[1]

The ancient Joseph, then, prefigured our Joseph in
his very name. "Remember," says St. Bernard, "the
ancient patriarch who was sold into Egypt, and know

---

1. "Quemadmodum Deus Josephum illum a Jacob Patriarcha progenitum praepositum
constituerat universae terrae AEgypti . . . ita temporum plenitudine adventante, alium
selegit Josephum, cujus ille primus typum gesserat."—*Decr. S. Rit. die* 8. *Dec.*, 1870.

that that man (Joseph) not only inherited his name but possessed, moreover, his chastity, his innocency, and his grace;"[2] nay, he inherited not only his name but the import and the substance of that name in a hundred-fold greater measure. Joseph in the Hebrew language signifies *increase;* hence the dying father of the ancient Joseph, when bestowing upon him the fullness of his benediction, said, "Joseph is a growing son; a growing son" (*Gen.* 49:22); meaning thereby, not only that his son Joseph himself increased in wisdom, in power, and glory, but that he increased for his brethren and his children, obtaining for them rich goods and possessions in the land of Gessen. But this double increase was far more verified in the second Joseph; first, by his own daily increase in the fullness of grace and in the Divine favor, and then by augmenting for us, his children and his brethren, the means of salvation, obtaining for us from God a continual increase of graces and benefits towards the attainment of our eternal inheritance.

The first Joseph was son of the patriarch Jacob, and the second Joseph was the son of another holy patriarch, Jacob, so that he resembled our saint not only in his own name but in that of his father; and the mother of the ancient Joseph, the beautiful Rachel, was buried near Bethlehem, whence sprang the second Joseph and where the Divine Redeemer was to be born. And even as at the birth of the first Joseph the servitude of Jacob to Laban was about to cease, and the way began to be opened for his return to his country, so at the birth of the second Joseph began to appear, as it were, the dawn of that day when the slavery of sin would be removed and the way re-opened to the blessed home of Paradise.

As the ancient Joseph grew in years he was of all his brethren the most gracious in manners, the most innocent and pure in his conduct. His father loved him with a special affection in preference to all his other sons, and, as a proof of his love, caused to be made for

---

2. *Super Missus est.* Hom. ii.

him a beautiful garment richly embroidered in various colors; by which it is signified that our Joseph should grow in grace and sanctity surpassing that of all the angels and saints, save Mary alone, and should be beloved above all by God, and by Him be clothed with habits of the most heroic virtues, so as to become an object of singular veneration and pre-eminently glorious among all the Blessed who have attained to glory. This was shown to the ancient patriarch in a marvellous vision, wherein it seemed to him that he and his brethren at harvest-time were binding their sheaves, and his sheaf stood erect, while those of his brethren which surrounded it bowed themselves down as if to adore it. In the literal sense this vision was fulfilled when, during the seven years of famine, his brethren came to him for bread, signified by those sheaves of wheat, and did him homage as the Viceroy of Egypt; but in the mystical sense it was accomplished in the second Joseph. The field in which he is found with his brethren is the Church; the sheaves of wheat are the accumulated merits, the fruits of grace. The foremost in gathering and binding full sheaves of holy works and heroic virtues in this great field was, after Mary, to be Joseph. The first who should follow him would also collect their sheaves, but these would never equal Joseph's sheaf, which would stand rich and glorious above them all; and, recognizing therein his superiority in merits and greatness, all would bow before him, beholding in him the reputed father of Jesus, the husband of Mary, the exalted patron of the Universal Church.

His glory and dignity were still more manifested in another admirable vision which the ancient patriarch saw, when he seemed to behold the sun, the moon, and eleven stars descend to adore him. This vision was fulfilled according to the letter when his father and his eleven brethren with their families came into Egypt to do homage to him on his throne; but more truly in a spiritual sense was it accomplished in our Joseph when, in Egypt, in Nazareth, in Jerusalem, he beheld Jesus, who is the Sun of Justice, "subject" (*Luke* 2:51) to him; his immaculate Spouse, Mary, who is fair as the moon, yielding him obedience; and now in Heaven beholds the Apostles and Saints all doing him homage and paying him the profoundest veneration. Now, if such bright stars do reverence to Joseph, what homage, what veneration, do not we owe to him, miserable little lamps as we are!

As the ancient Joseph became the victim of his brethren's envy and was led as a slave into Egypt, so our Joseph, through Herod's envy, was forced to become an exile in Egypt, flying thither with his greatest treasure, Jesus, and his most holy Spouse. And, as the former found grace with Putiphar, chief captain of Pharao's army, even to being made steward of his household, and set as governor over his whole family to order all things at his pleasure, even so the latter found grace with Jesus, his Lord, was constituted His minister-general, and promoted to the government, tutelage, and patronage both of the Holy Family and of the House of the Lord, which is His Church. The first Joseph in the house of Putiphar gave a signal proof of heroic chastity; and yet he was consigned for some time to the obscurity of a dungeon and was almost forgotten. The second Joseph gave a far more sublime example of angelic virginity, espoused as he was to the purest of all virgins; nevertheless, in order that the Divinity of Jesus and the Virginity of Mary might first be displayed in all their incomparable splendor, he chose to remain for some time hidden and almost forgotten in the Catholic Church.

While the first (says St. Bernard) receives from God intelligence in the interpretation of dreams, to the second He gives both the knowledge and the participation of heavenly mysteries. The former passed from the obscurity of a prison to the splendors of a court; the latter passed from the sorrows of exile to the celestial mansions, with the truly regal dignity of reputed father of the King of kings, spouse of the Queen of Heaven, and most powerful patron of the Universal Church. The exaltation of the ancient Joseph to the highest rank in the court of the king of Egypt could not more perfectly figure the elevation of our Joseph to the loftiest seats in the House of the Lord and the Court of Heaven. See how Pharao, having recognized the wisdom of Joseph in the true interpretation of his dreams, joyfully exclaims: "Can I find one wiser and one like unto thee? Thou shalt be over my house, and at the commandment of thy mouth all the people shall obey. Behold I have appointed thee over the whole land of Egypt." (*Gen.* 41:39-41). Then he took his ring from his own hand and placed it on Joseph's, and arrayed him in a robe of silk, and put a chain of gold about his neck, and made him go up into his second chariot, while a crier proclaimed that all should bow the knee before him, and acknowledge him as Governor of Egypt. Here, then, is an express figure of the second Joseph, when he was constituted by God head of the Holy Family and Patron of the Catholic Church. To our saint God in like manner said: "Whom shall I find wiser and more fitting than thou art to preside over My Family, and to be the Patron and Protector of My Church? Behold I set thee as the master and governor of My house, and all My children must do thy bidding." So it is: as the ancient Joseph, according to the saying of holy king David (*Psalms* 104:21), was made by Pharao lord of all his house and ruler over all his possessions, so, as Holy Church teaches us, the second Joseph was appointed by God lord of all His House and ruler over all His possessions; and so much the more powerful, the richer, and the more exalted as the House of Nazareth and the Catholic Church are more noble and more sublime than the perishable palace of Memphis, and his sway the more extensive in as much as the possessions of God in the whole earth are vaster than were those of the first Joseph in the land of Egypt.

So also the ring placed by Pharao on Joseph's finger was the sign of the great authority conferred on our Joseph by God; the silken robe typified the glorious gifts with which his pure soul would one day be invested; the chain of gold was the symbol of that intense charity with which his heart was ever burning. And thus, again, was Joseph elevated above the other saints, and raised, as it were, on a glorious chariot, to receive, especially in these our days, the praises of the whole earth; the supreme lawgiver of the Vatican, the immortal Pius IX, having proclaimed to the world that all are to bow down to Joseph, for that God has exalted him to the patronage and guardianship of the Universal Church.

Chapter IV

Joseph Prefigured in His Goodness, Clemency, and Generosity towards His Devout Clients, and Foreshadowed in Various Other Ways.

OUR compassionate Lord was pleased to ordain that the ancient Joseph should prefigure our glorious Patriarch not only in greatness and power, but also in his goodness, the gentleness of his soul, and the tenderness and magnanimity of his paternal heart. As long as the seven predicted years of plenty lasted few thought about Joseph; and possibly some may have scoffed at seeing him so intent on laying up so large a quantity of corn in the great storehouses of Egypt. But as soon as the years of terrible dearth had begun, then all remembered Joseph, and from all quarters men came to Egypt to buy for themselves their necessary food. And when the people cried out to Pharao for bread, the king told them to go to Joseph, and to do all that he should say to them; and Joseph opened in their behalf the vast granaries of Egypt. (*Gen.* 41:55, 56). Here we recognize the great facility and benignity of our saint in assisting those who in prosperous times ungratefully forget him. As the ancient Joseph laid up such store of grain that he might hereafter provide for the famishing people, so also did our Joseph during his lifetime accumulate such great store of merit that he might hereafter powerfully aid his clients. For, in consideration of his great merits, when the people, afflicted by private or public calamities, raise their suppliant voices to Heaven for aid, God replies: "Go to Joseph, and do whatever he enjoins you." Thus Joseph, after Mary, is appointed the perpetual dispenser of all heavenly favors; and, more generous in his gifts than the ancient Joseph, he opens to all the treasures of divine graces, not merely such as are earthly and temporal, but, what is much more, those which are spiritual and eternal. None need starve, knowing that Joseph holds open to them all the riches of Divine beneficence. And this would seem to be indicated in Holy Scripture, where it is said that in Egypt, that is, where Joseph was, there was bread; but everywhere else, that is, where he was not, universal death prevailed. How greatly, then, are the world and the Church indebted to St. Joseph; far more than was Egypt to the ancient patriarch! since, as St. Bernardine of Siena says, our saint has not merely provided for the Egyptians the bread which sustains the natural life, but has with the utmost solicitude nourished the elect with the Bread of Heaven; to wit, the most sweet Jesus, who infuses into us eternal life.[1] This, indeed, is distinctly stated and set forth in the solemn decree wherein St. Joseph was declared by our late holy Pontiff, Pius IX, Patron of the Universal Church.

Further, we may notice how the ancient Joseph treated his brethren, whom he recognized although they knew him not; how he filled their sacks with corn, and restored to them the price of it, besides giving them abundance of provision for their journey. They return, by his desire, with their youngest brother, Benjamin, in whom we see a figure of every innocent and dear client of St. Joseph. At the very sight of his young brother the patriarch is inwardly moved to tears, and says to him: "God be gracious to thee, my son." But for all he orders a rich banquet to be prepared in his apartments, and finally, unable any longer to restrain the swelling tide of his love, he makes himself known to his brethren, saying: "I am Joseph, your brother. Fear not; it was God who sent me

---

1. *Sermo. i. de S. Joseph*

before you for your preservation; it was God who made
me as it were a father to the king; it was God who constituted me lord over all his house, and governor over
the whole land of Egypt." (*Gen.* 44:4-8). So saying, he
presses them to his bosom, he sends immediately for
his father, Jacob, that he may come and share in his
joys and partake of his goods. He presents to Pharao
the good old man, his father, together with his brethren
and their families, and it is at Joseph's recommenda-
tion that the king right willingly concedes to them the
fairest and richest lands of Gessen. Who does not herein
behold a picture of our Joseph's conduct to those who
are devout to him? He grants largely to them what they
ask; nor does he need to be long entreated; he does not
sell his benefits, but bountifully adds more than he is
asked. As he receives with singular affection the innocent and implores for them a copious measure of Divine
mercy, so also he does not drive away the guilty who,
repentant, have recourse to him, but, after ingeniously
causing them to recognize the ruin brought about by
sin, he prepares for them a banquet of graces; and sometimes in the midst of their afflictions makes himself
known to his clients by such an abundance of heavenly
consolations as to move them to tears of tenderness.
"Come," he says, "come to my arms; I am Joseph, your
brother; I will protect you; I will defend you. It is God
who placed your salvation in my hands; He made me,
as it were, father to the King of kings; He made me the
reputed father of Jesus; He constituted me the patron
of His whole House, that is, of the Universal Church,
the sustaining arm of all the earth." Thus, fulfilling his
great office of loving protector, he presses all to his
bosom; he presents them before the throne of God; he
desires to save their entire families, and obtains for all
by his powerful mediation the blessed land of saints,
Paradise.

   To obtain all these immense advantages by means
of Joseph, the same condition must be observed which
the king of Egypt required of those who came to ask

for corn; namely, that they should strictly do what Joseph enjoins: "Go to Joseph; and do all that he shall say to you." (*Gen.* 41:55). God imposes the same condition on those who would obtain graces from St. Joseph; they must promptly and faithfully do what he bids them. And what else does Joseph tell us, both by word and example, but that we should fulfill the Divine law, even as he fulfilled it? Without the fulfillment of God's Commandments it is vain to hope for favors. But whosoever fulfills them perfectly, to him appertain, no doubt, all those heavenly and earthly blessings which the good old man, Jacob, at the close of his days called down on his son Joseph: "The blessings of thy father are strengthened with the blessings of his fathers: until the desire of the everlasting hills should come; may they be upon the head of Joseph, and upon the crown of the Nazarite among his brethren." (*Ibid.* 49:26). This prediction of Jacob was only partially fulfilled in the ancient Joseph, because he was not present, nor could he be present, at the coming of the Desire of the everlasting hills, the expected Messias. It was fully accomplished only in our Joseph, since in him alone, according to the Fathers, were summed up and epitomized all the blessings and all the virtues of the patriarchs who had preceded him; and Joseph alone had the exceptional privilege of being the first, after Mary, at the birth of the Desire of the everlasting hills, the first to see Him, to receive Him into his arms, to embrace Him, nurture Him, and possess Him as his dearest son. This is the reason why Jacob foretold that our Joseph would be blessed in preference to all his brethren; that is, that he would be privileged above all the other saints on earth and in Heaven. And it is, indeed, most consoling for us to behold this heavenly advocate of ours so clearly prefigured, not only in his wisdom, in his power, and in the high honor and esteem he enjoys in the presence of God, but also in the readiness and solicitude of the great charity he has for us, qualities which all combine to render his patronage most valuable and efficacious.

Wherefore, if he undertakes to plead our cause with the Eternal Judge, we are safe, we have won our suit.

But it was not alone in the person of the ancient patriarch Joseph that our saint was prefigured. We may see him also in Abraham's trusted servant, Eliezer, whom he sent to fetch a wife for his son Isaac from among his own kindred, and who escorted her in safety to her new and distant home. (*Gen.* 24). As Rebecca was a type of the Blessed Virgin, so was Eliezer a type of St. Joseph, whose office it was to watch over and protect his immaculate spouse during a large proportion of her stay on earth. Again, in Mardochai, the uncle and guardian of Queen Esther, herself also a figure of Mary, we cannot fail to recognize a typical resemblance to the holy Joseph, guardian and protector of the Queen of Saints and Virgin Mother of the Incarnate Son of God.[2] Indeed the Fathers of the Church and other spiritual writers have seen him mystically represented under many forms and in many passages of Scripture. Thus, in the Canticles it is said, "My Beloved"—that is, Jesus—"feedeth among the lilies" (*Cant.* 2:16); and what are these lilies? asks the Abbot Rupert. Certainly, after Jesus, there are none purer than Mary and Joseph, nor will there ever be. In Genesis (*Gen.* 28:12, 13) we read that the patriarch Jacob beheld in a dream a ladder which reached from earth to Heaven; and on the last step of this ladder the Lord Himself was leaning. This ladder is Mary, and the last step of this ladder, says the same spiritual writer, is Joseph, on whom Jesus Himself in His childhood leaned.[3] In Abraham, Sara, and Isaac the Fathers recognize the Holy Family; that is, in Abraham they see Joseph, in Sara Mary, in Isaac Jesus. Again, God willed that a veil of violet, purple, and scarlet, wrought with embroidery and goodly variety, should conceal the sacred ark from the profane, and divide the sanctuary from the holy of holies. This mysterious veil was a figure of

---

2. For the last two illustrations we are indebted to F. Coleridge's admirable chapter on "The Spouse of Mary" in his *Preparation of the Incarnation*, a work of which we cannot speak in too high terms of commendation.

3. *In Matthaeum*, cap. i.

Joseph, who was to hide from the profane the heavenly virginity of Mary and the Divine origin of Jesus. So also God commanded Moses to construct over the ark the propitiatory of purest gold, and to place two cherubim of gold at the sides, which, extending their wings, should guard and cover the propitiatory. (*Exod.* 25:18-20; 26:31-34; 37:6-9). This propitiatory is Jesus, and the cherubim of gold are Mary and Joseph, who guard, protect, and have the care of Jesus. If we are to credit the writer on Jewish antiquities, Arias Mentanus, one of these cherubim had the form of a beautiful young man, and the other of a lovely maiden. The prophet Isaias speaks of a sealed book placed in the hands of one who is learned, who, being bidden to read it, should answer, "I cannot, for it is sealed." (*Is.* 29:11). St. John Chrysostom, commenting on this passage, says: "What can this sealed book be save the most immaculate Virgin? And into whose care should it be consigned? Certainly into that of the priests. And to whom should it be given? To the artisan Joseph." Isaias, then, prophesied of Joseph. Further on also he points to Joseph, where he says: "The young man shall dwell with the virgin; and the bridegroom shall rejoice over the bride" (*Is.* 62:5): with reference to which Gerson and others say, "This is Joseph with Mary."[4]

I will conclude this chapter with a beautiful explanation which St. Francis de Sales has left us in his Spiritual Conferences of a passage in the Canticles which gives great honor to St. Joseph. In the said book (*Cant.* 8:8, 9) the August Trinity, gathered, as it were, in council for the execution of the great mystery of the Incarnation, speak thus: "Our sister, that is, Mary, is little, that is to say, most humble, and she is an immaculate virgin. What shall We do to our sister in the day when she is to be spoken to for marriage? If she be a wall, let Us build upon it bulwarks of silver; if she be a door, let Us join it together with boards of cedar." Thus the

---

4. Quoted by Trombelli, *Vita e Culto di S. Giuseppe,* p. i c. viii. n. 5.

Mother of God, according to the Divine council, was to be a virgin and a spouse; and her spouse, supereminently chaste, so far from being in the least degree an impediment to her virginity, was to guard and protect it, rendering it freer and more secure, and sheltered from every external contradiction. So that, if Mary by her vow of virginity should have raised, as it were, before her a golden wall of defense, God, to tranquilize her still further, gave her as her spouse St. Joseph, who was to be to her on all occasions as a bulwark of silver; and, though this House of Gold was closed with an adamantine door, God, in giving her Joseph, strengthened it with an incorruptible defense. Hence St. Francis de Sales says: "What is the glorious St. Joseph but a strong bulwark for Our Blessed Lady? Joseph was given to her as a companion in order that her purity might be more marvelously protected in its integrity under the veil and shadow of holy matrimony. If the Virgin be a door, said the Eternal Father, We do not choose that the door should be open, because it is the eastern door through which no one can enter or pass (*Ezech.* 44:1, 2); therefore is it needful to fortify it with incorruptible wood, that is, give her a companion in purity, even the great Patriarch St. Joseph, who for this reason was to surpass all the saints and angels, and the very cherubim themselves, in that eminent virtue of virginity."[5]

---

5. *Entretien,* xix.

Chapter V

Joseph of a Most Noble and Royal Lineage.

IT IS certainly a great glory to come of an ancient and a noble race, particularly when to this high lineage is united the memory of great deeds and integrity of life; and, although there is no virtue in being born great, yet may it greatly conduce to virtue. Nobility of birth is a boon from the Supreme Giver of all good not conceded to all, in which, nevertheless, its recipients must not take pride, but of which they must strive to profit, if they wish to become themselves worthy of honor and veneration. Hence we find Holy Scripture exciting us to praise these noble and holy personages who in their generation were truly glorious. (*Ecclus.* 44:1-8). Now, among all who deserve to be eulogized for their noble and exalted ancestry, the first in rank, after Jesus and Mary, is, no doubt, our great Patriarch St. Joseph. It is necessary, therefore, to exhibit his high genealogy with all possible clearness, solving all the doubts connected with it which might occur to the mind, that we may thus perceive how egregiously those err who regard St. Joseph as a poor plebeian, and hold him to have been a rough and ignoble artisan.

Joseph an ignoble plebeian! There is not in the whole world a more splendid genealogy than was his; among all the monarchs of the earth there is none to compare with him. God Himself desired that he should be thus privileged amongst the kings and patriarchs of the old

27

covenant, because the glory and splendor of his genealogy was to be wholly reflected upon Jesus and upon His Blessed Mother. The documents which record it are irrefragable, and its proofs unquestionable; for they rest, not on the testimony of men, but on that of God. God Himself, by means of His Evangelists, has been pleased accurately to enumerate all the generations which led in a direct line from Abraham to Joseph. The antiquity of a family is estimated by the uninterrupted number of ancestors it can reckon up to the remote stem from which it traces its origin. But what scion of a noble family can in this respect compete with Joseph? St. Matthew, descending from Abraham, through David, to Joseph, registers forty generations; and St. Luke, ascending from Joseph to Adam, counts as many as seventy-four.

It would, however, be of little value that a pedigree should be ancient, unless it were rendered illustrious by persons of noble rank and exalted dignity. Now, in the lineage of Joseph we find the most celebrated patriarchs, as Abraham; the greatest legislators and leaders of the people, as Zorobabel; the wisest and most renowned monarchs, as David and Solomon. And, if the greatness and the power of his ancestors went on diminishing after the return from the Babylonian captivity even to the time when the sceptre of Juda was usurped by an idolatrous and foreign king, as was Herod of Ascalon, nevertheless Joseph still remained the rightful successor and heir of the kings of Juda, as being descended from the family of David. On the other hand, the sceptre of Juda, according to the famous prophecy of Jacob (*Gen.* 49:10), was to be taken away, and to have ceased to be at the coming of the Messias; its failure, indeed, was to be the manifest sign of the coming of the Redeemer. Now, this removal of authority from God's chosen people occurred precisely at the period when Joseph appeared in the world, to be, as it were, the forerunner and the herald of the great Messias, who was to found a new kingdom, to wit, the Catholic Church, which was to "stand forever." (*Dan.* 2:44).

But Joseph was not glorious solely because the pure blood of the kings of Juda circulated in his veins, since others of the same stock could claim a like honor, but he was specially glorious in being, so to say, the last link of the regal genealogy which through his spouse united him to the King of kings; he closed the line of the ancestors of the great Messias, and beheld under his roof Him who was the Desired of all nations, the end and consummation of the law, born of his race and the Child of his Virgin Spouse.

Thus the genealogy of Joseph was to comprise the genealogy of Mary, his spouse, and also that of Jesus. For whence do we learn the genealogy of Jesus and Mary but from that of Joseph? He may be said to be its guardian, its depositary, its vindicator, its juridical witness. The Eternal Father had decreed that Jesus should be born of the tribe of Juda, of the race of David, and that He should have no earthly father, but be born of a most pure Virgin. In order, then, to fulfill this great counsel, He ordained that Joseph, the descendant of Juda and of David, should be espoused to Mary; and that of Mary, through the operation of the Holy Ghost, should be born Jesus. The Evangelists, following the custom of the Hebrews, who were not wont to give the genealogies of women, have not expressly left us the genealogy of Mary; and, as they could not give the direct genealogy of Jesus on the paternal side, since He had no earthly father, how were they to make it known save through the genealogy of Joseph? The Old Law provided that men were to intermarry with their own tribe and kin, and the women also, particularly if they had possessions, in order that their inheritance might not pass out of the family. (*Num.* 36:6-9). So that by the fact of knowing that Mary was the spouse of Joseph, we know also that she was of the tribe of Juda and of the race of David; and thus that Jesus, her Divine Son, was also of the same tribe and race. It is a great glory to St. Joseph that his genealogy should serve to make known to us those of Jesus and Mary, and should be, in fact, so identified with them as to be even called by the Evangelist the genealogy of Jesus: "The book of the generation of Jesus Christ, the Son of David." (*Matt.* 1:1). St. Bernardine of Siena, then, justly observes that the nobility of St. Joseph was so great that, if we may be allowed to say so, he, in a certain sense, conferred temporal nobility on God Himself in the Person of our Lord Jesus Christ.[1]

Although Mary's genealogy is not expressly mentioned, but has been sheltered under that of her holy spouse, it is really given; and, were this fact not recognized, serious difficulties would arise from the difference between the two genealogies, as recorded by the Evangelists St. Matthew and St. Luke. St. Matthew, who wrote his Gospel about eight years after the death of Jesus, for the benefit of the first Christian converts from Judaism, enumerates in direct descent the generations between Abraham and Joseph, that is, from Abraham to Juda, from Juda to David, and from David, through Solomon, Roboam, Jechonias, down to the transmigration of Babylon; and then from Jechonias to Mathan, who was the father of Jacob, "who begat Joseph, the husband of Mary, of whom was born Jesus, who is called Christ." On the other hand, St. Luke, the associate of St. Paul's travels, who wrote his Gospel about twenty years after Our Lord's Ascension, traced the genealogy of Joseph in an upward line, giving different names to his father and many of his ancestors from those assigned by St. Matthew. This is the form in which he casts it: he says that Jesus was beginning to be about thirty years of age, being, as was supposed, the son of Joseph, who was of Heli, and Heli of Mathat, and so on up to Nathan, the son of David. From him he mounts up to Juda, and from Juda to Abraham; but he does not stop there: he continues to ascend to Noe, and from him, through the antediluvian patriarchs, until he reaches Seth, "who was of Adam, who was of God."

1. *Sermo de St. Joseph.*

(*Luke* 3:23-38). Now, how is it possible that the Evangelists should contradict each other? Or, again, how would it be possible that Joseph should have two genealogies, and be at the same time the son of Jacob, according to St. Matthew, and the son of Heli, according to St. Luke? We proceed to solve this difficulty.

Chapter VI

Joseph the Son of Jacob and also the Son of Heli.

THE Emperor Julian, the Apostate, blasphemously declared that in tracing the genealogy of Joseph the Evangelists had shown themselves either dolts or liars. Rather it is he who was both dolt and liar, who denied the faith, turned back to an inane idolatry, and persecuted the Church of Christ. The Evangelists, inspired by the Spirit of God, who is the Spirit of wisdom, of truth, and of unity, could neither err, nor lie, nor contradict each other. It is, therefore, impossible that there should be a shadow of disagreement between them. Moreover, since St. Luke wrote considerably later than St. Matthew, and had therefore seen his Gospel, which was already circulated among the Christian converts, how is it conceivable that he should make contradictory statements in his own Gospel? The contradiction can only be apparent; it is impossible that it should be real, and equally impossible that Joseph could have had two genealogies and two natural fathers, Jacob and Heli. It remains to see in what sense each of the Evangelists wrote.

By generation, of course, Joseph could have but one true and natural father, and this father, according to St. Matthew, was Jacob: "Mathan," he says, "begat Jacob, and Jacob begat Joseph," thus asserting that Jacob was his father in the strict sense of the term. But St. Luke expresses himself in a different manner; he says, "Joseph was of Heli," not that Heli begat Joseph, even as at the close of the genealogy he says, "Adam was of God"; and we know that, although God was the father of Adam, it was not by generation. We conclude, then, that when the Evangelist places Heli in the position of Joseph's progenitor, he is understanding the parentage in a wider sense, and must mean that Heli was his legal father, his father by appellation, by affinity, by affection, as we shall see that he really was. Thus there is no contradiction between the two Evangelists: the true and legitimate father of St. Joseph was Jacob, according to St. Matthew's Gospel, and his father legally and by affinity was Heli, according to St. Luke. And in this all the Fathers and Doctors of the Church are agreed.

But what was the object of bringing Heli forward? What was St. Luke's purpose in informing us that Joseph had, besides his true father, a father according to law, particularly as the Evangelist does not explain the nature of this legal relationship? God does nothing without a purpose, and whatever we find in Holy Scripture has its just object and aim, and is written for our instruction. If, therefore, God inspired St. Luke to state the genealogy of Joseph in this wise, we may rest assured that it was with a view to His own glory and to our profit. As it was needful that St. Matthew should give us the natural genealogy of Joseph, so it was also needful, perhaps more needful, that St. Luke should give us his legal genealogy; and if he has not explained in what manner Joseph was legally the son of Heli, this was because the principal object of the Evangelists was, not to write the life of Joseph, but to manifest the life and character of the Messias; and of Him, indeed, they did not write everything, and what they did write was very brief, omitting much; for, as St. John says, if all had been written, the whole world, he thought, could not have contained the books which must have been written. (*John* 21:25). The remainder was left to tradition, that is, to the teaching of those Churches where the Gospel was preached, and to the

Fathers and Doctors, who should explain, according to the sense of the Church, what is wanting in Holy Scripture.

To understand, therefore, in what manner Joseph is the son of Heli let us refer to the Doctors of Holy Church. We find them expressing two chief opinions on this subject. The first is that of Julius Africanus, according to whom Heli, of whom St. Luke speaks, took a wife and died, leaving no children. Now, the law provided that in such a case the widow could oblige the brother of her deceased husband to marry her, in order to raise up children to him. The widow of Heli, therefore, according to those who maintain this opinion, would have appealed to Jacob, whom they suppose to be Heli's brother, to take her in marriage, and thus Joseph, their child, was naturally the son of Jacob, but legally the son of Heli. This opinion had followers even among the Fathers; and it cannot be denied that it was the most commonly adopted.[1] Nevertheless, be it said with all respect for those who professed it, this opinion, while on the one hand it involves no slight difficulties, on the other appears to add nothing of importance to the genealogy of Joseph, or to that of Mary and Jesus.

As regards the difficulties, it is well to quote the words of Scripture upon which this view is grounded. "When brethren dwell together, and one of them dieth without children, the wife of the deceased shall not marry to another: but his brother shall take her, and raise up seed for his brother: and the first son he shall have of her he shall call by his [brother's] name, that his name be not abolished out of Israel." (*Deut.* 25:5, 6). It is question, then, of brethren dwelling together; and it is prescribed that the first son that shall be born shall receive the name of the deceased brother. But nothing of all this do we meet with in the case before us. Jacob and Heli could not be brethren by birth, see-

---

1. It is the one adopted in the Douai Version of the Bible.

ing that, according to the Gospel, they had neither the same father nor the same grandfather; for we learn from St. Matthew that the father of Jacob was Mathan, the son of Eleazar, and from St. Luke that Heli was of Mathat, who was of Levi. Neither are we told that they lived together; on the contrary, it appears that, although they were of the same tribe and race, their families were distinct, since Jacob descended from David by Solomon, and Heli by Nathan. What possible obligation, therefore, could bind Jacob to marry Heli's widow?

However, setting aside this difficulty and supposing that he had married her, he was bound, according to the law, to give his firstborn son the name of his deceased brother. But we find, on the contrary, that Jacob called his son Joseph, not Heli. For these reasons, the above-mentioned opinion seems to want a sufficiently solid basis.

Let us now consider what importance it would add to the genealogy of Mary and Jesus, which is precisely what the Evangelists desired to place in a clear light by tracing the genealogy of Joseph. As it was known that women could not, ordinarily, be married to any save men of their own tribe and race, it was sufficient that St. Matthew alone should have informed us that Joseph, born of Jacob, was of the tribe of Juda and house of David for us to have drawn the conclusion that Mary, his wife, was also of the same tribe and race. What need was there that St. Luke should afterwards tell us that he was also legally the son of Heli? Of what interest was this fact as regarded Mary's genealogy, or what fresh light did it throw on the genealogy of Jesus? If Heli had no relationship with Mary, and was not in a direct line of descent with her, of whom alone was to be born Jesus of the tribe of Juda and race of David, what did it matter to us to know that he was legally Joseph's father? This being the case, we readily adhere to the second opinion, which confers a new and great importance on the genealogy of Joseph as traced by St. Luke.[2]

Now, according to this second view, the Heli mentioned by St. Luke is no other than the glorious St.
Joachim, the happy father of the august Queen of
Heaven and earth, Mary. This opinion is alluded to by
St. Augustine;[3] it was held by the author of the Sermon on the Nativity of the Virgin attributed to St.
Jerome; and it was entertained and discussed by the
celebrated Melchior Cano,[4] by Calmet, by Cornelius à
Lapide, and various others. The reasons alleged in favor
of this view are the following. All interpreters are agreed
in reckoning the three names Heli, Eliachim, and
Joachim as synonymous, and as being so used in Scripture. Thus in the fourth Book of Kings we read that
the king of Egypt changed the name of Eliachim, the
son of Josias, into Joakim; and we find the same statement in the second Book of Paralipomenon. (*4 Kings*
23:34; *2 Par.* 36:4). Philo Anianus also (quoted by Melchior Cano) informs us that with the Syrians and Egyptians the names Joachim, Eliachim, and Heli were
synonymous. Heli was but an abbreviation of Eliachim.
If, then, the Heli of St. Luke be in fact Joachim, the
father of Mary, the Evangelist had every right to say
that Joseph was of Heli, that is, not his son by nature,
but his son by affinity, his son-in-law, being the husband of Joachim's daughter, since it is usual thus to

---

2. Leaving in the text the arguments adduced by the Canon Antonio Vitali against
the solidity of the earliest opinions held on this subject, and without pretending to
choose between them and those of more recent date, it is only fair to state that
among the Doctors who embraced the opinion of Julius Africanus are to be found
some who, to obviate the difficulty suggested by the Canon that St. Luke's genealogy would, according to this view, add nothing of interest to that of Mary, say that
Jacob and Heli were brothers on the maternal, but not on the paternal, side, the
former of whom by his first wife was father of Joachim, the father of Mary, and of
Cleophas, called also Alpheus, who was the father of James the Less, Simon, Joseph,
and Judas named Thaddeus. Jacob's brother Heli having died without children, he,
in accordance with legal custom, married his widow, of whom he had a third son,
called Joseph. Joachim, therefore, and Joseph, according to this view, were brethren
on the father's side, and Joseph was uncle to Mary; so that both the Evangelists,
the one giving Joseph's descent through Jacob, his true father, from Solomon, and
the other through his father-in-law Heli, from Nathan, trace substantially the
genealogy of both Mary and Joseph, and consequently of the Saviour, according to
the flesh.
3. *Quaest. Evangel.* ii. q. v. *Vet et Nov. Testam.* q. lvi.
4. *Loc. Theol.* lib. ii. cap. v.

express this relationship, and in this way he would have traced for us Mary's genealogy without departing from the custom of the Hebrews, which was never to give genealogies on the woman's side. Melchior Cano observes, indeed, that those words, "who was of Heli," may refer rather to Jesus than to Joseph, and then the sense would run thus: Jesus, who was reputed the son of Joseph, was not of him, but of Heli, since, being born, without man's intervention, of His Virgin Mother alone, there was no one on earth of whom He could naturally be said to be the son except Heli, or Joachim, who was His grandfather according to the flesh. And, in order to create no surprise by passing straight from the grandson to the grandfather, the Evangelist at once assigns the reason, in that Joseph was not truly the father of Jesus, but only his putative father.

Thus, then, we learn that Jesus, born of the Virgin Mary, the daughter of Heli or Joachim, was truly of the tribe of Juda and descended in a direct line from David through his son Nathan, as Joseph, his reputed father, had the same descent through Solomon. Moreover, we have reason to believe that it was not through Joseph's genealogy alone that Jesus was the descendant of Solomon, for Benedict XIII, in one of his Sermons on the Life of Mary,[5] following in this opinion Cornelius à Lapide, Menochius, and others, maintains that St. Anne, wife of St. Joachim and the happy mother of Mary, was sister to Jacob, the father of St. Joseph: whence it follows that Mary was Joseph's cousin, and on her maternal side had the same regal descent from David through Solomon as Joseph had.

From all that has been said we must conclude that Joseph's genealogy is singularly glorious, not merely as illustrated by an uninterrupted series of patriarchs, kings, and renowned princes, but because it served to form and include the genealogy of the Mother of God and of the Divine Redeemer Himself. Well may the

---

5. *Sermo* ii.

crowned monarchs of earth bow their heads before St. Joseph, who for nobility of birth and ancestral glory far surpasses them all. His hand is more than worthy to grasp a regal sceptre and his head to be encircled with an imperial diadem. Call him no longer a plebeian, a common artisan. In him God has been pleased both to exalt nobility and to ennoble the labor of the artisan. St. Joseph is the glory of nobles and the consolation of workmen; he is the condemnation of those modern sectaries who, born of ignoble blood, desire to reduce all to one vulgar level, destroying every distinction of name, rank, or property, by which process society itself would soon be entirely destroyed. Let us fervently beg our exalted Patron, St. Joseph, by his powerful intercession to save the Church, the family, and society from such pernicious foes.

Chapter VII

Joseph Sanctified Before His Birth.

IT IS now an article of our faith that the Blessed Virgin by a singular privilege was prevented by grace and preserved in entire immunity from original sin. From Holy Scripture we also learn that some souls through the divine predilection, as those of Jeremias and of [John] the Baptist, were sanctified before they saw the light of day. Now, what shall we say of Joseph? Since in dignity and holiness he is inferior to Mary, we cannot assume with any certainty that God granted to him the same privilege as to her; and the Church has never made any utterance on the subject. Still, Joseph surpasses all the other saints in dignity and sanctity; we are, therefore, free to conjecture that, although this is not signified in Scripture, he must have been sanctified before his birth earlier than any of them, for all the holy Doctors agree in saying that there was no grace conceded to any other saint, except Mary, which was not granted to Joseph. As Mary, above all, was nearest to Jesus, so Joseph was nearest to Mary; and for the sake of Jesus, and also for Mary's sake, we may justly conclude that to Joseph must have been conceded a privilege second only to hers.

We have shown what a great end God had in view in the creation of St. Joseph, who was to be associated with the mystery of the Incarnation, and was thus comprised in the decree of man's redemption. Hence it is that he was pre-announced in Holy Scripture, and enno-

bled with so high a genealogy. Now, in order to correspond to so lofty a vocation, which, after that of the
Virgin Mother, was superior to all others, whether of
angels or saints, Joseph must needs have been sanctified in a most eminent degree, that he might be worthy to take his place in this most sublime order of the
Hypostatic Union, in which Jesus held the first place
and Mary the second. And, indeed, we find it to be the
constant doctrine of St. Thomas Aquinas, as well as of
all the Fathers, that those whom God elects and designs
for some great work, He also prepares and disposes so
as to fit them for its performance; and the Angelic Doctor adds that God gives to each grace proportioned to
the office which he is chosen to fill.[1] St. Bernardine of
Siena lays down the same doctrine, and he then proceeds to say that this was verified in the person of St.
Joseph, who was the reputed father of Jesus, the true
spouse of the Queen of the world and Lady of angels,
and was elected by the Eternal Father to be the faithful guardian of His two greatest treasures.[2] If, then,
Joseph was elected to such an office, which, after the
divine maternity, has none to equal it in Heaven or on
earth, he must have received of God for its discharge
a fullness of corresponding grace, superior to that vouchsafed to any other saint.

The election of God is from eternity, but sanctification takes place in time; and this sanctification is not
accomplished in all at the same hour. With some it has
been late, as with St. Paul. Some have been sanctified
at the sixth hour, some at the third, some at the first
hour, and some even before birth, as in the cases just
mentioned of Jeremias and [John] the Baptist. This is
a marvellous effect of the Divine Goodness, loving to
communicate Itself to a soul as early as possible and
with the greatest abundance of Its gifts. But to whom
more than to St. Joseph can It have loved thus to communicate Itself? In his case truly may we apply the

1. *Summa,* p. iii. q. xxvii. a. 4.
2. *Sermo* i. *de St. Joseph.*

words of the Psalmist: "Thou hast prevented him with blessings of sweetness; Thou hast set on his head a crown of precious stones." (*Ps.* 20:4). The grace of the Holy Spirit can have tolerated no delay in him, and, since God had prepared for Joseph the greatest grace of sanctification after Mary, He would not have awaited his birth to take possession of his soul, but in virtue of the merits of Jesus Christ, who was to be his reputed son, would have diffused into his heart such a flood of grace even from his mother's womb as to efface every stain of original sin and array it with the most splendid gifts, fitting it to be the abode of the Divine Majesty.

There are two ways in which this sanctification might be effected. His beautiful soul at the moment of its infusion into the body might have been guarded from contracting the stain of original sin; or at the second moment, that is, when the stain was scarcely contracted, it might have been instantaneously cancelled and purged by the grace of the future Saviour.

With regard to the first of these opinions, there have not been wanting pious writers who have held that Joseph was entirely exempt from original sin. The seraphic Bernardine de Bustis, a most devout Doctor, who flourished about the middle of the 15th century, and therefore previous to the Council of Trent, says that among the fervent clients of St. Joseph some did not hesitate to affirm that solely for the sake of Jesus, of whom he was to be the putative father, and of Mary, of whom he was to be the most pure spouse, he was not only sanctified in his mother's womb but, moreover, preserved from contracting original sin.[3] The said Doctor neither approves nor condemns this opinion, adding that it was known only to God, who from all men chose Joseph for His reputed father and for the spouse of His most holy Mother. A century later, Giacomo Lobbezio, of the Company of Jesus, also relates how some from their devotion to St. Joseph would maintain that the

---

3. *Mariale,* p. iv. *Serm.* xii. *de Despons. Virg.*

privilege conceded to his Blessed Spouse was also accorded to himself. This accomplished theologian adds
that he, too, would willingly subscribe to such a belief
in honor of this most holy Patriarch, but that he could
not venture to do so unless he had the authority and
witness of the holy Fathers and an intimation from the
Church and its Sovereign Pontiffs, which as yet we have
not had.[4] In the meantime the immediate rule of our
faith is the Church, the infallible mistress of truth;
and, however desirous we may be to see all the singular merits and privileges of our saint exalted, we must
not extend the range of even pious opinion beyond what
tradition or reason warrants.

Coming now to the other way in which Joseph's sanctification in his mother's womb may have been effected,
namely, at the second moment after his conception, as
theologians would say—the Blessed Virgin having been
sanctified at the first—it seems reasonable to believe
it; because it was not becoming that the putative father
of Him who came to take away the sins of the world
should remain for any considerable space of time with
the stain of sin upon him; it was not becoming that he
who was to bear in his arms, to tend, and feed Him who
came to vanquish Hell, should have himself remained
long under the yoke and slavery of Satan. It seems only
reasonable to believe that the Divine Saviour prevented
him with His grace. The mind of the Doctors of the
Church has been so freely expressed on this point that
it may be reckoned as a common opinion. Gerson, who
was most devout to St. Joseph, and who exerted himself so vigorously for the extinction of the schism which
afflicted the Church during his time, used loudly to
assert that in order to remove this tribulation it was
above all things necessary to honor and glorify in the
highest possible degree the great Patriarch, St. Joseph.
In the beautiful discourse which he delivered before the
Council of Constance on the Nativity of the Blessed Vir-

4. *Quaest. Theolog.* tom. iii.

gin,[5] he made the most splendid eulogium of her holy spouse, Joseph. In this sermon he openly professed that the Blessed Virgin was by a singular privilege prevented by divine grace in such wise as to preserve her from the least stain of original sin, so that she thus crushed the head of the old serpent, without having ever been trodden underfoot by him. Then, referring to Joseph, he uses these words: "As Mary before her birth was sanctified in her mother's womb, so may we believe was also her virginal spouse, Joseph"; from which observation it might have been concluded that he claimed the same immunity from original sin for St. Joseph as for the Blessed Virgin, except for the qualification which he subjoined: "although not in an altogether similar manner—*quamvis non omnino similiter.*" The similarity and the difference may be noted in this—that Joseph after the contraction of original sin was sanctified in the womb by the baptism of charity, *baptismo flaminis,* as was [John] the Baptist and as others have been; for so we read in the Jerusalem Office of St. Joseph. From these expressions we may gather that the learned preacher was persuaded that, if Joseph was not, like the Blessed Virgin, entirely preserved from the original stain, he must nevertheless have been speedily withdrawn from the hard slavery of Satan, so that his beautiful soul, enriched with every gift, shone resplendently before God from the first moments of his life. This doctrine was preached by Gerson at the Council of Constance, in presence of the very Fathers who had deputed him to place on record the conciliar decrees; and not only had these Fathers not a word to say in opposition, but they greatly applauded his discourse and ordered it to be published, accompanied by a notice that it had been delivered before them. This commendation served to promote the support of the doctrine by the most learned theologians.

In 1522 Isidoro Isolano, a Milanese Dominican Father, who had a very great devotion to the Saint, published

---

5. *Serm. de Nativ. B. V. Mariae,* Consid. ii.

his *Summary of the Gifts of St. Joseph,* dedicating it
to the Sovereign Pontiff, Adrian VI. In the 9th chapter
of this work he demonstrates that the opinion that St.
Joseph was sanctified in his mother's womb may be
held and piously believed.[6] Every sanctification of this
nature, he says, either is accorded on account of the
future exalted dignity of the sanctified, or is ordained
with a special reference to the Saint of Saints. Now,
both causes eminently existed in St. Joseph, who was
to be perfectly just, and was ordained, above all men,
to be nearest to the Saint of Saints, Jesus. If Jeremias
was sanctified before his birth because he was to proph-
esy expressly of Jesus, and [John] the Baptist also
because he was to point Him out present among men,
who can suppose that Joseph, on account of the close
knowledge he had of Jesus above all others, Mary alone
excepted, and his paternal education of Him, was not
also similarly privileged? If God was pleased thus to
sanctify His servants, how much more His putative
father, in order that he might be so reputed, and be
worthy of the name! Isolano adds that, if all the world
believes that the Mother of Jesus was raised to the
highest degree of sanctity in the womb on account of
the dignity of her Divine Son (and it is now an article
of faith that she was preserved from the stain of original sin from the very first moment of her conception),
why may we not believe that Joseph was likewise raised
to a certain degree of sanctity in his mother's womb,
since he was chosen by God to be called His father?
This, he adds, was also befitting the parity of the mar-

---

6. In this work of the Milanese Dominican we find (p. iii. cap. iii.) the following passage, which is very striking, partaking as it does of the nature of a prophecy, or,
at least, furnishing an instance of prescience bearing a close resemblance to prophecy.
"The mysterious action of the Holy Spirit will not cease to move and inflame the
hearts of the faithful, until the whole army of the Church Militant shall pay fresh
homage to Joseph, raising monasteries, temples, and altars dedicated to his name.
Yes, new and magnificent feasts will be celebrated in his honor, vows will be offered
under his invocation, and those whose petitions have been granted will gladly fulfill them at his altar. God will give deeper penetration to human intellects; and
learned men, meditating on the interior and hidden gifts in Joseph, will be fain to
acknowledge that no one ever possessed similar superheavenly riches. Others are
called the friends of Christ, but Joseph is called His father. The saints invoke Mary
by the title of Queen, and this Queen is the spouse of St. Joseph."

riage between the Blessed Virgin and St. Joseph.

Cornelius à Lapide treats of the same question, and after having noticed that several of the Fathers were of opinion that this privilege was accorded, not only to our saint, but to others whom he names, he comes to this conclusion—that God might concede this privilege to more than one, if He were so pleased, but, if to any of those specified He did in fact grant it, then, assuredly, it would seem that He would not have denied it to St. Joseph, the spouse of His Blessed Mother.[7]

St. Joseph, then, we see, is always, in the opinion of the Doctors of the Church, held to be, next to the Blessed Virgin, the purest and the most holy among creatures, and worthy, for the sake of the Divine Son and His Mother, to be liberated and purged from original sin immediately after his conception. And this doctrine, professed by great Doctors, and tacitly approved by the Church—a doctrine become familiar to preachers in their pulpits, to theologians in their academies, and to sacred writers in their works—may be considered as generally held and believed by devout Christians.

---

7. *Comment. in Mattaeum,* i. 16.

Chapter VIII

Concupiscence Subdued in the First Sanctification of Joseph by the Superabundance of Grace, Which was Greater in Him than in Any Other Saint except Mary.

ONE of the penalties of original sin is that rebellion of the flesh against the spirit which, according to the Council of Trent, proceeds from sin and inclines to sin.[1] Hence the Apostle said: "I see another law in my members fighting against the law of my mind, and captivating me in the law of sin that is in my members." (*Rom.* 7:23).

If it was fitting that Joseph should be speedily cleansed from the original stain, it was also fitting that he should by a special privilege be freed from this rebellion of the flesh which is its consequence. All in him was to be pure and holy; that conflict between the flesh and the spirit, that propensity to evil and difficulty respecting good could find no place in him, but there must be perfect subjection of the inferior powers to reason, perfect tranquillity and order in all his affections and in all the movements of his heart; which is equivalent to saying that the incentive to sin—*fomes,* as it is called by theologians[2]—was to be, as it were, extinguished in Joseph or, at any rate, vanquished and bound in such wise that it could not revolt against reason. Since Joseph was to be a pure virgin, in order to make

---

1. Sessio v. *Decretum de Peccato Originali.*
2. St. Thomas, *Summa,* p. iii. q. xxvii. a. 3.

him the worthy companion of the purest among all virgins, so also was it needful that he should be exempt from any movement of concupiscence which might cast a shadow on the white lily of his purity. God, certainly, did not fail to prevent and protect with this singular grace the heart of Joseph, so that the very slightest thought which was not perfectly chaste should never arise to trouble the serenity of his stainless soul.

Gerson, after having asserted Joseph's liberation from original sin, goes on to claim this privilege for him also. If, he says, the Lord would not confide His Mother, then a matron in age, to any but His virgin disciple, the Evangelist St. John, how much more when that Mother was in her tender youth! In like manner, since Jesus would not be born save of perfect virginal purity, that is, of Mary, so also He would not be nurtured save by one whose purity was spotless, that is, by Joseph.[3]

Echius, that eminent and learned doctor, follows and confirms this statement of Gerson in two Sermons which he composed in praise of St. Joseph, and which he dedicated to Pope Clement VII. "Christ," he says, "when hanging on the Cross and about to die, commended His Mother to the Apostle John. Doctors, enquiring why He did not rather commend her to St. Peter, or to some other of His disciples, give this reason: that He, a Virgin, commended His Virgin Mother to a virgin. It is also," he says, "to be considered, not only that Joseph was a virgin, but that God by a special grace had extinguished in him all the carnal fire of concupiscence, so that, free from all temptation, he could dwell with the most holy and most beautiful Virgin Mary." Whence it is just to infer that he was sanctified in his mother's womb, and that the rebellion of concupiscence was either extinguished or repressed in him. Nor should this surprise us, since, next to Mary, he was destined by God for the sublimest ministry, a ministry superior to that of all the angels and saints; and the holy Doctors are

---

3. *Serm. de Nativ. B. V. Mariae.*

unanimous in concluding that there was no grace, gift,
or privilege conferred on angel or saint which was not
conceded in a much higher degree to Joseph; otherwise
he would, doubtless, appear to be in some respect inferior to one or other among them.

Giovanni di Cartagena, who for his doctrine and piety
was so dear to Paul V, devoted thirteen of his beautiful Homilies on the mysteries of Christ and of Mary to
the praises of our saint. Having set himself to prove
that, with the exception of the Blessed Mother of God,
Joseph was superior to all the saints, he proceeds to
demonstrate the same with respect to the angels. "The
office of the angels," he says, "is the guardianship of
men; but to Joseph was committed a far higher and
more excellent office, since he was chosen to be the
guardian, not of a simple man, but of Christ the Lord,
God and Man, and to be the most faithful spouse of
His Mother."[4] St. Francis de Sales, the new Doctor of
the Church, enlarging on the praises of St. Joseph in
his Spiritual Conferences, exclaims, "Oh, what a saint
is the glorious St. Joseph! Not only is he a patriarch,
but he is the corypheus of all the patriarchs; not only
is he a confessor, but he is more than a confessor, because
in his confession is contained the dignity of bishop, the
generosity of martyrs and of all other saints"; and, later
on, he says that the Patriarch St. Joseph surpassed all
the saints and angels, and the very cherubim themselves, in the eminent virtue of virginity.[5] The great
Doctor, Alfonso Maria de' Liguori, pondering those
words of the holy Evangelist: "And He was subject to
them" (*Luke* 2:51), says: "This humility of Jesus in obeying causes us to know that the dignity of St. Joseph is
superior to that of all the saints, saving only that of
the Virgin Mother."[6]

If, then, it be now the common opinion of Doctors
that Joseph in his dignity, in his ministry, and in holi-

---

4. Lib. iv. Hom. ix.
5. *Entretien,* xix.
6. *Esort. alla Divoz. di S. Giuseppe.*

ness surpassed all the angels and saints, we are led to
the legitimate conclusion that from his conception he
was immediately enriched with gifts superior to theirs,
in order that he might be a fitting spouse for Mary,
and worthy to be the reputed father of Jesus. Therefore, if of the angels St. Augustine writes, that "God,
in creating the angelic nature, infused grace into it,"[7]
so likewise it must be true to say the same of St. Joseph;
otherwise the angels would be his superiors, not only
in their nature, but in the priority and abundance of
their grace. And what it is true to say of St. Joseph,
as compared to the angels, with still more reason may
be affirmed in respect to all the saints. If St. Joseph
had not been sanctified more speedily and with a fuller
amount of grace, in what respect would he have been
more highly favored than Jeremias or John the Baptist (*Jer.* 1:5; *Luke* 1:15), both of whom were sanctified
previous to their birth: of the Baptist it being declared
that he was "filled with the Holy Ghost even from his
mother's womb"? If, therefore, Joseph was superior to
the other saints, he must, not only have enjoyed like
privileges, but have had them in a much higher degree.
We have reason, then, to conclude that not only was
he freed without delay from original sin, but that his
beautiful soul was also delivered from concupiscence,
filled with the Holy Spirit and with the plenitude of
His gifts; nay, that he was even confirmed in grace, and
endued with the use of reason while yet in his mother's
womb, as we believe was the case with Mary from the
first moment of her conception.[8]

P. Paolo Segneri, a prince among sacred orators and
a profound theologian, in a splendid panegyric which
he pronounced on St. Joseph, after having demonstrated
how distinguished Doctors have agreed in affirming
that this privilege of sanctification before birth had
been granted to our saint, goes on to say how St. Thomas
teaches that the nearer anything approaches to its prin-

---

7. *De Civitate Dei,* c. ix.
8. St. Bernardine of Siena, tom. i. cap. i. serm. li.

ciple the greater and more perfect is its participation in the prerogatives or singular properties of that principle. Thus the brightness of the sun is more resplendent in its vicinity, and heat in proximity of the fire is more fervent; so also, if you draw water from a spring, you will find that it is clearer, more limpid, and more pure in proportion to its nearness to the source. "But, if this be so," he says, "how can any one suspect that Joseph, who by affinity and by office was so closely united to the universal Source of all sanctity, was made participant thereof in a lower degree and in less perfection than those who were much further removed from it? For this reason, then, we may well conclude, with very solid grounds of probability, that he was, not only sanctified in his mother's womb, but also confirmed in grace and exempted from all malice, so that no man on earth—let us boldly affirm it—was ever holier than was Joseph." And further on he says: "Have I erred in saying that no one ever exceeded Joseph in sanctity, always, of course, excepting, as she ever must be excepted, his Spouse? If such an assertion is to be esteemed temerity, then call Gerson, the famous Parisian Chancellor, temerarious, temerarious a Bernardine de Bustis, a Giovanni di Cartagena, an Isidoro surnamed Isolano, and, finally, a Suarez, whose judgment is equivalent to that of an entire university. And is it in ambiguous or obscure terms that Suarez expresses himself? Listen to his words: 'I do not see how it is a temerarious or improbable but, rather, a pious and probable opinion should any hold that St. Joseph in grace and glory surpassed all the other saints, for there is nothing in Holy Scripture repugnant to such a belief.'"[9]

If the venerable P. Segneri could thus speak in praise of St. Joseph two hundred years ago, and that eminent Doctor and great theologian, Suarez, a hundred years before him, what would they not have said, what would they not have written, in this our time, when the glo-

---

9. Suarez, tom. ii. disp. viii. sec. i.

ries of Joseph are more and more manifesting themselves in the whole world, and when from the sublime throne of the Vatican he has been declared the Patron of the Universal Church!

But Suarez goes further still. After having enumerated the various ministries in the order of grace, and said that the Apostolic ministry occupies the first rank, he adds, "There are other ministries which belong to the order of the Hypostatic Union, which in its kind is more perfect, as is apparent from the divine maternity of Mary; and in this order is the ministry of St. Joseph, which, therefore, surpasses the former, that of the Apostles."[10] If, then, according to Suarez, the ministry of St. Joseph belongs to the order of the Hypostatic Union, and this order is superior to the Apostolic, which is the first of all the rest, clearly Joseph, although he holds the third rank in the order of the Hypostatic Union, is superior even to Peter, who is first in the Apostolic hierarchy. Between the ministry of the Apostles and that of Joseph there exists this difference: the former is immediately for men, to conduct them to Christ; that of Joseph is immediately directed to Christ Himself, in order to preserve Him for men, and is therefore so much the more noble and sublime. "The ministry of Joseph," says Giovanni di Cartagena, "both as spouse of the Blessed Virgin and as adopted father of Jesus, was closely conjoined with the very Person of Jesus Christ, in such wise that its dignity appears, more than any other whatsoever, to approach the most sublime dignity of the Mother of God."[11] Benedict XIV himself thus concludes: "These graces, these spiritual prerogatives, of Joseph are great, are eminent, are most certain, and are so exclusively his that they have not been given to any other saint."[12]

Upon the authority, then, of such celebrated Doctors,

---

10. P. iii. q. xxix. sec. i.
11. Lib. iv. Hom. viii.
12. *De Servorum Dei Beatificatione et Beatorum Canonisatione,* lib. iv. p. ii. c. xx. n. 38.

we may safely hold that Joseph, being, next to Mary, superior in dignity and holiness to all the other saints, must therefore have received from God privileges proportionately greater, and was consequently speedily cleansed from original sin, filled with the gifts of the Holy Spirit, and even confirmed in grace, with concupiscence subdued, if not extinguished, from the first moments of his existence, that thus he might be worthy of being associated with Jesus and Mary, and form with them that august Triad upon earth which is the joy of the whole universe.

Some, however, would allege as an objection the declaration of Christ, who said, "There hath not arisen among them that are born of women a greater than John the Baptist" (*Matt.* 11:11); whence they infer that Joseph might, indeed, be equal to the Baptist, but could not surpass him. Nevertheless, we have the secure authority of Benedict XIV for considering that this praise of John detracts nothing from the pre-eminent glories of Joseph, since Jesus, in asserting that none had arisen greater than John the Baptist, was not speaking absolutely, but comparatively. He was speaking of him as compared to the saints and prophets of the Old Testament, and, moreover, was excluding from His general assertion those who ought to be excluded, and excepting those who ought to be excepted, as is the case in all general assertions. Thus from this declaration Jesus naturally excluded Himself and excluded Mary; and so also He excluded Joseph, as belonging to an order much superior to that of the Baptist. Hence Maldonatus, a very learned commentator, speaking of this declaration of Christ, wrote, "I answer briefly and easily that here the Baptist, as St. Jerome affirms, is compared by Jesus, not to all the saints, but only to those of the Old Testament."[13] Now, Joseph certainly belongs to the New Testament, and is the first after Mary. Therefore he is excluded. Moreover, St. Jerome, commenting on the words

---

13. *In Matthaeum,* cap. xi.

of Christ, observes that Jesus did not in this declaration prefer John to all the prophets and patriarchs, but only made him equal to them.

Others, indeed, and with much reason, maintain that John is not here compared by Jesus with all the saints, but only with the prophets, he being, in fact, the Precursor Prophet; and that it is clearly in this sense that He must be understood would appear from the context in St. Matthew's Gospel, where, speaking of John to the multitude, Jesus asked, "What went you out into the desert to see? A prophet? Yea, I tell you, and more than a prophet"; adding afterwards, "And if you will receive it, he is Elias that is to come." (*Matt.* 11:14). The meaning, therefore, of what Jesus proceeded to say was that among those who were born of women there had not risen a greater prophet than John the Baptist; and he was greater in this respect, that the other prophets beheld the Messias in spirit and announced Him long before, but John saw Him and announced Him as present. The words of Our Lord, as given in St. Luke's Gospel, confirm this view: "Amongst those that are born of women there is not a greater *prophet* than John the Baptist." (*Luke* 7:20). Zachary had foretold that his child should be called "the prophet of the Highest" (*Luke* 1:76); and Holy Church herself styles him the greatest of the prophets, and in her hymns declares the reason, namely, that the prophets who preceded him prophesied of Jesus from afar, but John pointed him out with his finger as present, and as the Lamb of God come to take away the sins of the world. (*John* 1:29, 36). Besides, in the very declaration which Jesus made He expresses a limitation of John's superiority, adding, "Yet he that is the lesser in the Kingdom of Heaven is greater than he"; by which we may understand he that is most profoundly humble; Jesus in these words alluding in a special sense to Himself, next to Mary, and then to St. Joseph, who for the greatness of his humility was, with the exception of the Blessed Virgin, unsurpassed by any saint. So, too, when His dis-

ciples asked Our Lord who was the greater in the Kingdom of Heaven He called unto Him a little child and,
setting him in the midst of them, He said, "Whosoever
shall humble himself as this little child, he is the greater
in the Kingdom of Heaven." (*Matt.* 18:1-4). Therefore,
since Joseph next to Mary excels in humility, it follows
that he is greater than all the other saints, including
the Baptist. Thus the superiority of St. Joseph is confirmed also by these words of Christ.[14]

Nothing in what has been said can be viewed as any
derogation of the high titles and sublime sanctity of
John the Baptist, who attained even to meriting the
praises of a God; the sole object being to remove all
doubt of the pre-eminence of Joseph, and to prove that
in his greatness and glory he must be reckoned, after
Jesus and Mary, as excelling all the saints and angels.

---

14. We have given Vitali's comment in his own words; but it may be well to cite a
contrary opinion. F. Coleridge writes: "This mode of explanation does not fully
meet the difficulty; for Our Lord says, not the lesser simply, but the lesser in the
Kingdom of Heaven. The words which presently follow upon these serve to confirm the supposition that Our Lord is here drawing a contrast between the greatest of the Prophets of the Old Law and the lowest offices of the New Kingdom;
and that this is the true explanation of these words about St. John. Great, indeed,
he was, as compared to the very greatest of the old Prophets, and yet he belonged,
with them, to the Old, and therefore greatly inferior, Dispensation, and thus it is
that his greatness is almost as nothing in comparison to the powers and digni-
ties of the ministers of that New Dispensation to which, indeed, he opened the
door, but to which he nevertheless did not by his office belong."—*The Training of
the Apostles,* part ii. p. 271.

Chapter IX

Joseph the Harbinger of Redemption—He
Belongs to the New More than to the
Old Testament.

A S after a long and deep night we first discern the
white light of dawn, to which the rosy aurora
succeeds, ushering in the resplendent sun, even
so, after the long and dismal night of error and corruption in the Gentile world, Joseph appeared, like the
early dawn, and after Joseph came Mary, who is the
celestial aurora, of whom was born Jesus, the true and
eternal Sun of Justice. Thus, as the dawn precedes the
aurora, and the aurora the sun, so Joseph preceded
Mary, and Mary Jesus.

And truly Jesus, the eternal refulgent Sun of Justice,
came to illuminate the world, immersed in the thick
darkness of false belief and sin, with the light of His
doctrines, His examples, and His miracles. "That was the
true light," says the Evangelist, "which enlighteneth every
man that cometh into this world." (*John* 1:9). But before
He arose, appeared the glowing and pure aurora, whose
roseate light rejoiced Heaven and earth, that is, Mary,
who in Scripture is compared thereto: "*quasi aurora sur-*
gens—as the morning rising" (*Cant.* 6:9)—and this beautiful aurora was to be preceded by the white light of
dawn, giving presage to men that the joyful day was at
hand; and this was Joseph. Wherefore it was with reason said that this blessed Triad on earth marks the confines between the ancient law and the beginning of the

55

new, even as the dawn, the aurora, and the sunrise mark the passage from night to day. Of the Blessed Virgin St. Thomas Aquinas says that she formed the transition from the Old to the New Law, as the aurora forms the confine between night and day; and of St. Joseph Isolano writes that he stood midway between the Synagogue and the Church, announcing the close of the one and the commencement of the other.[1] Whence we may argue that Joseph in point of time was the first sign of light, the first ray which shone upon the earth to give notice that the aurora was about to arise, from which was to emanate that longed-for Sun which was to dispel all darkness and bring in eternal day. Thus Joseph was the herald of Mary and Jesus; and he may be regarded as standing between the Old and the New Covenant. But to which does he belong? Does he belong to the Synagogue or does he belong to the Church?

The question is not a new one, but it may be considered as now resolved. Some doctors were of opinion that Joseph belonged to the Old Law, simply because when he departed this life there as yet existed neither Church, nor priests, nor Sacraments, but this is not altogether true; for, if the Church did not exist in its completed form, it existed in its commencement. The Catholic Church, according to St. Athanasius and other Fathers, began to have a visible existence even in the cave of Bethlehem; and Bethlehem, the House of Bread, received Jesus, Mary, Joseph, and then the shepherds and the Magi, who were the first-fruits of the true believers. Jesus was the Author, the Head of the Church, its corner-stone and its foundation-stone; Jesus was the High Priest by excellence; Jesus was the Giver and the Fountain of that grace which He afterwards lodged in the Sacraments. Mary was the first in this Church, nay, its Queen; after Mary, Joseph was the first and the most fervent of all the faithful, its first persecuted just

---

1. St. Thomas, *Sent.* iv. *Dist.* xxx. q. ii. a. 1; Isolano, *Summa de Donis S. Joseph,* p. iii. c. xvi.

one. It is, therefore, generally held by Doctors that St. Joseph undoubtedly belongs more to the Catholic Church than to the Synagogue; and Benedict XIV himself favors this opinion, where, in answer to the doubt proposed, he says that where it is question of origin, birth, and education in youth, Joseph belongs to the Old Testament, but where it is question of faith, spirit, profession, works, ministry, and co-operation in laying the first foundation of the Church itself, he belongs, without doubt, to the New Law.[2] For who, indeed, next to Mary, had more faith in the Divine Redeemer and more love for Him? Who had more knowledge of His spirit, and who was more imbued with it from his close and continual association with Him and with His Blessed Mother for thirty years? Who better observed His precepts and counsels? Who better discharged the ministry confided to him? Who, next to Mary, was enabled so immediately and so faithfully to co-operate in the mystery of the Incarnation, and thus, indirectly, in the foundation of the Catholic Church? Indeed, we may well think that, since Joseph saved Jesus from the anger of Herod, in Jesus he saved the whole Church, and from that time therefore merited the title and acquired the right to be the Patron of the same Church. Moreover, the whole Church has always regarded and venerated him as her own, and now more than ever in her sacred rites and feasts she exalts him as her incomparable Protector, her glory, and her defense.[3]

Another reply, both shorter and more simple, is that Joseph up to the time of his espousals with the Blessed Virgin belonged to the Synagogue, but that after his espousals and the most sacred day of the Incarnation of the Word he belonged incontestably to the Catholic Church; so much so as to be comprised with Jesus and Mary in the order of the Hypostatic Union, which is the highest order in the hierarchy of grace. Thus the

---

2. *De Canonizatione,* lib. iv. p. ii. c. xx. a. 14.
3. *Hymn. ad Matut. in Festo S. Joseph.*

seraphic St. Bernardine of Siena tells us that Joseph had in his hands the keys to open the gates of the New Law and to close those of the Law of Moses.[4]

---

4. *Sermo de S. Joseph.*

Chapter X

Joseph's Family and Parentage.

WE WILL now speak of the family from which Joseph sprang. The history of his ancestors is that of the kings of Juda. No more ancient, noble, or glorious race could be found in the whole world, but this is to say little; for the genealogy of Joseph is that of the King of kings Himself. St. Matthew, as we have seen, gives as His genealogy that of Joseph, calling it "the book of the generation of Jesus Christ, the son of David, the son of Abraham." (*Matt.* 1:1). On this Doctors of the Church have observed that the Evangelist enumerates all the ancestors of Joseph, not so much in order to trace Mary's descent and, consequently, that of her Divine Son as to make us understand that in Joseph were accomplished all the glories of his forefathers, all their hopes, all their prayers; that in Joseph all their virtues were combined, but in far greater fullness and perfection; that in Joseph was closed and terminated that line of great patriarchs who were the glory of Israel, but whom Joseph greatly surpassed from his incomparable election to be the destined husband of her of whom, by the operation of Divine power, Jesus was born. Thus, if Abraham was faithful and obedient, Joseph was still more faithful and obedient; if Isaac was solicitous and pious, much more solicitous and pious was Joseph; if Jacob was suffering and laborious, much more suffering and laborious was Joseph. Our saint was more patient than Job, more chaste than the first Joseph, more zealous than Moses; he was meeker than David, more fervent than Elias, more trustful than Ezechias, more courageous and intrepid than Mathathias.[1]

The Abbot Rupert observes that among the promises of the Messias made by God the fullest was that made to Joseph. God promised Abraham that of his race the Redeemer should be born, and that in him all the nations of the earth should be blessed. To David God promised that the Divine Saviour should spring from his family and inherit his throne forever. To Joseph, finally, who was of the house and lineage of David and a descendant of Abraham, God promised that His Divine Son, who was to be born of his Virgin Spouse, should "save His people from their sins." (*Matt.* 1:21). Thus in Joseph alone were the promises of God accomplished; whence the Abbot concludes that he was the last in time of the order of the Patriarchs, and that in him all the ancient promises were summed up and completed. Abraham, David, and the rest beheld them and saluted them from afar; Joseph saw them near to him, verified and fulfilled. The last promise was made to Joseph, but it was the best, the most desired, the fullest, the most complete.[2] Thus Joseph was the happiest, the most highly privileged, the most exalted, and the last of the patriarchs; last in time, but first in dignity.

In one sole respect did the other patriarchs surpass him; that is, in abundance of the comforts of life, of riches, of titles, of honors. The others were, for the most part, born in the enjoyment of wealth, or amidst the splendor of a court, or even with the regal sceptre in their hands; but not so Joseph. Joseph was born poor, though not a mendicant, in a humble but not an abject condition. A small house and scanty goods constituted

---

1. P. Patrignani, quoted with such high praise by Benedict XIV, says: "Joseph is the crown of the Patriarchs and progenitors of the promised Divine Messias. He inherited all their benedictions, and beheld their fulfillment. He was the original figured by Joseph, the governor and saviour of Egypt. He was the crown of the saints of the Old Testament; in him all their virtues were combined and perfected; and he was the crown of the saints of the New Testament."—*Novena di S. Giuseppe,* Gior. vi.
2. *De Div. Off.* lib. iii. c. xix.

the whole of his earthly possessions. He had a title to the throne of his ancestors, but the regal power had fallen into the hands of greedy procurators and foreign tetrarchs. He had, therefore, neither a royal palace, nor a long train of attendants; he had neither courtiers, nor treasure, nor domains, nor tribute, nor the homage of subject nations. Through the vicissitudes of the Babylonian captivity, the violent deeds of Antiochus, and the avidity of domineering potentates, the legitimate patrimony of his ancestors had been seized and dissipated. But, if Joseph was not born great in the eyes of the world, he was great before God for the abundance of graces with which He had liberally endowed and enriched him above all the kings and patriarchs, his progenitors. Jesus, who came into the world to condemn luxury, pride, and the insatiate desire of self-exaltation, was preparing for Himself a father, albeit only putative, who, if, on the one hand, he came of royal blood, so that the great ones of the earth could not be offended in him, was, on the other hand, humble, poor, lowly, that He might raise the miserable from their abjection, and thus fulfill the great end of His divine mission. Of the poor but most holy Joseph Jesus desired to form, as it were, a type, a perfect example, of every Christian virtue, to be afterwards proposed as a model to all the faithful, that they might imitate his piety, his religiousness, his patience, his obedience, his submission to the Divine Will, his fraternal charity, his unwearied activity in the fulfillment of his duties and in the exercise of every private and domestic virtue. God was preparing in Joseph a true friend, a protector, and a patron for those unthinking men of the people who become so often the sport and the prey of designing agitators. Jesus chose Joseph poor, as He subsequently chose His Apostles from among the poor, that the world might understand that He came to convert the whole earth, not by gold or by force, not by the pomp of secular power, but by the humility of the Gospel, by the poverty of the Cross, and by the admirable virtue of His example, of His word, and of the prodigies which He wrought, in order that the divine mission and divine origin of His Church might be the more manifest.

Having seen how Joseph was descended from Abraham and from the kings of Juda, and how, in particular, he was of the house and family of King David, we will now speak of his own parents. We are, as already observed, expressly told by the Evangelist St. Matthew the name of his father, for in closing his genealogy he says, "Mathan begat Jacob, and Jacob begat Joseph, the husband of Mary, of whom was born Jesus, who is called Christ." (*Matt.* 1:15-16). On this point, therefore, no doubt could arise. The difficulty suggested by the text of St. Luke has been already considered. Heli, there is the strongest reason to believe, is the same with Joachim, the father of Mary, and he became, therefore, the father-in-law, or legal father, of Joseph, his father by affinity, and whom, like his Blessed Spouse, he would call by that name. We owe much, therefore, to St. Luke, who, without departing from the custom of the Hebrews, has given in fact the direct genealogy of Mary. And this opinion acquires higher value if we admit—and we have no reason not to admit—the truth of what Menochius, Benedict XIII, and other Doctors assert, namely, that St. Anne, the mother of our Blessed Lady and the wife of Joachim, was sister to Jacob, the father of Joseph; whence it would follow that Joseph and Mary were first cousins, and that Mary, as also her Divine Son, was descended from King David by the double line of Solomon and Nathan; from Nathan on the paternal side and from Solomon on the maternal.

While, however, we know with certainty from Holy Scripture itself the names both of the actual and the adopted father of Joseph, it contains no notice of his mother. Tradition has been equally silent on the subject; yet we naturally conceive that she must have been a woman of singular virtue, to be selected by God to be the mother of a saint so highly privileged as was Joseph, who was destined for so exalted a dignity as the reputed father of His Eternal Son. Scripture and tradition are equally silent as to whether any supernatural signs preceded his birth, to foretell, as in the Baptist's case, the high mission for which he was designed, or, as under the Old Law, to announce the appearance of some great deliverer. It has pleased God that, if any such were vouchsafed to his parents, they should, like so much else that concerns the humble Joseph, be veiled in obscurity; one reason of which may be that his mission, although surpassingly great, was not to be of a public character. He did not come to speak to the world, and, in fact, we do not possess one recorded syllable from his lips. Be this as it may, we are left to our devout imaginations as to the character and even the name of the fortunate mother of our glorious saint.

But when did he first see the light of day? What was the date of his birth? What was the year, the month, the day? Waiving the difficulties which have arisen respecting the precise date of the Nativity, and accepting the common opinion of the learned Natalis Alexander[3] that Jesus was born in the year 4,000 of the creation of the world, there would still remain an uncertainty as to the year of St. Joseph's birth, unless we possessed some assured record of his age at the time of his espousals with the Blessed Virgin, of which more anon. As respects the month, the month of March · being throughout the Church dedicated to his honor, and, indeed, commonly called the Month of St. Joseph, some would have it that he was born in this month, and allege as proof that in the most ancient martyrologies the 19th of March, which we keep as his feast, is entered as his birthday; while the Christians of the East, particularly the Copts, Syrians, and Egyptians, commemorated the glorious death of the saint on the 20th of July. This feast, we are told by Isolano, in his *Summary of the Gifts of St. Joseph,* the Oriental Christians were in the habit of celebrating with great veneration;

---

3. Saec. i. diss. ii. q. 1.

whence it would follow that on the 19th of March his
birthday alone was kept. The same opinion has been
held in more recent times. Nevertheless, the reasons
given would seem insufficient to establish this point;
for the Church has always been in the habit of regarding the day when a saint departs from this life as his
natal day, since it is then that he is born to glory; and
when it desires to signify that the feast celebrates his
birth into this world the word "nativity" is expressly
used, as in the case of the Blessed Virgin and of St.
John the Baptist. Moreover, it is a question whether
there be not a confusion, in respect to this custom of
the Orientals, between our patriarch, who in the Gospel
of St. Matthew is characterized as "just" (*Matt.* 1:19),
with another St. Joseph who had also the cognomen of
Just and, along with St. Matthias, was proposed by the
Apostles as successor to Judas the traitor, the lot falling
on Matthias. (*Acts* 1:23). Now, the martyrdom of this
St. Joseph, or Barsabas, surnamed Justus, is in the
Roman martyrology on the 20th of July with these
words: "The natal day of St. Joseph, surnamed the Just."
Hence it seems more probable, and more in conformity
with the tradition of the Church, that it is St. Joseph's
happy death and passage to glory which we commemorate on the 19th of March. But, as the Church celebrates another festival in his honor, that of his
Patronage, on the third Sunday after Easter, we may
well feel that in this feast a memorial of his nativity,
which may have occurred about this season of the year,
is included; for in the first vespers Holy Church com-
mences her prayers and canticles with these words:
"Jacob begat Joseph, the husband of Mary, of whom
was born Jesus, who is called Christ,"[4] and then proceeds to congratulate St. Joseph on being constituted
as lord over His house and ruler over all His possessions; just as on the Nativity of Mary she says, "Today
is born the Blessed Virgin Mary, of the race of David,

---

4. *Antiph. in I. Vesp. Patron. St. Joseph.*

through whom has appeared to believers the Salvation of the World."[5]

As to the day of the week on which Joseph was born, we have nothing to guide us but the piety of the faithful, by the common consent of whom, and with the Church's approval, all the Wednesdays of the year have been dedicated to St. Joseph; the Roman Pontiffs having, moreover, enriched with indulgences the devout practice of honoring him specially on that day. We may, therefore, piously believe that it was on Wednesday our great patron was either born or died.

Four cities of Judea and of Galilee have disputed the honor of being this great saint's birthplace: Jerusalem, Capharnaum, Nazareth, and Bethlehem. It is urged in favor of the claims of Jerusalem, that his ancestors of the house of David dwelt on the hill of Sion, the city of the Great King, and, even in their depressed fortunes, continued to make it their place of refuge; so that it was here that Joseph was born, and not Joseph only, but Mary herself, the house which St. Joachim and St. Anne inhabited being pointed out to pilgrims and travellers. St. John Damascene confirms this opinion, saying that the Blessed Virgin was born in the house of Joachim near the Probatic Pool. Nevertheless, Jerusalem has not been able to establish its title to be the birthplace of either Joseph or Mary.

The pretensions of Capharnaum, standing on the shores of the Lake of Tiberias, were, according to Calmet, grounded on the familiar acquaintance which, as we learn in St. John's Gospel, the inhabitants claimed to have with Joseph, the reputed father of Jesus. "Is not this Jesus, they said, the son of Joseph, whose father and mother we know? How, then, saith He, I came down from heaven?" (*John* 6:42). But it does not necessarily follow that, because the people of Capharnaum knew Joseph well, therefore he was born in their city. He may have had frequent intercourse with them, as had Jesus

---

5. *Resp. pri. Noct. in Off. Nativ. B. Mariae Virginis.*

Himself, of whom, as we know, it was not the birth-place. "Bethlehem," says St. John Chrysostom, "gave to Jesus His place of nativity, Nazareth brought Him up, Capharnaum was His continued abode."[6]

In favor of Nazareth higher probabilities may be alleged. St. Luke in his Gospel says that, after the flight into Egypt, Joseph, Mary, and Jesus returned to *"their city Nazareth"*;[7] and St. John relates how Philip, hav-ing seen Jesus, said to Nathaniel that they had found the Messias foretold by Moses and the prophets, Jesus "the son of Joseph of Nazareth." (*John* 1:45). But, as regards the first text, it would appear that Nazareth was rather Mary's native place than Joseph's, and, if called his city also, it was but as the city of his domi-cile, where, after his espousals with Mary, he had his fixed abode. From the other text of St. John it is also clear that nothing further can be concluded. We know well that Our Lord was born at Bethlehem, and yet He is called "Jesus of Nazareth," and continued to be so called. The same may well apply to St. Joseph. Nazareth was, indeed, the birthplace of the Blessed Virgin, and became the permanent abode of the Holy Family; where-fore Jesus, as well as Joseph, was said to be of Nazareth, although it was the native place of neither.

In this contest Bethlehem must carry off the palm for the following reasons. The descendants of David through Solomon are said to have continued to abide in Bethlehem, where David was born, and to have returned thither after the Babylonian captivity, the site of the house of Isai, his father, and the cisterns belong-ing to it being still traditionally pointed out. The Fathers accordingly called Joseph a Bethlehemite, meaning, not only that he was of the house and family of David, but that there also he was born; and Isolano repeats an ancient Oriental legend in which it is expressly said that Joseph was a carpenter, born at Bethlehem, of the house of David. But the most substantial and conclu-

6. *Hom.* xiii. *in Mattaeum.*
7. St. Luke ii. 39; conf. St. Matthew ii. 23.

sive reason is the following: that in the census which Caesar Augustus commanded to be made all were to go for registration to their own native place, and Joseph, prompt in his obedience to every law, even human, so as it was not opposed to the divine law, immediately repaired with his holy spouse Mary, not to Jerusalem, nor to Capharnaum, but to Bethlehem. In Bethlehem Christ was to be born, and from little it was to become great, because, as the Prophet Micheas foretold, out of it was to come forth He who was to be the ruler of Israel. (*Mich.* 5:2). But previous to this honor of giving birth to the Messias, the Lord of the universe, it was also to be the native place of His reputed father, constituted by God to be the protector and patron of the Universal Church.

Let us in spirit betake ourselves to the dwelling-place of Jacob, and bend before the cradle of this blessed infant, upon whose serene brow repose the choicest graces of Heaven. Let us bend before him and venerate him, and present to him the devout affections of our hearts. He is already for us our star, our hope, and he will be our guide, our shield, our defense, our tutelary angel. Let us offer to him our congratulations, and, kissing his feet, bless our compassionate God for having been pleased to bestow on the human family, on the Catholic Church, next to Mary, the sweetest, the most holy, the most powerful Patron.

Chapter XI

The Birth of Joseph a Joy in
Heaven and in Limbo.

THE birth of the saints is, as St. Ambrose observes, the cause of joy to many. Thus, before John the Baptist came into the world the angel announced to Zachary that many should rejoice at his birth. (*Luke* 1:14). Now, Joseph was, next to Mary, the most eminent among the saints, and was to be born for the profit of all, since he was destined by God to be the Patron of all Christians. How, then, could it be possible that his nativity should pass unnoticed and not be the cause of joy in Heaven?

The Blessed Trinity rejoiced at the birth of him who by his wisdom and prudence, his virginity and his charity, should veil the admirable mystery of the Incarnation from the eyes of the profane until the day fixed for its revelation; him to whom the Eternal Father was wholly to confide His Only-Begotten Son for well-nigh thirty years; to whom this Only-Begotten Son was to make Himself subject (*Luke* 2:51), regarding him in the place of a father; to whom the Holy Ghost was in full confidence to entrust His Immaculate Spouse; and through whom the Most Holy Trinity would be eternally blessed, as It was afterwards to be in a yet higher degree by the birth of Mary, of whom St. Cyril of Alexandria wrote, "Through her the Trinity was glorified, Heaven exulted, and the angels were made glad."[1] More-

---

1. *Hom.* vi. *in Nestor.*

over, as a sign of predilection, the Blessed Trinity was pleased immediately to confirm our saint in grace, so that by a special privilege he should never commit even a venial sin, a privilege which was most fitting in him who was to be in the place of a father to the Son of God and the true spouse of His immaculate and holy Mother. Scripture itself tells us that the glory of fathers rests upon their children (*Prov.* 17:6); and so, too, the honor of a husband is reflected on his wife; wherefore the Blessed Trinity multiplied Its gifts and graces in Joseph, sanctifying him (as we have shown) in his mother's womb. The holy Doctor, Alfonso de' Liguori, preaching on the heart of St. Joseph, says, "God having destined Joseph to fill the office of father to the Incarnate Word, it must be held as certain that He conferred upon him all the gifts of wisdom and sanctity befitting such an office." And then he adduces in particular the threefold privilege which Gerson and Suarez attribute to him: that of being sanctified in the womb, confirmed in grace, exempted from the rebellion of concupiscence. "O blessed forever," he exclaims, "be the adorable goodness of God who so nobly exalted Joseph, for our advantage also and that of the whole Church!"

All the angelic hierarchies rejoiced at the birth of Joseph, because they beheld the time arrived when Heaven should be re-opened and the seats which were left vacant by the rebel angels should again be filled. On seeing him raised to an order superior even to the highest angelic choirs, seized with a holy wonder, they sang Glory to God, and joyfully honored him as the foster-father of their King and the spouse of their glorious Queen. But especially did those heavenly spirits rejoice who were chosen by God to guard him with loving reverence. To every human being, as we know, God appoints at his birth a guardian angel, who shall faithfully accompany, defend, and protect him in all the necessities and perils of life; and to one who is to hold high offices committed to him by God for the benefit of others, a second angel of a superior order is assigned, that he may be enabled more efficaciously to fulfill the mission with which he has been charged.[2] "Oh, how high," exclaims the great Doctor, St. Jerome, "is the dignity of souls, which from the moment of their birth have each of them an angel appointed by God as guardian!"[3] But if a soul is glorious which has a single tutelary angel given it, how much more glorious must that soul be which is surrounded by many sublime spirits of Paradise! And such we must fain believe was the case with our great saint.

But it may be asked, if Joseph was confirmed in grace and freed from the solicitations of concupiscence, what need had he of angelic guardianship? If he was thus specially protected by God, nay, was himself appointed to be the faithful guardian of Jesus and Mary, if he was placed in an order superior to that of the angels, does it not seem that these spirits should be given to him rather as attendants than as guardians? In reply to this objection we must repeat that if Joseph, as Doctors of the Church affirm, excelled the angels in dignity, he was not their superior in nature, since the angelic nature is undoubtedly higher than the human; and, indeed, in this was manifest the surpassing goodness of the Son of God towards us, that, when He would redeem the world from the bondage of sin, He humbled Himself to assume our human nature and not that of the angels.

Now, let us see if it was needful that Joseph should have the guardianship of angels, and in what sense it was needful. The Angelic Doctor, St. Thomas, speaking of man in his state of innocence, says that, although, through his possession of original justice, all within him was well regulated, nevertheless, as he was exposed to dangers from without, he needed the guardianship of angels. And the same great Doctor says, speaking of

---

2. A remarkable instance of this is recorded in the Life of M. Olier, the venerable founder of the Seminary of St. Sulpice, who himself relates the singular circumstance under which he was given an angel of his office in addition to his own angel-guardian.—Chap. iii. pp. 43, 44.
3. *Comment. in Matthaeum,* cap. xviii.

the Blessed Virgin, that, as she was not *in statu comprehensorum,* but was still *in via,*[4] she required while on earth to have angelic guardians. From all which we may infer that Joseph, albeit innocent and confirmed in grace, needed the same loving tutelage. For if it behooved the Blessed Virgin to have this guardianship, who was Mother of God and herself the Queen of Angels, how much more must Joseph, who was far inferior, have required it, both on account of perils from without, and also because he was in the state of *viator;* for it is precisely to such as are in the way that God appoints the angels as guardians (*Ps.* 90:11); with this difference, however, that, whereas to other men the angels are given as veritable guides, directors, and tutors, as superiors for the government of inferiors, who have actual need of being assisted and ruled in all things, to Mary and to Joseph they were assigned as guards of honor, who, clearing the way before them and removing every external peril, should bring them high messages from Heaven, and form their glorious retinue. A learned doctor, Tostatus Abulensis, thus sums up the purposes for which guardian angels were assigned to Joseph from his birth. 1) For his solace and comfort in life. 2) To guide him externally, and warn him of impending dangers.   3) To remove every impediment which men or devils should cast in his way. 4) For the fuller enlightenment of his mind. 5) For the increase of his merit. 6) To communicate to him the will of God. 7) To pay him honor as the spouse of Mary and the reputed father of Jesus.

And that not one angel alone but many were assigned to Joseph may be inferred from the fact that, when Divine Goodness elects any individual for a sublime position involving most important offices, it never fails to furnish him with the necessary means of fulfilling his obligations, among which, in addition to interior

---

4. *Summa,* p. i. q. cxiii. a. 4; p. iii. q. xxx. a. 2. By *in statu comprehensorum* is meant the state of those who have attained to their end, the beatific vision of God in Heaven; by *in via,* the state of those who are still traversing the way of this life.

gifts and graces, must be reckoned the consolations and external advantages which the guardianship of angels affords. St. Bernardine of Siena, quoting the opinion of St. John Chrysostom, St. George of Nicomedia, and St. Bonaventura, affirms that to the Blessed Virgin, already so specially protected by God Himself, many legions of angels were assigned as guardians. How, then, could it be that to Joseph, the spouse of Mary, to him who was honored by God not, indeed, as highly as was Mary, but, next to her, above all others, only one angel should be given, considering, moreover, the various exalted offices for which he was chosen, for each of which we may believe he had a special angel appointed to assist him? Some would have to serve as a guard to his person, others to pay due honor to his dignity, as the reputed father of Jesus and the spouse of Mary. Whence a pious writer, P. Patrignani, says that "St. Joseph was the most highly favored of men, being assisted and honored by angels. He received from them consolation in sufferings, light in perplexities, service and aid in toils and labors." Then, turning to the saint, he exclaims, "I marvel not, O most glorious St. Joseph, that thou wast so favored by the angels, since thou wast so like to them in thy own angelic purity. Neither do I marvel that they should be, so to say, ambitious of serving thee, seeing that they regarded thee as superior in dignity to themselves."[5] And these very angels, belonging even to the highest among the angelic hierarchies, who afterwards consoled him, accompanied him, and strengthened him in the numerous painful vicissitudes of his life, these same glorious spirits does Joseph now employ to succor so many who mourn, so many afflicted families, and, in fine, the whole Church Catholic placed under his protection; saying to them, in the language of the prophet Isaias, "Go, ye swift angels, to a nation rent and torn in pieces . . . to a nation expecting and trodden underfoot." (*Is.* 18:2). These angels, not only

---

5. *Il Divoto di S. Giuseppe,* Novena, Gior. vii.

joyfully fulfill his behests, but vie with each other in forestalling his holy desires; and no wonder, since, seeing that Jesus, their King, the King of angels and of men, made Himself subject and obedient to Joseph, they know not how better to honor so great a saint than by paying him the highest reverence and homage, the humblest and most entire subjection. Here, then, we perceive the reason why at his happy birth they surrounded him with such festal joy.

The joy they felt must have had its echo among the trustful inhabitants of Limbo, to whom angels, doubtless, reported the blessed tidings that the hour of their deliverance was approaching. The birth of Joseph was the first signal of the coming of Christ. Joseph was the morning star announcing the aurora which precedes the day. The rays of this star must have filled that gloomy abode with light. And, oh, with what exceeding complacency the holy Fathers, turning their eyes to Bethlehem, must have contemplated the infant Joseph, seeing how in him all their patriarchal and prophetic dignity was about to bear its promised fruit! How they must have blessed the birth of this child, whose appearance in the world brought with it the assurance that soon their bonds would be broken, their prison opened, their banishment ended, and that they would behold their long-desired Redeemer! The very thought must have caused them unutterable joy.

Chapter XII

The Birth of Joseph a Joy on Earth.

WHEN Heaven smiles, there must be responsive joy on earth, at least in some chosen hearts; and among these foremost must have been Joseph's fortunate parents. He was their first-born son, and as such, according to the custom of the Jews, a subject of much rejoicing. But although a veil is cast over his infancy and early years, and no reliable tradition has reached us on the subject, we can scarcely imagine that no wonderful signs preceded it, such as have announced the birth of saints much inferior to him both in office and in sanctity. If so many prodigies ushered in the birth of John the Baptist, who was a great prophet and the precursor of Christ, is it conceivable that no divine intimation preceded that of Joseph, the reputed father of Jesus, whom he brought up, and by whom he was so tenderly loved? But since nothing of the kind is recorded the matter must be left to the pious conjectures of his devoted clients.

One surmise, however, may be hazarded. On the eighth day the babe must have been circumcised, according to the command given to Abraham and confirmed by the law of Moses. On that occasion a name was always conferred on the child, and it was the father's place to pronounce what it should be; for we find that when the Baptist received that rite reference was made to Zachary as to how he would have him called, and he wrote "His name is John." (*Luke* 1:63). Jesus Him-

74

self received His Name on the eighth day, the day of His circumcision. The name of Joseph must, therefore, have been given to our saint on the day of his circumcision; and by whom was it given? Assuredly by Jacob, his father, in virtue of his paternal authority. But whence did the father derive this name? Who suggested it to him? Did he receive it from Heaven? We can hardly imagine that it was bestowed on this elect babe, as we might say, by chance, for in that case Joseph would have been inferior in this respect to many saints both of the Old and New Testament, who by a special favor received their names from God: as Abraham, Jacob, the Baptist, St. Peter, and others.

Now, since it is the common opinion of the Doctors of the Church that no gift or prerogative bestowed on the other saints, Mary always excepted, was denied to St. Joseph, it has been held by many writers to be most probable that the name of Joseph was revealed by an angel from God to his father Jacob, as was that of John to Zachary. Three reasons, according to Isolano, ought to persuade us that this name was given to Joseph by God Himself. First, its identity with that of the ancient patriarch Joseph, who on account of the wonderful things narrated of him has always been regarded as the type and figure of our saint. Secondly, the very fact that he was truly the spouse of the Mother of God and the foster-father of Jesus; for, if God gave their names to Abraham, Jacob, and Peter, with how much greater reason would He bestow a name on him who was to be brought into such close relations with His Divine Son! Thirdly, the signification of the name itself, which is interpreted as *increase,* a name most suitable to him in every way.[1]

The Angelic Doctor, St. Thomas, says that the names imposed by God on certain individuals are always significant of some gratuitous gift divinely conceded to them.[2] Thus the name given by God to Joseph, not only denotes the various gifts bestowed upon him for the fulfillment

---

1. *Summa de Donis S. Joseph,* p. i. c. i.
2. *Summa,* p. iii. q. xxxvii. a. 2.

of the great offices for which he was designed, but points
also to the continual increase of these gifts through his
co-operation and perfect correspondence with divine
grace. If the name of Mary, according to St. Bonaventura, was extracted from the treasures and jewel-
caskets of the Lord, from the same treasures and jewel-
caskets was drawn the beautiful name of Joseph. It
could not have been selected or imposed by men, because
it was to be closely and inseparably associated with
the Divine Name of Jesus and the holy name of Mary.
It was to be frequently pronounced by the august lips
of Jesus and to issue sweetly from the pure lips of His
Virgin Mother. It was often to be registered in the Gospel,
finding its place sometimes before, sometimes between,
sometimes after the blessed Names of Jesus and of
Mary. The angels were often to repeat it in their messages, and men often to invoke it in their needs. Many,
indeed, of God's people have borne this name, but in
them it was a simple appellation, void of special significance, but not so in our saint. In him it is full of
meaning, a name of great authority, of singular efficacy, of inestimable value. By interpretation it signifies, as has been said, *increase;* and so the ancient Jacob
said, prophesying, "Joseph is a growing son" (*Gen.* 49:22),
or, according to the Hebrew, "growing by a well." And
what is this life-giving fount near to which Joseph grows
and increases? First, it is Jesus, the well-spring of eternal life; secondly, it is Mary, who is the fountain conveying all the benedictions of Heaven. Close to these
two inexhaustible fountains Joseph grew, he increased
in all good; and not for himself alone, but also for us.
He not only grew, but flourished and bore fruit.[3] Hence
this name of Joseph imports for us likewise continual
increase, being so efficacious and powerful both with
Jesus and with Mary.

Joseph, sweet name, name sublime and powerful,
name which imparts gladness to the just, consolation

---

3. "Joseph est eritque filius fructificationis; id est, foecundus instar arboris sitae et
fructificantis juxta fontem."—Corn. à Lapide *(in loc.).*

to the afflicted, solace to those in tribulation, support to the feeble, courage to the timid, constancy to the wavering, confidence to sinners, and to the penitent the assurance of pardon! Name which is a deliverance in perils, a harbor in tempests, food in hunger, relief in destitution, peace in discords, victory in combats, health in sickness, and refuge in persecutions, a joy amidst tears, a shield, a defense, and a salvation in the last agonies! This name defeats every plot of the infernal foe, dissipates every baleful temptation, puts the devils to flight, and makes Hell itself tremble. Blessed is he who often in life invokes it; blessed he who is able to invoke it devoutly at death. He who has this holy name engraven on his brow and on his heart has a sure pledge of his salvation. St. Bonaventura, speaking of those who are devout to Mary, says that he who is stamped with her character, that is, with the love of her and of her virtues, and with the properties of a true devotion to her, will be registered in the Book of Life. And the same may be said of those who have the character, the love, the virtues of Joseph, and a true devotion to him. Blessed, then, is he who reposes under the safe shadow of the name and patronage of Joseph.

Chapter XIII

Joseph's Childhood and Youth.

THE rite of Circumcision being accomplished and the name bestowed, the offering of the firstborn in the Temple would next succeed. That Joseph was a firstborn son there can be no doubt. This opinion will hold good whichever of the two views that have been stated concerning his genealogy be the correct one. For if, according to the view with which we do not agree, Jacob married the widow of Heli, who had died without children, Joseph would still be the firstborn of this marriage. But we must own to a disinclination to believe that Joseph was the son of a mother who had been the wife of more than one husband. Such a mother scarcely seemed to befit him who was to be the pure spouse of a heavenly virgin and the reputed father of the Son of God Himself. Wherefore, we abide by the opinion that Joseph was the first-born of Jacob and of a young and holy spouse who had never been wedded to any other husband.

That Joseph was a first-born son we desire to establish, because under the ancient law it was esteemed an honor and a privilege to be so; and many advantages were attached to primogeniture. We can, therefore, well understand how when Esau recognized the great loss he had incurred by selling his birthright for such a trifle to his brother, he was filled with consternation and cried aloud for grief. (*Gen.* 27:34). Seeing, then, that primogeniture was an important prerogative, and that Joseph was to sum up in himself all the gifts and privileges of the patriarchs, he must needs have possessed the rights and advantages of a first-born son. This being so, Joseph, as we have said, was taken to Jerusalem to be presented in the Temple, and redeemed according to the prescriptions of the Law.

Jerusalem at that period had already begun to decline. After the profanations, the outrages, and the cruelties perpetrated by the monarchs who inherited the conquests of Alexander the Great in Syria, especially by Antiochus Epiphanes, the heroic resistance of the Machabees had obtained a temporary deliverance, but the Holy City had now virtually fallen under the domination of the Romans, who had appointed as procurator of Judea Antipater, the father of Herod. All who were of the race and family of David would court obscurity and concealment through the fear inspired by their jealous rulers. Nevertheless we may be certain that, although avoiding pomp and display, the pious Jacob and his spouse must have carefully fulfilled all the obligations of the law with respect to the infant Joseph, and have also brought him yearly with them to Jerusalem, as soon as his tender age permitted, for the Paschal solemnity. And with what ecstasy, may we well believe, would this favored child, when kneeling in the Temple, have joined in the exclamation of the Psalmist: "How lovely are Thy tabernacles, O Lord of Hosts! My soul longeth and fainteth for the courts of the Lord" (*Ps.* 83:1); and with what difficulty he would have torn himself away from the House of God, where willingly, like the young Samuel, he would have remained to spend his childhood and adolescence in the service and under the instruction of God's priests!

As time wore on, we may easily suppose that, when the parents of Joseph came up with their son to keep the feasts at Jerusalem, it would be to the house of Joachim they would repair, who at that period must have been already married to Anne, the sister, as we have already stated there is good reason to believe, of

Jacob, and therefore the aunt of Joseph. According to the testimony of St. John Damascene, and of a still living tradition, the house of St. Joachim and St. Anne was near the Probatic Pool[1] Here they dwelt for many years, until civil disturbances, probably, compelled their removal to Nazareth, where they had a small patrimony. Antipater had been succeeded in the post of procurator of Judea by Antigonus, the son of Aristobulus, but Herod his son, artful and ambitious, by ingratiating himself with the Romans, had himself named Tetrarch by the Senate, and two years later obtained the title of King of Judea, though some time elapsed before he was able to assume his authority. This Herod was (as we have said) the son of Antipater, an Ascalonite by nation, and an idolater. Although Judea had for some time been dependent on Rome and ruled, in fact, by her representatives, nevertheless the sceptre had not as yet departed from her. No stranger had been set up as king of the chosen people. Now, this was to be the sign of the approaching advent of the Messias, a thought which, under this new calamity, must have afforded consolation to those souls who were looking for the redemption of Israel; and they could not have been few in number, since the near accomplishment of the prophetic term of weeks, announced in vision to Daniel (*Dan.* 9:24, 25) as to elapse before the coming of Christ, furnished an additional token that the great Deliverer was at hand. And, indeed, we find that this expectation had reached the ears of the Gentiles and prevailed throughout the East, where it was generally known that the Hebrew people were looking for a King who would restore the glories of their nation.

Great consternation seized on the Jews at the news of the elevation of this foreign and idolatrous usurper to the throne of David. Had they not reason to dread the profanation of their temple, as in the days of Antiochus Epiphanes, the cessation of their sacrifices, the

---

1. Here was erected in the 6th century a church in honor of St. Anne, which remains to this day.

destruction of their altars, the dispersion of their priests, besides all the miseries which the conflict of this new ruler with Antigonus was certain to involve? Prayer was their only resource; and we may be sure that among the most fervent suppliants were Jacob and his young son, Joseph; nay, may we not piously believe that when, contrary to expectation, Herod subsequently, not only did not destroy the Temple, but largely reconstructed and adorned it, it was to the intercession of this holy child, who of all the dwellers upon earth at that time was dearest and most pleasing to God, that this happy result was mainly due? Two years after Herod's exaltation to the kingship of Judea he, with the assistance of the Romans, whose friendship he had bought, marched against Jerusalem, which during five months had to endure all the horrors of a siege; added to which, when its capture was effected, there ensued a fearful slaughter of the inhabitants by the Roman soldiery, enraged at the resistance they had encountered, and by the partisans of Herod within the walls.

Amidst all these dangers and calamities, Providence threw the shield of Its protection over the family of Joseph. But the early life of this great saint is so completely hidden in God that we must be contented to know that so it was, deprived as we are of details which would have possessed so high an interest for us. All we know for certain is that Joseph had to pass all his childhood and youth under the tyrannical rule of a proud, cruel, and jealous king; and hence always in peril, anxiety, and fear of fresh sufferings. History, so often unjust, has accorded to Herod the appellation of Great, simply because he was fortunate in his vices and in the success which his arrogance, his adroit cunning, and his cruelty won for him. Such an epithet ought to be reserved for those who have excelled in noble and signal virtues, whereas Herod was great only in his follies and in his crimes. The massacre of so many innocent babes in Bethlehem after Our Lord's nativity would alone suffice to blacken his memory and render it forever infamous. But besides this, he was continually staining his hands in blood; priests and lay- men alike, princes and high officers in his army, he would order to be executed, sometimes thirty at a time. He murdered his wife, Mariamne, and Alexandra, his sister-in-law, nay, even his own sons Alexander, Aristo- bulus, and Antipater, the last of whom he condemned to death only five days before he himself expired. To conciliate the people, however, he gave liberally when the country was desolated by plague and famine; he embellished Jerusalem, and enlarged the Temple; but this did not prevent the Jews from hating him as a tyrant, so that he had to fortify his regal abode and make to himself a citadel of the tower Antonia, which he built and named after his patron, Marcus Antonius. He was frequently accused at Rome both to Antonius and to Augustus, but he knew how to defend himself so dexterously that he returned triumphant to Jerusalem, where he put to death all whom he sus- pected of having been his accusers.

Under this impious and sanguinary king, then, Joseph had to pass his youth. As a descendant of the royal family of David, he had reason (as we have said) to live in continual apprehension. Jealousy and the fierce thirst of rule stimulated Herod to rid himself of any- one who he could so much as suppose might entertain the thought of depriving him of his usurped dominion. But that Divine Providence which had destined Joseph to co-operate in the great mystery of the Incarnation of the Son of God preserved and brought him safe through all the dangers which beset him. His meek- ness, humility, contempt for all the empty honors of the world, his peaceful temper, his submission to all the requirements of law, and the hidden and obscure life which he led, must have contributed to turn away all suspicion from this scion of the house of David. Accord- ingly, we do not hear of Herod's persecuting the fam- ily of Jacob, as he did all the partisans of Aristobulus and Hyrcanus. Jacob had one other son besides Joseph, the same, according to the historian Eusebius and others, who is frequently mentioned in the Gospel as Cleophas, or Alpheus, and whose sons are called the brethren of Our Lord (*Matt.* 13:55), that is, His cousins. So, too, Mary, the wife of Cleophas, who is also called in the first three Gospels the mother of James and Joseph, is styled by St. John the sister of the Mother of Jesus;[2] not that she was her sister in the literal sense of the term, but her sister-in-law and, indeed (as it is believed), otherwise nearly related to her.

An ancient Oriental tradition, which Isolano has inserted in his work on the Gifts of St. Joseph, records how our saint, when he must have been about twelve years of age, went to Jerusalem, as other youths were wont to do, there to learn science and wisdom from the Priests of the Lord, who were its sole teachers in those times. But however this may be, to render this science and wisdom truly perfect, God reserved for Joseph far more sublime instructors, the Incarnate Word Himself, and her whom the Church invokes under the title of Sedes Sapientiae, Seat of Wisdom, the Immaculate Virgin. In the school of Jesus and in the society of Mary for some thirty years Joseph must have become eminently perfect in the science of the saints. This consideration may serve to rectify a mistaken notion to be found even among some devout persons who, while esteeming Joseph to have been a very great saint, nevertheless imagine that he was simple and unlettered and endowed with but a slender amount of knowledge. No; Joseph had an exalted intellect, his judgment was profound, his wisdom surpassed that of the wisest among men. "God," says St. Bernard, "had found in Joseph, as in another David, a man after His own heart, to whom He could securely commit His heart's closest and most

---

2. *Matthew* 27:56; *Mark* 15:40, 47; 16:1; *Luke* 24:10; *John* 19:25. Mary, the wife of Cleophas, or Alpheus, had five sons and two daughters. The sons were Simon Zelotes, James the Less, and Jude, or Thaddeus, all three Apostles, Joseph surnamed the Just (*Acts* 1:23), and Simeon, a disciple of Jesus. The two daughters were Mary Salome (*Mark* 15:40; 16:1), wife of Zebedee and mother of James the Greater and John the Evangelist (*Matt.* 20:20; 27:56), and another Mary who is supposed to have been the mother of John surnamed Mark (*Acts* 12:12).

sacred secret; to whom He could manifest the secret and hidden things of His wisdom (*Ps.* 50:8), and communicate that great mystery which none of the princes of this world knew."[3] How, indeed, could it be otherwise? For, if of the ancient Joseph, who was but the figure of our Joseph, it was said that no one could be found like to him or wiser than he (*Gen.* 41:39), what must be said of our saint, who was not merely endowed with wisdom to interpret dreams, but was privileged to learn the secrets of Heaven, and to be admitted to the knowledge of the sublimest truths, revealed to him by angels, nay, taught him by the Son of God Himself and by the august Queen of all the Doctors of the Church?

---

3. *Super Missus est.* Hom. ii.

Chapter XIV

Joseph's Vow of Virginity.

IF HOLY SCRIPTURE nowhere expressly speaks of the chastity of Joseph previous to his espousals with Mary, we might well conclude it from the very fact of those espousals. We judge of the nature of a tree from the fruit which it produces; to know, then, that Joseph was the spouse of a virgin and of a Virgin-Mother such as Mary, was quite sufficient to persuade the great body of the Fathers to hold with security that Joseph was a virgin by his own election before he was chosen to be the husband of Mary. A few, it is true, too easily crediting the baseless statements of some of the Apocryphal books, which asserted that those who in the Gospel are called the brethren and sisters of Jesus were children of St. Joseph by a previous marriage, were led to withhold from him the gift and glory of perpetual virginity. But the great majority, and those of the highest authority, freely recognized this grace among those which enriched and adorned the spouse of the Blessed Virgin. As early, indeed, as the third century St. Athanasius spoke these short but weighty words of Joseph and Mary: that "both remained intact, as was proved by many testimonies";[1] and after him St. Jerome, defending the perpetual virginity of Mary against the heretic Helvidius, maintained that, not only Mary, but her spouse Joseph was ever a virgin, so that of this virginal marriage a virginal Son should be born. Hence

---

1. *De Incarnatione.*

St. Peter Damian asserts, in a letter to Pope Nicolas, and also in his work on the celibacy of the clergy, that such was the faith of the Church on this point; for that the Son of God, not content with having a virgin for His mother, willed that he who represented His Father should also be a virgin;[2] where we shall do well to observe that this great Doctor does not hesitate to qualify this belief as the "faith of the Church."

The Angelic Doctor, St. Thomas, enquiring how the most holy Virgin could give her hand as spouse to St. Joseph, seeing that she had made a vow of virginity, replies that the Blessed Virgin, before contracting espousals with St. Joseph, was certified by God that he had himself formed the same resolve of preserving perpetual virginity, and therefore that she exposed herself to no peril by her union with him.[3] Further, we find St. Francis de Sales, a most devout client of St. Joseph, strenuously maintaining his virginity and his vow. "How exalted in this virtue of virginity must he have been, who was destined by the Eternal Father to be the guardian or, rather, the companion in virginity of Mary herself! Both had made a vow to preserve virginity for their entire lives, and it was the will of God to join them in the bond of a holy marriage, not in any way to recall their vow, but rather to confirm it, and that they might strengthen each other to persevere in their holy resolution."[4]

From all these authorities it is clear that Joseph preserved through his whole life, and that by vow, the most angelic purity and virginity. Hence the Bollandists assert that the whole Latin Church, after St. Jerome, has ever held that Joseph lived and died a virgin.

The holy Doctors allege, moreover, other reasons, of a mystical order, to prove its essential propriety. It is a well-known saying of St. Gregory Nazianzen that the first virgin is the August Trinity. The Father is a vir-

---

2. *De Caelib. Sacerd.* cap. iii.
3. *In Quaest. Sent.* q. xi. a. 1.
4. *Entretien,* xix.

gin, who generates the Son in His eternal splendors; the Son is a virgin, who is generated by the Father without a mother; the Holy Spirit is a virgin, who proceeds eternally from the Father and the Son. After the image of this August Trinity the saints recognize a second Trinity on earth; of which the pious and learned Gerson said, "Would that I had suitable words to explain this most admirable and venerable Trinity, Jesus, Mary, and Joseph!"[5] Now, as the August Trinity in Heaven is the first and the altogether virgin, so also must the second Trinity on earth be altogether virgin. If Jesus is a virgin and Mary is a virgin, how should not Joseph, who completes this most virginal Trinity, be a virgin also? Jesus is the Head of virgins, Mary is the mother of virgins, Joseph is the guardian and patron of virgins.

That this glory belongs to Joseph may be seen still more clearly when we consider that he belongs to the order of the Hypostatic Union, in which, along with Jesus and Mary, prototypes of virginity, no one, assuredly, could be found who was not a spotless virgin. Hence Suarez says that Joseph shone so much the more in every virtue, especially in that of virginity, above all the other saints, inasmuch as he belonged to an order superior to that of all the other saints. It was fitting, therefore, that he who was immediately associated with the Most Sacred Humanity of Jesus should be altogether a virgin; otherwise he would be inferior to those saints who were ordained to a less intimate association with Jesus, as St. John the Baptist and St. John the Evangelist, and who, nevertheless, preserved perpetual virginity. And how could Joseph, who excelled in all virtues, fail of possessing this peerless gem, which was possessed by other saints far beneath him?

But more than this. Joseph, according to the opinion of St. Peter Chrysologus and of all other Doctors, was destined to occupy on earth the place of the Eter-

---

5. *Serm. de Nativ. B. Mariae Virg.* Consid. iv.

nal Father, and to represent Him in relation to His Divine Son. Now, perpetual virginity shines among the attributes of the Divine Paternity; wherefore Joseph, the representative on earth of the Divine Paternity, must needs, next to Mary, possess the beautiful virtue of virginity in the highest degree.

And are not the angels, to whom is committed the care of the world and the guardianship of men, pre-eminently virgins? Should not Joseph, then, to whom was committed the care and custody of Jesus and Mary, far excel the angels themselves in virginity? "And truly," says Isolano, "the virginity of Joseph was more noble, more acceptable, more profitable, more admirable, more perfect than that of the angels. More noble, because that of the angels is from nature, that of Joseph was from grace; more acceptable, because that of the angels is necessary, that of Joseph was voluntary; more profitable, because that of the angels is not meritorious, that of Joseph had high merit in the sight of God; more admirable, because that of the angels is in an impassible nature, that of Joseph was in passible and mortal flesh; more perfect, because that of the angels is only in the spirit, that of Joseph was in soul and body. Whence with justice does à Lapide write of Joseph that as regards this virtue he might be called an angel rather than a man."[6]

Joseph, then, was the first among men, as Mary was the first among women, to make a deliberate vow of perpetual virginity, notwithstanding the contrary prevailing custom; so that he may with reason be styled the Primate and Patriarch of all the religious and cloistered Orders, who consecrate themselves to God by a vow of perpetual virginity, as having led the way in embracing this first of the Evangelical counsels. And this determination on his part was so much the more heroic in that it was the earliest example of the kind, and appeared, not only opposed to the practice of the

6. *De Donis St. Joseph*, p. i. c. xiii.

people of God, but contrary to the scope and strict intention of the Law.

Whence, then, it may be asked, did Joseph derive this love of virginity, a state not encouraged by the ancient Law? It can hardly have had other source than a divine impression, produced in his soul by grace, of the excellence of this virtue, joined to a profound humility. For let us consider that St. Joseph must have conceived this design at the time when, the sceptre having departed from Juda, his nation had entered into new conditions, by being formally placed under the dominion of a foreign king; at a period, therefore, when the promises made by God to his house might be deemed near their accomplishment, and when, possibly, he himself, as being of the house and family of David, might be chosen by God to bear a part in the looked-for redemption of Israel. Hence we may perceive how solidly Joseph's virtue must have been based upon humility for him to esteem himself quite unworthy of having any share in an honor which for generations had been so coveted by his people. He resolved to remain chaste in the midst of the world, and thus excluded himself from the road to all human greatness and glory.

Let us, then, with all our heart congratulate the Patriarch of virgins, St. Joseph, on this his high prerogative. Let us rejoice with him for this most sublime gift, which God bestowed upon him that he might be a worthy companion of the Queen of Virgins, Mary. Let us earnestly beseech him to obtain for us from God the grace to be able, after his example, to lead pure and stainless lives on earth, that we may one day be with him in Heaven beholding the Face of God; for, as Christ has told us, it is only the clean of heart who shall see God. (*Matt.* 5:8).

Chapter XV

Joseph a Just Man—His Occupation.

GOD Himself, in the Holy Gospel, pronounces the encomium of St. Joseph by calling him "just." (*Matt.* 1:19). And the great Doctor, St. Jerome, thus expounds the term: "Joseph is called just on account of having possessed all virtues in a perfect degree." The word justice, in fact, comprehends every virtue, inasmuch as it leads man to render to each his due: to God, to his neighbors, and to himself; and when this debt is faithfully discharged, what else is wanting to true perfection?

Joseph rendered to God His due by the constant exercise of the three theological virtues, walking ever with the liveliest faith in the presence of God, with firm and stable hope expecting the near advent of the Messias, and with ardent charity loving without measure the sovereign goodness of God, and striving to the utmost of his power to make Him loved by others. He rendered faithfully to God His due by practicing all the duties of religion, continually praising Him, making Him oblations and sacrifices, sanctifying all His feasts, reverencing His Temple, honoring His priests. In one word, he gave himself wholly to God, and for His glory he would willingly have shed his blood.

To men he rendered their due by respecting them in their property, their honor, and their life. He loved them tenderly, was solicitous to assist them, and zealously edified them by his example. Compassion for the suf-

fering was, as it may be called, an integral portion of
his being. Like Job, he might have said, "From my
infancy mercy grew up with me." (*Job.* 31:18). This was
a gift specially infused into his soul by God in order
that, as he was to be the patron of the afflicted, his
heart should melt at once at the sight of misery and
be moved to give instant succor.

Finally, Joseph rendered to himself what was his
due: as respected his soul, treasuring up in it all the
virtues, all the merits, all the sound doctrine, and all
the holy operations necessary to salvation; as regarded
his body, procuring for it the fitting means for leading
an honorable life, even to the acquiring a handicraft
which might keep him holily employed and minister to
his temporal needs.

Thus abundantly furnished with divine grace, Joseph
had entered on the perfect possession of all virtues. He
is, therefore, with full reason styled "just" in the Holy
Gospel, and this, not merely to distinguish him from
other saints, as St. James the Less and Joseph called
Barsabas were styled just, but as being in reality perfectly just; just, not in an ordinary and common manner, but singularly and supereminently just. We have
here no slight indication of his sublime sanctity; for
while the people of God were expecting with earnest
longing the Just One by excellence, that is, the Messias, and were daily, in the words of the Prophet, praying that the clouds would rain down the Just (*Is.* 45:8),
behold, before the time, there appears on earth one who
is perfectly just. One who is just by grace precedes Him
who is just by nature. Joseph, adorned with all justice,
comes to figure and announce Jesus, who is called, and
is in fact, "the Lord, our Just One." (*Jer.* 23:6). Jesus,
who is the Sun of Justice, sends before Him this star
of justice, Joseph, who may thus be styled and is in
fact, after Mary, the first just one of the New Law; the
first justified and sanctified by the grace of the Redeemer
Christ; the first just one canonized expressly in the
Gospel by the Holy Spirit; first, not merely in the order

of time but in that of excellence, perfection, and dignity, always excepting the Most Blessed Virgin.

We have noticed how Joseph, to avoid idleness and procure an honorable livelihood, practiced a trade. Although the family of Joseph had long been shorn of its ancestral splendor and reduced to a humble state of life, we must not suppose that they were so far impoverished as even to be obliged at times to ask alms, which some have thought, grounding their supposition chiefly on the necessity in which, they say, Joseph found himself to practice a mechanical trade, and on the contempt in which he was on this account, according to them, held by his countrymen. To refute such exaggerations it is sufficient to refer to other special circumstances in Joseph's life, and to recollect the customs of his nation.

Joseph, indeed, was poor, but he was not a beggar; neither, because he worked at a trade which implied manual labor, need his state in life be regarded either as mean or contemptible. With the Hebrews, who still retained many of the simple and primitive customs of the Patriarchs, the profession of an artisan, if not noble or distinguished, was yet far from being esteemed as the lowest. The arts were respected as useful to society; and a good artificer was preferred to the richest merchant. Moreover, every father of a family was bound by the law to make his children learn some trade, even if they did not require to practice it, in order that they might not take to dishonest practices or become a burden to others. Accordingly, we find that St. Paul, born in possession of the freedom of a Roman citizen and a learned doctor in the law, which he had studied at the feet of Gamaliel, had been taught the art of tent-making, which he afterwards practiced when an Apostle (*Acts* 18:3; *1 Thess.* 2:9; *2 Thess.* 3:8), that he might be a charge to no man.

As for the supposed contempt implied in the language of his countrymen mentioned by St. Mark and St. Matthew, such is not its real or natural meaning.

In St. Mark's Gospel we read: "And going out from thence, He went into His own country; and His disciples followed Him. And when the Sabbath was come, He began to teach in the synagogue; and many, hearing Him, were in admiration at His doctrine, saying, 'How came this man by all these things? and what wisdom is this that is given to Him; and such mighty works as are wrought by His hands? Is not this the carpenter, the son of Mary, the brother of James, and Joseph, and Jude, and Simon? are not also His sisters with us?' And they were scandalized in regard of Him."[1] These words of the men of Nazareth seem to manifest astonishment rather than contempt, an astonishment, however, mingled with jealousy. They had not seen Him frequenting the schools; He was known to them as a carpenter and the son of a carpenter; and as, on the one hand, they were filled with wonder at the wisdom and learning He displayed and the miracles He wrought, so, on the other, they were offended at the authority with which He spoke; for, as it is said elsewhere,[2] He taught as one having power, and not as the Scribes and Pharisees. Their words and conduct implied nothing of contempt in regard either to His station in life or His occupation.

But, further, the employment which Joseph adopted was one that our Divine Master Himself did not disdain to practice in His youth, that He might set us an example of humility and laborious industry. Nay, He had already prepared in His reputed father an example which He Himself tacitly followed. For, admitting even the exigencies of his condition, we have every right to believe that Joseph gave himself to this avocation from his esteem and love for labor, and, what is higher still, a predilection for poverty. Every man is bound to employ profitably the gifts he has received from God, whether spiritual or corporal, each according to his state of life. God, as we read in the Holy Scripture,

---

1. *Mark* 6:2, 3; *conf. Matthew* 13:54-57.
2. *Matthew* 12:29; *Mark* 1:22; *conf. John* 7:15.

placed Adam, as yet innocent, in the terrestrial paradise in order to keep and dress it; and Joseph, instructed in this school, although sprung from a race of kings, not only was not ashamed to appear poor, but led from his tenderest years, as we have reason to conclude, a life of toil, thus avoiding idleness and that which is often its companion, dissipation, and the vices flowing therefrom. Many at all times have like him fallen into poverty and sunk to a low estate, but few know how to value it. Constrained to exercise a toilsome and servile art, few are they who know how to raise themselves to the consideration that what has become a necessity of nature to man ever since the fall may also be at the same time a heavenly boon; whatever art or profession they follow becoming thus in their hands a means calculated to promote their sanctification. But, if there are few comparatively now who know how rightly to value poverty, and, if in Israel under the Old Law such value was almost unknown, it was a perfection of St. Joseph, a perfection which was his many years before the Type of all perfection had appeared among men, before the Incarnate Wisdom had opened His mouth to announce to the world that consoling truth: "Blessed are the poor in spirit, for theirs is the kingdom of Heaven." (*Matt.* 5:3).

The merit of Joseph, then, did not consist in his having been born poor and living a life of poverty, neither was it on this account that God chose him for His representative in the house of His Son on earth, but because he willed and loved to be poor, seeing that God Himself so willed and disposed it. He was inwardly sensible of the perfection which lay in embracing a life of poverty, even as if he had a prescience that the moment was at hand when voluntary poverty would become one of the most splendid ornaments with which a creature could deck itself in the eyes of its Creator; a conviction quite opposed to that of the world of his day, not excepting the wise according to the flesh even in his very fatherland. The poverty, therefore, which was his by inheritance, he also chose for his portion on earth; so that he who was first poor by necessity became afterwards poor by election, because he was truly poor in spirit, and hence was a worthy instrument in God's hands for the execution of His designs regarding him.

Joseph, then, labored with his hands, but what was his precise occupation? The word which we translate carpenter is in the original one of general import, and may be applied to a workman in any material, whether wood, iron, stone, or even in the precious metals. Accordingly, there have been interpreters who maintained that Joseph worked in iron. St. Hilarion, adopting this view, says in reference to Jesus: "He was son of the smith who subdues iron with fire."[3] Others would have him to have been a builder or an architect; holding that, even as Jesus by eternal generation was the Son of the Eternal Artificer who formed the whole material universe, so also in His temporal generation He was believed and reputed to be the son of a builder.[4] Others, again, have even advanced the opinion that Joseph worked in silver and gold. But that which is now the commonly received belief, being grounded upon the best certified tradition, is that Joseph worked in wood; that he was, in fact, a carpenter, although he may have understood and occasionally employed himself in work of another character.

The testimony of St. Justin Martyr, who lived in the middle of the second century, and must therefore have known persons who had conversed with the Apostles, is of great weight. In his celebrated Dialogue with the Jew, Tryphon, he says, "Jesus came to John, being reputed the son of Joseph, the carpenter, or worker in wood, and He Himself was reckoned to be a carpenter; for while He dwelt amongst men He had performed carpenter's work, making ploughs and yokes, teaching us thus to lead just lives free from idleness." Ancient pictures, representing the Saint with the instruments

---

3. *In Matthaeum*, cap. xix.
4. S. August., *Serm.* i. *Dom. infr. Oct. Epiph.*

of a carpenter, confirm this testimony of St. Justin, as
also of other early ecclesiastical writers. That such was
the common opinion of the first centuries is also incidentally proved by the famous answer which a Christian schoolmaster in Antioch gave to the sophist Libanius
respecting the Emperor Julian the Apostate, who at
that time was fighting against the Parthians. Libanius, having asked him what the son of the carpenter
was doing now, he, speaking, as was believed, by a
divine movement, promptly responded, "He is working
at Julian's bier"; in which he proved to be no false
prophet, for soon after news came that Julian had fallen
mortally wounded in battle. We have another proof of
the general belief of primitive times in a remark of St.
John Chrysostom, when, expounding St. Matthew's
Gospel, he says, "Therefore was Mary espoused to a
carpenter, because Jesus, the Spouse of the Church,
was to work the salvation of the world by the wood of
the Cross." Such was also the decided opinion of St.
Thomas Aquinas, who with reference to the words in
the 13th chapter of St. Matthew, "Is not this the son
of the carpenter?" makes this comment: "Jesus was
reputed to be the son of Joseph, who was not a forger
of iron but a worker in wood." More proofs from other
holy and learned writers, forming a catena of evidence
down to the present day, including the last Doctor of
the Church, St. Francis de Sales, might be adduced,
but the opinion of the great Angel of the Schools may
well be left to close the list. The opinion expressed by
St. Ambrose that Joseph was expert in iron-work, as
well as in what more immediately belonged to a carpenter's trade, may suggest an explanation of all apparent discrepancies with regard to his occupation.

For this reason the holy Evangelists may have been
inspired to call Joseph's occupation by a comprehensive term, in order that all artisans, whether in wood,
iron, metal, marble, stone, or in the precious metals,
might recognize in him their special patron, and deem
it both a duty and a privilege to place themselves under

his particular protection. Thus, in this our age, when the question of the working classes is so prominently before the world, and certain evil teachers are abroad who would make them regard their condition as a misfortune and a wrong, and urge them to seek redress by forcibly appropriating the goods of others, it has pleased God to exhibit Joseph in all his glory as the most sublime model of the laboring man, so that all may turn their eyes upon him, learn from him their true dignity as Christian artisans, and, faithfully imitating his virtues, find under his patronage health to labor and needful employment for the support and maintenance of their families.

Let us admire, then, the profound humility of St. Joseph, who, although he came of royal blood, preferred the humble and laborious occupation of a carpenter to any other profession more noble and agreeable, in order the better to please God by a hidden and toilsome life, and avoid those perils which often attend a more elevated position in the social scale. Joseph, the scion of kings, from voluntary humility condemned his hands, worthy of bearing a regal sceptre, to wield instead the hatchet and the hammer, or, rather, he consecrated with his holy hands all the instruments of labor, teaching clearly thereby that it is the duty of all who in this transitory life have to gain their daily bread by the sweat of their brow to regard their life of toil as providentially assigned to them, in the mercy of God, to be the means by which they may work out their eternal salvation and secure to themselves an exalted position in the court of Heaven.

Chapter XVI

Birth of Mary—Her
Presentation in the Temple.

PROVIDENCE, which guides man along the path
of virtue to the fulfillment of his vocation, had
disposed that the very resolution which Joseph
had formed in the secret of his heart, and had long
maintained with perfect and constant self-abnegation—
a resolution by which he believed himself to renounce
all participation in the glories promised to the house
of David, and to make himself a stranger, so to say, to
that event which was to fill, not Israel alone, but the
whole universe with joy—was to be the very means of
fitting him to stand, next to Mary, in the closest relationship to the Divine Redeemer of mankind. Several
writers of high authority are of opinion that Joseph
went to practice in Jerusalem the trade which he had
learnt, in order to have constant access to the Temple
and take part in its sacrifices. This is highly credible,
and pious imaginations have loved to dwell upon the
thought that, possibly, he may even have been employed
in some portion of the work which Herod, in order to
gratify the Jews and make himself a great name, had
undertaken, namely, the enlargement and decoration
of their Temple. Joseph, who was so well acquainted
with the promises of God to His people, must have
known how the prophets Aggeus and Malachi had foretold that the glory of this latter house was to exceed
that of the former, for the Desired of all nations, the

Lord Himself, was to honor it with His presence. (*Agg.* 2:10; *Mal.* 3:1). To take any share and contribute in any degree towards its adornment, and thus employ his labor and skill directly for the greater glory of God, would have been a privilege most dear to his heart.

That he did so is, of course, matter of pure conjecture; but it rises above the rank of a conjecture, and may be considered as almost certain that he would frequently see his holy relatives, Joachim and Anne, when they came up to keep the great feasts at Jerusalem; Anne, as we have shown on good authority, being probably the sister of Jacob and therefore Joseph's aunt. For many years their marriage had remained unblest with any offspring, which was, as we know, considered by the Jews as more than a misfortune. Elizabeth's exclamation, "Thus hath the Lord dealt with me in the days wherein He hath had regard to take away my reproach among men" (*Luke* 1:25), would be sufficient proof, were such needed, that this was the general feeling. It pleased God to allow this affliction to weigh most heavily on this holy couple. Tradition tells us that having come up from Nazareth, where they dwelt, to keep the feast of the Dedication of the Temple,[1] and having made their offering, while they were kneeling in devout prayer, a priest named Isaac, or, according to others, Isachar, sternly rebuked St. Joachim in presence of all the worshippers, for daring to present himself within the sacred precincts when the curse of God rested upon him, as shown in the sterility of his marriage. If the youthful Joseph was present on this occasion, or, at any rate, being in Jerusalem, was cognizant of the humiliation of which his pious relatives had been the object, how must his tender heart have grieved, and how he must have exerted himself to raise their drooping spirits! They returned to the mountains of Nazareth, but not without having both of

---

1. The Hebrews kept three feasts of the Dedication of the Temple: the first, that of Solomon, in September; the second, that of Esdras and Zorobabel, in February; the third, that of Judas Machabeus, on the 25th of November. It was to this third feast that Joachim and Anne had come.

them been favored with angelic consolation and the assurance that God had heard their prayers and accepted their oblation. Epiphanius tells us that Joachim was praying in the solitude of a mountain and Anne retired in her garden, when they each of them separately received this divine favor. Joachim and Anne, says the historian Ludolphus, in his *Life of Jesus Christ,* having for twenty years been without offspring, had both of them promised, if their prayer was heard, to dedicate the child which should be granted them to God.

And behold, Anne, miraculously healed of her sterility, conceived in her womb her who was to be the delight, the life, and the joy of the whole world. Here was the commencement of a series of unprecedented prodigies. As this infant was to be the daughter of the Eternal Father, mother of the Divine Son, and spouse of the Holy Ghost, so her beautiful soul from the first instant of its creation and infusion into the body was, through the especial grace and privilege of God, and in regard of the merits of Jesus Christ His Son and the Redeemer of mankind, to be preserved free from all stain of original sin, and filled with every grace, gift, and perfection of which a human creature is capable.

The Virgin was born at Nazareth on the 8th of September, in the year of the world, as is supposed, 3986, and her happy nativity was the harbinger of joy to the whole universe. Her name, we cannot doubt, came from Heaven, and was revealed to Joachim, who gave it to her on the eighth day after her birth. "O name," exclaims that devout adorer of the Infant Jesus, St. Anthony of Padua, "joy to the heart, honey in the mouth, sweetest music to the ear!"[2] And St. John Damasus: "O happy couple, Joachim and Anne, what a debt of gratitude is due to you from every creature!"[3] On the eighth day after her delivery, Anne, accompanied by her holy spouse, must have borne in her arms this most lovely

2. *Sermo* iii. *Dom. Quadrag.*
3. *Orat.* i. *de Nativ. B. Mariae Virginis.*

babe to offer her to the Lord in the Temple, and perform, according to the law, the rite of her own purification. Scripture gives us no record of this act, but the devout mind loves to dwell upon it. For never before that day had so acceptable or pleasing an offering been made to the Most High. That sweet infant, but a few days old, was burning with the desire to consecrate herself entirely to God, that God whom she already knew so clearly and loved so ardently. For even in her mother's womb Mary enjoyed the use of reason and of her free will.[4] How could it be otherwise, since to John the Baptist this privilege was conceded, before he saw the light, in the sixth month of his existence? Her holy parents on their part, no doubt, renewed their promised consecration of the child which had been so miraculously given to them. According to a pious tradition, Anne possessed a flock on Mount Carmel and a house for its shepherds; and hither she and Joachim would often resort with their spotless infant. We can readily believe that it was here, on those heights of immemorial sanctity, that she, sweet child, who was one day to be invoked as Our Lady of Mount Carmel, besought her parents to fulfill their vow and allow her to go and enclose herself with other daughters of Sion in the House of the Lord.

It must have been a very painful sacrifice to this holy couple to part with their incomparable child, the joy and treasure of their life, but they loved God too much to refuse Him what He asked and what they had promised to Him. That the Virgin was three years old when she was presented in the Temple and devoted to the service of God is clear from the testimony of St. Evodius, successor of St. Peter in Antioch, as well as from that of St. Epiphanius, St. Jerome, St. Gregory Nazianzen, St. Basil and many others. There is, in fact, a whole catena of tradition on the subject. It was in the month of November, when the Hebrews celebrate

---

4. St. Bernardine, *Serm.* li.; Suarez, p. iii. disp. iv. sect. v.

the solemn dedication of the Temple, that Joachim and Anne brought the infant Mary to give her to God. Without objecting her tender age, or pleading for delay, they had at once acceded to the holy desire of their most innocent child. The sacrifice was willed by God, was pleasing to God: that was enough to cause them to bow their heads, and make the offering with all readiness of heart. What a beautiful example does Mary here present to the young, to follow without hesitation the voice of God calling them to a perfect life in the solitude of a cloister, without heeding for a moment the flattering allurements of the world; and what a splendid example do Joachim and Anne also offer to parents, not to oppose the religious vocation of their children, but to give them willingly to God, when it pleases Him to call them!

The presentation of Mary in the Temple is believed to have taken place in the year of the world 3989, and on the 21st of November, the day on which the Church celebrates the feast. The enclosure in which these young maidens had their abode was beside the Temple; that it was also attached to it we may gather from the Second Book of Machabees, chap. iii. v. 39, where it is said that the young virgins ran in consternation to Onias when they beheld Eliodorus rifling the sacred building. In memory of the abode of Mary in the Temple, the Emperor Justinian I erected in the sixth century, on its southern side, a church which was called the Church of the Presentation.

Chapter XVII

Mary's Abode in the Temple—Her Marriage with Joseph Decreed in Heaven.

MARY passed eleven years in the sacred retirement of the Temple, that she might, although all unknown to herself, acquire the necessary dispositions and have a fitting preparation to become the Mother of God, even as Joseph hid himself in the obscurity of a poor workshop to practice for many years the most excellent and most heroic virtues, that he might become like to Mary and worthy to be her spouse. Here, inwardly illuminated and guided by the Spirit of God, far more than by the instructions of her teachers, Mary rose to the loftiest height of perfection which a human creature can attain. Here, as Joseph had also done, she consecrated her virginity to God by a perpetual vow, conditional, however, on His good pleasure.[1] Hence, in accordance with the testimony of the ancient Fathers, the Angelic Doctor says that the Blessed Virgin stood, as it were, on the confines between the Old and the New Law; so that her vow was akin to the New Law in that it was a consecration of her virginity to God, and it savored of the Old Law in that it was made conditionally. To make an absolute vow of perpetual virginity would have been, so to say, to go beyond the spirit of the Mosaic Law, which favored, if it did not prescribe, matrimony; wherefore St. Bernard, speaking of Mary's vow, says that in making it she tran-

1. St. Thomas, *Summa,* p. iii. q. xxviii. a. 4.

scended the precepts of the Mosaic Law. But the condition which Mary prudently appended in no way diminished the value or weakened the strength of her vow; on the contrary, it embellished and enhanced it by the merit of obedience. From which we gather that, if virginity under the New Law ranks as one of the first and choicest virtues, it was certainly not the lowest under the Old Law. There it occupied, it is true, but a temporary place, being destined to be soon followed by the virtues of the married state, but it was not without its honor and its prerogatives. Holy Scripture alludes to it as to a privileged state, dear to God, who took pleasure in the prayers of chaste youths and pure young maidens, and who predestinated a virgin to be the mother of His Only-Begotten Son, and the Redeemer of the human race. "When the seers of Juda," says Orsini,[2] "unfolded to the elect but oft chastised people the prophetic picture of their miseries or their victories, they always introduced in it a virgin, either smiling or in tears, to personify provinces and cities. In the wars of extermination, in which the broadsword of the Hebrews cut down the women, children, and old men of Moab, the virgins were spared; and the high-priest, who was forbidden by a severe law to pay funeral honors even to the prince of his people, might assist without being defiled at the funeral of his sister if she had died a virgin. (*Lev.* 21:1-4). The virgins took part in the ceremonies of the Hebrew worship before that worship had a temple. Dancing choirs of young women, transplanted from Egypt into the desert, continued a long time, and ceased only when the ark was lost and the first Temple was destroyed. (*Ps.* 67:26). The virgins of Silo, who seem to have been in the time of the Judges more especially consecrated to the service of the Lord than the other daughters of Israel, were dancing to the song of canticles and the sound of harps, at a short distance from the holy place, during a feast of the Lord,

---

2. *History of the Blessed Virgin* (Husenbeth's Translation), pp. 73, 74.

when the sons of Benjamin carried them off." (*Judges* 16:19-23). "If the Jewish people," says P. Monsabré,[3] "mindful and proud of the oracles which promised them a Liberator born of their own race, esteemed marriage above all other states and regarded sterility as an opprobrium, they yet demanded continence from their priests at the periods when their sacred functions placed them in relation with God. They admired the holy reserve which (so to say) buried women in their widowhood. 'Because thou hast loved chastity,' said the high-priest, Joachim, to Judith, 'and after thy husband hast not known any other, therefore also the hand of the Lord hath strengthened thee, and therefore thou shalt be blessed for ever.' (*Jud.* 15:11). The pagans themselves recognized the beauty and greatness of a state which protested against the corruption of their manners. They sounded its praises by the mouths of their poets and their orators; they called celibacy and virginity to the service of their gods and their goddesses; Isis, Minerva, Ceres, and Vesta were surrounded by virgins. Only virgins were deemed worthy of guarding the sacred fire and of receiving the oracles of heaven; the virgins were reverend and holy; they merited the greatest honor; the *fasces* of the Lictors bowed before them; the first places were reserved for them at all the feasts where the majesty of the senate and people of Rome was displayed; and it was not thought too cruel to bury them alive when they betrayed their vows."

But to proceed: Mary did not give herself exclusively to the contemplative life; she also exercised herself in the active life; thus teaching thereby how in every state the two may be united. St. Epiphanius, St. Jerome, St. Ambrose, and St. Bonaventura, all describe this most holy child as occupied in the Temple in domestic work. Her hands plied the needle, the distaff, and the spindle, in labor for the poor, as well as for the decoration of God's House and making vestments for the priests.

---

3. *Sermon at Notre Dame on Palm Sunday,* 1887.

St. Epiphanius also tells us that the Blessed Virgin excelled all her companions in embroidery and in the art of working in wool, fine linen, and gold. The cedar spindles which she used were, we are told, preserved as a pious memorial in the Church at Jerusalem. Amongst all these occupations she found time to study and meditate profoundly the Sacred Scriptures, of which the Fathers attribute to her a consummate understanding. Her wonderful intellect, unrelaxing application, and the supernatural science infused by God had, indeed, already made her a true Seat of Wisdom. Marvellous things are related of this predestined child, of which the echoes have reached us through tradition: how she would rise alone to pray at midnight; how she would sometimes prolong her fasts for three days, and how angels would bring her fruits from Paradise;[4] how she enjoyed constant union with God, and was favored with the sublimest visions. And well may this have been so, since nothing which has been liberally bestowed upon the saints can have been wanting in the case of her who was to be the august Mother of God, the Queen of Angels and of Saints.

Thus was being prepared the accomplishment of the Divine Will, which had decreed to unite Mary and Joseph in marriage. Wonderful indeed are the ways of God! Who would have believed that Joseph, who had resolved to keep the Evangelical counsels, before the Son of God had appeared on earth to proclaim them, should bind himself with the ties of matrimony? This holy man's purity of mind and body seemed to raise him to a height far superior to the obligations of that state; and, if this be true of Joseph, what shall we say of our Sovereign Lady, Mary, the most perfect of all creatures, exalted to so sublime a height that in God's whole universe there was none equal to her? If Joseph did not seem created for the married state, still less could Mary; for, if the eminent virtue of this illustrious son of David

---

4. This tradition is credited by St. Gregory Nazianzen, St. Ambrose, St. Jerome, and others.

was too perfect for a condition of life in itself not the most perfect, must not the surpassing sanctity of Mary have placed her at a far greater distance from it? Yet this union had been decreed in the counsels of the Three Adorable Persons of the Ever-Blessed Trinity. The devout Andrew, Bishop of Crete, calls the Blessed Virgin a very world in herself, who within the narrow compass of her bosom enclosed Him whom the whole universe cannot contain.[5] Would it, then, be possible that God should take such particular care of all His creation as to set angels over the stars and the elements, to regulate their movements, their powers, and their influences, and be indifferent as respected the husband to whom He designed to confide the guardianship of this marvellous world, which alone exceeded in value thousands of worlds?

But it is not sufficient to believe that the Most Holy Trinity approved and ratified this marriage. If princesses, daughters of earthly monarchs, cannot contract an alliance without the consent of the sovereign, in order to obviate any union derogatory to their royal blood, much more was this needful in the case of Mary. She was, not only the daughter of the royal house of David, but a princess of a superior order, nay, in some sort, a divine order; for, though her origin was not divine, the blood in her veins was at least sufficiently pure to be converted into that of the God-Man. From all eternity Mary had been chosen by the Ever-Blessed Trinity for this incomparable dignity, and, when the fullness of time was come, had been fitted and prepared miraculously for it, and rendered as worthy of it as was possible for a pure creature to be. If, then, it entered into the Divine counsels to give her an earthly spouse for her protector, Joseph, assuredly, must have been also the special choice of the Triune God, Father, Son, and Holy Ghost; and, being so, it would not be conceivable that he should not have been rendered as worthy of

5. *Orat.* i. *de Dormitione Deiparae.*

this exalted honor as it was possible for him to be. Bernardine de Bustis teaches that, this marriage having been the most perfect ever contracted, the Blessed Trinity, which had decreed it before the world was, had also ordained that there should be between the two admirable contractors a more adequate similarity than in any who have entered into this state of life;[6] and this similarity between Joseph and Mary consisted, not only in externals and in the natural affections and inclinations, but more particularly in supernatural gifts. Joseph, therefore, was enriched with heavenly graces that he might resemble his blessed spouse, and be qualified to combine with her in the care and education of the Saviour of the world.

It is the common opinion of Doctors of the Church that, when the Blessed Trinity gave our saint as spouse to Mary, no other man could have been found so like to her. Both were in so high a grade of perfection that even as there would have been a great and unsuitable disproportion between the Virgin and any other spouse, so also would there have been a signal inequality between Joseph and any other consort who might have been allotted to him. St. Bernardine of Siena is of opinion that there never were two spouses so like to each other as were Mary and Joseph.[7] Not that any one pretends to affirm that an entire equality subsisted between them. Such an assertion would be both false and impious. Similarity and conformity do not, and could not, in this case imply equality. Their equality consisted in this, that Joseph was so exceedingly like to Mary that he had none like to him among men. Inferior to the Blessed Virgin alone, he was superior to all else besides. In that superiority, therefore, they were partners. What a singular glory was this, to be so like to the Blessed Virgin as to possess in a great measure common privileges with her, and to have a love for God of the same character as her own! And,

6. *Mariale,* Sermo xii.
7. *Sermo de S. Joseph,* t. iii. c. i.

in effect, Our Lady, as a learned interpreter observes, places no difference between the vehement sorrow and anxiety she experienced at the loss of her Son, and the sorrow, anxiety, and solicitude of her husband: "Behold Thy father and I have sought Thee sorrowing." (*Luke* 2:48). She thus gives us the liberty to compare the love which they both had for Jesus, and to hold as a consequence that Joseph was so similar to her that there was no one else who could enter into comparison with him.

Certainly we need no greater proof of the eminent sanctity of Joseph than is implied in the choice made of him by God to be the husband of Mary. We have only to look at *her* to know what *he* must have been. In the first marriage which was ever contracted, that of our first parents, God destined the man to be the model of the woman: "Let us make him a help like unto himself" (*Gen.* 2:18); but in the most holy of all marriages, that of Mary and Joseph, the wife was chosen as the model of her spouse; and thus the elevation of Mary furnishes us with a standard for conceiving how high must have been that of Joseph. The Blessed Trinity, in determining to give to Mary this companion, determined also that he should be a wondrous copy of her perfections and endowed with her incomparable qualities, while for his greater honor It decreed that he himself should meritoriously co-operate in the acquisition of them. Jacob served only fourteen years to win the beautiful Rachel, but Joseph during his whole life had been preparing for the dignity of spouse to the Queen of Angels. This Sovereign Lady, indeed, was of incomparably greater worth than was Laban's fair daughter, and a seraph after many centuries of devoted service might have deemed himself rich if he had obtained one word of recognition or one favorable glance from Mary. How great, then, was the honor which the Blessed Trinity conferred on Joseph!

This marriage having been decreed in the secret counsels of the Triune God, it was, moreover, to receive on

earth the highest possible sanction by becoming matter of deliberation and determination on the part of the
heads of the Jewish Church, the chief priests and doctors of the law, as we shall presently see.

Chapter XVIII

Testimony of the Synagogue to the Virtues of Joseph.

THE Divine Word, when appearing upon earth to redeem and renew our fallen race, would not, in assuming the nature of man touch anything that was defiled, but willed to be born of an Immaculate Virgin. This Virgin, however, as the Fathers have observed, must first be espoused to a husband, that he might be the shield and protector of her honor, which would otherwise be exposed to injurious aspersions when she became a mother, as well as to conceal for a time the secret of the Incarnation. That mysterious cloud which in the desert covered, as with a white veil, the Ark of the God of Israel, presents us with a striking figure of the office of Joseph, the most glorious of the Patriarchs, divinely elected to be the husband of Mary, the most highly gifted among all the daughters of Eve, in order to hide from every profane eye the adorable mystery which was to be effected in that true ark of the Living God, the bosom of Mary, wherein He was coming to abide as in His Tabernacle. God, who willed to accomplish this two-fold object, had in His wisdom provided His holy Mother with a spouse who, while united to her in the marriage bond, should not only be the guardian of her virginal purity, but be himself a virgin, and with the love of virginal purity so deeply rooted in his heart that it was to be like to her own, and receive additional luster from it, as does the white cloud from the rays of the orb of day which it veils from our view.

Such was to be this greatest and most perfect marriage. And we may well believe that it also entered into God's designs to honor and exalt the marriage-state in the espousals of Mary and Joseph. The Author of nature at the commencement of the ages had in Eden Himself instituted the marital bond, and had bestowed His blessing upon it and upon the first married couple; and the Author of grace, when pronouncing that tie indissoluble, also enriched it with such heavenly gifts that under the Gospel dispensation it was to be raised to the dignity of a Sacrament. Adam and Eve, although adorned with original justice, had fallen and become sinners before being parents, and thus had marred this divine institution. Now, the Incarnate Word, who came to repair all that the first man's sin had ruined, could not but restore honor to that which is the basis of the human family and of society. God would institute another marriage in reparation of His glory, and to remedy the defect of the first. Choosing, therefore, the most just of men, He gave him the most perfect of women for his spouse, who not only would not place him in danger of sinning, but would aid him to attain the highest summit of perfection. The glory of God required this; since, if Mary was to be His mother, Joseph was to be His father, though not by nature, yet by virtue of his office. He was to be His reputed father, fulfilling all the duties and obligations belonging to that relationship. The glory of God, therefore, required that He should give him a consort who would be truly an aid to him, as Eve was designed to be to Adam.

Seeing, then, that the knitting of this new tie was not only a most important work, but the most important ever as yet transacted in the world, God was pleased to employ in effecting it those persons who occupied the highest position in the Jewish Church. It is the universal opinion of the Fathers that it was the doctors, priests, and heads of the Synagogue who proposed and brought about this alliance. St. John Damascene, indeed, asserts that Mary was espoused to Joseph, not merely by the advice, but by the authority of the Synagogue; and that the priests were not content with determining the marriage of the Virgin, nor with selecting her spouse, but esteemed it an honor to conduct her themselves to Joseph, and consign her into his hands. It is certain, as St. Jerome says, that the priests were not in the habit of charging themselves with the establishment of the maidens confided to them for education in the Temple, but were wont to restore them to their parents at a suitable age, that they might provide for their marriage. But in this case they acted differently, whether from a particular inspiration, as was the opinion of St. Gregory Nazianzen, or that, the parents of the Blessed Virgin having died during her abode in the Temple (as is generally believed), they considered that it devolved upon them to provide for this holy maiden's future. She was a daughter of the house of David, and was, moreover, the heiress of whatever had belonged to Joachim and Anne. In such cases, where the woman represented her family and inherited property, the ancient law was particularly stringent concerning her marriage with a member of her own tribe, in other cases allowing a certain latitude.

We have reason to suppose that to many in Judea it must have been known that miraculous circumstances were connected with the birth of Mary; and, if we are to credit in this respect the author of the Book of her Nativity which has been by some attributed to St. Jerome,[1] her birth was preceded and followed by many prodigies indicating her surpassing excellence. What the priests of the Lord had witnessed must have strengthened in their minds, we may well suppose, the impression which may have been produced by such reports. They must have well remembered how when Mary arrived at the Temple, in age an infant of three

---

1. This book is regarded as apocryphal, and cannot be relied on; nevertheless it may contain true facts, along with doubtful statements and such as do not deserve credit.

years, but mature in grace and dignity, she had ascended the steps of the sacred edifice on the day of her Presentation with the devotion and fervor of a seraph. Moreover, the life which she had led for eleven or twelve years in this holy retirement was one of such perfection, such regularity, and was so marvellous in its character, as to inspire them with indescribable respect; so much so that some of the Fathers have asserted that she was admitted more than once to worship in the inner portion of the Temple, commonly inhibited to women. Be this as it may, the admiration excited in the minds of the priests by the sight of her virtues and the cognizance of supernatural facts connected with her life must have made them the more solicitous to select for this heavenly maiden a spouse who might be worthy of her.

And now the question occurs, did Mary, whose ardent desire it was to devote all her days to the service of God, and who, moreover, had consecrated to Him her virginity by vow, when made aware that it was the purpose of her tutors and governors, the doctors and priests of the Temple, to give her in marriage, allege as an obstacle the solemn promise she had made? Some, and among them ranks Canon Antonio Vitali, are of opinion that she did so, and would certainly have confided her dismay to her near relative, Zachary, who, as we know from the Gospel, took his regular turn of officiating in the solemn service of the Temple; indeed, he seems to take for granted that she had made her vow with his cognizance and sanction; but, as he does not allege any authority or tradition in favor of this view, we are at full liberty to form our own judgment in the matter. Objections will not unnaturally suggest themselves. As such a vow appears to have been without precedent amongst the maidens of Israel, it is difficult to imagine how Zachary, unless he were divinely illuminated, would have advised or sanctioned it. In the absence, therefore, of all light upon the subject, we are free to believe that Mary's promise to God, having been formed through the immediate inspiration of her inward Guide and Director, her secret also by the same dictation remained between herself and God.[2] Her silence on other occasions of an analogous kind would lead us to this conclusion: "My secret to myself." (*Is.* 24:16). But whichever view may approve itself to the mind, it is certain that the *Ancilla Domini* would have been prepared to submit to the will of Him who had prompted the vow, as signified to her by those whose authority over her made them His representatives in her regard. Moreover, she would feel persuaded that He would know how to guard the treasure committed to His keeping; and we are encouraged in this conviction by the testimony of saints and saintly persons, who have asserted that the Blessed Virgin herself had told them that she was assured by divine revelation that her virginity would not be endangered by her espousals. We have here been speaking exclusively of her actual vow of virginity, but there can be little, if any, doubt that the priests and guardians of Mary knew that her own desire would have been to dedicate herself to God in His Temple for the remainder of her days.

We may readily believe that among the young men of her kindred there must have been an eager competition for the hand of the daughter of Joachim and Anne, for Mary's perfections and endowments of every kind cannot, notwithstanding her secluded life, have remained concealed; and among these aspirants would be many who were rich, accomplished, and occupying honorable situations. Joseph was her nearest of kin, being, as seems most probable, nephew to her mother and nearly related to her also through Joachim, her father. Moreover, it is impossible to imagine that she could have been personally unknown to him. He may have seen this blessed infant in her cradle and witnessed her Presentation in the Temple; neither is it easy to conceive that his piety and sweetness of dispo-

---

2. We are glad to find that in this view we have the concurrence of F. Coleridge in his admirable work, *The Mother of the King.*

sition, coupled with his close relationship, had not endeared him to her holy parents. From humility and the love of poverty, more than from any absolute necessity, he, the lineal descendant of kings, had subjected himself to the daily toil of a mechanic, which, although it in no way degraded him in the eyes of true Hebrews, placed him in a position of some social inferiority. Such was the life he led at the time when it was in contemplation to bestow upon him the greatest honor which any man ever received; separated from the surrounding world, in a state of total renunciation and contempt of created things, retired and unnoticed, with no earthly desire but to remain in his obscurity, forgotten of all, and known only to God. Far, therefore, from aspiring to an alliance with Mary, or entertaining any solicitude on the subject, he would, apart from his vow of virginity, by which he had abandoned all thoughts of the married state, have deemed himself utterly unworthy of her. Joseph, then, was certainly not of the number of the claimants. Yet, notwithstanding his desire to eclipse himself, he had not been able so far to conceal his high sanctity and rare merits as to escape the observation of the priests who had the guardianship of the Virgin of Nazareth; at least we seem irresistibly led to this conclusion, since it was upon him that their choice fell; on him, the poor artisan, in preference to many who must have possessed higher worldly recommendations, and in spite of the exalted estimation in which they held the heavenly-gifted maiden, their ward, an estimation which laid upon them the responsibility of procuring for her the most suitable and most honorable marriage possible.

Chapter XIX

Betrothal of Mary and Joseph.

ST. EPIPHANIUS describes St. Joseph, not only as great among men and faithful in all his ways, but as reflecting the beauty of his interior holiness in his countenance and exterior. This striking sanctity, revealed in his person, might alone have served to give a sufficient explanation of the preference awarded him over all the competitors. Albert the Great, indeed, is of opinion that the Synagogue judged that it contributed to the glory of the most holy Virgin by choosing Joseph for her spouse, for that his virtue was so consummate and admirable that he might have conferred honor on the holiest alliance ever contracted, or to be contracted. Could there be a greater panegyric of our saint, could his rare qualities have received a higher encomium, than in the fact that the priests of the Temple and the doctors of the Law, in a body, after applying themselves with mature deliberation to make their election, as St. Gregory Nazianzen tells us they did, should have turned their eyes to Joseph, albeit a poor man, because the wealth of his virtues and the treasure of his merits raised him to an equality with the greatest and noblest man upon earth? Yes, one higher testimony he might have, and we have every reason to believe that it was awarded to him—the testimony of God Himself.

There is a general agreement among the Fathers and Doctors of the Church that Joseph was pointed out as

the spouse of Mary by a marvellous sign from Heaven.
St. Epiphanius, to whom allusion has just been made,
says that he was chosen by lot. Now, the lot, as used
on such occasions, and accompanied by prayer, was considered by the Jews as equivalent to a Divine pronouncement; as we see, for instance, in the choice of an Apostle
to fill the place of Judas. (*Acts* 1:26). St. Gregory
Nazianzen also speaks of the priests having selected
Joseph as husband and guardian for Mary by lot, over
which the Holy Ghost presided. In like manner, the
aged Patriarch of Constantinople, St. Germanus, says
that by a sign from God, and by the counsel of the
priests, the lot was cast concerning the Virgin; and the
great Chancellor of Paris and devout client of Mary,
Gerson, declared, before all the Fathers assembled in
council at Constance, that Joseph took a wife moved
thereto by the Holy Spirit. All speak alike upon this
point; but none of them explain in what manner the
lot was cast, or in what mode the Holy Spirit manifested His decision. A very ancient tradition, however,
supported by some Fathers and by many sacred writers, and resting also on popular belief, informs us that
the high-priest, divinely inspired, renewed the proof to
which Moses had recourse when it was question of the
high-priesthood of Aaron; God saying to him: "Whomsoever of these I shall choose, his rod shall blossom."
(*Num.* 17:5). All the unmarried men of the race of David,
and among them Joseph, being summoned to appear,
the high-priest[1] bade each of them bring a rod with his
name inscribed upon it, and whosesoever's rod should
be found the next day to have blossomed, he it was
who should be the spouse of Mary. So it was done; and
on the morrow, while the rods of all the rest had
remained dry and unfruitful, that of Joseph had bud-
ded and blossomed, and borne leaves and beautiful flowers. At the same time, a white dove was seen to descend
and light upon it. The aspirants were all filled with

---

1. P. Gabriele Valenzuella, Barnabite, in his *Life of St. Joseph*, says that this high-
priest's name was Abiatar.

grief and disappointment, and one of them in particular, it is said, a noble youth, possessing a rich patrimony, seeing his hopes deluded, broke his rod,[2] and, refusing to give his affection to anyone but Mary, retired to a grotto on Mount Carmel, where, among the disciples of Elias, he arrived at great sanctity, and built a chapel in honor of the most holy Virgin.

It is true that critics are not wanting who reject these traditions altogether, gathered, as they allow, from very ancient legendary writings, but writings which are apocryphal, that is, unauthentic and doubtful. But is this sweeping condemnation of all that is found contained in such writings reasonable? Hardly so. We have here to deal with a pious tradition, not gathered merely from these apocryphal sources, but handed down among the faithful. It has been alluded to by saints and Doctors, and adopted by devout and diligent historians of St. Joseph in later times. Moreover, from the earliest ages of the Church it has been depicted on tablets and sculptured in marble. Joseph, therefore, has every right not to see himself despoiled of his flowering rod, the sign and testimony of the miraculous choice made of him as the spouse of Mary. Many, indeed, have seen therein the literal fulfillment in symbol of that prophecy of Isaias: "And there shall come forth a rod out of the root of Jesse, and a flower shall rise up out of his root." (*Is.* 11:1). Was it difficult for God to cause a dry stick to blossom, and did not the importance of the choice seem to call for a supernatural sign, that all might acknowledge the Divine Will in this election? And because this incident is related in some apocryphal books, which contain other matter doubtful or undeserving of credit, its presence there ought not to suffice to invalidate its claim on our acceptance. If these books offer no guarantee of the truth of any particular affirmation contained in them, neither, on the other hand, is everything they relate to be nec-

---

2. This incident is delineated in Raphael's celebrated picture of the Betrothal.

essarily condemned as false.

What were the feelings of the humble Joseph when he found himself divinely singled out in preference to all these youths of far higher worldly pretensions, and for an honor of which he believed himself unworthy, it would not be easy to realize. We must be humble like him to conceive how abashed and confounded he stood before the assembly. Yet for one thing, we may be sure, he returned fervent thanks to God in his heart; he knew that, if called to embrace the married state, in espousing Mary his promise of keeping his virginity was safe. We have the authority of a great saint for believing this, that of St. Bridget, to whom Our Lady said: "Regard it as most certain that Joseph, before being espoused to me, knew by the inspiration of the Holy Spirit that I had made a vow of virginity."[3] St. Thomas, also, enquiring how it was that Mary consented to be espoused to Joseph when she had made a vow of virginity, thus replies to his own question: "The Blessed Virgin, before contracting marriage with Joseph, was certified by God that he had formed a similar resolve, and therefore that she exposed herself to no risk in espousing him."[4]

We have said that this marriage, having been decreed in Heaven, was also to receive the highest earthly sanction in the decision of the heads of the Jewish Church. It wanted now the consent of Mary, and consent is essential in the contract of matrimony. The Blessed Virgin, as has been observed, was certain to submit to the will of God in all that concerned her, but this must not lead us to think of her submission as simply blind and passive. It was a free consent, a reasonable consent. Even when an archangel was sent from Heaven to announce to her the Incarnation of the Word, we find her first pondering anxiously the meaning of Gabriel's salutation, and even asking a question for the removal of a difficulty and the satisfaction of her mind: "How shall this thing be?" before pronouncing the *Fiat mihi*.

---

3. *Revelations*, b. vii. c. xxiii.
4. *In Quaest. Sent.* q. ii. a. 1.

If, then, as is most true, she gave her consent to her espousals with Joseph, we may be sure that it was not without mature deliberation and examination of the obligations which she was about to assume. As a learned Doctor of our day[5] has said, no devout soul has ever embraced the profession of a religious life with such consummate prudence, or so closely examined and reflected on its vocation, as did Mary in contracting this marriage.

We must remember that, although Our Lady numbered only fourteen years at the time of her espousals, she had a mind fully enlightened; prudence, in her, had not waited for mature years, and God had infused into her from her tenderest infancy all that knowledge which is ordinarily acquired by study or experience. She, therefore, perfectly understood that she ought not to commit herself to the guidance of one who was not gifted with consummate prudence, for she knew that the head of the woman is the man, and God, who had liberated this Sovereign Virgin from the power of sin and of Hell, had not emancipated her from obedience to this law. It would be reprehensible in her to confide herself to the charge of anyone who was not most discreet and faithful, or trust her purity to a spouse who was not himself as pure as the heavenly spirits, or take any man to be the intimate companion of her life whose own standard was not of the most exalted virtue. She knew, in short, that in taking a husband she was taking a superior, a, confidant of her thoughts, a depositary of her secrets, a witness of her actions. He must, therefore, be eminently prudent, faithful, and chaste; in a word, he must be eminently holy. She knew also that she enjoyed perfect freedom as regarded her consent. The priests and doctors proposed to her a husband, but they could not command her to accept him. It did not appertain to them to do so. God alone can command a maiden contracting matrimony to choose such a one

---

5. Gregorius de Rhodes.

and no other for her spouse.[6] Nor are the relatives of
the Virgin likely to have brought any influence to bear
upon her in the choice she made. Relatives generally
think a good deal of temporal interests, and Joseph was
but a poor artisan. The acquiescence, therefore, of this
Sovereign Lady in taking Joseph for her spouse must
be regarded as the result of her own free election. Let
us see, then, all that is implied herein.

The opinion entertained by any person of another,
and the estimation in which he is held by that person,
derive their value from the wisdom and virtue possessed by the person forming this estimate. Wisdom is
needed to penetrate and discern the true interior merit
of the individual thus judged, and virtue to have a just
appreciation of the merit. Now, as the most holy Virgin had more wisdom than all men and angels, and as
her virtue exceeded that of all pure creatures, the honor
which she paid to anyone and the estimate in which
she held him must be considered to involve praise higher
than could be conceded by the united commendation of
all mankind and of all the angelic hosts. This being
presupposed, let us represent to ourselves Joseph and
Mary in the Temple of Jerusalem interchanging their
mutual promises in presence of the priests assembled
to witness the most holy, the most necessary, and the
most admirable matrimonial contract ever yet concluded.
The two words of consent which the Blessed Virgin pronounced sealed this contract, and at the same time
formed a more exalted panegyric than angels and men
united could have awarded to our saint; because by this
her consent she published that of all men Joseph was
the one who deserved to be her spouse; that she had
chosen him from all others, with full premeditation,
employing in the making of that choice all the virtue
and supernatural light of her soul, together with a full
and entire liberty; moved in this election by nothing
save the greatness of his merits, envying none of her

6. Maria d'Agreda tells us that God revealed to Mary that He designed her to enter
the state of marriage.

companions the great alliances for which they might be destined, but much preferring this poor artisan to all others, whatever might be their worldly advantages and endowments.

Such was the glory accruing to Joseph from Mary's choice of him, but its splendor would have been incomparably increased if the priceless riches which from that moment he received as the dowry which she brought him could have been manifested. Mary, as the daughter of the Eternal Father, had been endowed with incalculable treasures of grace; and St. Bernardine of Siena is of opinion that these, so far as he was capable of being their recipient, were communicated to Joseph when the Blessed Virgin, accepting him as her spouse, gave him her heart. For we must observe, with this holy preacher, that the glorious Virgin did not offer her heart to Joseph simply that he might know its movements and thoughts better than anyone else, though this was much—in fact, she told St. Bridget that she was known only to God and to Joseph; what an inconceivable honor!—but she also gave him her heart as his possession. And who can form any conception of what that heart contained? Solomon declared that it enclosed more interior riches than did all the just souls of ancient times: "Many daughters have gathered together riches; thou hast surpassed them all." (*Prov.* 31:29). "All the treasures of God and of the Saints were in Mary," says the Seraphic Doctor. Now this precious dowry was conceded to Joseph to be to him a glorious ornament, or, more strictly speaking, in order to establish a suitable uniformity in the alliance about to be contracted; that he might sustain with greater splendor the august dignity of Spouse of Mary.

Joseph, then, received in dowry a heart more perfect, more pure, than that of the angels, a heart full of virtues and of supernatural gifts, a heart full of God. And with what completeness did Mary bestow it! There is no question that of all spouses the glorious Virgin could bestow herself with the most absolute entireness, for never was any so completely mistress of herself and of all her faculties as was the Mother of God. Of all marriages, not only was that of Joseph and Mary the most holy and most perfect, but the union of heart was more intimate than it ever was in any other marriage. Our Sovereign Lady in giving her heart united it so closely with that of Joseph that together they had henceforth, as it were, but one heart; and the virtues and heavenly favors with which these beautiful souls were enriched became, in a manner, common to both. Speaking of Adam and Eve in Paradise, God said that they should be "two in one flesh" (*Gen.* 2:24); but of Joseph and Mary it might be said that they were two in one spirit. "They were one spirit," says St. Ambrose.[7] From the moment of their alliance the souls of Joseph and Mary possessed one same heavenly and divine life. The Holy Gospel seems to favor this idea, speaking always of Joseph and Mary with the same honor and as engaged in the same occupations. An angel reveals both to one and the other the Sacred Name of Jesus; both have the happiness of being the first who adored the Saviour, kneeling at His crib; together they presented their Son at the altar forty days after His birth; together they received Simeon's blessing. Jesus served equally His father and His mother; and, to add no more, God, who had deputed one of the highest angels as His ambassador to Mary, employed this same exalted prince of Heaven to declare to Joseph the mystery of the Incarnation. Amongst all that multitude of blessed spirits who encompass the throne of the Most High, Gabriel alone received the commission to treat with Joseph as with Mary.

To sum up what has been said. The Blessed Virgin in accepting Joseph as her spouse gave the most splendid confirmation to the high esteem in which his incomparable virtues were held. She also set the seal of her free consent to a marriage which had been decreed

---

7. *In Lucam.*

in the counsels of the Ever-Blessed Trinity and had formed the matter of solemn deliberation on the part of the heads of the Jewish Church. It was the *fiat* of this sovereign Lady.

Between the betrothal and the marriage of Mary and Joseph a certain period, according to the custom of the Hebrew people, intervened. It is supposed in their case to have been two months, their mutual promises being interchanged in November, and the marriage itself probably taking place on the 23rd of January, when the Church celebrates the feast of the Espousals of the Blessed Virgin.

Chapter XX

Age of Joseph at the Time of the Espousals—His Personal Appearance.

WE MUST pause here awhile to give a few words of consideration to the disputed question as to the age of Joseph at the time of his espousals with Mary. Three opinions have been held; one of which would make our saint far advanced in years. This opinion was accepted by some of the Fathers and ancient ecclesiastical writers, chiefly Greek; and in support of it has been urged the custom prevailing among painters of representing St. Joseph as an aged man, sometimes as almost decrepit. This view has, however, been strongly opposed, not only because it had no other ground to rest upon than the statements of Pseudo-Gospels which were current in the third and fourth centuries, and were coupled with the assertion that Joseph was a widower with many children, an assertion forcibly condemned by St. Jerome and a host of other Fathers and theological writers down to the present times, but also as in itself presenting insuperable difficulties. As we have already observed, these apocryphal writings, while probably recording some true traditionary facts, are entirely devoid of authority, and contain, moreover, much that we naturally reject as both improbable and unbefitting.

In the absence, then, of any authentic document on the point, it is reasonable to have recourse to arguments drawn from suitability and decorum. Now, when the tender age of Mary at the time of her espousals is considered, and the providential object of that marriage, which was to shield her reputation and to hide for a time the mystery of the Incarnation; to provide her also with a fitting companion and protector, who was to be an aid and a support to her, especially during their flight into Egypt and in all the labors and sufferings which their exile must have entailed; it would seem surprising, not to say incredible, in the absence of any solid proof, to suppose that it pleased God to select for her husband a man weighed down by the burden of years. Again, as regards the evidence to be drawn of Joseph's great age from pictorial representations, we may say that it has become quite valueless ever since patient research has brought to light monuments of much earlier date in the sculptures and paintings of the very first centuries. St. Joseph, the Cavaliere de Rossi tells us, is portrayed in the most ancient marbles and ivories as very young and almost always beardless. Later on, he was given a thick beard and a more mature and even aged appearance. Of the youthful representations he mentions many examples, one of which is even supposed to belong to the sixth century. However, it was in about the fifth century that the habit of depicting the saint of, at least, a mature age seems to have commenced. Clearly, then, as De Rossi observes, the most ancient monuments, those of the third and fourth centuries, are so far from following the apocryphal legend that, on the contrary, they picture to us the spouse of the Virgin in the flower of his youth. In the fifth century, when, without peril to the canonicity of the four Gospels, artists might be at liberty, if they pleased, to approximate to some apocryphal traditions, the practice of Christian art to which allusion has been made began to prevail. No argument, then, can be based upon this change; or rather, in the absence of any authoritative document, the tradition of the early Church, as gathered from the monuments of Christian art, is entirely unfavorable to the belief that Joseph was an old man. Thus they furnish support to those reasons to which we have just adverted, drawn from the unsuitability of supposing our saint to have been far advanced in years at the time of his espousals with the Blessed Virgin.

This notion being set aside, it remains for us to choose between the two other views: that is, whether St. Joseph was as young as he is represented in the early monuments, or whether he had already attained a mature age at the time of his espousals. In the absence of all direct evidence, it would seem that those who have given the subject the fullest consideration, and weighed and compared probabilities, consider that at the time of his marriage with Mary he was, most likely, approaching his fortieth year, and, therefore, of an age which can be reckoned neither young nor old, but in the prime of his strength, whether of mind or body.

Some remarks of Vincenzo de Vit, in his *Life of St. Joseph,*[1] are, we think, much to the point in this matter. He is speaking of the relative value of arguments drawn from monuments or tradition and those which rest on reasons of suitability, when it is question of a fact the realization of which depends, not on the will of man, but on the will of God, who disposes events in conformity with His own designs. "When it is question," he says, "of a purely human fact, reasons of propriety have not always the same value, either for or against our acceptance of it, as has the testimony of writers; but, in the present case, where it is question of a divine decree, according to which, as the holy Fathers affirm and the Church holds, the Son of God was to take human flesh in the womb of a married virgin, with the specific object of hiding (as we have said) this miraculous conception, as well as for other reasons which we have mentioned, seeing there is a total absence of all divine authority regarding the age of her spouse, reasons of propriety ought to take precedence of depositions of human authority, among which we include the

1. Cap. v.

testimony of monuments. For here it is no longer question of verifying a fact on the simple witness of historical writers who were not contemporaneous with the events they relate, but of examining whether the fact alleged corresponds with the object which we know to have been predetermined in the counsels of God. For, if once it be shown that the fact alleged is not suited to that object, we are bound to reject it." Applying this principle to the question before us, it is clear that for its solution we have only to consider what was the end proposed by God, and the adaptation to that end of the means which He thought fit to employ for its accomplishment; namely, a marriage which must be in every respect a most perfect one. Justly has it been said that "when Holy Scripture has in any case recorded nothing regarding the Virgin"—and the remark applies equally to St. Joseph—"all that remains to us is to enquire what is most agreeable to reason. Authority which contradicts reason in such cases is no authority at all."[2]

It is, perhaps, not difficult to conceive why painters, in portraying the Holy Family, should have had a bias in favor of increasing the apparent age of St. Joseph as compared with that of the young Mother. It must be borne in mind that it is here no question of actual likeness of either Our Lady, St. Joseph, or the Divine Infant; at most these pictures embody an instinctive Christian tradition, and are figurative of prevailing ideas rather than representations of personal appearance. Now, the primary idea of St. Joseph is that of the guardian, the protector, the support of the Virgin Mother, and this finds its natural expression, under the painter's brush, in a marked difference of age, and that to a greater degree than there is any reason for believing to have

2. Auguste Nicolas, in his work *La Vierge Marie,* part iii. chap. liv. (Paris, 1858), attributes this remark to St. Augustine, in a sermon on the Assumption of the Blessed Virgin. But the editors of the works of that Father refer it to an unknown author of the time of Charlemagne, a learned and pious writer, who drew largely from the works of St. Augustine, and to whose method of reasoning he was certainly no stranger.

existed. Then there is the typical and mystical view. St.
Joseph, as putative father of Our Lord, represents to us
(as we have seen) the Person of the Eternal Father, the
"Ancient of Days." We know that God is eternally young,
or rather that neither youth nor age can be predicated
of Him who is the Self-existing One, the ever-present
Now, the *I am.* Yet, in our impossibility to represent
God as He is, it is our habit, when desiring to indicate
the Person of the Father, to portray Him as a venerable and aged man, thereby figuring, not Himself, but
His Paternity. Even so, it seems a matter of course that
he who was chosen to be His representative on earth
should by analogy be pictorially portrayed in a similar
manner, without thereby implying anything as to the
actual age of our saint at the period in question. In conclusion, it may be added that we have also the symbolic
view. Gerson suggests it in the poem which he wrote on
the holy patriarch. Why was Joseph depicted as old? It
was to give us to understand that he possessed the
virtues attributed to age: prudence, holiness, and purity
of life. For in the Book of Wisdom we read "a spotless
life is old age." (*Wis.* 4:9).

Should it be objected that in the first three or four
centuries a different idea and type was adopted in depicting St. Joseph, and that he was represented as very
young, our answer may be gathered from what has
already been said. This difference arose most probably
from a desire to protest against the apocryphal legends
of the Saint's extreme old age. As an argument against
any such view the fact is certainly good, but we must
not strain it beyond its apparent object. It would not,
therefore, be fair to consider it also as a disproof of
what has been the persuasion of later ages and of the
present time, namely, that St. Joseph had already
attained to mature years, and was near to or not very
far short of forty, when he was espoused to our Blessed
Lady. The protest of the first centuries was clearly a
negative one; it was a protest against the assertion that
the spouse of Mary was in the decline of his days; and,

as it might be difficult to draw the precise line where maturity approaches to decline, these early sculptors and painters would be led to give to St. Joseph an unmistakable look of youth in order to reject and condemn the fables concerning his advanced age, which, we must remember, included also the denial to him of his aureole of virginity. For those passages in the apochryphal writings which ascribe to Joseph so advanced an age assert also that he was a widower with children, an idea equally repulsive to Catholic feeling and opposed to the tradition of the Church, both East and West, which from St. Jerome to our own day has united in declaring that Joseph, like Mary, was and remained ever a virgin.[3]

Tradition tells us of the surpassing beauty of the Mother of God, but scarcely any record has reached us of the personal appearance of St. Joseph, if we except the testimony of St. Justin Martyr—followed or corroborated, perhaps from additional sources, by Gerson and other Doctors—that in beauty and in bodily appearance he was most like to Our Lord; and this was fitting, in order that no suspicion might be entertained respecting his paternity or the virtue of the mother of the Divine Child. Whence we may gather that, next to Jesus and Mary, Joseph was the fairest of the children of men. But, apart from such rare intimations, we are left with nothing to draw upon but our own imagination, or what saints have told us who have beheld him

---

3. F. Coleridge is of opinion that these writings were "very considerably tampered with by heretical adulterations. On this account," he continues, "the class of literature to which the Apocryphal Gospels belong was under great suspicion, and it is most probable that, so to say, the innocent suffered with the guilty in the proscription which followed, and many a genuine morsel of ancient tradition was neglected and perished because it could not easily be discriminated from the spurious matter which had grown up around it. The word *apocryphal* is not in its proper meaning a word of necessarily bad import, for it may be applied to writings of the most perfect orthodoxy and the most complete veracity. But on account of the many dangerous and heretical works which had been put in circulation by the enemies of the Church, we find the Fathers speaking more severely of the whole class than some of its members deserved. It is clear that to a writer, for instance, like St. Jerome there was a great temptation to reject and proscribe the whole of a literature which might still contain many precious historical traditions."—The *Preparation of the Incarnation.* p. 234. (See also Mgr. Gaume, *Life of the Good Thief,* M. de Lisle's Translation, pp. 9-12.)

in their visions. Now, although private revelations can
never be quoted as authority, we cannot but regard
them with great veneration and interest after they have
been duly examined and tested; and when, moreover,
they happen to fall in with our own reasonable conjectures, we feel that they greatly strengthen and support
them. "Whatever of direct divine communication these
so-called private revelations do contain," says a distinguished Oratorian Father of our day, "is the reward and
seal of the ascetic and mystic contemplation of the mysteries of faith."⁴ That being the case, how could we,
apart from the possibility, not to say probability, of their
containing this divine element, fail to set the highest
store by them and immeasurably prefer nourishing our
devotion with them to indulging in our own unaided
fancies? The pictures which saints and other holy persons present to us are, surely, far more likely to resemble the truth than are such as we can construct for
ourselves; and yet, in the ordinary course of meditation on the mysteries of our faith, pictures of some sort
we are constrained to form. Sister Maria d'Agreda, whose
writings have been marked with high ecclesiastical
approval, speaking of Joseph when he was summoned
to appear among the descendants of the race of David,
that one of them might be selected as the spouse of
Mary, says that he was at that time thirty-three years
of age, was well-favored in person and of most pleasing aspect, of incomparable modesty and grave in
demeanor, and, above all, most pure in act, in thought,
and in disposition, having, indeed, from the age of twelve
years made a vow of chastity. He was related in the
third degree to the Blessed Virgin, and his life had
been most pure and holy and irreproachable in the eyes
both of God and men.⁵ This testimony, valuable on
account of the source from which it is derived, is also
precious to us as coinciding with our own natural sen-

---

4. F. Ryder, *Revelations of the After-World*, "The Nineteenth Century," February, 1887,
   p. 289.
5. *Mistica Citta di Dio*, tom. i. cap. xxii.

timents of suitability and propriety. As we felt to recoil from the idea of a decrepit spouse for the Queen of Heaven, so also is it hardly less repugnant to our notions that he should have been unprepossessing in his appearance. The ancient Joseph, who was the type of our saint and who even, prophetically, bore his significant name, is described as of "a beautiful countenance and comely to behold." (*Gen.* 39:6). Can his prototype have been less personally favored, destined as he was for incomparably higher honor? Sister Emmerich likewise describes St. Joseph as having in his whole person an expression of extreme benignity and readiness to be of service to others. She says he had fair hair. That of the Blessed Virgin, she tells us, was most abundant, and of a rich auburn; her eyebrows dark and arched; her eyes, which had long black lashes, large, but habitually cast down; her features exquisitely modeled; while in height she was about the middle stature, and she bore her attire, which for the Espousals was rich and becoming—the Sister describes it in elaborate detail— with much grace and dignity. St. Epiphanius, quoted by Nicephorus, has left us a very similar portrait of the holy Virgin, of whose admirable beauty so many other early Fathers speak. The saying of St. Denis, the Areopagite, who saw her, is well known: that her beauty was so dazzling that he should have adored her as a goddess if he had not known that there is but one God. From a motive of humility Our Blessed Lady would never again wear the robe in which, according to Hebrew custom, she was clad upon that day. The robe was preserved as a precious treasure in Palestine, whence it was sent to Constantinople about the year 461. The ground was of the color of nankeen with flowers blue, white, violet, and gold. It is now the sacred relic of Chartres, having been given by Charles the Bald to the Church there in 877. Many miracles have been attributed to it.[6]

---

6. See Orsini's *Life of the Blessed Virgin*, part i. chap. vii., who also mentions two tunics of Our Lady preserved in the East.

The nuptial ring of the Blessed Virgin is still preserved at Perugia in the Cathedral Church of San Lorenzo. The people of that city and of Chiusi are said to have formerly disputed in arms the possession of this treasure, nor was the difference appeased save by the decision of Sixtus IV and Innocent VIII.[7] It is related how, in days long past, a certain lady of high rank, named Waldrada, having had the rashness to place this ring on her finger, was punished by its immediately drying up. Others have obtained great graces by reverently honoring the holy relic on the altar where it is kept. The late august Pontiff, Pius IX, when he visited Perugia in 1857, paid public veneration to this ring.

---

7. Battista Lauri, *Storia del Santo Anello.* Benedict XIV, *Festa dello Sposalizio della B. Virgine,* sect. ii.

Chapter XXI

The Espousals of Mary and Joseph.

THE nuptials of Mary and Joseph were solemnized in the Temple, and, after receiving the sacerdotal blessing, the newly-married couple would be accompanied by their relatives and friends, walking in procession with music and rejoicing and the waving of myrtle and palm-branches, to their abode, the house which Joachim and Anne had occupied near the Probatic Pool. Perhaps—for this was a Jewish custom where it was designed to show honor—some of these branches would be cast under the feet of the Blessed Virgin and her spouse. Mary was to have her one scene of honor and pomp upon earth, as her Divine Son was to have His in His descent from the Mount of Olives on the road to His Passion, when He was to espouse to Himself the Church upon the Cross of Calvary. The friends of the bridegroom and the bride would on their arrival partake of the marriage-feast which had been prepared for them, an instance of which practice we see in the marriage at Cana in Galilee, where the Mother of Jesus was present, to which Our Lord, as well as His disciples, was invited, and which He honored with His presence and first public miracle.

After the feast, and as the sun went down, the guests would depart, leaving the married pair alone with God and with their good angels, who, we may piously believe, were now called to witness the interchange of those secret words which revealed the hitherto hidden vows, of the existence of which, however, we have reason to be well persuaded that the Holy Spirit had already interiorly assured them. It was now, then, that, according to the opinion of Fathers and Doctors, Mary and Joseph, while remaining bound together by the contract and tie of matrimony, renewed in a solemn and absolute form their respective vows of perpetual virginity. And thus, while continuing in the face of the law and in verity husband and wife, they were to live together as brother and sister, innocent and immaculate, like the angels of God in Heaven. They might be compared to a rose and a lily growing together in one vase. It was, indeed, an incomparable marriage, uniting all that is sweet and pure in the two estates; so that the devout servant of Mary and Joseph, John Gerson, speaking before the Council of Constance of this most pure marriage, gave expression to his ecstasy, when contemplating it, by exclaiming that in them virginity had espoused itself. Nothing in this marriage but what was heavenly, nothing savoring of earth. Holy doctors (as has been already observed) have interpreted the "sealed book" spoken of by Isaias the prophet (*Is.* 29:11), which should be delivered to one that is learned, as the Blessed Virgin, who is also called "a garden enclosed, a fountain sealed up" (*Cant.* 4:12), so that no foot of man should enter the former or profane hand invade the waters of the latter, and that it was to Joseph that this book was given. And when was it given? No doubt it was on the solemn day of his espousals with Mary that Joseph had this mystical book committed into his keeping. The book was the symbol of Mary's virginity, and it was given to the most pure Joseph in order that he might guard it in his virginal hands. And Joseph, knowing before his espousals that the Blessed Virgin had consecrated her virginity to God, understood the mystery of the sealed book, and received it into his custody only to respect and to guard it.

Let us listen to the great Bishop of Geneva on the

subject of Joseph's virginity. "In what degree," he says, "may we suppose that Joseph possessed holy virginity, a virtue which assimilates us to the angels, if the Blessed Virgin, was, not only the most perfectly pure and spotless Virgin, but, as the Church sings, Virginity itself, *Sancta et Immaculata Virginitas!* How highly exalted in this virtue must he have been whom the Eternal Father chose as the guardian of her virginity, or, rather I might say, as its companion; how great, I repeat, must he have been in this virtue! Both had made a vow to preserve virginity during their whole lives, and behold! God wills that they should be joined in the bands of a holy marriage, not that they might unsay their vow or repent of it, but to confirm them in it, and that they might be a mutual support in carrying out their holy enterprise; for this reason they now renewed their vow to live together as virgins for the remainder of their lives."[1]

But here some doubts may arise. If these two most holy spouses were already confirmed in grace and free from all incentives to evil, which in the one had never existed and in the other had by a singular privilege been extinguished or suppressed; if, albeit conditionally, they had both of them promised God to observe perpetual virginity, what need was there for them to bind themselves anew by an absolute vow to preserve in holy matrimony this unspotted lily of virginity? Were they inspired by God to do so? We cannot doubt it. For, indeed, they never did anything without diligently taking counsel of God, and God sent His angels to assure them of His good pleasure. If, then, this act was prompted by God, was pleasing to God, was accepted by God, without doubt it was of great advantage to themselves, and of profit to us; not that they feared lest they might fail in their holy resolve unless they bound themselves by this vow, for through divine grace they were already most firm in their determination, but because, being two most holy creatures, emulous

1. *Entretien*, xix.

of the highest perfection, and aware that the works of perfection are the more acceptable to God and have the greater merit and reward if performed by vow, partaking as they then do of the virtue of religion, they, in order that their virginity might be pleasing to God in the highest degree, resolved to consecrate and give it to Him by an absolute and solemn vow, as in fact they did. And thus Mary and Joseph, possessing all the graces and gifts of the conjugal state, were by their vow to have at the same time all the privileges and rare excellencies of virginity. It could not be that they should be deprived of this signal glory.

Then, as respects the profit to us. Mary was to be proposed for all future ages as the example, the mirror, and the model of all women, high and low, married and virgins, and especially of those who should consecrate themselves to God by a perpetual vow. And what is said of Mary as respects women must, in due proportion, be said of Joseph in regard to men. Joseph, so perfect before God, was to serve as an example and a model to all men, virgins as well as married, and particularly to those who have vowed perpetual chastity. He, too, was to be the first among men to make this generous and solemn vow, in order to become, as the Church styles him, the guardian of virgins and their great patriarch; and, in fact, the sublime example of Mary and Joseph drew numbers of saints of the New Law to follow in their steps, and oblige themselves, by vow, to lead a virginal life even in the state of holy matrimony, who have been held forth in ecclesiastical history as the admiration and marvel of the world.

Such, then, were the chief reasons why these two most holy spouses, although confirmed in grace, took an absolute and formal vow of perpetual virginity after the celebration of their marriage; and this is the common opinion of Fathers and Doctors. But, if they had made a vow before their marriage, and, not content with this, solemnly renewed it subsequently from their love of holy virginity, how, it may be asked, can their marriage be reckoned

true and valid? Is not the vow of virginity directly opposed
to the chief end of holy matrimony? Before applying ourselves to the solution of this difficulty, we may observe
that St. Thomas teaches that all that is essential to matrimony is that, between those who legitimately contract
it, there should be mutual consent and mutual engage-
ment of fidelity.[2] It is certain, as St. Augustine says, that
those are still true spouses who, after being lawfully
united in marriage, resolve in their hearts to remain ever
virgins. And the same Augustine denounces the heretic
Julian, of the sect of the Pelagians, who openly denied
the truth of the marriage between Mary and Joseph. This
being premised, we may further observe that it is clear
from more than one passage in the Holy Gospel that
Mary was truly Joseph's wife, and Joseph truly Mary's
husband, for she is expressly called the wife of Joseph,
as Joseph is called the husband of Mary (*Matthew* 1:16,
19, 20, 24; *Luke* 2:5). If Joseph be sometimes styled by
the Fathers simply the guardian, not the husband, of
Mary, this way of speaking was not intended to exclude
the reality of the matrimonial bond which united them,
but only to rebut any possible surmise which might arise
against their virginal purity.

But to return to the difficulty suggested respecting
the vows. St. Augustine, St. Thomas, and the Master
of the Sentences, not to mention others, firmly hold
that Mary and Joseph took two vows of virginity; the
first mental, simple, and conditional, that is, dependent
on God not disposing otherwise. This vow was taken
by each long before their union. The second vow was
absolute, perpetual, and without limitation, and followed immediately on their marriage. Neither of these
vows, however, could invalidate it. Not the first, because
simple and conditional, and such vows never invalidate
marriage, which a solemn vow alone can render void.
Neither can it be urged that, since it was a promise,
it was not lawful to break it; for it was a conditional

---

2. *Summa*, p. iii. q. xxix. a. 2.

promise, and the condition depended on God, who was pleased to release the two holy spouses from all previous promise, and, therefore, from all obligation. It is certain, also, that Mary and Joseph merited greatly by their obedience to what God had thus ordained; for, had not He decreed their union, they would have willingly remained in their solitary virginal state.

If the previous vow had no power to nullify the validity and reality of their marriage, still less could their subsequent vow, although absolute and unlimited. The contract was effected, the knot was tied; no subsequent disposition, however holy, could dissolve or break that holy matrimonial bond; it could only strengthen it by rendering it more holy. Everyone is at liberty to deny himself in regard to what belongs to him. Such a denial does not deprive him of the right of his own property. You may own an enclosed garden without culling or appropriating to yourself one of its flowers, and make an offering of all to God's altar. Mary did not cease to be Joseph's spouse because she had bound herself by a vow of virginity, nor did Joseph cease to be the true husband of Mary because he had consecrated to God his virginal purity. Thus a true marriage subsisted between them by mutual consent notwithstanding their vow, and all the more sublime in that it was more pure. The Church has always held such marriages to be true marriages, although accompanied by virginity, as we see in the examples of St. Thecla, St. Cecilia, the Emperor St. Henry of Germany, St. Edward the Confessor, and many other saints. How, then, shall we not hold as true, and most valid, the virginal marriage of Joseph and Mary? The proofs alleged by St. Thomas are irrefragable.

It may be further asked, if Jesus, who was essential purity, willed to be born of a virgin, why did He will that she should also be married? This question has also been fully treated by St. Thomas, who has given many reasons. Some of these have already been indicated by anticipation. Jesus, when born into the world, must be born according to the appearances of the world. His genealogy from Abraham, Juda, and David must also be clearly established; and a genealogy with the Hebrews was always traced on the father's side, the mother's, indeed, being (generally speaking) of the same descent and tribe; wherefore St. Jerome says that Jesus was conceived of a married virgin, in order that by Joseph's origin Mary's might be proved. It was also needful to hide the mystery from the profane, and also from the devil; against this adversary Jesus had a shield in Joseph; for, if Satan had discovered his vanquisher in the Babe of Bethlehem, he would at once have begun to wage fierce war against Him. Again, it was needful (as already observed) to guard Mary from dishonoring imputations on the part of those who were ignorant of the mystery, and from the penalties of the law, as also in order that she should be protected, maintained, supported, and consoled in toils and sufferings, especially during the flight into Egypt. To these reasons it must be added that in Joseph she would have an additional and unimpeachable witness that Jesus was conceived without an earthly father, and by the sole power of the Holy Ghost; and more credit would be given to her own declaration of her virginity, because, as St. Ambrose observes, if a virgin who is unmarried becomes a mother, it will certainly be assumed that in affirming her virginity she lies; but a married woman in such case has no inducement to lie, since it is in the order of nature that a married woman should have children. A mystical reason may also be given for this holy marriage; for the virgin espoused to the most pure Joseph was to be the type and figure of the Church, who was espoused as a virgin to a virginal Spouse, that is, to Jesus Christ, as St. Augustine says. Finally, in the person of Mary and Joseph the virginal and conjugal states were severally approved, sanctified, and glorified against ancient and modern heretics, who have furiously assaulted both the vows of virginity and the sacrament of matrimony.

Nor let it be objected that this marriage of Mary and

Joseph tended to hide and veil from men the virginity
of Mary, since this was the one chief object and desire
of these two holy spouses; that is, while jealously guarding and cultivating virginity, to withdraw it from the
observation of men and from their esteem, hiding it
through humility under the veil of matrimony, that they
might not be regarded as singular. Let us listen again
to St. Francis de Sales speaking of St. Joseph, and what
he says applies with still greater force to Mary: "Joseph
was very specially careful to keep the precious pearl
of his virginity concealed; for this reason he consented
to bind himself in marriage, so that no one should come
to know it, and that under the shelter of marriage he
might live concealed. Whereby virgins, both men and
women, who desire to live in chastity are instructed
that it is not sufficient to be virgins, but they must
also be humble." The virginity of Mary, according to the
Divine counsels, was to remain concealed until the
preaching of Christ, which was to manifest His Divinity; and until that time arrived, Joseph, like the veil
of the Temple, was to hide from the profane the Holy
of Holies; but, the propitious moment being come, the
mysterious veil was withdrawn, and the virginity of
Mary was displayed in all its splendor. It was proclaimed by Apostles, declared by Evangelists, and thence-
forth glorified throughout the world by holy Doctors.
And, along with the virginity of Mary, the virginity of
Joseph began by degrees to shine forth also, so that no
one can say that the reality of the marriage between
Mary and Joseph can in any way have effaced or
obscured the belief of their stainless purity. That thought
can only arise in the minds of carnal men, who (as the
Apostle tells us) (*1 Cor.* 2:14) discern not the things
that are of the Spirit of God.

If anyone should ask, would not a richer and more
powerful spouse have been more suitable for our Sovereign Lady, the reply is not far to seek. It is not power
or riches which attract the eyes of God. It is virtue,
rectitude, humility, poverty, and sanctity of life. Joseph

was given to Mary as her spouse because he possessed immense treasures of grace and of holiness, such as might have excited the envy of the celestial intelligences, because his singular endowments had rendered him pre-eminent above all, and because before God he occupied a more elevated and sublime position than that of all the kings of the earth. The Virgin was confided, not to the most powerful, but to the worthiest; not to the richest, but to the holiest; like to the Ark of the Lord, which was a figure of Mary, and was placed, not in the palace of kings, but under the lowly roof and in the charge of a simple Gethite, Obededom, upon whose house, in consequence, all the blessings of Heaven were showered. (*2 Kgs.* 6:10, 11; *1 Par.* 13:13, 14). It is manifest also that Jesus, coming into the world to condemn pride, arrogance, and the ill-acquired riches of men, willed that His most holy Mother and His foster-father should give the first example of a life, poor, frugal, modest, and laborious, such as might rebuke the insolent pride of the worldly, and be an abiding example and consolation to those who are placed in a poor and humble condition of life.

Chapter XXII

Life at Nazareth.

HITHERTO we have been considering Joseph as a young man, and living alone; we have now to regard him as he was in maturer years, and in the company of the Blessed Virgin, to which was soon to be added the company of the Son of God Himself, Christ Jesus. Up to this period the virtues of Joseph, although excellent and sublime, were private and hidden virtues, known only to the narrow circle in which he abode, but henceforward those virtues are to emerge into the light of day, and at length to become known to the uttermost parts of the earth below and the Heaven above. From constant association with Jesus and Mary, the virtues of Joseph acquired so brilliant and dazzling a luster as to be surpassed only by the sovereign splendors of the virtues of Jesus and Mary. Joseph, become the foster-father and guardian of Jesus, the spouse and protector of Mary, becomes, in consequence, the guardian and patron of the whole Church.

We left the holy spouses at Jerusalem, in their abode near the Probatic Pool. There, however, they did not long remain,[1] but went to establish themselves in Nazareth,

---

1. It would appear, from the view taken by Canon Vitali, that Mary and Joseph remained some time at Jerusalem, as though uncertain at first whether they would not reside there, and after their removal spent the following winter months at Nazareth. If their marriage was solemnized on the 23rd of January—and he expressly states his belief that it was so, the Betrothal having taken place, according to him, in the previous November—this would remove the Annunciation to more than a year after their nuptials; a supposition, we imagine, quite at variance with the general belief. Maria d'Agreda says that the Annunciation was six months after

where the Blessed Virgin owned a small house, inherited from her parents, along with some slender possessions in Sephora and in Carmel. What were the reasons which induced their removal we cannot know for certain. No doubt they sought counsel of God in prayer before taking this step, to which they may have been prompted by the painful feelings which the degeneracy of the Holy City excited in them, as well as by the rise of the malicious sects of Herodians, Sadducees, and Pharisees, and the spread of their false corrupting doctrines, not to speak of the cruel jealousy of Herod, which every day increased, displaying itself, not against his subjects only, but against his own wife and children, whom he mercilessly put to death. Mary and Joseph, being of the house and family of David, might, therefore, have just cause to dread becoming in some way the objects of his malevolent suspicions. Be this as it may, we have good reason to believe that the holy spouses never contemplated retaining the whole of the patrimony which Mary inherited from her parents, and which, moderate as it was, would probably have sufficed to raise them above the level of actual poverty. These two ardent lovers of virginity were also lovers of poverty, which they thus embraced by their voluntary act. Maria d'Agreda says that immediately after their marriage they divided what they possessed into three portions, one of which they gave to the Temple, one they distributed to the poor, and the third remained in the hands of Joseph for his administration, Our Lady reserving to herself the office of waiting on her

---

the marriage; in which case the Espousals on the 23rd of January would have been the Betrothal, the marriage itself, according to her, being celebrated in the September following, the month of the Blessed Virgin's Nativity. Having, however, laid down to ourselves the rule not to refer either for dates, or for the sequence of events, or any other matter of historical importance, to the revelations of saints, but simply, from time to time, to enrich and supplement the narrative with the pictures of what they saw in vision and have made known to us for our spiritual edification, we shall dismiss her view without discussion. That of Canon Vitali, we must own, seems to us scarcely admissible; and, as he alleges no authority whatever in its favor, we have felt at liberty to disregard it. If Mary and Joseph left Jerusalem for Nazareth immediately, or almost immediately, after their marriage, that would allow the space of two months to elapse between their nuptials and the Annunciation, a view more agreeable, we believe, to Catholic feeling and tradition.

holy spouse and performing all household work; for the same favored soul tells us that never did Mary interfere in external business, neither would she buy or sell; money, in short, never passed through her pure hands. Joseph was thus installed as head of the family, in the office of steward and administrator of the goods of what might truly be called God's house. The third portion of Mary's inheritance, which had been reserved, consisted chiefly, no doubt, of their humble house at Nazareth, whither they were about to retire, and where soon was to be accomplished the great mystery of the Incarnation.

We have seen how St. Joseph during his youth had exercised the trade of a carpenter. He now, we are told by a great contemplative, asked Our Lady if she wished him to continue it for her service, in order besides to have something to give to the poor, and also because it was well not to lead an idle and unemployed life. Of this the most prudent Virgin approved, telling him that the Lord did not wish them to be rich, but poor, and lovers of the poor and the refuge of the poor, so far as their means extended. Then—Maria d'Agreda, whom we quote, tells us—there arose a holy contest between the two blessed spouses as to which of them was to regard and treat the other as superior. Joseph in his humility esteemed himself as all unworthy of the treasure which had been committed to his charge; and so great was his veneration for Mary that he would have desired to take the place of her servant, seeking only to know and obey her will in everything. She, however, who amongst the humble superexcelled in humility, was the conqueror in this loving strife; for the most holy Mary would not consent that, the man being the head, the natural order should be inverted, so that it was her will to obey in all things her spouse Joseph, asking him only to allow her to give alms to the poor of the Lord, to which the Saint willingly agreed. It was a great sacrifice to Joseph to have thus to assume the place due to him as husband, and in doing so he, on his part, was practicing the virtue of obedience, even as Mary was on hers. The two spouses were, therefore, perfectly fulfilling the three evangelical counsels of chastity, poverty, and obedience.

The Santa Casa, now miraculously transported to Loreto, was, like the Nazareth houses in general, very small; and, as was the case with many of them likewise, it was built against the rock, with an opening into a cave or grotto at the back.[2] On the one side was an apartment in the rock, which to this day bears the name of the kitchen of the Madonna; on the other, at a very short distance, was what is still by tradition called the workshop of St. Joseph. The walls of the Santa Casa, wherein Mary had herself been born, and where she must have dwelt until taken to the Temple by her parents, were bare and unadorned, but we may be sure that her hands had soon placed everything in order, and, though there was nothing superfluous, the little they possessed was arranged with that neatness, modesty, and simplicity which invests a poor abode with a charm often wanting in the luxurious apartments of the rich. Mary had no servant, so that all the domestic work was performed by herself; and, as there was no water in Nazareth save at one fountain, distant about a quarter of a mile from their abode, the Blessed Virgin, with her water-pot on her head, might have been seen, like one of the daughters of the ancient patriarchs, going daily to draw water at the well for the supply of the house—lovely as Rachel, bashful as Rebecca in her whole person and bearing, or, rather, immeasurably surpassing in beauty and modesty all the daughters of Eve. The fountain was afterwards called by her name. Sometimes she would repair thither with a companion to wash the household linen, and Joseph, beholding her thus industriously employed, while thanking God in his inmost soul for having given him for his

---

2. See *Loreto and Nazareth*, by the late Father Hutchison of the London Oratory, where will be found a full description both of the Santa Casa and of the sanctuary at Nazareth. It may here be observed that what has been miraculously removed formed only a portion of the abode occupied or used by the Holy Family.

spouse, not a woman, but an angel of Paradise, grieved to see her, the daughter of kings and worthy of all the thrones of the earth, thus abasing herself to toil fit only for menials. Within the house, likewise, she never remained idle. She plied the needle and the spindle, as she had been wont to do in the Temple, and her exquisite workmanship helped to procure the necessaries of life. Maria d'Agreda, in her *Revelations,* has drawn out a marvellous parallel between her and the "valiant woman" of the Proverbs (*Prov.* 31:10-31), whom we may regard as the mystical type of Mary, as well as the example proposed to all women, but so ill followed by the greater number, especially in these soft degenerate days.

But first and foremost was her solicitude to minister assiduously to the wants and wishes of Joseph. She diligently prepared their simple meal and placed it on their little table, which had been made, we are told, by the Saint himself. Here were no rich viands or dishes of silver and gold. All spoke of modesty, economy, frugality. There was sufficient to support life, but no dainties to excite greed. There was peace and charity at that board. It was the "dinner of herbs" described in the Proverbs. "Better," says the Wise Man, "is a little with the fear of the Lord than great treasures without content. It is better to be invited to herbs with love, than to a fatted calf with hatred." (*Prov.* 15:16, 17). And if at that table there sat no company of noble guests, there was a band of heavenly spirits in attendance, sent by God to aid, guard, and comfort the holy spouses. The words which Joseph addressed to Mary were simple and brief, and brief and simple were her replies, but full of ravishing gentleness and sweetness. He seemed to be listening to an angel, or to more than an angel. Esteeming the virtues of her of whom God had made him the most fortunate spouse to be superhuman and heavenly, his respect was so great that it could not but manifest itself in his whole behavior. He could scarcely address her without inclining his head as to his lady and queen; and in all his words and actions there would never have been detected the slightest sign of that innocent freedom which commonly exists between good and virtuous spouses. Let us hear what St. Bridget tells us Our Lady said to her about her holy spouse. "Joseph was so reserved in his words," said Mary, "that none ever came from his mouth which were not good and holy, none that were idle or complaining. He was most patient and diligent in labor, most meek under injuries, most attentive to my every word, strong and constant against my adversaries, a faithful witness of the wonders of God, dead to the flesh and to the world, alive only to God and to heavenly goods, which alone he desired, conformed to the Divine will, and so resigned to it that he was constantly saying: 'Let the will of God be done in me; may I live as long as it is pleasing to God, that I may see His Divine will fulfilled.' He seldom conversed with men, but continually with God, whose will alone he wished to do; wherefore he now enjoys great glory in Heaven."

Joseph knew, says the pious and learned Gerson, that he was the head of Mary, because the husband is the head of the wife. Nevertheless, his veneration for her was so profound that he considered himself unworthy to be her companion, or even to kiss the ground on which she had trod; and he was always on the watch to render her some service, albeit unrequested, even as might some most devoted servant rather than spouse. And then he loved her so exceedingly, with a love like what the heavenly spirits feel for each other, and would have readily given his heart's blood for her: and as yet he knew not her incomparable dignity! Yes, he loved her exceedingly, and we may hold for certain that Joseph, as he was the first, so was he the most devoted servant of Mary—the most loving, the most faithful, the most assiduous, the most constant. He heads, we may say, the procession of her devout worshippers, the first

to raise his banner in her honor, unrivaled in his loy-
alty and devotion, nay, distancing all her other pious
clients with the rapidity of the eagle, the king of birds.

On the other hand, no less was the love and reverence which the Virgin had for him. She rejoiced to serve
him as her lord, respect him as her tutor and guardian,
and tenderly love him as her spouse, treating him with
all the honor with which Scripture records that Sara
treated Abraham, telling us that she called him "lord"
(*Gen.* 18:12; *1 Ptr.* 3:6), implying thereby much more
than the mere words express. Reflecting on all this, the
devout Gerson enthusiastically exclaimed before the
Council of Constance, "Marvellous is thy sublime elevation, O Joseph! O incomparable dignity, that the
Mother of God, the Queen of Heaven, the Sovereign
Lady of the world, should not disdain to call thee her
lord! Truly, truly," he continued, "O orthodox Fathers,
I know not which most to admire, the great humility
of Mary or the sublime grandeur of Joseph." Mary (says
Isolano) gave honor to Joseph, not only as her husband,
but as her tutor and guardian; she never departed a
hair's breadth from his wishes; she never determined
on anything without his advice, never moved a step
without his permission, nor undertook anything without his consent. In everything she depended on his will,
for in the will of Joseph she recognized the most holy
will of God. They were one heart and one soul: what
concord, then, what tranquillity, what peace reigned
between them![3] St. Bernardine of Siena writes: "Since
the Virgin comprehended how great was conjugal unity
in spiritual love, and knew that this spouse had been
given her directly by the Spirit of God, I believe that
she sincerely loved Joseph with the entire affection of
her heart";[4] and Isidoro Isolano adds that "the love of
the saints is the most ardent, the most perfect, and the
holiest of loves." John of Cartagena, indeed, argues
the eminent sanctity of Joseph above all the saints

3. *Summa de Donis S. Joseph,* p. ii. c. ix.
4. *Sermo de S. Joseph,* c. i. a. 11.

from the very fact of Mary's most ardent love of him; for "knowing," he says, "the obligation that lay upon her to love her spouse, she loved Joseph more than all the patriarchs and prophets, martyrs, Apostles, and angels."[5] What felicity for Joseph, and what an honor, to enjoy the whole love of her who with a single glance of her eye could enhance the joy of the angels of Paradise! Now it is that we can realize how the Evangelist, desiring to express the highest encomium of Joseph, comprised it in these few words: "Joseph the husband of Mary." The being Mary's spouse was the foundation and basis of all his dignity.

We cannot refrain from quoting here a passage from the writings of that great lover of Joseph, St. Leonard of Port Maurice. "Let the Evangelists be silent," he says, "concerning all they could tell us of Joseph, placing in array before us those virtues and singular prerogatives which serve as a noble accompaniment to his dignity. To me it suffices that they make him known to us as the husband of Mary, that is, the most like among all living beings to the most perfect of pure creatures who ever came out of the hands of God, even His own Blessed Mother. Spouse of Mary! that is, who came nearest to that highest pinnacle of sanctity which pierced the Heavens, which rose above the empyrean, and from the very bosom of the Eternal Father drew down His Only-Begotten Son. Spouse of Mary! that is, head of the first head in the world, for the husband is the head of the wife. Spouse of Mary! that is, lord of that sovereign Lady who well knew the precept of Genesis: 'Thou shalt be under thy husband's power, and he shall have dominion over thee' (*Gen.* 3:16); and who, most perfect in all else, was so also in the reverence and homage which she paid to her spouse, in which reverence and homage she surpassed all other wives. Spouse of Mary! that is, of the great Queen whom to serve is the highest dignity of the Dominations, the highest function of the

---

5. Lib. iv. *Hom.* viii. *de S. Joseph.*

Principalities, the deepest study of the Cherubim, and the most ardent desire of the Seraphim. . . . 'No more,' exclaims St. Bernard; 'you say all in saying he was like the Virgin, his spouse.' He was like her in all things: in countenance, in feature, in heart, in disposition, in manners, in sanctity, in virtue; so that, if Mary was the aurora preceding the Divine Sun, Joseph was the horizon illuminated by Its splendors."[6]

O truly happy spouse! Adam rejoiced when he received from God Eve for a companion, but his joy was soon turned into sorrow, for Eve brought to him irreparable woe; while Joseph's joy in receiving Mary for his companion was constant and enduring, for Mary was to him the cause of endless felicity. Mary brought him everlasting riches as her dowry, so that he might truly say, "All good things came to me together with her, and innumerable riches through her hands." (*Wis.* 7:11). Now, if the Virgin is wont to obtain such great graces even for sinners, enemies of her Son, how many favors must she not have obtained for her holy spouse, the guardian of her purity and the loving foster-father of her Divine Son! And if we, miserable creatures, often profit greatly from consorting and conversing with holy men, who are as nothing compared to the Virgin, how much may we not suppose Joseph to have profited by his association and conversation with the Queen of all Saints! "Mary," says Gerson, "for so many years inspired and communicated graces to Joseph by her looks, by her voice, by her example, by her conversation;" and again Cartagena: "What a vast increase of spiritual joy and virtue must we not esteem Joseph to have received from the society of the Blessed Virgin, from having been worthy of hearing so often the sweet voice of the Mother of God, contemplating her heavenly countenance, and enjoying, not only her blessed presence, but even her conjugal affection and intimacy!"[7]

We should overload our pages were we to cite all

---

6. *Panegir. di S. Giusseppe,* v.
7. Lib. iv. *Hom.* viii.

that Saints and Doctors have said touching the holy conversation of Mary and Joseph. We must be content with giving an extract from that *Conference* of St. Francis de Sales to which frequent reference has been made.[8] Speaking of the virginal nuptials of Joseph and Mary, he says, "Oh, how divine was the union between Our Lady and the glorious St. Joseph, a union which caused the Supreme Good, the Good of all goods, Our Lord Himself, to belong to Joseph—even as He belonged to Our Lady—not by nature but by grace; which made him a sharer in all the possessions of his dear spouse, and made him continually increase in perfection by his continual communications with her who possessed all virtues in so exalted a degree that no other creature, however pure and spotless, can attain to them! Nevertheless, St. Joseph was the one who made the nearest approach; and, as a mirror, when set before the rays of the sun, reflects them perfectly, and another set before the first so vividly repeats them that it is scarcely possible to see which of the two immediately receives them, even so Our Lady, like a most pure mirror, received the rays of the Sun of Justice, which conveyed into her soul all virtues and perfections, and St. Joseph, like a second mirror, reflected them so perfectly that he appeared to possess them in as sublime a degree as did the glorious Virgin herself."

Amidst the abundance of goods so many and so priceless, must not Joseph have deemed himself supremely blessed, and must not the holy house of Nazareth have appeared to him an earthly Paradise? The very knowledge that he was so ardently loved by Mary, the virgin spouse of the Eternal, the delight of angels and of saints, a miracle of beauty, the sweetest charm of Heaven and earth—was not this enough to transport him with unutterable joy? And to think that of so sublime a lady, visited by angels, blessed by God, he was the happy spouse, the protector, the

---

8. *Entretien,* xix.

guardian, the head, having, as Gerson says, authority, principality, dominion, and empire over her—this thought alone rendered him valiant to launch himself on any undertaking, however arduous, strong in sustaining every labor, patient under all adversities; this it was which made him insensible to all fatigues, rendered poverty itself still dearer to him than it had ever been; and, if anything grieved him, it was only that he could not provide for so great a lady all the honor due to her exalted rank and merits.

Chapter XXIII

The Annunciation.

THE Lord meanwhile was preparing for both of these holy spouses a high destiny, a grace and a dignity never conceded to any creature, earthly or heavenly. By the express command of God they had contracted holy matrimony in the presence of the priests of the Temple, and by His inspiration and movement had, immediately after their marriage, made a vow of perpetual virginity. But such a vow was a thing quite new, and the virtue of virginity itself was almost unknown to this carnal people. Mary and Joseph, in their humility, would hide from profane eyes this heavenly virtue under the veil of marriage. Nevertheless, they must have known that they would thus incur in the eyes of the vulgar the opprobrium of sterility. But what of that? So great was their love and devotion to virginity that they made no account of the disgrace, as it was reckoned, of infecundity, and cared not for the reproach it would bring upon them. God, however, who loves virginity and humility, did not will that this reproach should lie upon them, but purposed to reward their fidelity to these virtues in a wonderful manner. Others hastened to contract marriage, at the sacrifice of their virginity, with the hope of having the Messias born of their race, while these two holy spouses, on the contrary, had made a vow of perpetual virginity, reputing themselves unworthy of that honor; and lo! it was they to whom the Messias should be given

without loss of their angelic purity. They had hidden
it, heedless of what men would think on beholding them
childless. But God delivered the humble from the contempt of the proud, and to these virgin spouses divinely
conceded a Son, the fairest and the most exalted among
the children of men. Oh, how good is the Most High
God to the upright in heart! How gracious towards
those who are truly humble! Mary and Joseph knew
from the prophets that the time for the birth of the
Messias was at hand, and that He was to be born of
the tribe of Juda, and of the house of David, in the city
of Bethlehem; and, being themselves of that tribe and
house, they forego by their vow all possibility of being
themselves the happy progenitors, and conceal themselves in one of the obscure villages of Galilee. But,
precisely because they have such a lowly esteem of
themselves, God follows them, God singles them out,
and exalts them, bestowing on their virginal purity that
same Messias of whom they considered themselves so
unworthy, Him who had been the desire of all the mothers in Sion, and of so many patriarchs and kings; in
fine, the desire of the whole universe.

The winter was now past, and spring was returning
to gladden the earth. According to many Doctors of the
Church, it was the year 4,000 of the creation of the
world and the same season of the year in which God
completed that work of His hands. The 25th of March
had come, when the Lord God called to Him the
Archangel Gabriel, one of the seven spirits who stand
before His throne, the same who had been commissioned to reveal to Daniel the mystery of the seventy
weeks. That great prince of Heaven may, indeed, justly
be regarded as the Angel of the Incarnation. His name
signifies the Strength of God, a most fitting appellation for one chosen to announce the coming of Him who
was to vanquish "the prince of the power of this air"
(*Eph.* 2:2), the great adversary, the devil, and to destroy
his works. And to whom was this glorious messenger
sent? "To a virgin espoused to a man whose name was

Joseph, of the house of David; and the virgin's name was Mary." (*Luke* 1:27). This is the first time that the Evangelist names St. Joseph. By this mention of him he makes known to us the large share which he would have in the glories of Mary; for, if great was the dignity of the Virgin in being the Mother of God, great also was the dignity of Joseph in being the husband of her of whom the Son of God was born. Nor let the word "espoused" be understood, as by some it has been understood, as if Mary were at that time only promised in marriage, that is, betrothed. No. The nuptials had already been celebrated, according to the true sense of Scripture, a point which has been clearly established by the Holy Fathers and Doctors, and, in particular, by the Angelic Doctor, St. Thomas. Thus we find St. Matthew calling Joseph the husband of Mary, and Mary the wife of Joseph. (*Matt.* 1:19, 24). It may be remarked also that the term "espoused" is used again by the same Evangelist, St. Luke, on the occasion of the journey to Bethlehem (*Luke* 2:5), when no possible question could arise as to its signification. Those who contend that the marriage was not solemnized until after Mary's visit to Elizabeth, which lasted three months, and Joseph's discovery of her condition, raise an insuperable difficulty; for how in that case could one of the primary objects of their holy union have been attained, that of shielding the honor of the Blessed Mother of God?

To the great archangel, then, the Most High made known the embassage with which he was charged, and the words which he was to address to the Virgin of Nazareth. His Divine Majesty was at the same time pleased Himself to declare to the whole hierarchy of Heaven that the time for man's redemption was arrived, and that He was about to descend into the world and become incarnate in the womb of Mary, whom He had chosen, prepared, and adorned to be His mother. Although the ordinary manner in which the heavenly intelligences are enlightened is by communication from the superior to the inferior hierarchies, on this occasion it was not so; for, as Holy Scripture tells us, "When He bringeth in the First-Begotten into the world, He saith, And let all the angels of God adore Him." (*Heb.* 1:6; *Ps.* 96:7). No sooner, then, did all the orders of blessed spirits hear the voice of their Creator announcing to them this marvellous news, than they burst forth in one simultaneous canticle of praise and thanksgiving to the Triune God, magnifying especially the Divine condescension in honoring and exalting the humble: "Blessed be the name of the Lord from henceforth now and for ever. The Lord is high above all nations, and His glory above the heavens. Who is like unto the Lord our God, who dwelleth on high, and regardeth the things that are lowly in heaven and on earth?" (*Ps.* 112:2, 4-6).

Thousands of the celestial hosts followed Gabriel, as he flew with lightning speed to Nazareth, that they might adore the God-Man at the very instant of His conception, and pay their devoted homage to the Mother of the Eternal King. What was the hour? Midnight must have struck, for the 25th of March had begun; but it cannot have sounded long, for, as Jesus was born at the midnight hour at Bethlehem, so we may believe that He was conceived at a like hour at Nazareth, and may apply literally to the moment of His incarnation that passage in the Book of Wisdom which the Church has adopted for the Introit of Sunday in the Christmas week: "While all things were in quiet silence, and the night was in the midst of her course, Thy Almighty Word leapt down from heaven from Thy royal throne." (*Wis.* 18:14). But the whole universe, and God Himself, were awaiting Mary's consent. The Virgin was in the secrecy of her chamber, rapt in contemplation and fervent prayer for the coming of the Messias, that there might be an end of sin and prevarication, that iniquity might be cancelled, eternal justice be established, the prophecies be accomplished, and the Saint of Saints be anointed. This was, indeed, the continual subject of her petitions. Maria d'Agreda says that the Lord had caused her to make a nine days' prayer of special earnestness directed to that end, during which she was favored with visions and graces of a most exalted character; but she adds that, when Gabriel acquitted himself of his mission, the Most High left her in her ordinary spiritual state, withdrawing all unusual favors and graces from her soul, because this mystery was to be a "sacrament of faith," allowing the operations of that virtue, as well as those of hope and charity, to have their full exercise, that by believing and hoping in the Divine word addressed to her by the angel, she might merit freely the accomplishment of those things which were announced to her.[1]

The angel was to present himself in a visible human form, because, as St. Thomas says, he came to announce the advent of that God who, in Himself invisible, was about to become visible in human flesh; and he was also to assume a specially beautiful and majestic appearance, as befitted such a messenger and such a message. The Angel Gabriel came, says St. Augustine, all radiant in his countenance, glorious in his apparel, admirable in his bearing. That the movement of the angel was such as is proper to bodies seems to be signified by the Evangelist when he says, not that he appeared to Mary, but that he "came in" unto her, that is, entered the house and the room where she was, which was instantly flooded with light. The Virgin was suddenly roused from her ecstasy by this blaze of glory, but, if startled, she was not alarmed.[2] The visits of angels were not new to her, and a pious Oriental tradition asserts that she had even seen Gabriel himself once before near the fountain of Nazareth. The magnificence, however, of his attire, the majesty of his aspect, and the impressive grandeur of his ingress may well have filled her with peculiar awe and veneration. She was about to make him a profound obeisance when he presented her with his own reverential salutation, as

---

1. This seems to be implied in the words of Elizabeth. (Luke 1:45).
2. In the Office of the Annunciation it is said, *Expavescit Virgo de lumine;* but this need mean no more than that she was startled and astonished.

to his lady and queen. For times were henceforward changed, and men were no longer to adore the angels after the manner of the people of God under the Old Testament, which was "ordained by angels in the hand of a mediator." (*Gal.* 3:19). The Apostle also calls it "the word spoken by angels," and adds that "God hath not subjected unto angels the world to come," signifying thereby the kingdom of Christ. (*Heb.* 2:2, 5). The angels, in fact, under the Old Law, before the Incarnation, not only acted the part of messengers from God to men, but not unfrequently personated Him and spoke in His Name. Hence we find them receiving on these occasions a vicarious adoration directed to God.[3] But when human nature was united to God Himself in the Person of the Word men were no longer to be under the ministerial rule of the angels, but were to be their companions and brethren,[4] and Mary was to be their queen as well as ours.

So Gabriel bowed low before the Virgin of Nazareth, and said, "Hail, full of grace, the Lord is with thee. Blessed art thou among women." Sublime salutation, with which, as St. Ambrose says, the Virgin alone could be saluted, for she alone obtained that grace which no other ever merited; that is, to be full of Him who is the author of grace. Mary is saluted as full of grace, says St. Jerome, because to others grace is given in part and by measure, but in Mary the whole fullness of grace was infused;[5] whence, as St. Bernard adds, she is full of grace for herself and has a superabundance of grace for us. Mary, then, being so full of grace from the moment of her conception, it was meet that the Lord should be

---

3. Numerous instances in proof of this might be cited: e.g., *Gen.* 32:28, 30, where the "man," or, as Osee calls him (xii. 4), the "angel," who wrestled with Jacob, says, "If thou hast been strong against God," etc.; and Jacob himself called the name of the place Phanuel, saying, "I have seen God face to face, and my soul has been saved"; also *Judges* 13:22, where Manue says to his wife after the angel's visit, "We shall certainly die, because we have seen God"; and, in particular, *Gen.* 18:17-33, where the angel who remained to speak with Abraham is repeatedly called "the Lord."

4. This is the reason given by the angel in the Apocalypse (22:9), for refusing the homage which St. John the Evangelist would have paid him, and may serve to explain the angel's disclaimer, of which heretics have availed themselves to deny the lawfulness of the honor rendered by Catholics to these spirits of Heaven.

5. *Sermo de Assumptione B. Mariae Virginis.*

with her, not in an ordinary and common manner, but
in one that was extraordinary and unprecedented. God
is with all by His essence, His power, and His presence, and with the just by His grace; but He was with
Mary, not only in all these modes, but in one altogether
new and singular. He was with Mary by a certain peculiar union, since the Son of God was about to take
human flesh in her womb and, with a human soul
united to the Person of the Word, was to be called and
truly to be the Son of Mary, wherefore Mary was to be
truly called and truly to be the Mother of God. No one
in the world, whether among angels or among men,
was ever so closely united to God as was Mary, no one
was so near to the Divinity; so that the Angelic Doctor does not scruple to affirm that the dignity of Mary
has something in it of the infinite. Well, therefore, might
she be styled blessed by the angel, blessed among all
women. All other women shared the malediction of Eve;
Mary alone was exempt. From Eve began malediction,
and benediction began from Mary. From the first instant
of her being she triumphed over the infernal serpent,
and was in herself and in her children eternally blessed.
Jahel, it is true, who was a figure of Mary, was saluted
by Debbora as "blessed among women" (*Jgs.* 5:24),
because she had slain Sisara, the enemy of God's people, but this blessing of Jahel was simply one of words,
whereas the blessing of Mary was in very deed; it was
intrinsic and full of measureless grace, from the peculiar presence of that God who is the author of grace;
so that, as St. Ambrose says, the form of blessing used
by the angel to Mary was reserved for her alone.[6]

At these words of praise the most humble virgin was
"troubled" and, casting her eyes on the ground, reflected
within herself what could be the import of the salutation. This was the cause of her perturbation, and not,
as some have imagined, the appearance of an angel in
human form. What need to seek further when the Evan-

---

6. L. ii. *in Lucam.*

gelist speaks so plainly? The angel gently comforted her, saying, "Fear not, Mary, for thou hast found grace with God"; as if he would say, whoever has found grace has no cause to fear; it is for those only to fear who have lost grace; and then immediately follow the words, given by St. Luke, in which he acquitted himself of his embassage: "Behold thou shalt conceive in thy womb, and shalt bring forth a son; and thou shalt call His name Jesus. He shall be great, and shall be called the Son of the Most High, and the Lord God shall give unto Him the throne of David, His father, and He shall reign in the house of Jacob for ever: and of His kingdom there shall be no end." (*Luke* 1:30-33). At hearing this glorious offer, which of the daughters of Sion would not have exulted with joy? Which of them would have hesitated for an instant in accepting the divine maternity? Nevertheless, Mary retains her heavenly calmness, and pauses before giving her assent. She well understood the meaning of the offer made to her, and never doubted for a moment the omnipotence of God. She believes the mystery, but, prudent and most tender of her virginity, which she has solemnly vowed to God, she desires to comprehend how the two can be reconciled. She seeks, says St. Augustine, to know the mode in which the mystery can be accomplished. Venerable Bede says that she had read in Isaias (*Is.* 7:14) that a virgin should conceive and bear a son, but she had not read how this was to be, and this she sought to learn from the angel; that is, how her beloved virginity was to remain safe and intact: as if she were ready (as saints have said), had she the choice, rather to renounce the divine maternity than lose her virginal purity, so enamored of it was she. She is not incredulous, she does not ask for a sign, as did Zachary (*Luke* 1:18), to enable her to believe. She simply seeks a solution of the difficulty. Although the works of God, perfect in themselves, need no justification before men, nevertheless, when the human reason is called on by God to give its assent, and some contradiction is discernible by it, though only apparent, God is willing to come to the aid of the infirmity of human nature, that, all obstacle being removed, the adhesion given to His Will by the intellect may be more entire and the homage more perfect. And this was precisely Mary's case. If the vow she had made was from God, of which she had no doubt, and if equally from God was the maternity now offered by the angel, whose veracity she never questioned, then it was certain that the latter must take place without violation of the former. But by what means could two things be reconciled which presented themselves to the intellect as so diametrically opposed. Wherefore Mary, who had heard her own praises in silence, now speaks, and inquires of the angel, "How shall this be done, because I know not man?" These words of Mary are a manifest testimony to her own virginity and that of Joseph. St. Augustine draws from them an indisputable argument to prove that both she and Joseph had bound themselves thereto by a perpetual vow. And because this question of Mary was not one of vain curiosity or cold mistrust, but was dictated by that consummate prudence with which she was endowed, the angel promptly satisfied her. "The Holy Ghost," he said, "shall come upon thee, and the power of the Most High shall overshadow thee. And therefore, also, the Holy which shall be born of thee shall be called the Son of God." (*Luke* 1:35). By these words Mary was assured that, this conception being the marvellous work of the Spirit of God, she should become the Mother of God without detriment to her virginity; whence St. Peter Chrysologus says, "Mary is truly blessed, in that she possesses at once the dignity of a mother and the merit of virginity."[7] "This glory," exclaims St. Bernard, "of having the joy of maternity and the honor of virginity belongs to Mary alone, who in this privilege had none either preceding or following her. It is her exclusive privilege, which shall never be given to another. It is a privilege

---

7. *Serm.* cxliii.

at once singular and ineffable."⁸ St. Bernard deduces
from the angel's words two other great truths. The mystery of the Most Holy Trinity, or of the Three Divine
Persons, is clearly and distinctly revealed for the first
time in the Annunciation. The angel names the Father,
the Son, and the Holy Ghost. The other truth is that
the whole Blessed Trinity took part in this great mystery, although the Second Person alone became incarnate. Gabriel added, "And behold thy cousin Elizabeth,
she also hath conceived a son in her old age; and this
is the sixth month with her that is called barren; because
no word shall be impossible with God." (*Luke* 1:36, 37).
The angel made this known to Mary, not only that she
might rejoice at the happy tidings, but that she might
go and visit the mother of the Precursor.

A great wonder it is, no doubt, and worthy of our
highest admiration, that the accomplishment of all these
mysteries and of everything involved in them should
be left by the Most High in the hands of a humble
maiden, and that all should depend on her *fiat;* but
securely was it left to the wisdom and fortitude of this
"valiant woman," who did not betray the confidence
reposed in her. The works accomplished within God
Himself need not the co-operation of the creature, nor
do they admit of its participation; therefore God awaits
not the consent of creatures to act *ad intra.* But in His
works *ad extra,* His contingent works, it is different.
Among these the greatest was His being made man;
and He would not effect it without the co-operation of
the most holy Mary or without her free consent; and
this in order that with her and by her He should give
this fulfillment and crown of all His works, and that
we should recognize the benefit as coming to us from
the Mother of Wisdom and our Reparatrix. Moreover,
God desired that Mary should give the assent of her
whole being, intellect, heart, will, and that her reply
should be therefore such as befitted the most exalted

---

8. *Serm.* iv. *de Assumpt. B. Virg.*

of mysteries. And Our Lady discerned all that was implied in the stupendous offer made to her; she saw all that depended on her answer—the fulfillment of all the prophecies and of the promises made by God, the most pleasing and acceptable sacrifice ever offered or which could be ever offered to Him, the opening of the gates of Paradise, victory and triumph over Hell, the redemption of the whole human race, satisfaction and compensation to Divine justice, the foundation of the New Law of grace, the glory of men, the joy of the angels, and all that would be contained in and result from the Only-Begotten of the Father taking the form of a servant in her womb. All was before the magnificent and divinely illuminated intellect of this great Lady. Having, then, conferred with the angel and within herself concerning this most sublime mystery, her spirit was fortified and raised to such a height of admiration and reverence, and she made so intense an act of the love of God, that her most chaste heart, by the force of this act and under its pressure, gave forth, says Maria d'Agreda, three drops of its pure blood from which the Holy Ghost formed the Body of Christ our Lord, so that the substance of which the Sacred Humanity of the Word was made was furnished by the most pure heart of Mary, through a true and ardent act of love: a beautiful thought, which, when once suggested, we do not willingly relinquish, as it makes us realize more fully and deeply the co-operation of the Blessed Virgin in the work of our redemption.

At the same moment that love had this supernatural effect within her, she bent her head with the profoundest humility, and, joining her hands, she said, "Behold the handmaid of the Lord; be it done to me according to thy word." The salvation of the world was awaiting Mary's consent. Mary has given her consent, and the world is saved. In one instant is accomplished in her the work of the Incarnation, and Mary is the Mother of God. The Virgin remains absorbed in an ecstasy, flooded with torrents of heavenly joy. She has become the tabernacle of the Living God; legions of angels have descended to honor her as their queen and adore the Divine Word made Flesh within her; and Gabriel having fulfilled his mission, after making a profound genuflection, returns to the courts of Heaven.

Chapter XXIV

The Visitation.

WHEN Mary awoke from her ecstasy, in which saints have asserted that she was raised to the intuitive and beatific vision of God, she comprehended the dignity of her lot and how He that was Mighty had done to her great things. To this exaltation she responded by plunging herself deeply into the thought of her own nothingness. Humbly prostrate with her face on the ground, she long adored within herself the majesty and goodness of God, whom with maternal tenderness she could now also invoke by the sweet name of son. But we must not imagine that Mary had a vision only of joy and glory. She had pondered well all the prophecies concerning the Messias, how He was to be offered for the redemption of a sinful world, and cannot have failed to be familiar in particular with the description of His sufferings given by Isaias, who has been styled the fifth Evangelist, and the detailed reference to them which abounds in the Psalms of her own kingly ancestor, David. The shadow of the Cross must have lain upon her, and a vision of the lance and the nails, and all the ignominies and torments of the Passion must have arisen before her. But, like her Divine Son, who, when coming into the world to offer Himself as the true sacrifice for sin, said, "Behold I come, to do Thy will, O God; I have desired it, and Thy law is in the midst of My heart" (*1 Ps.* 39:8, 9), so also Mary accepted all the suffering and the agony which was to

167

be her portion, the Holy Spirit strengthening and supporting her by the certainty of the immense good
which the whole human race would derive from the
Passion and Death of the Incarnate Son of God. Nevertheless, if by the power of divine grace Mary ever
continued strong, resigned, and tranquil, still, in the
very midst of these her maternal joys the sword which
was one day to pierce her soul must have been visible to her even before Simeon's prophecy had been
addressed to her. So much was the world's salvation
to cost Mary!

Meanwhile, Joseph as yet knew nothing of the sublime dignity to which his spouse had been exalted. Mary
met him as usual, with the same loving reverence, kneeling down to wash his feet when he returned wearied
with his labors; but we are fain to believe that he must
have experienced an undefined impression of veneration for her, and would have preferred to cast himself
humbly at her feet. If favored souls are sometimes sen-
sibly conscious of the presence of the Blessed Sacrament in our churches, how much more must holy Joseph,
whose spiritual senses were so delicate and refined,
have felt his heart burn within him with divine charity, from the nearness of Him who now dwelt in Mary
as His living tabernacle! But she said nothing; perhaps
was even more silent than was her custom. She went
about her usual employments, she prepared the frugal
meal, and all was the same, yet not the same, for a
glory must have shone in the countenance of the august
mother, and a fragrance of Paradise have pervaded that
lowly dwelling. But why did not Mary confide in Joseph,
for hitherto he had been the depositary of all her
thoughts? First, because the secret which the angel had
revealed to her she understood to have been intended
for herself alone, wherefore she would not communicate it even to Joseph, fearing to go beyond the Divine
will. Moreover, the Virgin was possessed of much discretion and forethought. If she made known to him that
the Son of God had become incarnate within her, she

knew, indeed, that he would believe her, but she knew also his humility and reverent spirit, and may have thought that, awed by so much majesty, he would perhaps retire and leave her. She waited therefore until the mystery should be divinely manifested to him; and, finally, being herself perfect mistress of humility, she dared not utter any word which would turn to her own praise.

And so Mary kept silence; she knew that it is "good to hide the secret of the King," but she knew also that it is "honorable to reveal and confess the works of God." (*Tob.* 12:7). Accordingly, while concealing the mystery that had been accomplished in her, to wit, the Incarnation of the Divine Word, she acquainted her beloved spouse with the prodigy which God had wrought in their cousin Elizabeth, and with her desire to go and congratulate her on the favor which had been shown her. Zachary's dumbness, with which it seems probable they were well acquainted, since it was now of six months' duration, must have made him also worthy to receive a visit of sympathy from them both, bound as they were to the holy couple, not only by ties of kindred, but by intimate association. Zachary's frequent presence in Jerusalem, where he came to serve in his sacerdotal course, must naturally have brought this about; and, though Scripture makes no mention of it, we have reason to conclude that, during Mary's abode in the Temple, she must have become closely united in affection with her saintly cousin, Elizabeth. Anyhow, Joseph, who considered the smallest wish of Mary as a law to himself, was sure to give his ready consent. St. Luke says that Mary, "rising up in those days, went into the hill country with haste, into a city of Juda" (*Luke* 1:39), by which we are not to understand that she set out that very day, the haste alluding rather to the rapidity of the journey. The Evangelist says, "in those days," not "that day," and Cornelius à Lapide is of opinion that there was a delay of two or three days. We can well understand that such might be necessary in order to make some few slight preparations.

But wherefore did Mary undertake this journey, and make it with haste? Heretics, with their habitual and injurious rashness, reply that she made this fatiguing journey in order to ascertain with her own eyes if what the angel had announced to her was true; thus making the Blessed Virgin incredulous or doubtful concerning his message to herself. "But no," exclaims St. Bernard; "Mary was neither incredulous nor doubtful of the truth of the angel's words."[1] She fully believed, and promptly gave her assent; and on this account she was praised for her faith by Elizabeth herself. Mary went to visit her cousin that she might rejoice with and assist her, and God Himself disposed the journey in order to give occasion to all the prodigies which took place at this blessed Visitation. And the Virgin went with haste because, as St. Ambrose says, the grace of the Holy Spirit knows no delay. Mary, he adds, was neither incredulous nor uncertain on hearing the angel's announcement, nor was she doubtful concerning the example he gave her of God's omnipotence in the case of her cousin, Elizabeth; but, as one joyful at the mystery accomplished, pressed by charity to aid her kinswoman, and eager to rejoice with all in the common gladness, she took her way towards the mountainous country of Judea.[2]

Here some have raised a doubt, seeing the Evangelist does not name Joseph, whether he accompanied Mary on her visit. All are agreed that the most holy Virgin at her tender age cannot have exposed herself to making this long and arduous journey alone, but it has been opined that she may have taken as her companion some matron well acquainted with the road. Yet, if Joseph is to be excluded simply because Scripture does not name him, so also must the supposed matron be excluded, of whom not a word is said in the sacred text; and when it becomes a question of suppos-

---

ing who might have been Mary's companion, certainly it is only reasonable to conclude that Joseph was the person. True, the Evangelist does not say that he went, but neither does he say that he did not go; nor, again, does he say that Mary went by herself. Not to mention a circumstance is, assuredly, not the same thing as to deny it; and this applies peculiarly to the Gospel narratives. Clearly they do not record everything, often leaving what they omit to be supplied by tradition, and even by reason and common sense. As for another objection which has been made, that, if Joseph had accompanied Mary, he would have heard Elizabeth's testimony to the Incarnation, it has little, if any, force. It is not necessary to suppose, nor is it likely, that Joseph straightway followed Mary into the interior of the house. Those pictures which represent Elizabeth as meeting the Blessed Virgin at the threshold and saluting her are purely imaginary, and do not, in fact, accord with the Gospel statement; for St. Luke tells us that Mary "entered into the house of Zachary, and saluted Elizabeth." (*Luke* 1:40). Trombelli says that the opinion that Joseph was not introduced along with Mary into Elizabeth's apartments receives a confirmation in the custom of Orientals, who assign separate rooms to the women of their families. Add to this, that the careful Joseph would never have allowed Mary to make this long and rugged journey entirely on foot, but would surely have taken with them an ass for her accommodation. He would, therefore, naturally on arriving have seen first to providing this animal with shelter, and then have sought his kinsman, Zachary.

But it is, in fact, the common belief that Joseph was Mary's companion on this journey. One of the principal ends for which God gave him to her as her spouse was that he might always be to her a companion and guardian, a guide and protector, in all the various necessities and vicissitudes of life. This office had become for him a duty. It is impossible, then, to suppose that on this first grave occasion he could have failed to fulfill the obligation which God had laid upon him; towards her, too, whom he beyond measure loved, and whom he regarded as his greatest earthly treasure. Can we imagine his suffering her to go without him, exposed to all the perils of the road and to all its inconveniences and discomforts? Joseph, besides, was, as well as Mary, the near relative of Elizabeth, and as desirous as Mary herself to show her and her husband cordial affection. What would they have thought at seeing his wife arrive by herself? Friends and relatives, and, indeed, all who knew them, would assuredly have had cause to wonder, and to blame him for his indifference and neglect. And Mary, too, brought up in the sanctuary, far from the noise and tumult of the world, bashful and timid as a dove, who with trusting faith had united herself to Joseph, to be henceforth his inseparable companion, how could she ever have consented to leave him, and, moreover, for so long a time?

But it is needless to go in search of proof when we have the authority of saints and Doctors on our side. St. Bernardine of Siena and St. Bernard are entirely agreed upon this point, and the latter enlarges on the blessedness of the house which contained such holy persons, and on the joy which Joseph, in particular, must have experienced in accompanying Mary on this journey. Isolano goes so far as to say that no rational person, or possessed of Catholic feeling, could admit for a moment that Our Lady at that tender age went unattended, or that Joseph, for any cause whatever, could have allowed his virgin spouse to make so long a journey without accompanying her.[3] Gerson, Vida, Echius, Gaetano, Salmeron, and the learned Suarez held the same opinion. We may close the list with St. Francis de Sales, who was so devout to the mystery of the Visitation that he desired that the Congregation of religious women which he founded should receive its name. He alludes to Joseph being Mary's companion on the road as to an unquestionable fact. Speaking of Mary's

3. *De Donis S. Joseph*, p. ii. c. vi.

haste, mentioned by the Evangelist, he says that the first movements of Him whom she bore in her bosom must necessarily have been most fervent. "O holy eagerness," he exclaims, "in which there is no disquiet, and which hastens without hurrying! Angels prepared to accompany her, and Joseph to be her willing guide. I would fain know something of the conversation between these two great souls; but I imagine Mary spoke only of Him of whom she was full, and breathed only the Saviour; and St. Joseph on his part respired only after the Saviour, who was darting secret rays into his heart, awakening in it a thousand inexplicable feelings, and, even as the wine enclosed in casks acquires insensibly the odor of the flowering vines, so the heart of this holy Patriarch experienced, without knowing how, the fragrance, the power, the strength of the Divine Infant who had blossomed in his fair vineyard. O my God, what a pilgrimage! The Saviour serves them as staff, food, and drink."[4]

It may have taken them three days to reach the city where Elizabeth and Zachary dwelt, which is commonly supposed to be Hebron. It was on the mountains of Judea, and was one of the sacerdotal cities of which the Lord, as we learn in the Book of Josue (*Jos.* 21:13, 39) allotted forty-eight to the tribe of Levi. The Evangelist calls it "a city of Juda," which evidently designates only the name of the tribe to which it belonged, for there was no city of that name in Israel. There was, it is true, a city called Jota (*Jos.* 15:55), which was also a sacerdotal city, on the mountains of Judea and near to Hebron. At the period of the Crusades, and even earlier, there was a popular local tradition that Zachary and Elizabeth dwelt at Ain-Carem, which the Catholic pilgrims called "St. John on the mountain," and which was, perhaps, identical with the ancient Ain mentioned by Josue, in connection with Jota or Jeta (*Jos.* 21:16), and distant from Jerusalem

---

4. *Lettres,* dccxxv.

scarcely six miles. In favor of the claims of Ain-Carem are the sanctuary of the Visitation of Mary to Elizabeth existing there, and another pointed out as the birthplace of John the Baptist, as also the spot where he was concealed from the rage of Herod, and the desert and grotto where he abode from his tenderest years. But no written record remains to testify to any ancient tradition on the subject. The general opinion of Doctors is that the city of Juda mentioned by St. Luke is Hebron, the ancient Cariath-Arbe (*Luke* 14:15; 21:11), a sacerdotal city, and one of the cities of refuge. It could boast of the highest antiquity, higher even, it has been said, than that of Memphis. It was the abode of the earliest Patriarchs, and when Abraham came into the land of Canaan, he pitched his tent near an oak by the plain of Mambre, which is in Hebron. (*Gen.* 13:18). There he received the three angelic guests, who came to promise to him, in the name of the Lord, that in his seed all the nations of the earth should be blessed. Here it was, as St. Jerome says, that he saw the day of Christ and rejoiced to see it. In Hebron David reigned seven years and six months, and there he was consecrated king in the presence of the ancients of all the tribes of Israel. (*2 Kgs.* 2:11; 5:3, 5). But never had the hills of Hebron received so high an honor as when the Incarnate Word traversed them enclosed in the womb of the most pure Virgin, accompanied by David's true heir and the greatest of patriarchs and saints, her holy spouse Joseph. The sacred bones of Abraham, Isaac, Jacob, Sara, Rebecca, and Lia, which lay buried in the double cave of Ephron (*Gen.* 25:9, 10; 49:29-31), must have been moved within their tombs when Mary and Joseph approached and, in passing, piously saluted the venerable relics of their ancestors.

Chapter XXV

Mary and Joseph's Abode in Zachary's House.

THAT Elizabeth was Mary's cousin is of faith, because we have the angel's word for it, as recorded in the Gospel. How she was thus related we learn from tradition. Jacob, the son of Mathan and father of Joseph, had two sisters, Anne, the happy mother of Mary, and Sobe, the mother of Elizabeth, so that Mary and Joseph were Elizabeth's cousins in the same degree. That Sobe should have married into the tribe of Levi need cause no surprise. The law which obliged maidens to marry in their own tribe was peculiarly stringent as regarded orphans or such as were otherwise possessed of property, in order to prevent the inheritance passing out of their tribe; but in other cases there was more license, especially after the return from the Babylonian captivity, when the tribes had been almost entirely dispersed, and particularly in the case of the tribe of Levi, which was scattered among the rest, and had no inheritance apart.

Immediately on arriving, Mary, as the Evangelist tells us, entered the house of Zachary, and saluted her cousin Elizabeth. This salutation, as we know, was followed by the first homage which the Divine Infant received after that of His Blessed Mother. The babe in Elizabeth's womb heard and understood, and leaped for joy, when straightway, filled with the Holy Ghost, Elizabeth exclaimed: "Blessed art thou among women, and blessed is the fruit of thy womb. And whence is this to

me that the mother of my Lord should come to me?"
(*Luke* 1:41-44). The Blessed Virgin then uttered that
glorious canticle of humility which the Church continues to repeat in her honor. Mary, no doubt, entreated
her cousin not to divulge the secret which had been
revealed to her. But what are we to think of that blessed
house of Zachary, which had now become a sanctuary
of the Most High, the temple of God—and more than
a temple, an earthly paradise? Its holy occupants, we
may be sure, spent the greater portion of their time in
prayer and in the praises of God, in conversing on the
Holy Scriptures and the ancient Fathers, dwelling specially on what the prophets had foretold concerning the
Messias, now so soon expected to appear, but whom
Mary and Elizabeth and the unborn Precursor could
adore as already present. The Paschal solemnities must
have occurred during the early part of Mary and Joseph's
sojourn at Hebron, and those faithful observers of the
Law will not have failed to fulfill their devout obligation by repairing to the Holy City for a few days, returning afterwards to resume their charitable offices in the
house of Zachary. Mary, no doubt, would diligently assist
Elizabeth in preparing all that would be needful for the
expected infant; and what a boon for the Precursor to
be enveloped on his birth in the swaddling-bands which
her blessed hands had fashioned!

The as yet dumb father must have found a great
solace and support in the company of holy Joseph. Some,
indeed, of those writers who are ready to admit that
Joseph accompanied Mary on her journey are disposed,
on what would seem insufficient grounds, to question
his having remained during the three months. The interests of his business as carpenter would, they maintain,
have been alone reason enough for his not absenting
himself from his workshop for so long a time. But this
conclusion is based upon a supposition which has been
shown to be purely gratuitous—viz., that Joseph's means
were so narrow as to necessitate on his part continual
daily toil for procuring sustenance, when, as we have

good reason to believe, it was more from humility and to avoid an idle life that he had embraced the humble trade which he practiced, than from absolute need. Besides, Zachary was a priest with ample means, well able to extend hospitality to a relative whose society far more than compensated him for any additional outlay which his presence could have caused. Would he, indeed, have suffered him to depart? We can hardly conceive it to be possible. Moreover, ever since God had committed to Joseph the charge of Mary as his most pure spouse, there can be no doubt that he reckoned his station to be wherever she was. How could he otherwise acquit himself of his office of her protector, guardian, and guide, an obligation so sacred in his eyes? But, leaving the region of conjecture, let us have recourse to authority. Cardinal Cajetan, the famous commentator of the Angelic Doctor, clearly states that Mary went to visit Elizabeth, accompanied by Joseph, and with him abode three months in the house of Zachary.[1] Gerson had previously held the same view, after Gerson St. Bernardine of Siena, and before them both, St. Bonaventura in the 13th century.

A question has been further raised as to whether Mary remained with her cousin until the birth of the Baptist. The Evangelist says that she "abode with her about three months, and then returned to her own house." (*Luke* 1:56). After stating this, he narrates what occurred at the birth of John. Those doctors who adhere strictly to the letter maintain that, from the Evangelist's words, it would appear that Mary returned to Nazareth before Elizabeth brought forth her son; and they, moreover, think that this was more suitable to the most pure Virgin than being present on such an occasion and assisting at the gathering of kinsfolk and friends which followed. But those who attend to the spirit, as well as to the letter, hold that Mary waited for her cousin's delivery. She had come for the express

---

1. *Comment. in* p. iii. *D. Thomae*, q. xxix. a. 2.

purpose of assisting and consoling her in her condition, and is it credible that she should have abandoned her at the last moment, to the deep disappointment of the holy couple? Who would impute to Mary virtue of so stiff an order? Must not Elizabeth have reckoned on her taking the infant into her arms and blessing him? Mary, surely, must have desired to press this child of promise to her bosom; and the babe himself, who already, in the obscurity of his mother's womb, had recognized the Son of God, and received the use of reason, was he to be denied the happiness of adoring Him when he came forth to the light of day, and of being folded so close to Him in Mary's embrace?[2]

Benedict XIII considered her presence as the general and the most secure opinion, and it is supported by the authority of both ancient and modern Doctors. Origen, Bede, Comestore, St. Bonaventura, St. Antoninus of Florence, Gerson, St. Bernardine of Siena, are all at one on this point, and the opinion is also strenuously defended by the learned P. Calmet. St. Bernardine of Siena assures us that Mary did, indeed, visit Elizabeth in order to serve and assist her, but more still to sanctify the Precursor of her Son, to behold him, take him in her arms, and lovingly tend him. St. Ambrose had long before expressed a like opinion, and given us to understand that the object for which Mary tarried so long at Hebron was, not merely to be of service to Elizabeth, but mainly for the spiritual advantage of so great a prophet as her infant was to be.[3] It is inconceivable that, with such an object in view, she should have departed without caring to see him, embrace and bless him, and without remaining for his circumcision, thus not so much as becoming acquainted with the name he was to bear. Gerson says expressly that Mary, along with the rest of her kindred, congratulated Elizabeth when she had brought forth her son, and that from this union of congratulation Joseph is not to be

2. *Sermo de S. Joseph,* a. ii. c. i.
3. *In Lucam,* cap. i.

excluded.[4] The order observed in St. Luke's narration need form no difficulty. He finishes one subject and returns to take up another. Such inversions in point of sequence of time are common with him. We have two examples of the kind; one in his second chapter, where, after relating (v. 18) how the shepherds went away and recounted the wonders they had witnessed, he goes back (v. 20) to speak of their returning and glorifying God for all the things they had heard and seen; the other, in his third chapter, where, after saying (vv. 19, 20) that John was cast into prison by Herod the Tetrarch, he goes back (v. 21) to speak of his baptizing Our Lord in the Jordan.

As for the objection to Mary's presence on account of her virginity, we must remember that in the eyes of the world there could be no impropriety, since she occupied the position of a married woman, while in the eyes of the angels, and, indeed, of all who knew her, she was a pattern of modesty. As regards herself, therefore, suffice it to say, "To the clean all things are clean." (*Titus* 1:15). Maria d'Agreda says that Mary was not actually present at the infant's birth—his mother, out of reverence to her and the Incarnate Word, not having requested her to be so—but was engaged in prayer while the delivery took place. Then, bidden interiorly by Our Lord, she at once repaired to Elizabeth's bedside, and received the newborn child into her arms, at his mother's desire, offering him to the Eternal Father. Maria d'Agreda adds that, unperceived by others, Mary, while thus engaged, was in an ecstasy, and, so long as it lasted, the happy babe lay upon her bosom, on which so soon the Son of God was to repose. The child understood all, and, so far as he was able, testified his joy and solicited the caresses of God's holy Mother, and Mary caressed and blessed him, but never once kissed him—the "kisses of her mouth" (*Cant.* 1:1) she reserved for her Divine Son.

Again, as for Mary's association with the congratu-

---

4. *Serm. de Nativ. Virg. Mariae,* Consid. iii.

latory meeting of kindred and friends, her withdrawal, we must recollect, would have been an ungracious act, according to Jewish notions; and, indeed, had she not already been at Hebron, it would, probably, have been incumbent on her, if possible, to repair thither for the purpose. There is, moreover, nothing in Our Lady's whole life to make us view her retirement and solitude as of that austere order which would exclude the courtesies of life. Do we not find her afterwards at the marriage-feast of Cana, and interesting herself so much in what would be felt important by the givers and partakers of the festivity, as even to obtain a miracle in their favor from her Divine Son, and that His first public miracle?

But enough of this. Mary and Joseph must have remained until after the infant's circumcision, and been present at the wonders which accompanied it: the unloosening of Zachary's tongue, and the glorious canticle in which, filled with the Holy Ghost, he burst forth announcing the coming Messias, and the office which the child John was to fill. Mary and Elizabeth would have comprehended the full import of Zachary's prophecy, and their hearts must have overflowed with joy. Joseph, too, must have rejoiced exceedingly that the Orient from on high, the Redeemer of Israel, was at hand, though as yet he knew not that He had become incarnate in Mary's womb. But, as we are more than once told in the Gospel that Mary pondered in her heart the words she heard (*Luke* 2:19, 51), so also must we fain believe that Joseph, who was so like to her, also dwelt interiorly upon what he had seen and heard in the house of Zachary, as together the two holy spouses made their homeward journey to Nazareth.

Chapter XXVI

Joseph's Trial.

HAVING regained their home, Mary and Joseph resumed their former tenor of life—their occupations, their labors, their exercises of piety, with even increased fervor. The poor and the sick rejoiced at their return, for in them they beheld their constant benefactors. All superfluities, the fruit of Joseph's toil—that is, all that was not strictly needed for the maintenance of Mary and himself—were regarded as their patrimony. His hands labored for it, and her hands dispensed it. Like her mystical figure in the Proverbs, "she opened her hand to the needy and stretched out her hands to the poor; and the law of clemency was on her tongue" (*Prov.* 31:20, 26), that kindness which adds such sweetness to a gift, and is itself an alms more prized by the suffering than even the material relief. Neighbors and friends, too, rejoiced to see them again, for their goodness, gentleness, and courtesy had endeared them to all.

The nearer the time approached for Mary's divine delivery, the more exalted were the graces of which she was the privileged recipient. Not only was she continually favored by familiar visits of angels, who came to adore and serve the Incarnate Word within her, but we have reason to regard as most true what saints have asserted, that she was admitted at times, so far as is possible for a human creature still abiding on earth, to behold God in His Divine Essence. That great authority, Suarez, says, "I affirm that it may be piously and with probability believed that the Blessed Virgin was in this life sometimes elevated for a short space to the clear vision of the Divine Essence."[1]

Nor need this surprise us when we consider that, with the exception of the hypostatic union, there could be none more intimate, more sublime, than that which existed between Mary and the Incarnate Word,[2] the flesh of Christ being the flesh of Mary; from whence, indeed, St. Thomas deduces that the Blessed Virgin, being the Mother of God, possesses a certain infinite dignity derived from the Infinite Good, which is God;[3] and Suarez says that "the dignity of the Mother of God is in its kind infinite."[4]

Joseph, meanwhile, in the midst of his labors and his poverty esteemed himself superlatively rich, because in Mary he possessed the rarest and most precious treasure on earth. Her presence was paradise to him. One glance from her countenance of heavenly modesty and of the glory which beamed from it was sufficient to kindle in his soul the fire of divine charity such as burns in a seraph; the sound of her voice, which had awakened to the light both of reason and of grace the unborn infant, must have made his heart often bound within his bosom. He felt the nearness of God in her, and was blessed beyond expression. As, however, it is scarcely given to mortals to enjoy for long such perfect felicity on earth, we may well imagine that the fear of losing it could not have been absent from his mind, and that a strange prescience concerning his virgin spouse, fostered by all he had recently seen and heard, may have dwelt in its secret depths. Respecting these things, and many more, Scripture is silent, though the veil has been lifted at times in the visions with which saints have been favored.

Thoughts such as these he may have pondered on

---

1. In p. iii. disp. xix. sect. iv.
2. B. Dionys. Carth. lib. ii. *De Laud. Virg.*
3. *Summa*, p. i. q. xxv. art. 6.
4. In p. iii. disp. xviii. sect iv.

after their return from Hebron, when one day the fact of the pregnancy of his most pure spouse flashed upon him unmistakably. We will adhere to the Gospel words, for nothing is said in vain: "She was found with child of the Holy Ghost." (*Matt.* 1:18). "By whom," asks St. Jerome, "was she found with child? Certainly by no one but Joseph."[5] Others would never have supposed that she had conceived by Divine power, but would have recognized in her condition nothing but the natural fruit of a lawful marriage. Not so her spouse Joseph. He was well acquainted with the inviolable virginity of Mary. He also knew well what was her unapproachable sanctity. He knew that she lived an angel's life on earth. What wonder, then, if what he beheld should have suggested to him the thought that possibly she was the destined mother of the Messias, the Virgin foretold by the prophet Isaias, who was to bring forth the Emmanuel! Joseph, we must remember, was deeply versed in the Divine Scriptures, and, according to St. Francis de Sales, was wiser than Solomon. Not he alone, but others far less enlightened than he was were anxiously looking out at that period for the coming of the Redeemer. (*Luke* 2:25, 38). All knew that He was to be of the tribe of Juda and of the house of David, and all who were familiar with the prophecy of Isaias must have known that He would be born of a virgin. Moreover, Joseph must have recalled all that had preceded and accompanied his espousals with Mary; and that which had taken place in the house of Zachary, whom he had heard declaring by the movement of the Holy Ghost that the child miraculously given to him was to go before the face of the Highest, must have been fresh in his memory. Does it not, then, seem most highly probable that all these signs and tokens combined must have brought wonderful evidence to the mind of Joseph concerning the mystery attaching to Mary's state? And not only must we feel this to be highly probable, but

5. *Comment. in Matthaeum,* cap. i.

it is even difficult to imagine that it could have been otherwise. A thought which in other men might have awakened feelings of self-complacency, pride, and exultation, in the most humble Joseph caused such confusion, and what we may call dismay, that we may imagine him repeating to himself words such as these: "The Mother of God my spouse! The Son of the Most High born in my house!" No, such an honor was not for him. His place was not there. Could he in the face of the world continue to accept, recognize, and treat Mary as his wife, who had conceived by the power of the Holy Ghost? Could he appear to claim as his son the Holy One who was to be born of her? He shrank with holy consternation from the very idea. In his just mind such conduct assumed the appearance of acting out an impious falsehood.[6] No, his place was not there. What could he do, then, but privately depart, and go to hide himself among the deserts and solitudes of the Jordan, there to weep over his own unworthiness? Such, we may believe, must have been the thoughts which filled Joseph's mind when he made this discovery, and not that distressing alternation of doubts and suspicions of the fidelity of his immaculate spouse which some pious orators have dwelt upon, causing pain, we cannot but think, to many of their devout hearers.

It is true that some of the ancient Fathers held that doubts and perplexities concerning Mary's state arose in Joseph's mind,[7] but the more general opinion of Doctors and Fathers, ancient and modern, coincides with

---

6. F. Coleridge in his volume entitled *The Nine Months,* chap. xiii., has admirably drawn out and explained the trial of St. Joseph, and in particular has shown most lucidly how he could not venture to take upon himself the high office which would have sprung out of the changed relationship between him and Mary.

7. Several of the early Fathers speak of the painful perplexity of Joseph in what may be called ambiguous terms, one while asserting that he could not doubt the chastity of Mary and at another that he could not question the evidence of his senses. St. Augustine, in particular, certainly uses words implying that Joseph was tried by doubts of the fidelity of his spouse, and that these were the cause of his resolution to abandon her. But the opinion of one Father, however eminent, cannot outweigh the contrary belief of many others equally learned. St. Jerome, for instance, was St. Augustine's contemporary, and was a strenuous maintainer of Joseph's confidence in Mary's innocence. Now, he, if anyone, must have been thoroughly acquainted with the traditions of Palestine, and had made the deepest study of the text of Scripture.

that which we do not scruple to adopt, namely, that
Joseph thought of withdrawing secretly from the Virgin out of reverence to the Divine Maternity. The first
view is grounded on the letter of the text, viewed on
its surface; the second also rests on the letter of the
text, but carefully examined; whereby it is plain that,
so far from contradicting, it is really favorable to the
view which is most honorable to Mary as well as most
worthy of Joseph. It also removes, or rather precludes,
all those difficulties which the other various interpretations raise without solving. We will, then, examine
the text a little in detail.

We have just observed that the Evangelist distinctly
says that Mary was found to have conceived of the Holy
Ghost. But Joseph alone could have known this, because
he alone knew of the mutual vow of virginity which
together they had made. Others could never have imagined the existence of this vow. The text proceeds:
"Whereupon Joseph, her husband"; and here we will
pause to notice once more how Joseph is expressly called
her "husband." What is narrated cannot, therefore, have
taken place in the interval between the betrothal and
the nuptials, as some have maintained. Had this been
so, the discovery of Mary's state would have been made
by others, not by Joseph, as she could not have been
residing with him. Add to which, that their marriage,
which, according to this view, took place immediately
after the angel's appearance to Joseph, would not have
shielded the honor of Our Lady.[8] The birth of Jesus less

8. *Matthew* 1:18-25. Those who suppose that Joseph was as yet only betrothed to Mary
when she was "found with child" avail themselves of the expression, "*antequam
convenerunt*—before they came together." They say that it shows that Joseph and
Mary were living apart, not being yet married, but that after the angel's appearance to Joseph in his sleep (v. 20) the nuptials were celebrated and he took her to
his home. What such a view involves is shown above. As for the expression in question, it must be regarded in the same light as that which occurs in a subsequent
passage (v. 25); where it is said: "And he knew her not *till* she brought forth her
firstborn son": with regard to which it will suffice to quote the note appended
thereto in the Douai version: "From these words Helvetius and other heretics most
impiously inferred that the Blessed Virgin Mary had other children besides Christ.
But St. Jerome shows, by divers examples, that this expression of the Evangelist
was a manner of speaking usual among the Hebrews, to denote by the word *until*
only what is done without any regard to the future. Thus it is said (*Gen.* 8:6, 7)
that 'Noe sent forth a raven, which went forth and did not return *till* the waters

than six months after their union would have been a circumstance sure not to be forgotten in Nazareth. Now, the legitimacy of His birth was never questioned by His unbelieving countrymen, or the slightest slur ever cast upon Him or Mary, His mother, by His malicious enemies, who would have been sure to avail themselves of any report of this kind had it ever existed.

To continue. The Evangelist says: "Whereupon Joseph, her husband, being a just man, and not willing publicly to expose her, was minded to put her away privately," or, in other words, separate himself from her and leave her; for the Greek word rendered in the Vulgate by *dimittere* has this signification, as may be often seen in Scripture. It is the word, for instance, used in the Gospel of St. Matthew 19:5: "For this cause shall a man leave (*dimittet*) father and mother," where, assuredly, the term *dimittet* could not signify to put away or divorce. Neither can it be the meaning in the case of which we are speaking. Joseph could not have repudiated Mary by a private bill of divorce, or any other form, without its becoming known, and therefore without defaming or publicly exposing her, the very thing which, it is said, he was not willing to do.

Then, again, as regards Joseph being a just man, which is the reason given why he did not act in this manner by his spouse, the text does not say that he was compassionate; it does not say that he was merciful; nor does it use any expression which might seem to countenance the idea that there was anything to forgive or condone on his part. It says simply that he was just. But the epithet "just," according to St. Jerome and the other Fathers, signified (as we have already

were dried up on the earth'; that is, did not return any more. Also (*Is.* 46:4) God says, 'I am *till* you grow old'. Who dare infer that God should then cease to be? Also in 1 Machabees 5:54: 'And they went up to Mount Sion with joy and gladness, and offered holocausts, because not one of them was slain *till* they had returned in peace;' that is, not one was slain before or after they had returned. Again, God saith to His Divine Son (*Ps.* 109:1): 'Sit Thou on My right hand *till* I make Thine enemies Thy footstool.' Shall He sit no longer after His enemies are subdued? Yea, and for all eternity. St. Jerome also proves, by Scripture examples, that an 'only-begotten son' was also called 'firstborn' or 'first-begotten' because, according to the Law, the first-born males were to be consecrated to God (*Ex.* 13:2)."

seen[9]) the perfect possession of all the virtues. In every case it would, at least, point to a faithful fulfillment of all the injunctions of God's law. St. Luke describes Zachary and Elizabeth as being both of them "just before God, walking in all the commandments and justifications of the Lord without blame" (*Luke* 1:6); that is, fulfilling all the precepts of the Law of Moses. Now, the Law of Moses did not leave to a man the choice either of retaining his wife, if guilty of adultery, or even of concealing her crime, if it became known to him. If Joseph, then, did not denounce Mary, and was desirous that no suspicion should be directed to her, it is manifest that he did not himself suspect her of infidelity; otherwise the epithet "just" would not have been strictly applicable to him, since he would not have been an exact observer of the Law, in that he sought to conceal the sins of others. (*Lev.* 5:1; *Prov.* 18:22). St. Jerome uses this very argument in defense of Joseph. "If," he says, "it was a precept of the Law that, not only the guilty, but those who had knowledge of their guilt, were under the penalty of sin, how could Joseph, in concealing the sin of his wife, be styled *just?*"[10] Yet it was precisely because he was just that he would not denounce her, being persuaded that she was innocent, and that, if she were with child, it was through the power of God. But, if she were innocent, why does he not remain with her? The reason, as we have said, is clear. Having become persuaded from so many signs that she is the mother of the Messias, he, reckoning himself unworthy to abide under the same roof with her, and with the Desired of all nations, comes to the determination to leave her privily, so that her reputation may remain undamaged. Had he abandoned her publicly how many questions and suspicions concerning the motives of his behavior would have arisen! But, departing thus quietly, people might naturally suppose that his work had called him away for a time, and that

9. See chapter xv.
10. *Comment. in Matthaeum,* cap. i.

he was executing some order which he had received in the neighborhood, or, possibly, that for some cause or another he was making a fresh journey into Judea.

Still, it may be asked, how could Joseph have the heart to forsake a wife so tenderly beloved, and in such a condition; leaving her, too, without a companion and without aid amidst all her trials? Did he not give a thought to the grief which he would cause her? Yes, Joseph we may be sure thought of everything, but the awe and reverence he felt at the presence of an Incarnate God was more powerful in him than the love and tenderness he bore his spouse. Without ceasing, therefore, to love her, he meditated concealing himself from her sight, convinced that, having with her a God, she had greater aid, security, and comfort, and better company, than he could have afforded her. This separation was a great sacrifice to him, and caused him unutterable pain, but it seemed to him to be necessary, and he purposed to effect it.

Now, having seen that the Gospel text, so far from being opposed to the interpretation we advocate, is favorable to it, we will refer to the Fathers. If we are to credit so great a saint and Doctor of the Church as St. Bernard, there is a very general agreement among them on the subject. He reasons thus: "For what cause did Joseph think of leaving Mary? Hear upon this point, not my opinion, but that of the Fathers. Joseph wished to separate himself from Mary for the same reason as made Peter desire to leave the Lord, when he said, 'Depart from me, for I am a sinful man, O Lord' (*Luke* 5:8); and for which the centurion would dissuade Him from coming into his house, saying, 'Lord, I am not worthy that Thou shouldest enter under my roof.' (*Luke* 7:6) In like manner, Joseph, reputing himself a sinner and unworthy, did not think it fitting to live familiarly with one whose surpassing dignity inspired him with awe. With a sacred dread he beheld in her the indubitable token of the Divine Presence, and, as he could not fathom the mystery, he desired to leave her. Peter was confounded at the greatness of the Divine power, the centurion by the majesty of the Divine presence; and Joseph also, as a man, was struck with fear at the strangeness of so great a mystery, and therefore was minded privily to leave her. Do you marvel that Joseph, beholding her pregnancy, should esteem himself unworthy to abide with his virgin spouse when you hear St. Elizabeth, unable to sustain her presence without trepidation and awe, exclaiming, 'Whence is this to me that the Mother of my Lord should come to me?'"[11] Thus St. Bernard. His words need no comment.

But who are the Fathers to whom he alludes? There are an Origen, a Jerome, a Basil, a Remigius, author of a fragmentary work which has been attributed to St. Chrysostom, a Theophylact, and others. "Joseph," says Remigius, "sees that his spouse has conceived; he beholds with child her whom he knows to be chaste; and, because he had read in the Prophets, 'There shall come forth a rod out of the root of Jesse, and a flower shall rise up out of his root' (*Is.* 11:1), he did not question or doubt but that this prediction was about to be fulfilled in her." And again, elsewhere he exclaims, "More possible does Joseph believe it that a woman should conceive without the concurrence of man, than that Mary should sin."[12] To the names we have mentioned we may add those of Aimon, St. Thomas Aquinas, Gerson, St. Bernardine of Siena, and Isidoro Isolano. Here are St. Thomas's words: "Holy Joseph pondered in his humility not to continue to dwell with so much sanctity."[13] But, leaving all the rest, let us listen to the great Doctor of the Church, St. Francis de Sales. Echoing the sentiments of St. Bernard and the other Fathers, he writes thus: "The humility of St. Joseph, as St. Bernard explains, was the cause of his desiring to abandon Our Lady when he perceived her to be with child. St. Bernard

---

11. St. Luke 1:43. *Super Missus est,* Hom. ii. sect. 14.
12. *Comment. in Matthaeum.*
13. P. iv. disp. xxx. q. ii. a. 2.

says that he reasoned thus within himself: 'What is this? I know that she is a virgin, for together we took the vow of preserving our virginity and our purity, in which she would certainly not have failed. On the other hand, I perceive that she is with child, that she is a mother. And how can maternity and virginity subsist together? How should not virginity be an obstacle to maternity? Might it be,' he then said, 'that she is that glorious Virgin of whom the Prophet declares that she shall conceive and bring forth the Messias? If this be so, far be it from me to abide any longer with her, I who am unworthy to do so. It were better that I should secretly leave her on account of my unworthiness, and not live any longer in her company.' Marvellous sentiment of humility!"[14]

---

14. *Entretien,* xix.

Chapter XXVII

Joseph's Vision.

WE ARE told that Joseph had such complete command of all his senses that they never participated in or betrayed the movements of his inward self, but that on all occasions he behaved with the same unvarying equanimity. Accordingly, he concealed from Mary the trouble which he was enduring, but she was interiorly cognizant of it, and, knowing well his reverential spirit, she knew also that he was meditating some step which would be most painful to her. Why, then, does she not reveal her secret to him? Why does she not reassure and tranquilize his mind? Should she delay much longer, she may be too late. Tomorrow, before the dawn of day, Joseph will have crossed the threshold of his home, and gone forth a wanderer on the face of the earth. What, then, is the Holy Virgin doing? She is silent. She knows the faith of Joseph, his humility, his perplexity, his confusion, and it pains her acutely that she cannot console him; yet she perseveres in her silence, because she does not think herself authorized to speak, and because she shrinks from uttering her own praises. She remembers that the angel did not give her permission to divulge the mystery. The secret of God must be kept, and if He should be pleased to make it known, He will Himself reveal it to Joseph, as He did to Elizabeth and to the unborn infant, John. She is silent, therefore, and waits. She knows how to wait; not like Saul, who lost a kingdom and God's favor

because he could not wait. Patience is an attribute of
holy souls. Saul lacked it. "Forced by necessity," he said,
"I offered the holocaust." (*1 Kgs.* 13:12). The Queen of
Saints knows of no necessity save that which constrains
her to wait on God. In her patience she possesses her
soul, but she prays, and that in great anguish of spirit,
and fervently implores her Divine Son, whom she bears
in her bosom, speedily to free Joseph from so great suffering, to enlighten him, and send him counsel and comfort in his trial.

Mary's prayer was quickly heard and granted, for
the interpreters of Holy Writ consider that Joseph was
left but a short time in this state of perturbation; indeed,
according to an ancient Eastern legend, not a single
night was allowed to pass before he was delivered from
it, an opinion which the wording of the text may be
almost said to favor: "But while he thought on these
things, behold the Angel of the Lord appeared to him
in his sleep, saying, 'Joseph, son of David, fear not to
take unto thee Mary thy wife, for that which is conceived in her is of the Holy Ghost. And she shall bring
forth a son; and thou shalt call His name Jesus: for He
shall save His people from their sins.'" (*Matt.* 1:20, 21).
This is the first time that we hear of an angel appearing to Joseph, but it does not follow that he had never
previously received a heavenly visit. It does not appear
to have excited any wonder in him, as in one not conversant with angelic communications, for he immediately recognized the messenger who addressed him as
being sent by God, although he spoke to him only in
his sleep. Hence we may form a high estimate of Joseph's
faith, to whom so little sufficed to make him believe.
The angel was, doubtless, Gabriel, who had already
appeared to Mary, and he knew how to convey to the
mind of Joseph such certainty of his mission as to leave
no room for doubt. But this implies a corresponding
state of mind in Joseph, a holy preparation of soul
which rendered him alive to spiritual influences, for
God never forces conviction upon anyone; it implies

that Joseph was a discerner of spirits, and it may even
be said a prophet, for in the Book of Numbers the Lord
said: "If there be among you a prophet of the Lord, I
will appear to him in a vision, or I will speak to him
in a dream." (*Num.* 12:6). It will be observed, too, that
the angel called him by his name, Joseph. Blessed are
those whose names are known to God and are written
in the Book of Life. And the angel not only called him
by his name, but added, "Son of David," to remind him
of the promises sworn by God to that king and now
fulfilled in his virgin spouse.

He then proceeds to tranquilize his mind, saying,
"Fear not to take unto thee Mary thy wife, for that
which is conceived in her is of the Holy Ghost"; that
is, fear not to remain with Mary thy wife, and to consider and accept her as such. This is the true sense of
the angel's words, and not, as some have supposed, that
he commanded Joseph to take Mary to wife, as if he
were not already bound in marriage to her, abiding as
he was in the same house with her, and called her husband, as Mary was also called his wife, by the Evangelist himself. "The word of the angel," says Benedict
XIV, "by which he bade him not to fear to *take* unto
him Mary for his wife is a Hebrew mode of expression,
which does not signify the commencement of an act,
but the continuation of an act already begun. The meaning of his mandate is this: 'Retain and keep the wife
you have taken, and do not forsake her'; and such is
the interpretation of those who are adepts in the
Hebrew idiom."[1] The angel bids him remain with Mary,
and not fear to do so, albeit he is now infallibly informed
that she has conceived of the Holy Ghost; and he is to
remain with her precisely because he is designed by
God to be the tutor and guardian of both herself and
her Divine Son. Joseph, with all a father's rights, without having had any part in His conception, was to give
Him the name of Jesus. "And thou shalt call His name

---

1. *De Festis B. Virginis; in Festo Annuntiationis,* cap. iii.

Jesus," that is, Saviour; for Jesus, by His Passion and
death, was to save the human race from eternal perdi-
tion: "He shall save His people from their sins." We see
how the angel's words entirely coincide with the view
here presented of the cause of Joseph's perturbation
and the motives urging him to his proposed flight. He
does not bid him discard his suspicions, for Joseph had
none, but abide without fear with the Divine Mother
as his wife, and assume the legitimate rights and position of a father; for the imposing of the name was the
father's special office. The angel says not, "His name
shall be called Jesus," but "Thou shalt call His name
Jesus": words which are most significant as regards the
office and dignity of Joseph.

The verses which follow seem to be plainly a commentary of the Evangelist himself: "Now all this was done
that it might be fulfilled which the Lord spoke by the
prophet, saying: Behold a virgin shall be with child,
and bring forth a son, and they shall call His name
Emmanuel, which, being interpreted, is God-with-us."
(*Matt.* 1:22, 23; *Is.* 7:14). But, however this may be, certain it is that the angel's message entirely satisfied
Joseph and set his mind at rest. The infallible assurance now given to him of the sublime dignity of Mary
doubtless increased in his heart a thousand-fold his
faith and his reverence, but the command coupled with
it had extinguished every importunate idea of flight
and separation. On awaking from sleep the thought
that he was dwelling under the same roof with God
Himself must have absorbed every faculty of his soul,
and we may imagine that he straightway prostrated
himself on the ground in deepest adoration. He recalls
the oracles of the prophets; and the glories, the humil-
iations, and the sufferings of the Redeemer unfold themselves before him. He reflects how he is to act as father
to the Son of God, and the weight of so much dignity
well-nigh overpowers him. He reflects how he is spouse
to the mother of the long-promised Messias, and he
knows not how he can duly correspond to what is

required of him, and worthily bear himself under the tremendous responsibilities laid upon him.

No doubt but Mary was immediately apprised how Joseph had been enlightened by the angel concerning the high mystery which had been wrought within her, and how the overwhelming respect and awe which had seized upon him prevented him from so much as raising his face from the earth. With the morning light she would speedily seek her holy spouse, in order gently to console him, and, kneeling down, would invite him to adore with her the Majesty of God present with them, and beg the Lord to make known to them His holy will in all things. Perhaps she again repeated the inspired canticle of the *Magnificat,* with which she had replied to Elizabeth's salutation; and, when she arrived at that verse which says how God has cast down the proud and exalted the humble, Joseph, feeling that these words applied to him as well as to Mary, will have been moved to shed tears of profound self-abasement and gratitude, not knowing how sufficiently to return thanks to God who had regarded his lowliness also. The more, indeed, we reflect upon these mysteries, dwell upon them and penetrate them by meditation, the more we shall be struck with the close analogy between Mary's high election and that of Joseph. He, too, had his trial and probation, and on his behavior under them, on his correspondence with grace, and his free consent, seemed to depend the fulfillment of the divine decree appointing him the foster-father of Jesus and investing him with a paternity which for its sublimity and specially high characteristics has never had its parallel on earth.

We can readily imagine that there would be a renewed contest, so to say, the only possible one, between these holy spouses as to which was to render submission and obedience to the other, for henceforward Joseph felt that, as the Mother of God, he could only regard and treat her as his sovereign and empress. But Mary, we know, cannot have allowed of any reversal of their natural relationship, but must have implored him to continue to regard her, not only as his spouse, but as his handmaid in all things, telling him that she should always render to him the homage and obedience which was his due, as a father and guide, her guardian and the protector of her virginity, as God had appointed. Thus would they together join in serving Jesus and co-operating in the great work He had come upon earth to accomplish. St. Bridget tells us in her *Revelations* how the Blessed Virgin assured her that, when Joseph beheld her with child by the operation of the Holy Ghost, he feared exceedingly, suspecting no evil of her, but, remembering the words of the prophet which foretold how the Son of God would be born of a virgin, reputed himself unworthy to serve such a mother, until the angel in sleep bade him not to fear, but to minister to her with charity. And Our Lady added. "From that moment Joseph never ceased to serve me as his sovereign, and I humbled myself to the lowest offices to show him my submission."

This behavior of Joseph towards the august Mother of God was, we must be sure, quite compatible with his filling the position in the Holy Family of its head, which he was bidden and bound to assume, even as it was compatible with what is far more amazing still, his acceptance and, subsequently, his exercise of the superiority which, as His reputed father, was conferred upon him over the Son of God Himself, who, though the Lord of all, was more perfectly subject to Joseph than the most dutiful of sons ever was to his parent.

Chapter XXVIII

The Paternity of Joseph.

JOSEPH'S virtue was sublime and exceptional; therefore was it subjected to a great and singular trial. But, as he heroically surmounted this trial, so God was pleased, not only to console him, but to exalt him to a dignity of extraordinary glory. What this glory was which the Ever-Blessed Trinity conceded to Joseph we learn from the Evangelist. He tells us that when Joseph had risen from his sleep he faithfully fulfilled the mandate of the angel, that is, the command of God by the mouth of His angel, namely, to recognize as his true spouse her who had conceived by the power of the Holy Ghost, and was about to bring forth a son to whom he should give the name of Jesus. In this command all the Three Divine Persons concurred. The Son, who was to be born of Mary, had no earthly father. It belonged to His Heavenly Father to confer upon Him His name: that is the father's office and right; and the Eternal Father transferred this right to Joseph, willing that in His place he should impose on Him the name of Jesus, and, in doing so, He constituted him His representative in all a father's rights, and expressly confided to his paternal care His Only-Begotten Son. Jesus, the Son of God, who was to be born of the Virgin Mary, willed that she should be joined in marriage and live with a virgin spouse, so that men should not repute His birth as illegitimate; and He willed to recognize this virgin spouse as His father in affection, adoption, government and education, and to be constantly obedient and subject to him. The Holy Ghost, who had operated the incarnation of the Son of God in the womb of Mary, willed that to Joseph this His spouse should be entirely confided. He was to be the zealous guardian of her virginity, her guide, her aid, her support, and her inseparable companion through all the vicissitudes of life. And where, apart from the Divine Maternity, can so great a dignity be found upon earth as that which was conferred on Joseph by the Three Divine Persons of the Most Holy Trinity?

We will here pause awhile to reflect on this high dignity, for the paternity of Joseph is a mystery which deserves our deepest consideration. We may view the announcement of the angel to Joseph as the counterpart, so to say, of the Annunciation. Mary then became the mother of God. Jesus was to be truly born of her, and to be Flesh of her flesh. In the vision which came to Joseph he was appointed to be—though not in the way of generation—the father in a peculiar and ineffable manner of the Eternal Son. It is important, then, in estimating the glory of Joseph, to consider that it is not sufficient to suppose that he was only held to be the father of Jesus in popular credence, for there was a sense in which he was truly what he was called. This august dignity which was conferred upon him was, as has been observed, altogether singular and incomparable. Although inferior to that of the Blessed Virgin, inasmuch as she conceived in her womb and brought forth the Son of God, and was therefore His mother according to the flesh, and more entirely His parent in that regard than any earthly parent ever was of her child, nevertheless, in its lower degree, Joseph's dignity of father of Jesus stands alone; and his title pointed to a reality, and did not merely serve to conceal from view (as, however, it also did) the fact of the Incarnation. The Gospel language and the testimony of Mary are significant tokens of this truth, which has been dwelt upon and commented by several Fathers and Doctors of the Church.

If Joseph had been the father of Jesus only in the estimation of others, it would have been a great honor to him, and this honor is undeniably his; but we should take a restricted view of the dignity bestowed upon him if we did not believe that this title had moreover a true and real signification belonging to it. God does not give a mere name. His word is creative, and imparts a corresponding reality. Among those eminent interpreters of Scripture who have treated of the paternity of Joseph St. Augustine must be numbered as expressly asserting his claim to be called the father of a God-made-Man. The devout Abbot Rupert is of opinion that Joseph's supereminent faith constituted a sufficient title to that appellation. Observing that St. Augustine holds that the Blessed Virgin was in a certain manner mother of the Saviour even before the Incarnation, and that it would have availed her nothing to conceive the Son of God in her chaste womb if she had not first conceived Him by the brilliant light of faith, it appears to him that St. Joseph's paternity may be established on the excellence of his faith, which conferred greater honor on it than the ordinary mode of generation could have imparted. As Abraham *by faith* (*Heb.* 11:8-19) became father of his race, so faith produced in Joseph a still more wonderful paternity. The learned Bishop of Christopolis, Jacob Valentia, in his *Treatise on the Magnificat,* makes some very striking remarks on the character of the paternity of Joseph, who, he affirms, was in a singular manner the spiritual father of the Messias. That illustrious prelate gives us to understand that St. Joseph concurred as an exemplary cause, or model, in the production of the Sacred Humanity. He says that the Holy Spirit in preparing the body to which the Divine Word was to unite Himself observed the temperament, the disposition, the inclinations of Joseph. He attended to his beauty, to his form, to his physiognomy, to copy it when organizing the body of the

Saviour; and, indeed, this resemblance seemed fitting in order to corroborate the popular opinion that the son of Mary was also the son of Joseph. The Eternal Father begat His Son by the sole knowledge of Himself. The Blessed Trinity contemplated Itself to reproduce Its living image in the creation of our souls. The body of the first Adam, Tertullian says,[1] was molded by God as a model of the Humanity of the Second Adam, whom in the course of ages He designed to bring into the world. But when the Holy Spirit formed the Body and created the Soul of Jesus He contented Himself with looking at Joseph, that the one and the other might be perfectly alike. If, then, our saint co-operated as an ideal cause in the production of the Humanity of the Divine Word, may we not believe, with the learned Bishop, that Joseph was His father after a spiritual and most singular manner? That we have a right to believe as much is unquestionable, since it is the general doctrine of the Fathers and theologians of the Church that Joseph is the father of the Saviour on most assured titles; and that, with the exception of generation, there is nothing which can be attributed to any man worthy of the name of father which was not pre-eminently possessed by him.[2] We need not, then, fear believing too much or holding exaggerated notions concerning a mystery which probably far surpasses our unaided intellects fully to conceive.

But we have by no means exhausted the subject. We will look at it from another point of view, which confers no less honor on our saint. Jesus Himself elected Joseph to be His father, and always treated him as such. This, too, is the teaching of the holy Fathers. We find, for instance, St. John Damascene declaring that Jesus raised Joseph to the glorious dignity of His father by a special election and privileged adoption;[3] and St. Epiphanius also saying that no one can deny that Joseph

---

1. *De Resurrectione Carnis,* cap. vi.
2. See, in particular, Suarez, *Tract. de Incarnat.,* t. ii. disp. viii. sect. 1: also Salmeron, *Tract.* iii.
3. *Orat.* iii. *de Nativ. B. Virg.*

is the father of the Son of God, adding that the origin of this paternity was the love of this same Son, who adopted him for His father. St. Bernard in later days echoes the same sentiment.[4] Of all the sons of men, the Saviour alone had the power to choose His own father. With other men this was impossible; they were incapable of choice before they existed, and could therefore give no preference to one man more than to another. Even Jesus Christ Himself, as Son of God, did not elect His Eternal Father, not only because His generation was necessary, but also because He in no way preceded His own eternal generation, and therefore exercised no deliberation or choice concerning Him who begat Him from all eternity. But this same Divine Saviour could, without doubt, designate the father whom as Son of Man he was to acknowledge, because, as the Word of God, He preceded him, and there was nothing to constrain Him to prefer one man to be His father more than another. On the Cross He adopted St. John the Evangelist for His brother; but long before He had honored St. Joseph by adopting him for His father. The adoption of John was made at the death of the Saviour, the adoption of Joseph had already been made in the first instant of His life. If it was, as we have said, a high honor to Joseph to be chosen as the spouse of Mary and accepted by her, what must we say of the dignity conferred on him in being chosen by the Son of God Himself to be His father? And, as he was truly the spouse of Mary, not merely such in name, so was he also by adoption the true father of Jesus. Jesus in adopting him made him His father supernaturally, and this belief is surely more honorable to the Saviour than to suppose that every time He gave him that endearing name it was one empty of any true signification. No; the paternity of Joseph was a real paternity, and, albeit in a mysterious and spiritual sense, had a reality far surpassing that of any ordinary father.

---

4. *Super Missus est,* Hom. ii. 16.

And how often, and with what affection, in the course of the well-nigh thirty years during which Jesus conversed with Joseph, did He not pronounce that sweet name! It seems most probable that the first time the Incarnate Word spoke it was to say "father and mother," according to the prophecy of Isaias (*Is.* 8:4), and to imitate little ones in all His ways. Be this as it may, how often must the Divine Infant have called Joseph father! How often, embracing him and, after the manner of children, clasping and clinging to his neck, must He not have said, "O father, My dear father!" The angels know how often, for the words of the Saviour would be duly counted by those blessed spirits. Again, the very fact of Jesus having so often during His public ministry called Himself the "Son of man," is not perhaps without a peculiar meaning as regards Joseph's paternity. The learned Cardinal Toleto[5] has drawn attention to this, and says that, making use of a general term significant of both sexes, He would show that, although His mother alone had conceived Him, nevertheless He wished all the world to know that He recognized Himself as the son of Joseph; and, as often as He honored him with the name of father, He conferred upon him the right to be truly so called. The words of God, as we have said, are effective and creative: "He spake, and they were made; He commanded, and they were created." (*Ps.* 32:9). That which Omnipotence pronounces is simultaneously accomplished. When, therefore, God names Joseph His father He makes him so. A word of the Most High had sufficed to draw a whole universe from the abyss of nothingness, and this word had so much power, St. Ambrose says, that its execution did not follow, but accompanied it. In like manner, the Son of God needed but a word for the subsistence of a new quality in Joseph, that of father, in the possession of which he was manifestly placed by the mere fact that Jesus called him father. As St. Augustine and St. Gre-

---

5. *In S. Joannem,* Annot. xvii.

gory the Great teach, God, both in the Old and the New Testament, speaks by acts as well as by words. That Jesus treated Joseph as His father for so many years— no son having ever shown so much respect and obedience to his parent—is in itself a striking proof of the true paternity of Joseph. The acts of the Son of God are not less significant than were those of patriarchs and prophets; hence we have every reason to affirm, with Cardinal Cajetan, that Jesus Himself teaches us that He is verily the son of Joseph. But on this subject, His marvellous subjection to Joseph, we shall have more to say hereafter.

St. Augustine, speaking of our saint, says that he owed the august title of father of Jesus, and consequently the Saviour's choice of him, to that which in other men is incompatible with paternity, namely, his extraordinary love of virginity and his study to perfect it in himself. And, in effect, if Mary's virginal purity inclined and drew the Son of God, as St. Bernard says, to abide in her chaste womb, it is highly probable that this same virtue, which flourished so sweetly in the breast of Joseph, moved the Saviour to choose him for His father. But He alone knows the motives of His choice; one thing we know, as St. Jerome says, that there was in him such a fund of merit that nothing more was needed to cause him to be preferred to all other men.

We must now take a glance at his title to paternity founded on his espousals with Mary. Jesus was the virginal fruit of a virginal marriage, for Joseph was the husband of Mary of whom was born Jesus. It was not as when a woman takes a second husband, and her children by the former marriage call him father because he is legally such. Everyone understands this practice, in which a claim to real paternity is neither made nor implied. But Joseph was the husband of Mary, not only of whom Jesus was born, but when He was born, and also at the time of His conception. Jesus was not only born of a virgin but, as Scripture expressly states, of "a virgin espoused to a man whose name was Joseph." (*Luke* 1:27). If it had so pleased God, the Annunciation and the Divine Conception might have taken place a day or two before the Espousals, for the marriage of Joseph and Mary would have equally served in that case to shield her honor, but no; the Virgin Mother was to have a husband, and that husband was Joseph.

We are so accustomed to the brief words of the Scripture narrative that we are apt not to take sufficient pains to fathom their deep import; yet their very briefness bespeaks their depth. None are superfluous or casual. All have their meaning, and, not seldom, several meanings. Now, we may notice that the Evangelists, while taking marked care to state that the Incarnate Word was divinely conceived, so that man had no part in His generation, which was the sole work of the Holy Ghost, speak also of Joseph in terms and give him a position hardly to be accounted for or fully understood unless we hold his paternity in a true and special sense of its own. Joseph was father of the Saviour because of his holy marriage with the glorious Virgin, for, according to the opinion of the Abbot Rupert, it was impossible for him to be the husband of Mary without being the father of Jesus. "If," he says, "he is the husband of Mary, then he is the father of the Lord."[6] Many centuries ago, St. Augustine, that strenuous defender of the paternity of Joseph, availed himself of the same reason to justify the language of Scripture in calling him the father of the Son of God: "Whence is he called father but because he is the husband of Mary?"[7]

This great Doctor of the Church further strengthens his opinion by an argument which, if it was not put forth by one of his high authority, would be deemed perhaps by some to make too arrogant a claim on behalf of our saint. Yet it would not be easy to confute it. He says that Jesus might be called the son of David, even if the Blessed Virgin had not been descended, as, in

---

6. *Comment. in Matthaeum*, cap. i.
7. *De Consens. Evang.* c. i.

fact, she was, from that great king; for it was sufficient that the Saviour was truly the son of Joseph for him to be incontestably recognized as the son of David. For if David can justly claim the august title of father of the Messias, because Joseph connects him with Him— and that so it is the genealogy of Joseph given by St. Matthew testifies—it is easy to infer that this same saint may be also justly held by all men, and declared without fear of error, to be the father of Jesus. Such is the doctrine of St. Augustine, which, before him, was taught by Origen,[8] who, though not so high an authority as the great Bishop of Hippo, records at least the opinion of very early times.

Perhaps sufficient attention has not been paid to the witness which the New Testament genealogies give in favor of St. Joseph's substantial claims. They are often regarded in the light, if not of a difficulty, yet of something needing explanation. Why, it is asked, is it Joseph's genealogy which is given? The object being to prove the Saviour's descent, according to the flesh, from David, it was surely Mary's, not Joseph's, genealogy which was needed. Moreover, Joseph's descent is introduced in these clear and formal terms: "The book of the generation of Jesus Christ, the Son of David"; and ends by saying: "Jacob begat Joseph, the husband of Mary, of whom was born Jesus." (*Matt.* 1:1, 16). Now, it is true that a satisfactory explanation has been given, as has already been noticed, namely, that the Hebrews were not in the habit of tracing genealogies on the female side, and that Mary, being near of kin to Joseph and of the house of David, was included in the same descent. Besides which, the genealogy given by St. Luke is by some interpreters, though not by all, considered (as was pointed out) to be Mary's, Heli being identified with Joachim, her father; but any way, the significant fact remains that the name of Joseph here also, where the descent is traced upwards, heads—as in St. Matthew's Gospel, where it is traced downwards, it closes—the genealogy

8. *Hom.* xvii. *in Lucam.*

of Our Lord; both being therefore, on the face of them, designed to establish His title to being the son of David through Joseph, whose natural descent from that king is given by St. Matthew, as his legal is given by St. Luke. St. Matthew, after recording this genealogy, immediately proceeds to state how the generation of Jesus was the work of the Holy Ghost; and St. Luke, by his expression, "Being (as it was supposed) the Son of Joseph, who was of Heli," incidentally declares the same; namely, that Joseph had no part in the generation of the Son of God. Hence we find the two Evangelists, while clearly asserting that Jesus was not the son of Joseph by natural generation, at the same time giving testimony to His being his son in another sense, by connecting His right to the title of son of David with the husband of His Blessed Virgin Mother.

The Virgin belonged to Joseph by marriage, and, if we are to credit the pious and learned Chancellor of the University of Paris, Gerson—who preached, not merely without rebuke, but with commendation, of the lofty privileges of our saint before the Council of Constance—the Holy Spirit would not take the small portion of the blood of the most pure Virgin needed to form within her the Body of the Divine Word, without Joseph's implied consent; so that the Word in assuming a portion of the substance of Our Lady appropriated what, in a manner, depended on Joseph, inasmuch as He united Himself to the flesh of her over whom this great saint had rights; and thus, in becoming the son of Mary, He became also, in a certain sense, the son of Joseph, for He was not the son simply of a virgin, but of a virgin married to Joseph. "Joseph was His father by generation, not his own, but of Mary, his wife." These are Gerson's words; and it is in the same sense that the strong expressions of some Doctors in past times must be interpreted; such as the following of Antonio Perez, Bishop of Urgel, in his commentary on St. Matthew: "Joseph obtained the right of a father to Christ, in that He was bone of his bone, and flesh of his flesh, to wit, of Mary his spouse"; and those of the learned Paschal Rathbert, Abbot of Corbie, who lived in the middle of the eighth century, when he said that the Saviour belonged to Joseph even according to the flesh.[9] We might also quote as an authority the Venerable Bede, who, apparently following St. Augustine, judges that Joseph, in virtue of his marriage, has the same title to be called the father of Jesus as he has to be called the husband of Mary.[10] And, as it is the incontestable doctrine of the Church that Joseph was the true husband of Mary, it must be inferred that he thereby justly merited also the title of father of Jesus. And would it not seem that God, by not allowing the conception of His Son to precede Mary's marriage, designed to give Joseph an authentic title to that name, that all men might be able to say, as does the learned Tostatus, that "Christ was the offspring of the marriage of Mary and Joseph";[11] and, as the learned Bishop of Christopolis affirms, that He was "born of this sacred, virginal, and inviolate marriage"?[12] It was God's Will, in short, that it might rightly be maintained that the Saviour was, not only the "Blessed Fruit" of Mary's chaste womb, but, as St. Thomas observes, and, before him, St. Augustine, the fruit of the alliance of Joseph and Mary, and at the same time the son of both the one and the other.

We have still to make some allusion to Mary's own transfer of a share in her rights to Joseph; for, according to many theologians, Mary may be said to have had the rights, not only of a mother, but, in the absence of any human parent on the other side, of a father also. Yet that she fully conceded his share in these rights to Joseph, so far as they belonged to her, there can be no doubt. We have only to refer to the words she addressed to her Divine Son after finding Him in the Temple: "Thy father and I have sought Thee sorrowing" (*Luke* 2:48), giving Joseph the first place. She does not say, "My

9. *Expos. in Matthaeum.*
10. *In Lucam, Rom.* ii.
11. *In Matthaeum,* cap. i. q. xxxii.
12. *Tract. super Magnificat.*

spouse and I," or "Thy servant, Joseph, and I," but "Thy father and I." And the Evangelist himself adopts our Lady's language, and speaks of them both as the parents of Jesus, (*Luke* 2:41) as if their claims in that respect were on an equality. But upon this remarkable incident we shall not here further dwell, as we shall have occasion to recur to it in the course of the narrative.

In conclusion, it must be added that (as Gerson observes) the Holy Ghost substituted Joseph in His place to be Mary's visible spouse. It is an undoubted doctrine of the Fathers of the Church that the Virgin was the spouse of the Holy Ghost, and, as that Adorable Spirit heretofore, brooding over the waters, imparted fecundity to them, so also by an operation wholly divine He caused Mary to conceive. Being, however, Himself invisible, He gave her in His stead a visible spouse, who should accompany her everywhere and render her faithful service. It was as when the Saviour on ascending into Heaven withdrew His visible presence from the Church, His spouse; He appointed Peter as His Vicar in the care and government of that Church, investing him with all His powers and making him His personal representative; and, even as Peter, in his quality of Vicar of Christ, could call the Church his spouse and her children his children, who, on their part, also gave him, and still give, his successors the name of father— Papa—so also the Holy Ghost invested Joseph with His authority and rights, and taught the Evangelists, as we have seen, to call him father of Jesus, and record his genealogy, not that of his spouse, Mary.

There is a further reflection which must naturally suggest itself to everyone who ardently desires to see St. Joseph honored and exalted. While Jesus remained on earth He was believed and reputed to be the son of Joseph. Now, though the Divinity of Our Lord was fully known only to a chosen few, all men regarded Him as a great prophet mighty in word and work, and there was even a widely spread expectation that He would prove to be the promised Messias, the inheritor of David's throne, the people more than once desiring to take Him by force and make Him their king. Can we think that the Saviour would allow Joseph to lose any portion of the honor which at one time thus accrued to him from his paternity? His very name signifies increase; how, then, could he suffer diminution? But more than this: while on earth, dwelling in the humble house of Nazareth, Jesus called Joseph father, and treated him lovingly as such; and now that He is sitting in glory at the right hand of His Eternal Father, together with His mother, the crowned Queen of Heaven and earth, and Joseph, too, clothed in his glorified body, as it is piously believed—for how could it be otherwise?—can we imagine that our dear Lord, who on His exaltation turns to Mary and calls her mother, has ceased to address Joseph with the endearing name of father? If so it could be, then would it follow that to our great Patriarch and Patron earth proffered a glory and a blessing which Heaven denies him. But this is not so. God's gifts are real, not nominal gifts; and they are, moreover, as we are told, "without repentance." (*Rom.* 11:29). He does not give and then take away. He increases, He develops, He causes to fructify, but He never resumes, as though it were a mere loan, what He has once conferred; nay, even that which is entrusted to us as such, the talents which we receive to trade withal until His coming, He makes ours on the day of reckoning, with increase and recompense incalculable. And shall not Joseph, who served Him so tenderly and faithfully as His father on earth during thirty years, enjoy forever, in eternal bliss, the dignity which during his mortal life, spent in poverty and obscurity, had exalted him far above any man who ever had lived or ever should live—his Paternity?

Chapter XXIX

Interior of the Holy House—Journey
to Bethlehem.

MARY, as we have said, besought Joseph to allow her to continue to serve him as before, and not to pay her the profound homage which, since he had become acquainted with the mystery of the Incarnation, he desired to do. The feelings of Joseph, we may imagine, bore some resemblance to those of a devout Catholic in presence of the Blessed Sacrament. He would willingly have been always on his knees, except when engaged in performing the domestic work, from which he most ardently desired to relieve his spouse, ever since it had been made known to him that she had become the tabernacle of God. Maria d'Agreda records touching revelations of the holy contention between the two spouses on this subject. The Blessed Virgin, she tells us, was deeply grieved at being hindered in the practice of humility, and that the relations which God had appointed between them as husband and wife should be changed and disturbed; for, though apparently yielding to her entreaties, Joseph nevertheless was constantly endeavoring to anticipate her, or taking advantage of times when she was retired in prayer to do her work for her. She now tenderly besought the Lord to oblige her spouse to desist from his purpose, both in this respect and in the external homage which he strove to pay her. Her prayers were heard, and the guardian-angel of Joseph spoke interiorly to him, bidding him not to thwart her who was superior to all creatures in Heaven and earth in her desires for self-abasement, but to allow her to minister to him in outward things, while in the depths of his heart he venerated her and adored the Incarnate Word, whose will it was that He and His Blessed Mother should serve and not be served; thus instructing the world in the excellence of the virtue of humility. He permitted him, however, to help her in anything which involved fatigue, and bade him ever honor within her the Lord of all.

Joseph acquiesced in God's Will, but it was with much confusion that he allowed himself to be waited upon and served by her whom he knew to be the Sovereign Queen of angels and of men. By this obedience he made abundant compensation for those other lowly acts which he left to his holy spouse, seeing that this abstention was to him a far greater act of humiliation and self-renouncement than their performance would have been. He, however, more frequently now than formerly, left his workshop to see if Mary needed any assistance, and also to hold sweet conferences with her on divine things, in which he received great illumination from her in whom were inexhaustible treasures of wisdom and of knowledge, while she in her humility and modesty sedulously avoided the appearance of being his instructress.

Joseph was also favored with many interior graces, and even with visions of the unborn Babe. He and Mary were alone in their humble abode. The Evangelists have not described to us their life and conversation, and they themselves never spoke of it to anyone. That God, however, should have favored some of His saints and privileged souls, while engaged in contemplation, with marvellous glimpses of scenes so touching and edifying can be no matter of surprise; and this seems to be an occasion when it is legitimate to borrow from their revelations a few details to aid us in our meditations on the hidden life at Nazareth. From them we learn that the angels in attendance on the Divine Mother held frequent converse with her, and often joined her in singing canticles of praise to their Incarnate God. But not only these glorious spirits, but even the animal creation would bear their part in honoring her and their Creator. Sometimes, we are told, at the summons of the Lord, birds of exquisite beauty would come and visit her; they would salute and do her reverence as their mistress, bring her flowers in their beaks, and unite their voices with hers in a concert of sweetest harmony; nor would they depart until she had blessed them. In inclement weather they would take refuge with this compassionate mother, and she would welcome and feed them with the tenderest kindness, loving them for their innocence and glorifying God in His admirable works. For none of His works did she esteem to be trivial and of no account, but held all to be worthy of respect, as manifesting, more or less, one or other of His attributes or perfections. He had created them, and that sufficed. They are steps, too, whereby the mind ascends to the contemplation of spiritual truths; they are mirrors in which we behold the invisible God reflected. A special gift of the Holy Ghost, that of science [knowledge], is given to us for this end, and Mary possessed all these gifts in the most eminent degree. Joseph also was favored with witnessing a visit of these feathered songsters, and, full of astonishment and delight, he believed, in his humility, that these simple creatures acquitted themselves of their obligations towards their Queen and the Divine Infant better than he did himself, or was permitted to do.[1]

---

1. Instances of the confidence and affection shown by animals to man are frequent in the lives of saints. How much more, then, should we expect them in the case of one who bore in her womb their Creator and her own! It is sufficient to allude to St. John the Evangelist and the partridge, St. Francis of Assisi and the wolf, St. Benedict and the raven, St. Gregory and the dove. The Lives of the Fathers of the Desert abound in facts of a similar order—showing that innocence and sanctity have the gift of recovering for man the power over the brute creation which he possessed in the primeval Paradise. But, indeed, such incidents, extraordinary as they are, differ only in their singularity or in their marvellous character from those which are of familiar experience to persons who have cultivated the friendship— we use the term advisedly—of animals and enjoy their confidence. Their willing submission and self-restraint, their intelligence, their sympathies, and their gratitude, are similar in kind to the instances which are narrated in the annals of

As we have said, Mary and Joseph were alone. They had no servant, and not seldom found themselves in a state of destitution on account of their great liberality to the poor, giving them always what they had to give; for, unlike the children of this world, they were not solicitous to lay by for the morrow, saying what shall we eat and what shall we drink, and wherewithal shall we be clothed? and this not from improvidence, which cannot expect any reward from God, but from charity, love of poverty, and faith in Him who feeds all things living, and never fails those who rely upon Him. The greatness of soul, the faith and liberality, of Joseph, were similar to those of his spouse. Never could a feeling resembling cupidity find entrance into his heart. He labored diligently, it is true, as also did Mary, but never did they put any price on the work of their hands, but left it to those for whom it had been performed to make what remuneration they pleased, receiving it from them, not so much as payment, but as voluntary alms. Such was the sanctity and perfection which Joseph had learned in the school of Heaven, and which he practiced in his house; and thus it would sometimes come to pass that he was not paid for his work, and then want visited the lowly house of Nazareth, and even needful food for the support of life would fail its holy inmates. On these occasions they waited patiently until the Lord was pleased to provide for their sustenance. One day (so Maria d'Agreda tells us), the usual hour for their repast having arrived, there was nothing for them to eat. For this deprivation they thanked God, and, waiting until He should be pleased to open His omnipotent hand, continued in prayer until late in the day. In the meantime the angels prepared a meal for

---

hagiology. Animals, moreover, are susceptible of an ardent affection for human beings; they show a preference and. an attachment to individuals of a purely personal nature, quite irrespective of services rendered to them; and cases are well authenticated in which they have even died of sorrow at being deprived by death of those they loved, bemoaning their loss, and refusing to eat or to be comforted. Here, as ever, the natural is the groundwork of the supernatural.

them, laid out the table, and placed on it fruit, pure white bread, and fish, besides a species of conserve of such exquisite sweetness that earth could never have supplied the like. Then they called the holy spouses to come and partake of this Paradisical feast, which they did with tears of gratitude to the Sovereign Lord who had so miraculously supplied their needs.

Time flowed on, and the nine months of Mary's pregnancy were drawing towards their close. Already had her blessed hands prepared the swaddling-bands in which she was to envelop the Infant God-Man; and Joseph, we cannot doubt, had lovingly fashioned the cradle in which He was to rest. He little thought of the rough manger and the straw which was to be the Saviour's first bed on earth, as the hard cross was to be His last. And so it seemed as if in green Nazareth the bud of Jesse was to blossom. But what said the Scripture? "And thou, Bethlehem Ephrata, art a little one among the thousands of Juda: out of thee shall he come forth unto me that is to be the ruler in Israel; and his going forth *is* from the beginning, from the days of eternity." (*Mich.* 5:2). This prophecy was well known among the Jews, for we find that when King Herod inquired of the chief priests and scribes where Christ should be born, they replied, "In Bethlehem of Juda," quoting the prediction of Micheas. If so, is it possible that to Mary and Joseph, so conversant with Holy Writ, it can have been unknown? And yet we find them remaining on at Nazareth without doubt or question. If this surprises us, it is only because the strength of their faith and their complete abandonment to the leadings of God's Providence are beyond our shallow perception. God would know how to bring about His Will in the manner He pleased, and they left all in His hands. If Mary was divinely illuminated with respect to His designs, we may be certain she would say nothing, but leave to Joseph, her appointed head and guide, the direction of all her actions. To Joseph no angel was sent to bid him go to Bethlehem, and in the absence of light from on high he certainly would neither plan, nor speak, nor move.

God, however, who disposes human events in order to the accomplishment of His high purposes, brought about the fulfillment of His word to the prophet by an edict of the Roman Emperor, Caesar Augustus, that "the whole world" subject to him "should be enrolled." (*Luke* 2:1). Everyone was to repair to his own city to have his name set down in the public register. Among other expositors of Holy Scripture, Tirinus says that in this general census women and children were included. Whatever motive may have prompted the Roman Caesar to send forth this decree, whether it were the pride of knowing exactly how many individuals were subject to his sway, or for the sake of the tax thereby collected, or for other reasons suiting his policy, he was, unknown to himself, serving the secret designs of Him who was his Lord as well as of the millions who were to be enrolled as his vassals. Joseph and Mary were of the house and family of David. Bethlehem, consequently, was their city. Thither, therefore, must they go to be inscribed. Thus were the words of Micheas to be literally accomplished; thus, too, as St. Thomas has pointed out, no one, whether Jew or Gentile, should be able to raise a question as to the birth of Jesus, His name being registered in the tables of the Roman census, which could be seen, even in the days of St. John Chrysostom, who alludes to them. Scarcely was He born, says the Venerable Bede, but He was inscribed in Caesar's census, and to render us free, made Himself a subject; and St. Alfonso dé Liguori says that, not only did Mary and Joseph pay the tribute and enter their names in the book as Caesar's subjects, but the Child of Mary, Jesus Christ Himself, who was the Lord of Caesar and of all the princes of the earth, was also inscribed therein.

But to return to our narrative. It wanted but a few days of the time at which Mary's divine delivery might be expected when Joseph heard the Imperial decree proclaimed with sound of trumpet in Nazareth. It must have deeply concerned him, not for himself, for nothing which only personally affected him could either grieve or disturb him, but through his solicitude for Mary, and the pain he felt at her having to make this journey of ninety miles in her present state, and in the depth of winter. Whether Mary already knew that she should have to repair to Bethlehem for the birth of her Divine Infant, or Joseph brought her the first intimation, the handmaid of the Lord would sweetly accept whatever might be the will of God in her regard, and her cheerful acquiescence must have encouraged and consoled her spouse. Nor let it be supposed that, while it was a virtue in Mary that nothing could trouble the serenity of her soul, it was an imperfection in Joseph to suffer anxiety. God, in making him the husband of Mary and the adopted father of His Son, had endowed him with all the tenderness which belongs to and becomes those relationships, or, rather, with far more than ordinary wedlock and paternity bring with them; and, moreover, he increased his merits by the patience with which he bore the pressure of these high responsibilities upon his loving heart. As Mary's compassion was afterwards to constitute her martyrdom and her participation in the Passion of her Divine Son, when the sword pierced her soul at the foot of the Cross, so may we piously believe that Joseph's meritorious sufferings came to him much more through the love he bore the two heavenly treasures committed to his keeping than from any of the bodily labors and trials which he endured for their maintenance and protection. The Evangelists are sparing of their words; they seldom record feelings; or, at least, we have to content ourselves with a few scattered hints, all the more precious and all the more significant from their fewness. That one testimony given by Mary, to which allusion has already been made, "Thy father and I have sought Thee sorrowing," throws a flood of light upon the martyrdom of love which consumed the heart of

Joseph during those thirty years.

There was no delay; they set out at once. A small supply of provisions to meet probable deficiencies on the crowded roads was laid upon the ass which was to carry the Mother of God and the Incarnate God Himself. Was it the same which had previously been similarly favored when Mary visited her cousin Elizabeth? Probably it was. Blessed animal! which was also to be present at the Nativity, to recognize and adore its Creator, and even be permitted to render Him a service, when His own people had shut their doors against Him. May we be excused for pausing here to express our unfeigned wonder why a creature so singled out for honor in Scripture history should be commonly, in our day, meanly thought of, often hardly treated, and its very name made a reproach? It was Balsam's ass, not the proud horse, whose mouth was opened; it was an ass that, not only carried Jesus while yet in His mother's womb, but bore Him on his triumphant entrance into Jerusalem, the type of His glorious coming at the last day, of which circumstance the prophet had made special mention: "Behold thy King will come to thee, the just and saviour; He is poor and riding upon an ass, and upon a colt the foal of an ass." (*Zach.* 9:9). Perhaps it is for this very reason that this singularly intelligent and patient animal is not more esteemed. He bears the sign of the cross on his shoulders and back, and the obloquy of the cross appears to cling to him.

We may imagine what was the state of the roads at this time, when such numbers were pressing hither and thither to repair to their respective places of enrollment; how every possible conveyance was in requisition, and every beast of burden, the poor making their way as best they might on foot; how the inns were crowded—and by inns we must not imagine houses of entertainment, offering the comforts which we expect to find in such places. They provided shelter, and food could probably, though not always, be procured, but for other accommodation travellers would have to supply themselves with what they wanted. Anyhow, what was to be had was sure to fall to the lot of the richest and the most importunate. But Joseph and Mary, carrying all the riches of Heaven and earth, travelled in the garb of poverty, and were humble, modest, and retiring. We may be certain, therefore, that the five days they are believed to have spent on the way to Bethlehem were days of privation, fatigue, and discomfort of every kind. But they did not travel alone; they had an escort. In the Canticles we read: "Threescore valiant ones of the most valiant ones of Israel surround the bed of Solomon, all holding swords and most expert in war, every man's sword upon his thigh, because of fears in the night." (*Cant.* 3:7, 8). But many more were the valiant ones, princes of the armies of Heaven, who invisibly surrounded and protected the bed of the True Solomon by night and by day. Thousands of angels attended on Mary, to guard her, to shield her from the cold blast, and, what to her would be far more distressing, the rude gaze of the throng. Perhaps, for the consolation of Joseph, whose only thought and solicitude was for his holy spouse, he was allowed a vision of the protecting wings which surrounded her. If this privilege was vouchsafed to him he would lie down in peace, and after the day's fatigue sleep the sleep of the just until the dawn of another winter's day saw them once more on the road to the city of David. Doubtless he would think with satisfaction that when they had reached Bethlehem, where once he had lived and must still have friends, Mary would have ample compensation under some hospitable roof for all the trials of the way. This hope he would naturally express to her, and she would gently assent, even though interiorly she might know it would be otherwise.

On the evening of the fifth day they drew near to Bethlehem, and the crowd thickened as they approached the town. We can figure to ourselves Joseph leading the meek ass, and making way with difficulty for the animal and its Divine burden, no one giving them the slightest heed or scrupling to push rudely by; Mary calmly seated with her veil drawn around her. What an entry into his regal city of the inheritor of David's throne, or, rather, of Him who was the sovereign of earth and Heaven! In this lowly fashion they moved on till they reached the chief hostelry of the place, Joseph being solicitous to secure at once accommodation for Mary, were it only a night's shelter, for darkness was closing in. But the guest-house was full. The Evangelist simply says, "There was no room for them in the inn." (*Luke* 2:7). They were turned away from the door, and had to seek a lodging elsewhere. As they passed the Imperial office, where the names were entered and the tribute-money paid, Joseph would give his own and that of Mary his wife, as a little later he was to give the Name that is above every name. The injunction of the law thus accomplished, Joseph resumed his fruitless search. Although the Evangelist mentions no other place but the inn, we may be sure that Joseph left no house untried where there was the least hope of being received. Maria d'Agreda says that they went to no less than fifty, but everywhere they met with the same repulse and that cold indifference which it is the lot of the poor so often to experience. Saints, indeed, tell us so; for St. Vincent Ferrer, in a sermon on the Holy Innocents, says that, because the Bethlehemites would not receive the Virgin, nor Joseph, her spouse, therefore did God provoke the wrath of Herod against them. Jesus had come to His own, and His own received Him not. Hard, indeed, is it to explain how Joseph in his own native place could find no kind friend and no shelter for Mary, in a condition, too, which called for sympathy and compassion from all. Cleophas, the brother of Joseph, had, no doubt, removed to Capharnaum some time previous; and of his other relatives there might now be none in Bethlehem. If he applied to former friends they no longer knew or acknowledged him, for Mary and he were treated as strangers at every door. None was opened to receive them. Goats of the left hand were these hard-hearted Bethlehemites: "I was a stranger and ye took Me not in." (*Matt.* 25:43).

Let us admire the sweet serenity and patience of Mary. We can scarcely imagine that she did not know what would be the result of each successive application, but she kept silence, committing herself without reserve to the guidance of Joseph. Fatigued and exposed to the chilling December blast, she had to pass from door to door, but, far more than the wintry wind, did these cold denials pain her. The wind was the obedient instrument of the good pleasure of the Most High, which she loved and adored; but the Bethlehemites, with hearts closed to the sweet influences of divine grace and even of natural kindness, were rebels to His holy will; nay, they were driving the Lord Himself from their doors. But neither must we fail to turn a look of tender compassion on Joseph, whose soul was filled with such anguish as no words could tell. We know what it is to be powerless to do aught for those most dear to us, and who depend upon our care, when they are exposed to straits and perils. But what is the fond love of any of our poor hearts compared to that of Joseph? Let us think, too, of the responsibility laid upon him, and the corresponding strain upon his mind and affections: the care and guardianship, not only of the Blessed Mother of God, but of the Incarnate God Himself!

Chapter XXX

The Stable at Bethlehem.

WHITHER were Joseph and Mary now to turn? At no great distance from the inhabited houses, there was, on the slope at the eastern end of the place, a cave or grotto, hewn in the rock on which stood the inhospitable city. It served as an occasional stable, of which travellers availed themselves for their beasts, as well as a place of refuge for shepherds on cold and tempestuous nights. Joseph, who had lived at Bethlehem, must have known its surroundings well, and have been acquainted with the existence of this rough excavation. It might be vacant, and would, at least, afford some kind of shelter for the remainder of the night. Hither, therefore, he directed his steps, leading the ass which bore the Redeemer of the world and His august Mother. The cave was unoccupied; how poor and uninviting it must have been is proved from this very fact. Bethlehem was full to overflowing, yet no one had stopped to profit by this rude stable. He who came to take the lowest place had reserved it for Himself.

The Evangelists, St. Matthew and St. Luke, both say that Christ was born in Bethlehem of Judea, to distinguish it from another Bethlehem in Galilee, but they do not specify whether the place of His birth was within or outside the city. No reasonable doubt, however, can be entertained as to the locality. Tradition was fresh in the days of St. Helen, mother of the Emperor Con-

221

stantine, who built a large and sumptuous church on
the spot, including within its area the cave of the Nativity, at the eastern limit of Bethlehem, on the incline
looking northwards. Further, the Fathers invariably
affirm that Jesus was born outside, and not within, the
town. St. Justin Martyr, who lived in the third century,
was a native of Sychar in Samaria. He is, therefore, an
excellent authority in this matter. Now, in his Dialogue
against Tryphon, he writes thus: "Since Joseph did not
find where to lodge in the village of Bethlehem, he
repaired to a certain grotto near to it; and being there,
Mary brought forth Jesus and laid Him in the manger,
where the Magi, coming from Arabia, found Him." Eusebius of Pamphylia also says: "The place is still shown
near Bethlehem where the Virgin brought forth to the
light and laid the Divine Infant." It is noticeable also
that the Fathers always give the name of cave, grotto,
or den to the spot where Jesus was born,[1] but caves,
grottoes, and dens are not to be met with in peopled
cities. It is clear, then, that Jesus was born outside of
Bethlehem, beyond the walls, even as He willed to suffer outside the gate of Jerusalem; in which we discern
one of the mysteries of His immense charity in the face
of all the ingratitude and contempt of men.

A miserable receptacle was this cave, with the
neglected stall and manger of beasts. We may imagine
the confusion and sorrow of Joseph at having nothing
better to offer to his august spouse. Yet was he truly
thankful to find any shelter for her; and, when we speak
of Joseph's sorrow, we must ever remember that this
sorrow existed only in the sensitive portion of his soul.
His joy, his delight, was to fulfill the will of God. His
devotion to that holy will we have already noticed as
having been revealed to St. Bridget by Our Lady. The
words are brief indeed in which the Evangelist records
the birth of the Saviour, an event which has no paral-

---

1. Origen (lib. i. *contra Celsum)* calls it *spelunca.* Eusebius *(in Vita Constant.* lib. iii.)
calls it *antrum. St.* Jerome calls it a little cavern of the earth: "In this little cavern of the earth the Creator of the heavens was born."—*Epist. ad Marcellam.*

lel for greatness in the world's history. We long for particulars, for something on which our imagination can feed, and thus nourish in us pious affections. In the entire absence of all detail, we may gladly avail ourselves of the picture presented to us in a vision with which a holy soul was favored. Maria d'Agreda beheld the most holy Mary and St. Joseph entering the hospice which Divine Providence had prepared for them, and of which, from the light given by the attendant angels, they could at once perceive the rudeness, the nakedness, and withal the complete solitude and seclusion, which was their desire. The two holy pilgrims sank on their knees to return thanks to God with tears of gratitude. Our Sovereign Lady understood the mystery, indeed, better than did St. Joseph, though he, too, was full of faith and submission to the appointments of God's wisdom; for no sooner had Mary's feet touched the floor of the cave than she felt an overflowing fullness of interior joy, so that she immediately poured forth a prayer to God that He would liberally reward the Bethlehemites, who by closing their doors against herself and her spouse had been the occasion of obtaining them so great a boon as the occupation of this tranquil retreat.

Mary's angels stood around her, like a guard of honor, visible to her in human form, and to Joseph also, such consolation being due to him in his anxiety and as a preparation for the great mystery about to follow; for as yet he was ignorant that Mary's delivery was to take place in this abject abode. Mary, however, knew it, and determined to clear with her own hands the place which was to serve as a royal palace to the Eternal King, discharging thereby at once a lowly office and paying due reverence to her Divine Son. But Joseph, regarding the majesty of his most holy spouse, of which she herself took no account, intreated her to leave to him the work she desired to do, and began at once to sweep the floor of the cavern, Mary still lending her aid; and then the angels, as if fired with a holy emulation, came to her help, and had soon cleansed the whole interior, which they, moreover, illuminated and filled with a heavenly fragrance. It was fitting, indeed, that, humble as it was, the place should be purified where the Lord of Heaven, Purity Itself, was to repose. Joseph kindled a fire, with the means of doing which he had come provided, for the cold was great, and Mary and he sat by it, partaking of some frugal viands which they had brought with them, although Mary ate only to conform herself to Joseph's wishes, for she was becoming more and more absorbed in the contemplation of the approaching mystery. Knowing that the hour was drawing nigh, she presently besought her holy spouse to go and take some rest; and he, complying with her desire, begged her to do the same; with which view he laid coverings upon a rude manger that was there, to serve her as a couch. He then retired apart into a corner of the cavern, and, being immersed in prayer, the Spirit of God came upon him, with a plenitude of power and sweetness which ravished his soul in ecstasy, during which he had a vision of all that took place in that blest spot. Nor did he return to consciousness till he heard the voice of his august spouse calling him; and this deep sleep into which Joseph had been cast was more marvellous and more sublime than that of Adam in the terrestrial Paradise.

Meanwhile Mary had received a call from the Most High which exalted her far above all created things. This ecstasy was one of the highest and most admirable to which she was raised during her most holy life; and by it she was so transformed and illuminated as to fit her for the intuitive vision of God.[2] During this rapture her Divine Son declared to her that the time of His birth was come. Mary, prostrate in profound humility, gave glory and thanks to God on the part of all creatures, begging for herself new light and grace, that

---

2. Several theologians, and among them St. Antoninus and Suarez, are of opinion that it is highly probable that the Blessed Virgin was raised to the clear vision of God at the hour of the Nativity, as also at the Annunciation, if not more often, as saints have held.

she might know how to treat, and serve, and pay homage to the Word-made-Man, whom she was to receive into her arms and nourish at her breast, for she esteemed herself utterly unworthy of such an office; and, because she thus humbled herself, the Lord magnified her, bidding her, as His true and legitimate mother, to exercise this office and ministry, and to treat Him as at once the Son of the Eternal Father and the offspring of her own womb. This rapture, accompanied by the beatific vision, continued for above an hour, and concluded with her divine delivery, which, so far from causing her pain, filled her with ineffable bliss, of which, not the soul only, but the body partook, which became so spiritualized, beautiful, and refulgent that she no longer seemed to belong to this earth. Rays of light emanated from her countenance, which wore a most majestic aspect. She was on her knees in the manger, her eyes raised to Heaven, her hands joined before her bosom, her spirit raised to God, and herself, as it were, all deified; and it was in this attitude, when the hour of midnight had struck, that she gave to the world the Only-Begotten Son of the Father, and her own son too, our Saviour Jesus, true God and true Man.

He came forth from His virginal cloister even as the rays of the sun penetrate without impairing the crystal glass, as hereafter He was to pass through the stone of His monument and the closed doors of the Coenaculum. He came forth leaving His mother's pure virginity, not only inviolate and unimpaired, but more resplendent than before. He came forth, Himself most pure and most beautiful. It was a birth, although a true and real birth, free from all those humiliating accompaniments which our fallen nature has inherited. Moreover, although He had taken our passible nature, and, having done so, withheld from His body that participation in the glorious endowments which were its due, yet the Divine Wisdom decreed that the glory of His most holy soul should be communicated to the body of the Infant God when coming into the world; even as on Thabor, when He was transfigured in the presence of the three Apostles; for it was the will of God that the Blessed Mother should behold her Son for the first time in glorified form; and this for two ends: the one, that by the sight of His grandeur she should conceive with what reverence she was to treat the God-Man, her Son; for, although she knew this already, the Lord ordained that she should also realize it experimentally, and receive a new grace corresponding to this divine experience. The second object was to bestow on her by this marvellous sight a reward for her fidelity and love, in that her most chaste eyes, which had never rested on anything earthly from the affection she bore her Divine Son, should be rejoiced by beholding Him born all glorious and resplendent.

St. Michael and St. Gabriel were seen by the favored soul whose vision we are briefly describing, standing at a short distance from Our Lady, and when the Divine Infant came forth they received Him into their arms with incomparable reverence, and held Him up before the eyes of His Virgin Mother, as the priest elevates the Host for the adoration of the faithful. The Son and the Mother looked at each other—His heart filled with unutterable love for her, and she elevated and transformed into Him. The mystical language of the Canticles could alone render what then passed between the God-Man and her who is symbolized as the beloved in the Song of Songs: "My dove, my perfect one, the only one of her mother, the chosen of her that bore her. The daughters saw her, and declared her most blessed. How beautiful art thou, my love, how beautiful art thou! thy eyes are dove's eyes. Thou art all fair, O my love, and there is not a spot in thee. Thou hast wounded my heart." (*Cant.* 6:8; 4:1, 7, 9). And she replies: "My beloved to me and I to him. My beloved is white and ruddy, chosen out of thousands. Behold, my beloved speaketh to me. Arise, make haste, my love, my dove, my beautiful one, and come." (*Cant.* 6:2; 5:10, 2:10). The Divine Infant spoke audibly, at least, to the heart of His mother. He told her that she was to resemble Him, so that, as she had given Him His human nature, so would He henceforth give her a new being of grace, which, although that of a pure creature, should nevertheless be most like unto His, which was divine. And the beloved replied: "Draw me: we will run after thee to the odor of thy ointments." (*Cant.* 1:3). But who can express what passed in that mysterious but brief colloquy of love? The grace which Mary then received accompanied her through life, when she became the living pattern and mirror, and the exact similitude, so far as was possible to a pure creature, of Christ, true God and Man. The Divine Infant then suspended the miracle, or, rather, He returned to that miraculous state wherein the gifts of glory were withheld from His most holy body. He manifested Himself to His mother without them in His passible nature, and in that state, profoundly adoring Him, she received Him into her arms from the holy archangels, offered herself to Him to serve Him as His handmaid, and forthwith offered Him to the Eternal Father for the salvation of men. Then, looking at her Divine Son, the joy of her heart, she besought Him to admit her to that kiss which is the desire of all creatures: "Let him kiss me with the kiss of his mouth" (*Cant.* 1:1); and so she pressed her most pure lips to His, and received the loving embrace of her God and her Son. And in her arms, which served Him as an altar, all the angels of Heaven came to worship Him. Heaven was well-nigh empty that Christmas night, or, rather, the court of Heaven was in the stable of Bethlehem, for the other Persons of the Blessed Trinity were present in a special manner at the Nativity of the Word made Flesh.

It was now time for the most prudent Virgin to call her faithful spouse, Joseph, who, as has been said, was in an ecstasy, and had known by revelation all the mys-

teries of this Divine Birth. It was now fitting that he
should with his bodily senses see, touch, reverence, and
adore the Incarnate God, and this before any other mortal man. Returning, then, from his ecstasy, at Mary's
call, the first object on which Joseph's eyes rested was
the Infant God in the arms of His Virgin Mother, leaning against her cheek and sacred bosom. Here he adored
Him with profound humility and many tears, and kissed
His feet with such joy and admiration that if divine
power had not supported him he would have died for
very joy and love. Our Lady now, with unspeakable reverence, wrapped the Infant Saviour in the swaddling-
bands which she had prepared, and then, as St. Luke
says, laid Him in the manger, in which Joseph had
strewn some hay and straw to render the bed less hard
for His tender limbs.

Having now been adored by angels and men, the God-
Man was to receive the homage of those inferior creatures of His hand whom we are in the habit of styling
brute beasts. They had an honorable post on this occasion. In the stable was an ox,[3] together with the ass
which had borne Mary and her precious Burden; and
at the voice of their Sovereign Mistress the innocent
animals knelt down before the Infant in the manger.
Then, drawing nigh, they stood on either side and warmed
Him with their breath, thus doing Him both the homage
and the service which men had denied Him. Let us gaze
for a moment at this touching scene: God-madeMan,
wrapped in swaddling-bands, lying in the manger
between two animals, as the Church records in the Divine
Office for Good Friday.[4] Then was literally fulfilled the
prediction of Isaias (*Is.* 1:3): "The ox knoweth his owner,
and the ass his master's crib; but Israel hath not known
me, and my people hath not understood." St. Jerome is

---

3. It has been held by several Doctors, quoted by Benedict XIII, that the ox also
belonged to Joseph, and was brought by him to carry such few things as he thought
might be needed.
4. The Septuagint Version has this rendering of the passage in the prophecy of Habacuc
iii. 2.

an authentic testimony to this tradition, for, writing to Eustochium, he tells her how her mother, the noble matron Paula, so devout an adorer in the Holy Places, having entered the cave of the Nativity, beheld the stall in which the ox knew his owner, and the ass the crib of his master. St. Gregory Nazianzen and St. Gregory of Nyssa affirm the like; and the Church, as we have said, lends her venerable sanction to this pious and touching belief.

Tradition has also preserved the memory of many wonders said to have taken place on the night of the Nativity, to which more or less credence has been attached; others have been alluded to by ecclesiastical writers. From the living rock in this blessed grotto a vein of pure water began to flow; it was still to be seen in the time of the Venerable Bede. When we recollect the marvel of the grotto of Lourdes in our own day, we feel that such a miraculous occurrence was more than probable. The vines of Engaddi blossomed; the oracle of Delphos was silenced;[5] idols fell to the ground, both at Rome and in Egypt; the Emperor Augustus is said to have seen in the air the Virgin and Child on the summit of the Capitol, where now stands the Church of Ara Coeli; a fountain of oil sprang from the Taverna Meritoria, on the site of the present sumptuous Basilica of Santa Maria in Trastevere, and ran as far as the Tiber. These and other signs are said to have accompanied the birth of the Saviour of the world; and it is worthy of remark that even to our day, and among the Protestant peasantry of our own land, pious beliefs are

---

5. "The oracles are dumb,
    No voice or hideous hum
        Runs through the arched roof in words deceiving.
    Apollo from his shrine
    Can no more divine,
        With hollow shriek the steep of Delphos leaving.

Our Babe, to show His Godhead true,
Can in His swaddling-bands controul the damned crew.

And all about the courtly stable
Bright-harness'd angels sit in order serviceable."—Milton, *Hymn on the Nativity.*

still cherished concerning the marvels said to be
repeated on each night of the Nativity.[6] There is a
sweetness in the memory of that joyful mystery of our
Catholic Faith which lingers on in spite of the chilling, poisonous atmosphere of unbelief.

---

6. As an instance, the blossoming of the Glastonbury thorn may be mentioned, and
another, not so well known, current among the peasantry of that once most Catholic-
county, Devonshire, that on Christmas night the cattle go down on their knees in
their stalls. The writer has this on the authority of a native of Devonshire, now a
Catholic, who in her youth was assured that this always takes place. We give the
fact for what it may be worth; it is a testimony, at least, to the undying hold of
Catholic traditions on our poor.

Chapter XXXI

The Adoration of the Shepherds.
The Circumcision.

ON this blessed Christmas night our great patriarch St. Joseph entered on the exercise of his high prerogative of father of Jesus. That paternity, as has been shown, was far superior to a mere legal, that is, adopted paternity. Jesus, although not his true son, was much more than his adopted son. An adopted son is one who, born of strangers, is received into another house where the marriage has been unfruitful, and formally invested with this title. Not so Jesus. Jesus was born miraculously from the virginal espousals of Joseph and of his true and legitimate spouse. He was born in Joseph's house, not by a legal fiction, but by a divine ordinance. Joseph, therefore, is more than the putative or reputed father of Jesus; and, if the Church calls him so, it is, says the learned Estius, to exclude the idea of natural generation.[1] On the night of the Nativity he entered practically on all the essential prerogatives and attributes of paternity imparted to him by God, which, as the Blessed Canisius, a profound theologian who was at the Council of Trent, observes, are chiefly three: affection, care, and authority.[2] He had paternal affection; for, as the Abbot Rupert assures us, the Holy Spirit, who formed the members of Jesus of Mary's blood, infused into Joseph's heart

1. Lib. iv. *Sent.* dist. xxx. sect. x.
2. *Tract. de B. V. Deipara,* lib. ii. cap. xiii.

231

the most tender love for the Divine Infant who was
about to be born.[3] Also the Eternal Father, who begets
His Son from all eternity, willing, in a certain sense,
to share with Joseph His paternity of Jesus born in the
fullness of time, caused, as it were, a spark of the infinite love which He bears to His Divine Son to descend
into the bosom of Joseph; and this new paternal affection, joined to his already boundless charity, began from
this moment to kindle in his heart such a flame of love
towards Jesus that, next to that of Mary, its like was
never found among men, nor ever shall be, not even
among the angels themselves. His solicitude and care
for this Divine Son were inexpressible; for no father
ever did so much or endured so much for his children
as did Joseph for Jesus. And, finally, he had paternal
authority. This is why Jesus was always submissive
and obedient to Joseph, and why Joseph himself,
notwithstanding his deep reverence for Jesus, ventured
to fill the father's position of command.

In virtue of his paternal rights Joseph had also become
the head, the arbiter, and administrator of the Holy
Family. The devout Bernardine de Bustis says that it
is of Joseph, set over this sovereign family of God, that
these words of Jesus reported by St. Luke and St. Matthew may be understood: "Who, thinkest thou, is the
faithful and wise steward whom his lord setteth over
his family?"[4] It is almost as if He had named Joseph.
Now, who can measure the greatness of this dignity, to
be head, and ruler, and administrator of Him who is
King of kings and Lord of lords, and of her who is
Queen of Heaven and earth? This dignity, says the
learned Cartagena, without doubt far surpasses all principality, whether human or divine; and clearly did the
Eternal Father mark that to Joseph was committed the
care and rule of this most Holy Family, when to him
alone, through His angels, did He dispatch His messages from Heaven, telling Joseph what he was to do,

---

3. *In Matthaeum,* cap. i.
4. Luke 12:42; *conf.* Matthew 24:45.

whither he was to go, and what road he was to take in order to place those most dear pledges, Mary and Jesus, in safety. In him, in short, was fulfilled what had been prefigured in the ancient Joseph, who by the great king Pharao "was made lord of his house and ruler of all his possession." (*Ps.* 104:21).

In that blessed night also Joseph became the patron, the vicar, and the patriarch of the whole Catholic Church. It is certain, St. Athanasius tells us, that the stable where Jesus was born is "a figure of the Church, whose altar is the manger, whose vicar is Joseph, whose ministers are the shepherds, whose priests are the angels, whose great High-Priest is Jesus Christ, and whose throne is the Blessed Virgin."[5] Since, then, this grotto and crib is the figure of the Church, and Joseph is its vicar, as representing the High-Priest, Christ Jesus, and acting in His place, well did it become our late venerated Pontiff, Pius IX, to proclaim Joseph Patron of the Universal Church. There is yet another reason. The Church took its beginning from Jesus Christ, who was its Divine founder. The first to form part of that Church was Mary; the second was Joseph. But of this nascent Church, limited as yet to the Holy Family, who was the tutor, the protector, the head? Joseph. And, if he filled this office towards the Church at its birth, he did not cease to exercise it after its birth and diffusion throughout the world. Wherefore, with greater reason than Abraham can he be called, as truly he is, the Father of the Faithful.

But we will now return to contemplate the grotto of the Nativity, where Mary and Joseph are adoring the newborn Infant. The first exercise of Joseph's paternal solicitude (to which allusion has already been made) was the endeavor to render the hard bed of the manger more tolerable to the tender limbs of the Babe. Nor can we doubt that he lost no time in employing his carpenter's skill in constructing out of such rude materials as were available a more suitable cradle for the Divine

5. *Hom. in Censum B. Mariae Virginis et S. Joseph.*

Child. That he did so is certain, for this is the cradle which is still venerated at Santa Maria Maggiore in Rome, called on this account *Santa Maria ad praesepe.*[6]

While the mystery of the Nativity was being accomplished in the stable of Bethlehem, there were at the distance, perhaps, of a thousand paces, near the Tower of Edar (or the Flock), some simple shepherds "keeping the night-watches over their flock," in that fair plain where Jacob of old pastured his sheep (*Gen.* 35:21), where Booz, the great-grandfather of David, commanded his reapers to drop some corn, that the beautiful Ruth might return from gleaning with her hands full (*Ruth* 2), and where David, tending his sheep, was called to be anointed king by Samuel. (*1 Kgs.* 16:4, 13). Suddenly, in the midst of the darkness, a great light flashed upon them, illuminating the whole heavens. "And behold," says the Evangelist, "an angel of the Lord stood by them, and they feared with a great fear. And the angel said to them: Fear not; for behold I bring you good tidings of great joy which shall be to all the people; for this day is born to you a Saviour, who is Christ the Lord, in the city of David. And this shall be a sign unto you: you shall find the infant wrapped in swaddling clothes and laid in a manger. And suddenly there was with the angel a multitude of the heavenly army, praising God, and saying, Glory to God in the highest, and on earth peace to men of good-will." (*Luke* 2:8-14).

God had promised by the mouth of His prophets that He would send a Redeemer to the world, and that He should be born in Bethlehem; and He had now punctually fulfilled His promise. But, as this promise had been made to His chosen people, so also was the chosen people the first called to know and adore the newborn Messias. The first manifestation which Jesus made of Himself was to the shepherds of Bethlehem; the second was to

---

6. Pope Theodore, a native of Palestine, saved this cradle during the Mahometan invasion, in the year 642, and caused it to be carried away, together with the body of St. Jerome, who had been its faithful custodian, and brought to Rome, where the precious relics were received with the greatest reverence and joy, and deposited in the Basilica Liberiana, afterwards called *Santa Maria ad praesepe.*

the Gentiles, that is, to the Magi, the first fruits of the Gentiles. Jesus revealed Himself first to simple and blameless shepherds, because He loves to converse with the simple; and it was to shepherds that He made Himself known, to show that He, the Pastor of pastors, came to call new pastors, who were to feed His new flock, the Church. He surrounded them with a bright light, to signify that with His heavenly doctrine He came to enlighten all men. And, finally, He called and instructed them by the mouth of an angel, because they were believers, whereas He called the Gentiles to Him, that is, the Magi, by means of a star, a thing unendowed with reason, and a miraculous sign, because (as St. Gregory observes) to the faithful the language of faith is the most fitting, but to non-believers the language of miracles. And St. Paul, before him, had already clearly said that the voice of prodigies was not for the faithful, but for the unfaithful in order that they might believe, and the voice of revelation is not for the unfaithful but for the faithful, who already believe in God.[7]

We need not suppose that this refulgent light which struck the eyes of the shepherds was limited to the spot where they were keeping their night-watches. It probably illuminated the whole neighborhood, and shone all around the city of David, so that, if any had been awake, they might have supposed that a new sun had arisen in Bethlehem, and that night had been turned into day; but the Bethlehemites were plunged in profound sleep, and none saw it, or none noticed it. This light may have been visible even as far as Jerusalem, which is not many miles distant, giving a literal application to the words of the prophet Isaias, when he cried, "Arise, be enlightened, O Jerusalem; for thy light is come, and the glory of the Lord is risen upon thee." (*Is.* 60:1). But we do not hear that a single living soul gave heed to that heavenly portent save a few poor shepherds, for all were sunk in sleep, symbol of the gross

---

7. "Wherefore tongues are for a sign, not to believers but to unbelievers; but prophecies, not to unbelievers but to believers." (*1 Cor.* 14:22).

darkness in which the world was plunged.

But who was that glorious angel who announced the good tidings to the shepherds, and who seems to have been the leader of the angelical army which suddenly burst upon their sight. According to the Fathers and Doctors of the Church, it was the Archangel Gabriel. He who was to announce the highest of mysteries must needs be an angel of highest dignity, as St. Gregory the Great observes. Gabriel was also the special angel of the Incarnation (as Cornelius à Lapide points out) to whom all the solemn embassages connected with that sublime mystery were entrusted, beginning with the revelation to the prophet Daniel of the period of the seventy weeks.

When the angels had departed, the shepherds said one to another, "Let us go over to Bethlehem, and let us see this word that is come to pass, which the Lord hath showed to us." They lost no time, for the Evangelist adds, "they came with haste." (*Luke* 2:15, 16). The angel had, perhaps, indicated to them the precise spot where they would find the newborn Saviour, or the angelic light issuing from the cave may have guided their steps. "And they found Mary and Joseph, and the Infant lying in the manger, and seeing, they understood of the word that had been spoken to them concerning this child." (*Luke* 3:16, 17). How much is comprehended in that word "understood"! They saw, and they adored with undoubting faith. It is to the simple and the child-like, such as were these shepherds, that the Lord unveils the mysteries of His kingdom. We are reminded here of those words which He afterwards uttered: "I confess to Thee, O Father, Lord of heaven and earth, because Thou hast hid these things from the wise and prudent, and hast revealed them to little ones. Yea, Father; for so it hath seemed good in Thy sight." (*Matt.* 11:25, 26). We may imagine with what grace and kindness Mary and Joseph received these good men, listened to their narration, replied to their questions, and gave them what further instruction they needed.

Nor can we suppose that this was the only visit which these shepherds paid to the stable in the rock, or the only time that they had the happiness of adoring the Divine Infant. During the remainder of the time that Mary and Joseph tarried there they would surely return again more than once, bringing probably some little offering out of their scanty means. When the Gospel says that "all that heard wondered, and at those things that were told them by the shepherds"; and that "the shepherds returned glorifying and praising God for all the things they had heard and seen" (*Luke* 2:18, 20), the action alluded to was probably their return to their own homes, and after the departure of the Holy Family from the cave. So, at least, thinks Maria d'Agreda, and that Divine Wisdom so decreed it. Had their report been immediately published and generally believed— which in the first instance, however, it was perhaps not likely to be, coming from ignorant rustics, as they would have been reckoned—there would, if only from curiosity, have been some concourse of other inhabitants of the neighborhood, of which we hear nothing, and which would have entailed a publicity which did not enter into the designs of God. Maria d'Agreda says that among those who credited the report which subsequently spread was Herod, and that among the martyred innocents were some children of these holy men, who offered them with joy to suffer for the Saviour whom they already knew. But how many in number were these shepherds, and what were their names? Scripture does not inform us, but, as we know from the authority of ancient writers that near to the Tower of Edar was subsequently built a church in honor of the holy angels and the three shepherds, it would appear that those who went that happy night to Bethlehem were three in number. And when that church had fallen, on its site remained the grotto called after the shepherds, nearly a mile distant from Bethlehem. The descent into it is by a few steps, and the memory of the shepherds is still venerated there. Baronius, on the authority of the

Venerable Bede, says that there was a church or oratory there, containing memorials of the three shepherds
who had knowledge of the Divine Nativity.[8] Tradition
has not preserved to us their names, but between the
grotto of the shepherds and Bethlehem there is a little village called Bethsaur, that is, House of the Dawn,
and this is supposed by some to have been the native
place of the three shepherds who had the honor of
beholding and adoring the Sun of Justice on His first
rising, and being now numbered among the saints.

There is no reason to suppose that the Holy Family
immediately removed into a house within the town.
Tradition is adverse to any such idea; neither has it
been adopted, we may say, by the Church, which always
supposes the Circumcision and the visit of the Magi to
have taken place where Jesus was born. Joseph, no
doubt, made every endeavor to render their humble
abode as habitable as possible. There was, however, no
water in the immediate vicinity of the cave; and we
have already alluded to the tradition of a miraculous
issue from the rock of a spring of water, for the supply of the Holy Family, and that the Venerable Bede
mentions its existence in his day.

We must not omit to add that, according to the authority of Tertullian, it was at the coming of Christ that
the waters of the Probatic Pool in Jerusalem acquired
their curative virtue. When Jesus was conceived, says
Genebrard,[9] this pool, which previously had only served
for washing the sheep intended for sacrifice, was shaken
as by an earthquake, and poured forth a prodigious
quantity of water. Then the Archangel Raphael began
to make his descents into it, which ceased after Our
Lord's death. Voices, indeed, were heard in the air, saying, "Let us depart hence, let us depart."[10] Near the

---

8. *Annal.* ann. i. n. 14.
9. *Chronic.* b. i.
10. Josephus, in his *Wars of the Jews,* b. vi. c. v., relates how from the interior of the
    Temple on the day of Pentecost voices were heard saying, "Let us depart hence,
    let us depart." They proceeded from the guardian-angels, who were abandoning
    the Temple.

Probatic Pool was the house of Joachim and Anna (as has already been observed), where, in the sixth century, during the reign of Justinian, a beautiful church was erected. Some of the learned even say that the ground on which was the pool had been their property, and, consequently, afterwards that of Mary.

When the eighth day after her delivery had come, the time had arrived for the circumcision of the Infant. It was prescribed by God to be performed on that day, although it might be postponed for any serious reason. But Mary and Joseph were too exact observers of the Law to wish to delay it for an instant beyond the appointed time. Circumcision might be performed in any place, even in private houses, and by any person, the father or mother of the child, or by a stranger; it was not necessary to have recourse to the priest. Thus we read that Sephora, the wife of Moses, circumcised her son (*Ex.* 4:25); and the Apostle Paul circumcised Timothy. (*Acts* 16:3). That Jesus was in no way bound by this law of circumcision is plain, inasmuch as that rite was a remedy for sin, and He was essentially holy, nay, Holiness Itself, and had come to cancel sin in others. Nevertheless, as He had come, not to destroy but to fulfill the Law (*Matt.* 5:17), He willed to submit Himself to this painful and humiliating rite in order to give to all a sublime example of obedience, mortification, humility, and purity; and He, no doubt, interiorly made known to His Blessed Mother that such was His desire. The Angelic Doctor points out further reasons for which Jesus willed to be circumcised like others: namely, to prove the reality of His human nature against heretics, who would have said that He had but an apparent, shadowy body, an ethereal body brought from Heaven, not formed in the womb of the Immaculate Virgin; in order also to mark the importance of the divine precept given to Abraham, and to prove that He was truly of the race of Abraham, thereby removing all pretext from the obstinate Jews not to recognize Him as the true Messias promised to Abraham, and demonstrating that, being come to cancel the sins of the world, He did not refuse to submit Himself for our sakes to the remedies of sin.[11] St. Leo adds another reason, namely, that the devil should not discover that Jesus was the looked-for Messias; and St. Ambrose, in order that the Mosaic law should be buried with honor; finally, St. Augustine, in order that all carnal concupiscence should be circumcised, and Christian virginity and chastity reign in us. That Jesus was circumcised where He had been born, we have the authority of St. Epiphanius: "Born in Bethlehem," he says, "circumcised in the cave, presented in Jerusalem."[12] This is the opinion generally embraced by the Doctors of the Church.

But who was the minister of the rite? The Evangelist is silent on this point. Imagination has accordingly allowed itself full scope, and painters have been pleased to introduce into their representations a priest in his sacerdotal vestments; but we have no authority for supposing that any priest came to the stable of Bethlehem to circumcise Jesus. The opinion of those Doctors who believe that the minister of the circumcision of Jesus was Joseph appears the most probable. St. Ephrem the Syrian, a most ancient writer and contemporary of St. Basil, one who was well acquainted with the traditions of his native land, and highly esteemed both for his science and his piety, says expressly that it was Joseph who circumcised Jesus. Writing in confutation of those heretics who ascribed to Our Lord a phantastic body, he says: "If Jesus Christ had not true flesh, whom did Joseph circumcise?"[13] Thus he refers to it as to an unquestioned fact. St. Bernard, Suarez, and many others also believe that Joseph circumcised Jesus, because he who circumcised an infant was the same also who imposed the name; and it was Joseph who gave Jesus His name. This opinion, then, has been generally adopted. The precept of circumcision was addressed to

---

11. *Summa*, p. iii. q. xxxvii. a. 1.
12. *Haeres*, xx.
13. *Orat. de Transfigur. Domini.*

the heads of families; it was the office of the father, unless a priest took his place. Joseph, then, as Isolano says, circumcised Jesus as his son.[14] On him we may believe devolved this solemn and painful duty. Jesus was circumcised by Joseph on Mary's knees, no other eyes beholding the first drops of the Precious Blood flow except those of the holy angels, and no other ears save theirs hearing the wail of the Divine Infant. In this act Joseph accomplished three sacrifices in one: the sacrifice of Jesus, who began the great work of our redemption by suffering in His innocent members; the sacrifice of Mary, who with indescribable sorrow, but with perfect resignation, offered her Son to the Eternal Father, and held, as it were, the victim bound; and the sacrifice of himself, who had to nerve his hand to perform an act so painful and repugnant to his tender heart. It was an act of heroic obedience and fortitude on his part, greater, St. Bernard says, than was that of Abraham in sacrificing his son Isaac; for Joseph loved Jesus incomparably more than Abraham did his son Isaac, and well knew the difference between the son of any mortal man and the Son of the Eternal God. Thus the knife which cut the flesh of Jesus wounded the heart and pierced the soul of Joseph. Here there was no angel to stay his hand. The act must be accomplished, and in performing it Joseph was, indeed, more than a martyr.

Then, too, was that name pronounced over the Divine Infant at which "every knee," as the Apostle tells us, should bow of those who are in Heaven, on earth, and under the earth (*Phil.* 2:10); and it was by the lips of Joseph that it was pronounced. St. Luke only says that His name was called Jesus (*Luke* 2:21), without specifying by whom; but from St. Matthew it would appear that it was Joseph; for the angel had said to him: "Thou shalt call His name Jesus." (*Matt.* 1:21). It was, indeed, no little glory to Joseph to receive an embassage from

---

14. *De Donis S. Joseph,* p. iv. c. i.

Heaven commissioning him to confer this name. Jesus is the Son of the Eternal Father; to the Eternal Father, therefore, it belonged to impose the name; and yet He commissioned St. Joseph to exercise that right in His place. Joseph, says Isidoro Isolano, is the Enos of the New Testament, who first began to invoke the Name of the Lord. (*Gen.* 4:26). That profound theologian, Salmeron, who was present at the Council of Trent, did not scruple to say that in this sole act of giving to Jesus His name was declared the whole paternal office of Joseph, as by the sole act of feeding the sheep of Christ was signified the full power and jurisdiction of Peter over the Church. Whence Isidoro Isolano draws the conclusion that Joseph in God's sight is superior to all the other saints, because no other was exalted to so high a dignity.

Chapter XXXII

The Adoration of the Magi.

JESUS was visited and adored first by the poor and simple, the despised of this world, which loves grandeur and looked for a Messias who was to come in kingly state. Yet He was not to want the homage of the rich, the noble, and the great. After the shepherds were to come the Kings. The Epiphany, that is, the Manifestation of Christ to the Gentiles in the persons of the holy Magi, was always for us, the descendants of Gentiles, a very joyous and consoling mystery, reminding us of our vocation to the True Faith. It has been called, indeed, the Christmas Day of the Gentiles. All the Fathers in their homilies to the people spoke of it with great eloquence, and with ardent love; and the memory of it has been held in singular reverence throughout the Christian world. At Rome especially its octave is celebrated with great pomp.

St. Matthew's account of the coming of the Magi is contained in a few simple words: "When Jesus, therefore, was born in Bethlehem of Juda, in the days of King Herod, behold there came wise men from the East to Jerusalem, saying, Where is he that is born King of the Jews? For we have seen his star in the East, and are come to adore him." (*Matt.* 2:1, 2).

The question naturally arises as to who were these wise men, or Magi, what were their names, whence had they come, and what had been the motive of their journey? It has been the commonly received opinion that

they were men skilled in astronomical science, who
watched the movement of the stars; and, as St. Leo
says, it was not possible in those days for any to dedicate themselves to that science save those who held
the highest rank in society, men adorned with wisdom,
and on that account rulers amongst their people. That
such were the Magi there can be no doubt, and hence
they are called indiscriminately wise men and kings.
They were, in fact, so many little kings in the different regions from which they came. We have an example of this kind of sovereignty in the five kings whom
Abraham, with his three hundred and eighteen followers, defeated, rescuing Lot from their hands. (*Gen.* 14:14-
16). The Magi are, accordingly, always styled kings by
the ancient Fathers. St. Leo, St. Augustine, St. Jerome,
St. Hilarius, St. Cesarius, and others, all give them this
title. Tradition is invariable as to their being three in
number; so much so, that Calmet calls this opinion the
common and universal opinion of the Church. We may
see this truth expressed in sacred sculpture and pictures prior to the time of St. Leo, where the Magi represented as adoring the Divine Infant are always three;
and, indeed, we see this indicated in Scripture itself
by the three distinct gifts which they offered—gold,
frankincense, and myrrh. (*Matt.* 2:11).

We do not find their names mentioned in the early
writers; but they must have been handed down traditionally, since the Venerable Bede says that they were called
Gaspar, Baldassar, and Melchior. The churches of
Cologne and of Milan have constantly venerated them
under these names; and it is under these names that
they are to this day known to the faithful.

As to the motive cause of their journey, we must
remember how, fifteen centuries before, the prophet
Balaam was sent for by King Balak to curse Israel, and,
having mounted a hill, whence he beheld the Hebrews
encamped in the desert, seized by the Spirit of God, he
began instead to bless them, exclaiming, "How beautiful are thy tabernacles, O Jacob, and thy tents, O Israel!

. . . I shall see him, but not now: I shall behold him, but not near. A star shall rise out of Jacob, and a sceptre shall spring up from Israel." (*Num.* 24:5, 17). The holy Magi were well acquainted with this prediction, which had been preserved in their country; and since, as we have said, they were constant observers of the heavenly bodies, scarcely had they noted on the night of the Nativity the appearance of a new star of extraordinary splendor, when they believed that they beheld the fulfillment of Balaam's prophecy, and that this luminary announced the birth of the great King. This observation, and the conviction resulting therefrom, came to the three kings separately at the same time; for they must necessarily have been apart from each other, residing in the several districts which they ruled. All three, however, beholding the star simultaneously, and simultaneously illuminated by divine grace, understood that it announced the birth of the promised Redeemer, and forthwith set out to follow its guidance. Thus, we may believe they met and prosecuted their road together, with their respective trains of dromedaries, and with their eyes fixed aloft upon this wondrous star, which was not, like the other luminaries, in the distant vault of heaven, but in mid-air above their heads.[1] We cannot, indeed, conceive of it otherwise, if its movement was to act as a guide to the direction they were to take.

The Evangelist tells us that these three wise men came from the East, but does not specify their country. Opinions have consequently varied on this subject; but the most probable, and the most generally received, is that they came from Idumea and from Arabia Felix, near to which are Saba, Madian, and Epha. There are several reasons in its favor, and it has the authority of many ancient Fathers—St. Justin, Tertullian, St. Cyprian, St. Epiphanius, and others. Idumea and Arabia are truly eastward as regards Bethlehem; in Arabia was uttered the prophecy of Balaam, called hither by

---

1. St. Thomas, *Summa*, p. iii. q. xxxvi. a. 7.

the King of Moab; and Moab, as St. Jerome observes, is a province of Arabia; it would retain, therefore, a vivid remembrance of the prediction. Arabia also abounds in gold, frankincense, and myrrh, the gifts offered by the Magi as the products of their country. Here, then, would have been the beginning of the fulfillment of prophecies which await a much fuller accomplishment: "The kings of the Arabians and of Saba shall bring gifts; to him shall be given of the gold of Arabia." (*Ps.* 71:10, 15). "The dromedaries of Madian and Epha, all they from Saba shall come, bringing gold and frankincense." (*Is.* 60:6).

That the kings set out as soon as they saw the star, and that the star appeared at the moment of Christ's birth, may be gathered from the words of the Evangelist: "When Jesus was born in Bethlehem, there came wise men from the East." He does not say, "in those days," allowing a certain interval, but gives us to understand that these holy men suffered no delay to intervene; they made straight for Jerusalem, the capital of Judea, where they might assuredly expect to find the newborn King of the Jews whom they had come to adore. But, as they approached Jerusalem, the star suddenly disappeared. The miraculous light was withdrawn; but God had not left them deprived of guidance. They entered the city, enquiring, "Where is he that is born King of the Jews, for we have seen His star in the East, and are come to adore Him"; but they could get no reply. Instead of joy, Jerusalem was filled with perturbation and dismay. The one absorbing idea, doubtless, was the fear of the jealousy of the tyrant Herod, when this report of a competitor for his throne should reach his ears, which it presently did: "and King Herod, hearing this, was troubled, and all Jerusalem with him." (*Matt.* 2:3). Miserable blindness of God's own people! These Magi came from afar to seek in Judea the King, the Messias, whom the Jews themselves neither sought nor recognized in their own land. Yet they had at hand the means of recognizing Him had they desired it, and could even point the way which none of them cared to follow.

Herod, concealing his fears, assembled the chief priests and scribes, and asked of them where Christ should be born. They gave him the true reply, quoting the prophecy of Micheas. (*Mich.* 5:2). Herod then called the Magi privately, and made minute enquiries of them as to the time when the star appeared, and bade them, when they had found the Infant, to return and tell him, that he, too, might go and adore Him. When the kings issued from Jerusalem, and were taking the road to Bethlehem, the star, which had disappeared when they entered the city, again shone forth; at which, the Evangelist says, "they rejoiced with exceeding great joy." The spot where they again beheld it was at a well about half-way between Jerusalem and Bethlehem, which is still called the Well of the Star, or the Well of the Three Kings. They no longer needed a guide, for the star, as the Evangelist says, "went before them, until it came and stood over where the child was." (*Matt.* 2:7-10). Maria d'Agreda saw it in vision enter the grotto, and not disappear until it had rested over the head of Jesus, and had dissolved into a luminous aureole of light encompassing Him. It had done its work, and had brought the holy pilgrims to the feet of the Infant God, enthroned on His mother's knee, as we may believe, for the Evangelist says: "They found the Child with Mary His mother," not meaning thereby to exclude the presence of Joseph, but simply to indicate that He was in His mother's arms when the Magi, who were divinely illuminated with the knowledge of the mystery, found Him and fell down before Him, adoring Him and presenting their gifts.

Some have seen in St. Luke's employment of the phrase "entering into the house" a proof that the Holy Family had removed from the cave of the Nativity into a house in the city, but no such inference can be drawn from the use of a word which in Scripture we find indiscriminately applied to all the habitations of living beings, including even those of birds and beasts. Hence in the Psalms we find the "highest of the trees of the field" spoken of as the "house of the heron." (*Ps.* 103:18). But the authority of St. Jerome, who lived in the holy places, and is the surest witness of the sacred traditions which had been there preserved, ought to be alone sufficient to remove all doubt on the question. Writing to Marcella, a Roman matron, and speaking of the grotto of Bethlehem, he says: "Behold, in this little hole in the earth was born the Creator of the Heavens; here He was wrapped in swaddling clothes, here visited by the shepherds, here pointed out by the star, here adored by the Magi."[2] St. Augustine, St. John Chrysostom, not to speak of other Fathers and Doctors, are of the same opinion, which the learned Suarez also maintains as the commonest. Indeed, the Church herself sings on the feast of the Epiphany, and through the whole octave, "Today the star brought the Magi to the crib." The devout feelings of the faithful certainly echo the Church's tradition, and they cannot reckon for nothing. Even had they less solid warrant than they can lay claim to in this instance, they are, as we may say, the passive voice of the Church. For the God-Man, the King of the Universe, to be born in what St. Jerome forcibly describes as "a hole in the earth" is, we know, the setting forth of a great mystery—the mystery of His humiliation and abasement, as also of the lesson of poverty and self-denial which He came to teach, and by which He was to rebuke and condemn the pride of the world. Mary and Joseph knew this well. Nor can we suppose that for mere accommodation's sake they would remove from their lowly and symbolic "hole in the rock" as soon as the diminished concourse of strangers at Bethlehem rendered it possible to find shelter in an ordinary house. This, at least, is not an idea which recommends itself to Christmas devotion. It clings to the stable and the crib. Here Our Lord received the adoration of the shep-

---

2. *Epist.* xvii. *ad Marcellam.*

herds, figures of His chosen people: this is certain; and here, also, we may well feel sure, He received the homage of the Kings of the East, representatives of the Gentiles, and not in a hired lodging. St. John Chrysostom speaks of their not being scandalized in that they found nothing of this world's greatness, but only this narrow cabin, mean crib, and a poor mother, in order that we may learn that they came, not to honor a mere man, but to adore a God Incarnate, the Author of all good.[3]

Many even believe that the Virgin did not leave the grotto of the Nativity until the forty days of her prescribed retirement after childbirth were accomplished, when she went to Jerusalem to present her Son in the Temple, and submit herself to the rite of purification. Be this as it may, the adoration of the Magi preceded the Presentation by many days, and we may therefore confidently rest on the Church's tradition that on the sixth of January, that is, twelve days after the birth of the Divine Infant, the Magi adored Him in the stable of Bethlehem where He was born. This period of twelve days allows ample time for the journey of the Kings from Arabia, including their brief pause at Jerusalem. It is true that some who have held that the Kings came from very distant regions of the East, which would have rendered it impossible for them to have arrived twelve days after the Nativity, have referred their visit to a later period, and have supposed it to take place a year and twelve days after the birth of Jesus. But this opinion seems to involve several insurmountable difficulties, to overcome which as many gratuitous suppositions must be accepted, always a strong objection when it is question of proving an alleged fact; and it must be confessed that it seems to jar not a little with all our devotional ideas, and to break up, so to say, the cluster of beautiful mysteries which gather round the Birth of the world's Redeemer and adorn our Christmas festivity, when we love to gaze upon Him reigning from the

---

3. *Hom.* viii. *in Matthaeum.*

Crib, as hereafter He was to reign from the Cross. To
the two only reasons which might appear to militate
plausibly in its favor, we shall briefly allude anon.

As it especially regards the honor of our saint, we
must not pass over in complete silence the opinion of
some that Joseph was not present at the adoration of
the Magi, because he is not mentioned as being so. But
surely this omission cannot be thus regarded. How much
have the Evangelists omitted as regards Mary, the
Mother of Jesus; how much as regards Jesus Himself!
St. Matthew does not say that Joseph was not present,
and it seemed scarcely necessary to state that he was
present. Where should he be? And why should he be
absent? There was no need to conceal or put him out
of sight from fear of misapprehension on the part of
the Magi. Their very gifts prove that they knew the
mystery of the Incarnation, and that it was a God-Man
to whom they had come to do honor. Gold they offered
as to their king, incense to their God, and myrrh to
His sacred humanity, which He had assumed to Himself that He might by His Passion and death redeem
a fallen world. The Fathers and the Doctors of the
Church are all agreed that, while outwardly guided by
the light of the star, they were inwardly illuminated
by the Holy Spirit. If anything is to be concluded from
the silence of the Evangelist concerning St. Joseph, it
can only be a tribute to his humility. We may, indeed,
imagine that when the kings entered he withdrew into
the background, for Joseph ever sought to hide himself, that the divinity of Jesus and the glory of his
immaculate Virgin Spouse should alone be manifested.
And does it not seem as if his humble desire had been
seconded by the Evangelists? He is mentioned by them
all; it could not be otherwise; but it is worthy of notice
that not a syllable of his is recorded by them. Mysterious silence, symbol and token of his profound humility! But tradition has recorded what the Evangelist
failed to mention; namely, his presence at the visit of
the Magi. St. John Chrysostom, speaking of the sor-

rows and the joys of St. Joseph, says that the grief he had felt upon learning that the ferocious Herod had been troubled, and all Jerusalem with him, on hearing of the birth of this new King was succeeded by great joy on beholding the star coming to rest on the head of the Divine Infant, and the adoration of the Magi. In all the sculptures and pictures of the early times of the Church representing this mystery we see the figure of our saint, a little behind Mary, leaning on his flowering staff, in rapt contemplation of the glory of the Divine Child; and one of the most learned and diligent historians of all that appertains to the life and worship of St. Joseph boldly asserts that it must be regarded as an undoubted truth that he was present when the Magi came to visit the Infant Jesus and offer Him their mystical gifts.[4] After adoring their God and King, and paying their homage to His august Mother, they turned, no doubt, with loving reverence to Joseph, honoring in him the head of the Holy Family, appointed by the Eternal Father to represent His paternity; and to his care they would consign the precious treasures they had brought.

We are unwilling to believe that these holy pilgrims, who had come so far, and for so high an object, would have returned immediately; and, though Scripture only records their arrival, adoration, and departure, it seems probable, as with the shepherds, that their visit to the cave was not a solitary one, their attendants, with the dromedaries, finding accommodation in Bethlehem, where the influx of strangers had now ceased. If Holy Church celebrates her greater feasts with octaves, and, in the case of the greatest, continues her Alleluias much longer, may we not well conceive that the devotion of the Magi, who were not commemorating a feast, but keeping it in very deed at its glorious origin, was extended over several days? If so, their delay may have been a Providential dispensation by which the execu-

---

4. Trombelli, *Vita e Culto de S. Giuseppe,* p. i. c. xxii.

tion of Herod's murderous purpose was suspended. The hypocritical tyrant had enjoined them to return to him; he would wait, therefore, until he had received from them certain and accurate information as to where to find his intended victim, and would probably take no step until he had dismissed them to their own country, ignorant of his design. Time may thus have been afforded for Our Lady's accomplishment at Jerusalem of the rite of purification. Whether any misgivings as to compliance with Herod's injunction arose in the minds of the Magi we do not know. It would seem that they could hardly be long in Judea without hearing of some of his deeds of violence and blood; and if, as St. John Chrysostom says, it was one of St. Joseph's sorrows to learn how Herod and all Jerusalem with him were troubled at hearing of the birth of the King, he can hardly have been silent on the subject when it became question of the Magi's return. Be this as it may, we may well feel assured that these holy men, so remarkable for their faithful correspondence with divine light, did not fail to seek by fervent prayer to learn the will of God; and that will, the Gospel tells us, was made known to them in a dream. "Having received an answer in sleep that they should not return to Herod, they went back another way into their own country." (*Matt.* 2:12).

We hear no more in Scripture of the Magi. Whether they subsequently heard of the preaching of Jesus and the wonders He wrought we are ignorant; but of this we may be certain, that, if God had called them again, they would have revisited Judea as promptly as before, to confess and adore Him. Certain it is that their faith did not remain idle in them. They performed the Apostolic work of preparing their people for embracing the truth; and, after the Ascension of our Lord, the Apostle Thomas, we are told, ordained them bishops in their own country, where they co-operated admirably in the extension of the Church, making a holy end, full of years and of merits. The Bollandists say that Melchior died at the age of a hundred and sixteen, Gaspar at the age of a hundred and nine, and Baldassar at that of a hundred and twelve, about the middle of the first century. From Arabia, where they died, St. Helen, mother of Constantine, transported their relics to Constantinople; from thence they were transferred, Constantine still reigning, to Milan, where they were deposited in the church of St. Eustorgius. Finally, in the year 1162, Frederic Barbarossa, having taken and spoiled Milan, gave them to Raynold, Archbishop of Cologne, who placed them in the church of St. Peter, where to this day they still repose, and receive, as for centuries they have done, the veneration of the faithful.

Chapter XXXIII

Purification of the Blessed Virgin and Presentation of Jesus in the Temple.

THE Eternal Word, when born into the world, willed to conceal the splendors of His Divinity under His human nature, but not to such a degree as to prevent some flashes of its glory from illuminating His nativity and the first days of His life on earth, so that those who did not recognize Him as their God would be inexcusable. In His lowly crib He received the conjoined testimony of Heaven and of earth. Angels and men came to adore Him; the stars of the firmament and the beasts of the field gave witness to Him as the Creator and Lord of all things. The first few Gospel pages which speak of His infancy are a succession of contrasts or alternations between abasement and glorification. No sooner have the Kings of the East and their trains departed than we find Mary and Joseph making preparations for her, the Immaculate, to go to Jerusalem to receive the rite of purification after childbirth, designed for the fallen daughters of Eve, who conceive in sin and bring forth in sorrow, whereas Mary's divine conception and joyous delivery had only enhanced the glory of her pure and spotless nature. Our Blessed Lady, however, would claim no exemption, but would imitate her Son, who had submitted to the law of circumcision ordained for sinners. By so doing she also gave an example of obedience to the established law of God; she paid honor to it, and removed all occasion of

254

scandal. This rite of purification was to be accompanied by the oblation and redemption, for a few sicles, (*Num.* 3:47), of her Firstborn Son,[1] of Him who had come to redeem the whole world by the priceless offering of His own Precious Blood. It might have been imagined that the gifts of the Magi would have enabled Joseph and Mary to present the offering of the rich, but they were not minded to apply them to this purpose. They made the offering of the poor, the two turtledoves, and it is supposed that they divided what the Kings had brought between their indigent neighbors and the Temple of God at Jerusalem.

The morning of the fortieth day saw them preparing to leave the grotto, which had become a place sacred in their eyes. Possibly God may have favored them with a divine prescience that, having been consecrated by the presence of the Incarnate Word, and sanctified by so many heavenly mysteries, it was never to fall again into a like neglect, but, tended by the piety of the faithful, was afterwards to see a sanctuary raised over it which was to become a center of pilgrimage to the whole Christian world. Mary and Joseph, then, went forth, Mary bearing in her arms her Divine Son, and Joseph leading the ass laden with the few things which they carried with them, including the gifts for the Temple. As they cannot have been ignorant that they had become objects of search to the suspicious Herod, there was the more merit in this act of obedience to the Law, as fear might have suggested a speedy return into Galilee. But Mary and her holy spouse never acted on the impulse of feeling or passion. They followed God's guidance, and committed the consequences to Him. Joseph, to whom it appertained to direct all the movements of the Holy Family, was himself a docile instrument in God's hands.

---

1. The expression "firstborn" among the Hebrews, it need scarcely be observed, did not imply that there were subsequent children. When all the firstborn were smitten in Egypt no one imagines that such as were the only sons of their parents were exempted. There is a sense, however, in which Jesus is called, and is indeed, "the firstborn among many brethren." (*Rom.* 8:29). Of these He, on the Cross, made Mary the mother, in the person of St. John, the beloved disciple.

That some human fears for the safety of his precious charge must at times have pressed painfully on his tender heart we may well suppose, without detracting from his merit; nay, they even added to it. He would, doubtless, also in the same human way, derive some consolation from the reflection that, now that the Kings had returned without communicating to Herod the information he required, the very poverty and obscurity of himself and his blessed spouse would be a shield to her and to the Child, little imagining the sweeping massacre which the cruel tyrant would adopt to make sure of the newborn King not escaping destruction. But his great consolation and the never-failing source of his trust was the protecting arm of Providence.

Mary, out of reverence to her Divine Son, whom she was carrying to present as an oblation to the Eternal Father, wished to make the journey on foot, and even (so says Maria d'Agreda) to perform it barefoot; but this Joseph would not permit, and she obeyed him without remonstrance. Wearied by the way, when they had passed the Well of the Star, or of the Three Kings, Joseph besought her to rest herself under the friendly shade of a lordly terebinth, or turpentine-tree. Tradition has faithfully preserved this fact, and a beautiful legend attaches to it, that the tree bent its branches at the approach of Jesus to honor in Him the God of Nature. Pilgrims, from the earliest ages of the Church, used devoutly to kiss it, in memory of its having sheltered the Mother and the Divine Child;[2] and in that tree we may see a figure both of Jesus and of Mary, for Wisdom, in Ecclesiasticus, says, "I have stretched out my branches as the turpentine-tree, and my branches are of honor and grace." (*Eccles.* 24:22). After resting a while, they resumed their way.

This journey from Bethlehem to the Holy City was the most solemn and sublime procession which earth

---

2. For sixteen centuries this tree under which Mary rested was believed to have a hidden virtue in it, and to have effected a multitude of cures. (Martorelli, *Terra Santa,* cap. vii. p. 155.) The tree was destroyed in the seventeenth century, but the memory of the spot where it stood has been preserved.

had ever beheld, or which had ever entered the gates of the Temple, poor and mean as was its outward appearance, for it was accompanied invisibly by troops of angels, as a guard of honor; and how great is the splendor of these glorious princes of Heaven may be imagined when we remember that the sight of one alone, sitting on the stone at Christ's monument, made the Roman soldiers who watched it become as dead men for fear. His countenance, St. Matthew tells us, was like lightning, and his raiment of dazzling whiteness. (*Matt.* 28:3, 4). What, then, must have been the refulgence of thousands of these exalted beings! But, if their majesty was great, words fail when we consider the unspeakable grandeur of which they were only the attendants: the King of everlasting ages, His mother the Queen of angels and of men, and her holy spouse who was honored with the title and office of father to the Son of God Himself. What Holy Church thinks of this august procession—and where can we find a safer guide than the spirit of our mother, the Church, embodied in her ritual—is shown by the procession she organizes to solemnize what we call Candlemas Day, once a day of obligation when England was Catholic—the thurifer going before with incense burning, the cross borne aloft by the sub-deacon following, then the clergy in their order, and the faithful—all, clergy, acolytes, and people, carrying lighted candles which have been previously blessed by the celebrant. And let us listen to the beautiful antiphon which is intoned as soon as the solemn words, "Procedamus in pace," have been pronounced by the deacon, and the response, "In nomine Christi," has been given by the choir: "Adorna thalamum tuum, Sion, et suscipe Regem Christum; amplectere Mariam, quae est celestis porta; ipsa enim portat Regem gloriae novi luminis; subsistit Virgo, adducens manibus Filium ante luciferum genitum, quem accipiens Simeon in ulnis suis, praedicavit populis Dominum esse vitae et mortis, et Salvatorem mundi"—"Adorn thy chamber, O Sion, and receive Christ the King; embrace Mary, who is the celestial gate; for she bears the glorious King of the new light; remaining ever a Virgin, she brings in her hands the Son begotten before the day-star, whom Simeon, receiving into his arms, proclaimed to the people to be the Lord of life and death, and Saviour of the world."

Among the devout Israelites who were waiting at that time for the Redeemer's advent was a holy old man named Simeon. His longing desire and heart's prayer was that he should behold that day. His prayer had been granted, and he had received an answer from the Holy Ghost that "he should not see death before he had seen the Christ of the Lord." Simeon was not a priest, but he was truly a prophet. "The Holy Ghost was in him" are the expressive words of Scripture; (*Luke* 2:25-27) "in him," making his soul a palace of light, and acting as a lamp to direct his ways. "Thy word," says David, "is a lamp to my feet and a light to my paths." (*Ps.* 118:105). Of such a man no act is fortuitous or meaningless; he "walks at large," with the freedom of those who have escaped from the tyranny of self, because he has sought God's commandments, not his own will and pleasure. God has become his inward guide; and so the Gospel says that Simeon "came by the Spirit into the Temple." This whole Psalm, indeed, admirably describes the mind of such a man as Simeon, who has taken the testimonies of the Lord as an inheritance forever because they are the joy of his heart, and whose soul has fainted after His salvation.[3] The law which the Virgin came to fulfill prescribed three things: 1) the purification of the mother; 2) the offering and redemption of the firstborn son; the oblation of a lamb by the rich, and of two turtledoves or two young pigeons by the poor. At this rite the husband must be present also, joining in the offering. When, therefore, as the Evangelist says, "His parents brought in the Child Jesus to do for Him according to the cus-

---

3. *Psalm* 118:45, 81, 111. The Arabs give Simeon the title of Siddik (he who verifies), because he bore witness to the coming of the true Messias in the person of Jesus, the Son of Mary.—D'Herbelet, *Bibliothèque Orientale*, tom. iii. p. 266.

tom of the Law" (*Luke* 2:27), Simeon at once knew Him
by that inward revelation which brings assurance with
it; not as the shepherds knew Him, from the miraculous vision of Angels and from hearing their heavenly
announcement, but by the direct voice of the Spirit of
God, who was ever abiding in him; and so "he took Him
into his arms and blessed God," and poured forth from
the depth of his soul that canticle of the "Nunc dimittis" which we know so well.

St. Luke says: "His father and mother wondered at
these things which were spoken concerning Him"
(*Luke* 2:33); not that they did not know these high
mysteries already, but to hear the great works of God
published is ever to hear and know them afresh; and
then the intuitive knowledge which God had given to
this holy man, without the intervention of any sensible prodigy, was matter for deep and devout admiration; moreover, Simeon was the first to proclaim
publicly that the Redeemer was come, come to His
Temple, as the prophet Aggeas (*Agg.* 2:8, 10) had foretold, rendering its glory greater than that of the first.
The adoring of the shepherds and that of the Kings
of the East had taken place in a secluded cave of the
earth, but the voice which proclaimed the Child "a
light to the revelation of the Gentiles and the glory
of His people Israel" (*Luke* 2:32), sounded in the courts
of the Lord and before His holy altar. If few heard, it
was because few were there, and still fewer attended
to the words spoken to a poor mother and her Babe.
Simeon blessed both Mary and Joseph, but to Mary
alone did he speak of the sign of contradiction which
her Child was to become, and of the sword which was
to pierce her soul (*Luke* 2:34, 35), for Joseph was not
to live to behold the Passion and death of Jesus. When,
indeed, the lance of the centurion pierced His side and
penetrated the agonized soul of the mother, Joseph
was with Him in the Limbo of the Fathers, which had
been transformed into Paradise by His presence. Nevertheless, we may be certain that the holy Patriarch

deeply shared her sorrow when this prophecy, which, no doubt, brought into still more vivid light the prescience she already had of her Son's sufferings, was addressed to her, a prescience which was never to leave her, but amidst all the joys of her maternity was to make her by anticipation the Mother of Dolors. Simeon predicted that Jesus was "set for the fall and for the resurrection of many"; not that He would be the efficient, direct, and positive cause of the ruin of the former, as He is of the salvation of the latter, but only the incidental, indirect, and negative cause; inasmuch as, in order not to perish, they must believe in Jesus, love Jesus, obey Jesus, and they would obstinately refuse to believe in Him, love Him, and obey Him, and would thus be lost eternally. In the same manner would He be a sign of contradiction, in that many would adore Him as God, bless and serve Him faithfully, and many would deny Him and blaspheme Him, and instead of serving Him would prefer to serve the devil, their malicious enemy. This sad presage embittered also the soul of Mary, and was to her a continual martyrdom, which the tender soul of Joseph shared, though his eyes were to be closed in death before their accomplishment began to manifest itself in the hatred and hostility of the Jews against Our Lord. Indeed, it must have been a source of additional poignant grief to his generous and loving heart to know—as he must have known long before his death—that when this prophecy was verified he, the protector of Jesus and Mary, would not be there to defend and console them.

To temper a little the pain inflicted on the hearts of Mary and Joseph by Simeon's prophecy, God directed the steps of an ancient and holy woman into the Temple. It was Anna the Prophetess, the daughter of Phanuel, of the tribe of Aser. After the death of her husband, with whom she had lived seven years, she had made the Temple her continual abode, serving God with fastings and prayers night and day. (*Luke* 2:36, 37). Mary must have been well-known to her; indeed, it is supposed that this venerable woman had been the instructor and trainer of the young maidens brought up within the precincts of God's House. Coming in at the moment when Simeon was restoring the Divine Babe to His mother, she also was ravished in spirit and gave testimony to Him as the true Messias. Nor was her testimony limited to that moment, for we are told that she spoke of Him to all who were looking for the redemption of Israel. But what of the priests of the Lord? As the humble Virgin advanced with her Infant in her arms to perform the three acts prescribed by the Law, was there not one of them to behold in spirit the immense glory with which the presence of the Lord of all, the Orient from on high, the Desired of all nations, was filling the Temple? We do not hear of one. The Virgin placed herself on her knees, having given the Divine Babe to Joseph. Most humble in her aspect, with eyes modestly cast down, her head inclined towards the ground, and her hands joined over her bosom, she awaited the coming of the priest. He came, prayed over her; and thus did she seem to be purified who was herself brighter than the sun, fairer than the moon, and purer than the stars of heaven.

The offering and redemption of the Child followed. As the inner court of the Temple was interdicted to women, Mary remained kneeling, and in her heart and mind accompanying the solemn oblation made of her Divine Son to the Eternal Father, while Joseph, bearing Him in his arms, went into the Court of the Priests to present Him. Jesus, High-Priest according to the order of Melchisedech, enters into His Temple, and the band of Levites who minister there do not hasten to receive Him with reverence, do not surround Him with their homage, do not honor Him even by a look. They had no eyes to see, so He hid His face from them. The unworthiness of the Levitical priesthood God had already declared by the mouth of the prophet Malachias: "The son honoreth the father, and the servant his master: if, then, I be a father, where is My honor? and if I be a master, where is My fear?" (*Mal.* 1:6). And by the same prophet He had exposed the cause of their blindness and irreverence, namely, their covetousness, their pride, and their love of worldly things. Therefore he had declared to those priests, who despised His name, that He had no pleasure in them, and would receive no gifts at their hands.[4] More than thirty years later, with His own divine lips, He was to reprove them for these very vices, and announce to them their approaching rejection: "The kingdom of God shall be taken from you, and given to a nation bringing forth the fruits thereof." (*Matt.* 21:43).

A priest drew nigh to take the Divine Child and offer Him to the Lord; and never had oblation so acceptable been made to God, but, in truth, it was Jesus, Priest and Victim, who, through the Spirit (*Heb.* 9:14) and by the hands of Mary and Joseph, made an unspotted offering of Himself to His Eternal Father. Joseph then paid the small sum of money required, to redeem Him who was the Redeemer of all,[5] and took back the Divine Victim to feed and tend Him, and rear Him up to complete the Sacrifice on Calvary. All that remained now to perform was to offer the doves, the one as a holocaust, the other as a sin-offering. These innocent creatures Joseph consigns to the priest, who ascends with them the steps of the Altar of Holocausts to make the oblation. Mary had accompanied in spirit all these solemn acts of religion; but within this Court of the Priests no sign occurred such as those which had just before marked the arrival of the Holy Family at their entrance into the Temple. Among the priests not a few were courtier-like partisans of Herod; possibly there

---

4. *Malachias* 1:7, 10. The luxury and avarice of the chief priests of Jerusalem was past belief. The pontiffs sent people into the country to take the tithes in granaries, and appropriate them to themselves, which left the inferior priests to die of hunger. At the least remonstrance, the miserable Levites were accused of revolt and insubordination, and delivered up to the Romans. The Governor Felix alone cast forty of them into prison, out of complaisance to the doctors and princes of the synagogue.— *Life of Josephus,* quoted in Orsini's *History of the Blessed Virgin,* chap. xiii.

5. For this reason the Doctors of the Church agree in giving to Joseph, in a certain sense, the title of redeemer of the Redeemer.—Cartagena, lib. xviii. Hom. xiv.

might be some who were hereafter to sit in the Sanhedrim which was to pronounce Jesus guilty of death. Such men were not worthy to behold a ray of the glory of the Lord.

All the ceremonies being completed, Joseph returned to the outer court, and restored the Divine Infant to His mother's arms. Then they departed. If it be true that a portion of the offerings of the Magi had been set apart by them as a gift for the Temple, Joseph will have taken it there alone, secretly and silently, so as to attract no notice. It would have been an inconsistency to allow it to accompany the public offering of the poor which they made; such a display also would not have harmonized with the character which marks all the acts of Mary and Joseph, namely, a profound and retiring humility. It would, moreover, have attracted to them an attention which must have been perilous under present circumstances. The Virgin most prudent and the discreet and thoughtful Joseph, her spouse, were sure to shun carefully any such risk. They came to Jerusalem in obedience to an ordinance of God; in order to perform God's Will natural fears must be laid aside, but when all had been accomplished, the safety of the Divine Infant must have been their one leading thought. It is scarcely probable, therefore, that they remained in the neighborhood of the jealous tyrant longer than was necessary to complete the religious rite which had brought them to Jerusalem, but they will have at once turned their minds, if not their steps, towards the homeward journey.

Chapter XXXIV

A Question of Dates.

BEFORE proceeding farther, it will be well to give some attention to the two chief reasons adduced by those who suppose that the visit of the Magi and the flight into Egypt took place a year later than is commonly believed.

The first is the silence of St. Luke, who, after relating all that occurred in connection with the Purification, says: "And after they had performed all things according to the Law of the Lord, they returned into Galilee, to their city Nazareth" (*Luke* 2:39)—omitting all mention of the flight into Egypt and of the massacre of the Innocents. We should, therefore (they contend), gather from his words that Mary and Joseph returned at once to their home at Nazareth, and that these events all occurred at a later date. But, in the first place, those who attach importance to this argument seem not to perceive that it would prove too much; it oversteps its object, and, in doing so, neutralizes all its force. That St. Luke should omit the account of the flight into Egypt, which is given by St. Matthew, who on his part never alludes to the Purification, is intelligible; but that his history of the Infancy should be irreconcilable with it, and leave no place for it, is not intelligible, for this Evangelist goes on to say: "And the Child grew, and waxed strong, full of wisdom; and the grace of God was in Him. And His parents went every year to Jerusalem at the solemn

264

day of the Pasch" (*Luke* 2:40, 41); and then follows the narration of what took place on one of these occasions, when Jesus was twelve years old. While the exile in Egypt lasted, it is plainly impossible that Mary and Joseph should have gone up every year to keep the Pasch. Where, then, is space left for their abode in Egypt, allowing even for the shortest computation of its length? St. Luke, in this case, would not only have omitted all mention of it at the time to which it is commonly referred, but have put it out of the question, so to say, at any future time. This could not be. If it be urged that, though St. Luke says "every year," this may be understood of every year during which they abode at Nazareth, all account of the exile into Egypt being omitted because St. Matthew had already related it, this contention would apply, and much more legitimately, to the having passed it over at an earlier time. The argument, consequently, would prove too much, or it would prove too little. It would remove no difficulty, and would create others; for instance, an apparent discrepancy with St. Matthew, who plainly connects the visit of the Magi with the Nativity: "When Jesus was born in Bethlehem of Judea, there came wise men from the East to Jerusalem." (*Matt.* 2:1). Moreover, the adoration of the Magi unquestionably took place at Bethlehem. If, therefore, the afore-mentioned supposition be admitted, we shall have to account for the Holy Family's stay at Bethlehem a year later, and that not at the time of the Pasch, which would have led them into its vicinity.

The difficulty which this hypothesis is intended to remove may be met by a much simpler explanation. St. Matthew, as has been observed, makes no mention of the Purification, and from his account we might conclude that the angel appeared to Joseph and bade him fly into Egypt immediately after the departure of the Kings, whereas time must have intervened for the Purification, which could not take place until the fortieth day had been completed; of this St. Matthew takes no notice, but follows up his subject to its close. St. Luke, in like manner, after relating the circumstances attending the Purification, continues his own subject of Mary and Joseph's fulfillment of the prescriptions of the Law and, passing over the interval of the flight into Egypt, records their return to settle in their own city of Nazareth. We have the authority of the great St. Augustine for this view.[1]

Maria d'Agreda has an observation on the subject which is much to the purpose. After saying that the perfect accordance of the two Evangelists had been shown to her, she draws attention to the fact that St. Luke, when speaking of the return of Mary and Joseph to Nazareth, immediately adds the words to which reference has been made: "And the Child grew, and waxed strong, full of wisdom; and the grace of God was in Him." Now all this, she remarks, would not have been manifested until the years of early infancy had been passed; but the observation would naturally find its place after the return from Egypt, when Jesus had attained the age in which children begin to show the full use of reason. At that date, therefore, we may presume, St. Luke takes up and pursues his narrative.

It would be a mistake to judge the Gospel narratives as though they were designed to be independent and complete histories of Our Lord's life. They were apparently written, each of them, with a leading object in view, and relate chiefly the facts which serve to establish it. Moreover, St. Luke, who was evidently and, we might say, necessarily well acquainted with all that had been previously written, introduces fresh facts, while he omits those which St. Matthew and St. Mark had recorded. The same may be observed of the Gospel of St. John, which was written later than the others, and contains much additional matter, while avoiding repetition of what had been narrated by his predecessors. Thus the several Gospels may be said

1. *De Consensu Evangelistarum,* cap. v.

to be supplementary to each other.[2]

The second reason alleged; which at first sight seems plausible, is that when Herod perceived that he had been deluded by the wise men, he sent "and killed all the men-children that were in Bethlehem, and in all the borders thereof, from two years old and under, according to the time which he had diligently enquired of the wise men." (*Matt.* 2:16)—that is, the time when he had learned from them that the star appeared. All children between the age of two years and that date were to be slaughtered. Now, if the Infant was just born, why, it is argued, slay all the children of two years old? Does not this very fact go to prove that, from the information he had obtained, Herod had reason to believe that Jesus might possibly be approaching that age, and was, at least, above one year old? But the question may be reversed. Why, if he believed that the Child was between one and two years of age did he cause the newborn infants to be slain among whom He would not in that case be found? Does it not seem more probable that his jealous suspicions would suggest to him that the star which had summoned the Magi had possibly appeared subsequently to the birth of the Infant; and, as to him the shedding of blood was no more than the spilling of so much water, he would desire to make sure of his victim by including older children in the slaughter? "If," says St. John Chrysostom, "Herod commands the massacre of all children born within two years, let it cause no wonder; because, fear and fury raging in this tyrant, he, from excess of caution and unbridled power to persecute, included a longer time, so that none who had reached that age, and among them especially He on whose account the rest were killed, should escape him."[3]

Local tradition, never to be lightly disregarded, points to Bethlehem as the place where Joseph was in sleep

---

2. As an instance of how one Evangelist will place events in juxtaposition which we know from another Evangelist were separated by other incidents, we might point to St. Mark's account of Our Lord's appearances after His Resurrection, as given in his concluding chapter, especially from the 14th verse to the close.

3. *In Matthaeum,* Hom. vii.

bidden by the angel to take the Child and His mother
and flee into Egypt. The Holy Family, it is said, had
returned thither, not, however, to the cave of the Nativity, but to a small house not far distant, known afterwards as the house of Joseph, near to which was a little
grotto. Tradition has ever preserved in Bethlehem the
memory of this grotto, calling it the Grotto of Milk,
because the Blessed Virgin is said to have often nursed
her Divine Son therein.[4]

Orsini, however, in his *History of the Blessed Virgin,*
advances the opinion, for which he quotes the authority of St. John Chrysostom, that, after they had performed all things according to the Law of the Lord,
they returned into Galilee to their city Nazareth; and
this, with the view of reconciling the words of St. Luke
with St. Matthew's account. At Nazareth, then, he
believes, Joseph received the divine command, and
thence commenced his journey into Egypt, taking Bethlehem on the way. We cannot but think, however, that
in thus disposing of the difficulty created by this apparent discrepancy, far more serious difficulties are created. From Nazareth, where they would have been in
comparative safety, the Holy Family, according to this
account, would have returned to the very focus of danger. The tradition of their having been at Bethlehem
before the flight is too marked, however, for Orsini to
think of setting it aside. "Whatever," he adds, "was the
motive which led Joseph and Mary to the crater of a
volcano, there is no doubt that they stayed there only
a few hours, and that they made haste to reach a mar-
itime town of the Philistines in order to join the first
caravan going to Egypt."[5]

Another difficulty in regard to this view of the return
to Nazareth may be perceived in the time necessarily

---

4. The piety of the faithful afterwards raised an altar within this grotto, where Mass
used to be said every Saturday. The place was held in much veneration by nursing mothers, not Catholic only, but even Mahometan and Hebrew.—Martorelli, *Terra
Santa,* chap. vii. p. 166; Fr. Lavinio da Hamme, *Guida Indicatrice dei Santuari e
Luoghi Storici di Terra Santa,* pp. 342, 343.

5. Chap. xiv.

consumed (about ten days) upon the journey to and from that place. Even supposing, then, that Joseph received the angel's commands immediately on arriving there, this adds considerably to the interval between the departure of the Magi and the massacre of the Innocents. We have reason, therefore, to conclude that the Holy Family after the Presentation returned at once, not to Nazareth, but to Bethlehem.

It may be asked, however, why should Joseph and Mary have returned to Bethlehem after accomplishing all their legal obligations at Jerusalem. It did not lie naturally on their road to Nazareth and made, to all appearance, an unnecessary delay and prolongation of their journey. For this a reason has been suggested which certainly, we cannot but think, has high probability in its favor. Did Joseph and Mary really purpose to return to Nazareth? Had they not rather resolved to settle at Bethlehem? Joseph had taken Mary thither by a Providential dispensation, the compulsory enrollment of every family in the place to which they belonged. Here she had brought forth her Divine Babe; here His birth was celebrated by the Angels of Heaven; here He was adored by the shepherds on the night of His Nativity; here he was circumcised and received His Name of Jesus; and here He was visited and worshiped by the Magi. Might not this constellation of divine mysteries clustering round Bethlehem have appeared in Joseph's eyes as so many signs from God that he should take up his abode in the city of David? There are certain indications in the Gospel itself of such a purpose having been entertained by him. We find later, on the return of the Holy Family from their exile in Egypt, that Joseph was, apparently, not intending to go back to Nazareth, but that, when he arrived on the confines of Judea, and heard that "Archelaus reigned *in Judea* in the room of Herod his father, he was afraid to go thither." It was to Bethlehem, then, that he had probably contemplated taking Mary and Jesus. If he had been on his road to Galilee, this news would not have alarmed him, neither would he have needed the angel's warning, which caused him to "retire into the quarters of Galilee." (*Matt.* 2:22).

To this supposition no slight countenance is given by St. Matthew's observation, "that it might be fulfilled which was said by the prophets: that He shall be called a Nazarite" (*Matt.* 2:23); by which he seems to imply that Joseph had intended to go to Bethlehem, but that his progress was arrested by his fear of Archelaus, and, being warned in sleep, he turned aside to Nazareth, and thus was led unconsciously to fulfill what the prophets had said. Joseph did not go to Nazareth in order to fulfill the prophecy. The prophecy had its fulfillment independently of his will, and from one of those circumstances which escape all human calculation, but have formed part of the Divine counsels.

Chapter XXXV

Flight Into Egypt—Massacre of the Innocents.

ALL things, it has been shown, combine to render it most probable that Joseph, after the Purification, returned to Bethlehem, and with the purpose of settling there, believing that all the signs which had accompanied the Nativity of the Divine Infant marked it as the place befitting Him and agreeable to the will of God signified thereby. If Mary had any inward illumination on the subject she would be silent. Joseph was the head of the Holy Family and its appointed ruler, guide, and provider. They probably left Jerusalem immediately; and, if not on that very night, probably on the next, Joseph was again visited in sleep by the Archangel Gabriel. St. Matthew says, "And after they," that is, the Magi, "were departed, behold an angel of the Lord appeared in sleep to Joseph, saying, Arise and take the Child and His mother, and fly into Egypt, and be there until I shall tell thee. For it will come to pass that Herod will seek the Child to destroy Him." (*Matt.* 2:13).

It is evident that God, having an infinity of means in His power by which He might easily have placed His Son in safety, and shielded Him from Herod's fury, was pleased to choose that which was the greatest abasement to the Saviour, flight, but at the same time the greatest honor to Joseph: an angel was sent by the Eternal Father to convey the commission to him to carry His Son into Egypt. To our short-sighted views it might have appeared more convenient that the Divine Infant should have been borne gently and swiftly through the air by this exalted spirit than that He should have to journey slowly and wearily along the earth in the arms of a man. Nevertheless, God did not confer this office on any of those blessed spirits whom He beheld kneeling in thousands and tens of thousands before His throne, and burning to execute His Will and to render some act of homage and service to the Incarnate Word. To Joseph alone was to belong the glory of preserving a life whose every instant was of incomparably more value than the united lives of all created beings. All men contributed to the death of the Saviour, one alone saved Him from death in His infancy; so that, as to one alone among women, Mary, was He indebted for His life as man, so to one alone among men did He owe its preservation. Thus St. Joseph has been called the saviour of the Saviour, seeing that he saved Him from death by murder and by starvation.

Oh, what a glory was it to this virgin father to clasp in his embrace the Son of God and bear Him away in safety from His persecutor! Truly might we reply with Origen[1] to anyone who should ask why Joseph is called the father of the Saviour, that it is because he gave Him protection against all the dangers of the journey into Egypt. He preserved His life, and thus earned a fresh title to be called His father, inasmuch as the preservation of anything ought to be as highly esteemed as its original production. God commissioned angels to convey prophets and preachers of the Gospel from one place to another, but to Joseph alone did He entrust His Son and the charge of conducting Him to a place of safety. Joseph did not make his journey from Bethlehem to Egypt as rapidly or as easily as did the angel who bore Habacuc from Judea to Babylon, or as St. Philip the Deacon, taken away by the Spirit of the Lord, was transported from the desert road of Gaza to

---

1. *Hom.* viii. *in Lucam.*

Azotus,[2] but this only enhances his glory; because the journey cost him so dear, being full of labors, fatigue, suffering, and peril to his own liberty and even life, undergone to save that of Jesus. More glory had he in carrying the Son of God into Egypt than had the great legislator, Moses, in delivering the people of God from that house of bondage, or than all the angels who contributed to that deliverance, nay, than any of those blessed spirits who announced the Birth of the Incarnate Word, who ministered to Him, and spread a table for Him in the Desert, who comforted Him in His agony, or who watched at His sepulchre to proclaim the glad tidings of His Resurrection.

Out of regard to the higher dignity of Mary we might have thought that the angel would have been sent to her; nevertheless, it was not to her, but to Joseph, that he was bidden to go, that it might be known that he was the recognized head, tutor, guide, governor, and guardian of both Jesus and Mary, and that he it was who was responsible for their safety. The angel, moreover, does not say, Tell Mary to take her Son, but bids him take the Child, signifying that to him is committed the charge of conveying Him into Egypt; and, not the Child only, but the Mother. What an unspeakable honor did God thus confer on Joseph, in that He confided to him entirely the safety of His most beloved and precious treasures, Jesus and Mary! The angel adds, "Fly into Egypt"; he does not say, "Fly with them," for Joseph is the head and representative of the Holy Family. He is, as it were, one with Jesus and Mary, he is inseparable from them. Where Joseph is, there also are Jesus and Mary. Joseph, belonging to the order of the Hypostatic Union, forms, in fact, with Jesus and Mary that glorious Triad on earth which represents the Most August Trinity in Heaven.

Many reasons may be given why it was decreed that

---

2. Daniel 14:32-38; Acts 8:39, 40. Cornelius à Lapide says that the agent employed was probably the same angel who had bidden Philip take the road to Gaza (v. 26); and for this he cites, as his authority, among others, St. Jerome *in Isaiam,* lxiii. 9.

the Son of God should seek refuge in Egypt. St. Matthew mentions only one, after his custom of showing how all prophecy was accomplished in Jesus: "that it might be fulfilled which was spoken by the prophet, Out of Egypt have I called My Son." (*Osee* 11:1; *Matt.* 2:15). Isaias and Ezechiel had also predicted that the Saviour should enter into Egypt, and that the idols should fall down at His presence. (*Is.* 19:1; *Ezech.* 30:13). We may discern other reasons in the abode which the patriarchs, Abraham, Jacob, and Joseph, made in that land. The destinies of the chosen people had, indeed, been intimately bound up with Egypt for centuries; and we may well believe that God had a purpose of mercy towards that country in decreeing that the Holy Family should seek refuge there, thus illuminating and sanctifying those regions, which were afterwards to give so many martyrs to the Faith, and to be peopled with so many holy anchorites, of whom St. Chrysostom says that there were not in Heaven so many constellations as Egypt contained habitations of hermits and holy virgins.

The angel bade Joseph remain there until he should bring him word again. This uncertainty must have been, naturally, very painful to our saint, but, perfect model as he was of obedience, he asked not a single question. How many difficulties and objections the great lawgiver, Moses, made before he would consent to undertake the work of bringing back the people of Israel from that same land, although the Lord promised to be with him and do signs and wonders! Joseph is bid to fly, no help is promised to him, no directions are given to him, and he says not a word upon receiving this unexpected commission. St. Francis de Sales observes[3] that herein the angel treats Joseph as a perfect religious; he simply says: Take the Child and His Mother, and fly into Egypt. How many questions might he not have asked! It was then dark night; was he to wait till day should dawn? To what part of Egypt was he to go? Was he to

---

3. *Entretien,* iii.

bear the Infant in his arms during the whole journey, or permit Mary to share that charge with him? Alone, ignorant of the way; exposed to danger from wild beasts and robbers; in the winter season; unprovided with means; to have to pass into foreign lands, not knowing what reception they would meet with—all this might have prompted much anxious enquiry. But Joseph was silent. He had heard, and that sufficed. So he arose, and did as the angel had bidden him: he took the Child and His mother by night, and fled into Egypt. St. Peter Chrysologus says that this journey was so arduous that the very angels were struck with wonder when they beheld the Saviour required to make it.[4] To face all these evils St. Joseph at once generously devoted himself, setting out at the very moment he received the command, although, as Cardinal Cajetan observes, the angel did not precisely bid him fly during the night. Even this one circumstance of his life must show how singular and perfect was the obedience of Joseph. Albert the Great believes that it would be impossible for anyone to exhibit more readiness of body and spirit than did our saint, not tarrying to make provision or enquiry, nor even questioning the angel as to the road he was to take. So perfect was his docility to the divine command that a Doctor of modern times pronounces it to be an especial work of the Spirit of God.[5] There is something very significant in the brief and, as we might call them, decisive words in which the Evangelists always state the obedience of Joseph. No careful reader of the Gospels can fail to notice this. What they leave unsaid strikes us as much as what they say. There are volumes for meditation and instruction in those short passages, and they seem to make us understand our saint better than the most detailed description would have done.

Joseph hastened to apprise Mary. Perhaps she already knew all by interior revelation; but, whether or no,

---

4. *Sermo* cli. *De Fuga Christi in Ægyptum.*
5. Claudius Guilliadus *in Matthaeum,* cap. x.

Mary's heart was always prepared for suffering, and her will to conform itself to the expressed will of God; she never complained, she never uttered a lamentation. She had soon collected the few things they would carry with them. Joseph laid them on the meek ass, their constant companion and assistant, and, as we may believe, added some of the necessary implements of his trade. Then he besought Mary to place the Divine Infant in his arms, and pressing Him to his bosom, and folding his mantle over Him to shield and conceal Him and at the same time to protect Him from the inclement blast, he went forth, with his august spouse, in the darkness and silence of the night. But which way were they to turn? To ask their road would be a peril. He who sent a star to direct the steps of the Magi, and who led Israel in the desert by a pillar of cloud in the day and a pillar of fire at night, would be sure not to leave the Holy Family to make this long and dangerous journey alone and deprived of guidance. We may, then, readily believe—it would be difficult not to believe—that Mary's guard of honor, the angels appointed to be her attendants, were again visible, if not always, yet in the hour of need and doubt, to throw light upon their path.

It is supposed that they took the direction of Gaza; and, if so, they passed near Hebron. Mary must have longed to communicate with her cousin Elizabeth, that she might set her on her guard against any risk for the safety of her son John, but their journey allowed of no delay, however short. "Take the Child and His mother, and fly into Egypt": such was the command addressed to Joseph, and it would admit of no reserve. But Mary may have commissioned one of her guardian angels to bear a warning message to the house of Zachary.

That vale of Hebron was rich in fruits, in figs, vines, olives, and pomegranates, as it was also in pious memories. It was there that the explorers of the land sent by Moses gathered rich figs and that marvellous bunch of grapes which required two men to bear it, as a sample of the produce of the land. (*Num.* 13:24). It was also on the hills of Hebron that, according to Hebrew tradition, Noe planted his first vine. (*Gen.* 9:20). Now He was passing who was to be trodden in the winepress of God's anger against sin, and to pour forth all His Precious Blood as the wine of our salvation. Not venturing to enter the city, the Holy Family stopped to rest in a country-shed on the summit of a hill about a mile to the north of it. The spot has preserved to this day the memory of the Mother of God by bearing her name, which the Arabs still give it. It has also been a place of pious pilgrimage to Catholics.[6] If Elizabeth and Zachary were able to see their holy relatives as they passed, it must have been here. We love to dwell on the possibility, and on the joy which it must have caused to the infant Baptist to behold again, and adore, and interiorly converse with Jesus, the God-Man, of whom he was the chosen Precursor and whom he was to be the first to proclaim as the Lamb of God, who taketh away the sins of the world. The meeting, if it took place, must have been very brief, for the fugitives would pause for repose no longer than necessity imperatively demanded, until they had passed the frontiers of Herod's dominions and set foot in the land of the Philistines.

Scarcely had the Holy Family left the confines of Bethlehem when cries and shrieks began to rend the air. Herod, furious at seeing himself deceived by the Magi, had sent forth his cruel order, which his satellites hastened to fulfill to the utmost, and even beyond the limits of his orders. Troops of soldiers had entered Bethlehem, and, with drawn swords in their hands, had burst into every house and butchered all the male infants, tearing them from their cradles, and from the arms of their distracted mothers, whose screams filled the city and every household with consternation. Whoever attempted resistance was slain. Concealment was

---

6. Martorelli, *Terra Santa,* cap. x. p. 197.

the only resource for the unhappy women; but where and how conceal their babes, whose innocent wailings betrayed their hiding-place? "They knew not how to be silent," says St. Augustine, "because as yet they knew not how to fear."[7] From Bethlehem the carnage spread to the surrounding villages. The ground reeked with blood, and was strewn with the mangled corpses of these innocents, and the whole country was filled with desolation and mourning. "Then," says St. Matthew, "was fulfilled that which was spoken by Jeremias the prophet: A voice in Rama was heard, lamentation and great mourning; Rachel bewailing her children, and would not be comforted, because they are not." (*Matt.* 2:17, 18; *Jer.* 31:15). Rama was a city of the tribe of Benjamin, on the borders of Bethlehem, and the prophet represents Rachel as weeping for her children, not because all these slaughtered infants were actually her descendants, but because, being buried close to Bethlehem, she had acquired, so to say, the rights and the name of mother of these babes.[8]

Herod's cruel order was limited to children who were not above two years old; but how many may have perished who had passed that age! The male children alone were to be the victims of his fury; but how many female infants may have been also recklessly slaughtered! How many mothers were slain by the same sword that pierced their babes lying on their bosoms! How many fathers and brothers, casting themselves between the children and the armed soldiers to protect them, mingled their blood with that of these martyred innocents! The executioners swept through all the neighboring villages, and, tradition tells us, reached even Hebron, the infant Baptist being saved by his mother, who, as soon as she caught a sight of Herod's soldiers, ran with him to the top of the mount still called "St. John on the mountain," where a rock is shown which miraculously opened to conceal the mother and her son from their murder-

---

7. *Sermo* i. *de Innocentibus.*
8. St. Jerome, lib. i. *Comment. in Matthaeum,* cap. ii.

ous pursuers.[9] Macrobius says that in this manner even
a son of Herod perished who had been put out to nurse
at Bethlehem. Other accounts state three; which made
Caesar Augustus, the Roman Emperor, exclaim, when
he heard of this brutal act, that it would be better to
be a pig than Herod's son, since in the capacity of a
Jewish proselyte he would spare swine, while he put
his sons to death. Happy sons, if so indeed it was, to
be numbered among the Holy Innocents, instead of growing up to tread, perhaps, in the steps of their father!
What was the number of these slaughtered babes we
know not. Some of the ancient Doctors extend it to an
amount which would seem incredible, after making every
allowance for the larger population of Bethlehem and
its adjacent territory than at the present time. The
Greeks and Abyssinians in their liturgy have retained
the number of fourteen thousand, but the Holy Roman
Church, in the absence of any precise statement in
Scripture or tradition, simply says that Herod, enraged,
slew many children.[10]

That they were true martyrs of the New Law there
was never any question; because they died for Jesus,
and martyrdom consists, not in the pain of death, but
in its cause. The Church, indeed, addresses them as
the flowers of the martyrs, because, in the opening of
life, the fierce persecutor of Christ cut them off as the
blast cuts off the budding roses.[11] They were also the
first who shed their blood for Christ, and the saying

---

9. Joannes Phocas, saec. xii., quoted by Martorelli, *Terra Santa,* cap. xxiii. p. 402, n. This desert grotto, where St. John is believed to have lived an eremitical life, previous to his entering on his office of Precursor, has been now transformed into a chapel by Mgr. Valerga, where Mass is daily offered by an anchorite, who has taken up his abode among some neighboring ruins, eating only bread and dried fruit sent to him by the nuns of Our Lady of Sion, and drinking only of the spring which used to quench the Baptist's thirst. Here he spends his time in prayer, meditation, and the cultivation of a small plot of ground. He is a Frenchman, a native of Villeneuve-les-Avignon, and had been an officer in the French army, but was afterwards on the staff of Don Carlos. Quitting the service, he became a Trappist, but subsequently, by the advice of superiors, studied for the priesthood, was ordained, and belonged for seven years to the secular clergy, when, having made a pilgrimage to the Holy Land, he was attracted to his present life of religious solitude by a visit to the monastery of St. John in the Desert. (See *Catholic Missions,* July, 1887, p. 39.)
10. Office of the Holy Innocents.
11. *Hymn. Ad Laud. SS. Innocentium.*

this offers no contradiction to the assertion that St. Stephen was the Protomartyr of the New Law, since he was the first of the holy martyrs who, after the Passion of Our Lord, confessed the Faith both by word and deed; but the Holy Innocents confessed the Faith, not with their tongues, but by their death, which was to them a baptism of blood. Hence the Church, in her prayer for their feast, says of them, "Non loquendo, sed moriendo, confessi sunt—they confessed, not by speaking, but by dying."[12] When the Empress St. Helen built the Church of the Nativity over the grotto of Bethlehem, many of the little bodies and relics of the Holy Innocents were collected by her and placed in that church, where subsequently a subterranean chapel was constructed and consecrated to them. Besides the ancient accounts, we may refer to the pages of a modern traveller, who thus describes what he saw: "From the chapel of St. Joseph you pass, descending five steps, to that of the Holy Innocents, whose precious memory has been exalted to high honor by the Infant God for whom they died. A pillar supports the subterranean vault of the little sanctuary, and there is a small cave under the altar, in which repose some relics of their tender bodies, innocent victims of the dark and ferocious jealousy of Herod, who from the loving embrace of their mothers were carried by the angels to the bosom of Abraham."[13] Of them the Church sings: "Vos prima Christi victima, Grex immolatorum tener, Aram sub ipsam simplices Palma et coronis luditis—You, the first victims of Jesus, tender flock of the slain, simple little ones, play under the altar with your palms and crowns." A worthy resting-place it was for these martyred babes, the spot where He was born who is the God of the innocent and of the persecuted.

---

12. *Orat. SS. Innocentium.* It has been piously believed by some that these infants, at the moment of their martyrdom, were gifted with a premature use of reason, and enlightened to know the cause for which they died, thus enabling them to add merit to the innocency of their sacrifice.

13. Martorelli, *Terra Santa,* chap. vii. p. 163.

Chapter XXXVI

Journey in the Desert—Destruction of Idols.

SCRIPTURE does not tell us by what road the Holy Family fled into Egypt, but there can be little doubt that it was by the way that goeth down from Jerusalem to Gaza, which, as we read in Acts 8:26, was desert. It was by that road that the minister of Candace, Queen of the Ethiopians, was returning to his country when Philip overtook him. But he was a great man, seated at ease in his chariot, where he could beguile the way by reading, and surrounded by his servants, ready to minister to his wants. How different was the case of the Holy Family, alone, without attendance, and with the most scanty provision for their needs! But they had to face a worse desert after leaving Gaza. Passing through the land of the Philistines, they directed their steps, as is commonly believed, to Heliopolis. This was the easiest, shortest, and least perilous road; nevertheless, the holy travellers would have to traverse full seventy leagues, of which about fifty were solitary and desert.

Many wonders are related of this journey which are here omitted, as lacking sufficient proof, but there is one which cannot be passed over in silence, abundantly supported as it is by tradition. Gaume, in his admirable *Life of the Good Thief,* gives several versions of this incident, but in the main points they agree. It is related by many learned writers, and therefore must not, as Pope Benedict XIII[1] observes, be laid aside as apoc-

1. *Sermo v. de Vita Mariae.*

281

ryphal or doubtful. True, it is first mentioned in one of the earliest apocryphal writings, but, as we have already observed, this, if not in itself sufficient authority, is far from being a reason for its rejection; and its adoption in one form or another by so many early ecclesiastical writers furnishes a strong ground for believing that the tradition was based on fact. When we find the story accepted by such great saints and scholars as St. Augustine and St. Anselm, not to speak of others, we may be sure that the evidence in its behalf was satisfactory in their days. It runs thus: The Holy Family having crossed the torrent Besor, which is the torrent of the desert, and entered a thick forest of ancient trees, found themselves suddenly in presence of a band of robbers. Men of this class were ready to seize on unprotected travellers, and pitilessly spoil, if not murder them. If this could happen on the frequented road between Jerusalem and Jericho, where, according to Our Lord's parable, which possibly embodied a true incident, a certain man fell among thieves, who stripped and wounded him, leaving him half dead, well might the like occur in this lonely and trackless wilderness; nevertheless, these ferocious ruffians, strangers to compassion, were arrested by the sight which met their eyes. They stayed their hands; and their leader, stepping forward, was so much struck by the majestic sweetness of the Infant, the beauty and modesty of the Mother, and the simple dignity of Joseph, that he not only forbade his followers to injure a hair of their heads, but treated them with courtesy, and conducted them to his own tent, where he harbored them for the night. On the following morning, having furnished Joseph with provision for the way, he accompanied them a certain distance, and, in taking leave of them, having discerned, bad man as he was, the holiness of his guests, he asked for their prayers, and the Virgin benignantly promised him that for the charity which he had shown them God would not leave him unrewarded. And this man, the same story asserts, was Dismas the Good Thief, who, having years afterwards fallen into the hands of justice, was condemned to be crucified in punishment of his many crimes. His cross was on the right of that of Jesus, the side on which Mary stood; and, then and there repenting of his sins, he confessed Jesus as the true Messias, and besought Him to remember him when He came into His kingdom; to which Jesus replied: "Today thou shalt be with Me in Paradise."[2]

The Holy Family cannot have traversed the desert in less than fifteen days, and that, too, amidst continual perils of wild beasts and robbers, and all the sufferings of exposure and privation incidental to travelling through so desolate a region. This was the desert in which Elias took refuge when he fled from the vengeful wrath of Jezabel, and in which he was comforted by an angel, who brought him a hearth-cake and a vessel of water, in the strength of which miraculous food he walked forty days and forty nights to the Mount of Horeb. (*3 Kgs.* 19:2-8). God also poured down manna on the people of Israel to feed them in the wilderness. Would such favors be wanting now at His hand? For here it was no longer to supply with sustenance a prophet of the Lord, or an ungrateful and stiff-necked people, but to preserve the natural life of Him on whom the Eternal Life of the whole human race depended, and the life of His Blessed Mother and of His holy foster-father, to whose charge He had been committed. It would not seem to have been possible for the Holy Family to have carried with them, or even to have obtained on the way, more than the scantiest provision when they entered on this trackless sandy desert of a hundred and fifty miles' extent, so that, even granting that the charity of the Good Thief replenished their little stock, it must have been exhausted long before they could reach a land of fruits and fountains. Here, then, was assuredly a call for miraculous interposition; and we

---

2. John 24:40-43. Dismas, it is thought, was an Egyptian by birth, and there is a tradition in Palestine that he had dwelt in a village between Nob and Nicopolis, now called Latrun.—Lavinio da Hamme, *Guida Indicatrice de Santuarii e Luoghi Storici di Terra Santa*, p. 59.

may reasonably believe that the angels, who afterwards
ministered to Jesus when He had fasted forty days and
forty nights in the desert, supplied the wants of the
Holy Family when all natural means of support had
failed them. Maria d'Agreda confirms this view in her
visions of the flight into Egypt.

On leaving the desert the holy exiles would enter on
the fertile lands of Gessen, where large possessions
were assigned to Jacob and his sons by the ancient
Joseph, when Viceroy of Egypt; and here the question
presents itself: Did they direct their course immediately to Heliopolis, which tradition points to as the
place of their abode while in Egypt, or did they make
a circuit, visiting other cities by divine direction? For
it is not to be overlooked that local traditions point to
their presence elsewhere. Without relying on the visions
of saints as precise authorities in questions of this character, which, as we have already stated, was not our
intention, it is well to allude to whatever may serve to
throw a light on facts apparently contradictory, but having all a certain degree of traditionary evidence in their
favor.

The flight of the Incarnate Word into Egypt, as Maria
d'Agreda observes, had other ends in view besides the
escape from Herod's fury, mysterious ends which had
been shadowed forth in ancient prophecy. Our Lord, so
to say, made this flight the means of accomplishing
them, and passed into Egypt to work in that land the
miracles of which Ezechiel and Osee (*Ezech.* 30:13; *Osee*
11:1), and, still more expressly, Isaias, had spoken:
"Behold the Lord will ascend upon a light cloud, and
will enter into Egypt, and the idols of Egypt shall be
moved at His presence, and the heart of Egypt shall
melt in the midst thereof."[3] Now, all this came to pass
when the Infant Jesus, borne in the arms of His Immaculate Virgin Mother, symbolized by a light cloud, came
into that land. Maria d'Agreda says that, before set-

---

3. Chap. xix. i. "Light cloud" is in the Douai Version translated "swift cloud."

tling at Heliopolis, the Holy Family was led by angelic guidance to visit various other places where the Lord designed to work wonders and pour blessings on the benighted people, for the whole land was given up to idolatry and superstition. Every little village was full of idols; many possessed temples which were tenanted by devils, whom the poor ignorant inhabitants adored with sacrifices and rites enjoined by these same demons, receiving answers to their prayers and questions, by which they were deluded and led away. It needed the strong arm of the Lord, that is, of the Word made Flesh, to rescue this people from the tyranny of Satan. To obtain this victory over the infernal enemy, and to illuminate those who lay in the region and shadow of death, the Most High was pleased that Christ, the Sun of Justice, should, only a few days after His nativity, appear in Egypt, and make a progress through the land to enlighten all by His divine power. The Infant Jesus, says Maria d'Agreda, had no sooner entered the inhabited territory with His Mother and St. Joseph than, joining His hands, He prayed to His Heavenly Father for the salvation of these slaves of the devil, and immediately used His divine and royal authority to precipitate into the abyss the evil spirits who dwelt in the idols. At the same time, the idols themselves tottered and fell to the ground with a great noise, and the altars and temples became heaps of ruins. The cause of these wonders was well known to Mary, who inwardly accompanied her Divine Son in all His petitions, as Co-operatrix in the salvation of the human race; so also did Joseph well know that all these works were accomplished by the Incarnate Word, and with holy admiration blessed and praised Him; but the devils, although they felt the compelling force of the divine power, were ignorant whence it proceeded. So God willed. If, of old, the image of the Philistine god, Dagon, was prostrated to the ground by the Ark of God (*1 Kgs.* 5:3-5), in which the glory of the Lord dwelt only representatively by the ministry of His angels, how much more might we expect

that the idols of the Gentiles should be broken to pieces
by the presence of the Word of God Himself!

The Egyptians were moved to wonder by this strange
event. True, some light still lingered among their wise
and learned men, through a tradition come down from
their ancestors, who had heard the voice of the prophet
Jeremias, when he abode amongst them, declaring that
the Lord was the true God, the everlasting King, before
whom the earth should tremble, and that the gods,
which were the work of the artificer's hands, should
perish from the earth, and from those places that are
under heaven. (*Jer.* 10:11). These and many other truths
concerning the great King who was to come they must
have dimly known, but from the multitude they were
hidden. Accordingly all was fear and confusion, and, as
Isaias expresses it, the heart of Egypt "melted"; each
man asked his neighbor what might this thing mean.
And some, beholding with curiosity the strangers who
had come amongst them, would draw nigh and accost
Our Lady and St. Joseph, speaking of the ruin of their
temples and their gods. Mary was so sweet and gentle
in all her words, which had a heavenly efficacy in them,
and her countenance was so divinely beautiful, that
many were attracted to listen to her as she spoke of
the true God, who made all things, and the vanity and
falsehood of idols. To Joseph, the head of this wandering and wonderful family, many questions were sure to
be addressed; but in this case we are not left to conjecture, or to the revelations of saints, for ecclesiastical tradition confirms us in the opinion. St. Jerome,
indeed, believed that Joseph frequently disputed concerning the truths of religion with the Egyptians, in
order to draw them out of their gross errors. The sanctity of his life contributed equally with his conversation towards their conversion; and it was assuredly
fitting that the new Joseph should be the Doctor of
Egypt, as was the ancient, whom, as we read in the
104th Psalm, the King had "made master of his house
and ruler of all his possessions, that he might instruct

his princes as himself, and teach his ancients wisdom."
If this be so, the aureole of Doctor as well as of Apostle cannot be denied to our Joseph.

Heliopolis, at any rate, seems to have been the terminus of the Holy Family's journey, whatever may have been the extent of their wanderings. In this city was the famous Temple of the Sun,[4] so celebrated by ancient writers, in which no less than three hundred and sixty-five deities are said to have been worshiped. When Joseph, then, with the most holy Virgin and the Divine Infant entered this city and paused awhile in front of the temple, it is a constant tradition, authorized by many Fathers and Doctors of the Church,[5] that all the images of those lying gods which it contained were shaken, and fell to the ground; as if to demonstrate, says P. Segneri,[6] that in presence of the true God no false god can stand. Tostatus adds that, when the idols in Heliopolis fell down, the same catastrophe occurred in all the other temples throughout the land of Egypt. We have given the two accounts without pretending to examine, still less to decide, which may be the more accurate statement as to the order of events, of which the substance remains the same whichever view we adopt. The learned Cartagena's words might, indeed, be applicable to either, for he says, in a general way, that when Christ entered into Egypt there was no temple throughout the land in which the idols were not cast down.[7] Tradition also relates how Aphrodisius, the High-Priest of the Sun, having heard the fatal news, hastened to the spot full of wrath, but that when he saw Jesus in the Virgin's arms and the humble Joseph, he was struck with such awe and reverence that he at once recognized in this Babe the true God, and, casting himself on his knees, adored Him, saying to all the people who had flocked to the scene of destruction, "If

---

4. Aseneth, the mother of the first Joseph, was the daughter of Putiphare, priest of Heliopolis (*Gen.* 41:45).
5. P. Donato Calvi, *Proprinom. Evang.* Risol. v. Tostatus, q. lx. *in Matthaeum,* cap. ii.
6. *Manna dell' Anima,* 16 Maggio.
7. Lib. ix. Hom. ix.

this were not the God of our gods, they would not have prostrated themselves before Him, and, if we do not the same, we shall incur the peril of Pharao."[8] We are also told that he offered the Holy Family hospitality under his roof, but that Joseph would not accept it, and retired with Jesus and Mary to a neighboring village; nevertheless his house, it is said, would always have been open to them. This same Aphrodisius was subsequently instructed by St. Paul, and, after being pontiff of an idolatrous worship, became a priest of the New Law, and was ultimately ordained Bishop of Béziers, in Gaul, where he closed his holy life by a glorious martyrdom at the age of 101, along with three companions, whose names have also been recorded: Caralippus, Agapitus, and Eusebius. The Gallican Martyrology assigns their united feast to March 12th, saying that Aphrodisius hospitably received as guests for seven years the Divine Infant with His Mother and St. Joseph. But this statement can hardly be accepted literally, believing, as we do, that Joseph knew that it was he who was commissioned to support the Child and His Mother, and that he would therefore not have consented to see this obligation discharged by another. It is, however, reconcilable with the supposition that Aphrodisius placed his house at their disposal, which gave him the merit of a hospitality which he was not permitted to exercise. Some also say that he gave the Holy Family the cottage which they occupied. The Roman Martyrology fixes the feast of St. Aphrodisius and his companions on April 28th.

There is a village between Heliopolis and Memphis called Matarieh by the Arabs. Here is a garden of balsam shrubs, and, as olive trees still survive in the Garden of Gethsemane, we may well imagine that this sweet and salutary plant, fit emblem of Him who was come to be the Healer of the Nations, flourished in the days when Joseph took the Child and His Mother to dwell in its vicinity. In this village they remained until

---

8. Tostatus, *ibid.*

the angel signified to Joseph the divine command to return to Judea. Memphis and even Hermopolis and Alexandria are said by some writers to have been the abode of the Holy Family, as well as old Cairo, situated between Memphis and Matarieh. At this place the spot to which they are believed to have retired is now enclosed within the monastery of St. Sergius; and in order to see it a descent of twelve steps must be made, which recalls to mind the grotto of Bethlehem. Very likely, as has been observed, they may have made a passing sojourn in these various places, but the many religious memories which have clung to Matarieh, and which cannot be recognized elsewhere, seem to confirm the most reliable tradition which we possess on this subject. In Matarieh there still exists a sycamore of enormous girth, standing in a vast garden—it might rather be called a forest—of orange trees. Under its spreading shade the Holy Family are said to have rested.[9] This tree is much venerated in the East, Mahometans even calling it the tree of Jesus and Mary. Fifty paces from it is the Fountain of the Virgin, to which a miraculous origin is attributed. God caused it to spring forth to allay the thirst of Mary and Joseph in a country parched by the burning rays of the sun. The water of this spring was pure and sweet, whereas that of all the rest in the neighborhood was brackish and bad. Here Mary used to go to draw water in her little amphora, and here, too, tradition says, she used to wash the swaddling-bands of the Infant Jesus; for which reason the sick and infirm come to drink thereat, and often, it is said, recover their health. A short way from it is a large stone upon which the Virgin Mother used to spread the linen to dry. All these spots are reverenced by Mahometans as well as by Christians.[10] The Empress Eugénie, when she visited Egypt after the opening of the Suez canal, went to see the ancient sycamore, and

9. See P. Geramb's account of his journey from Jerusalem to Mount Sinai. This sycamore, it is supposed, must be a shoot from the parent stem. The ancient tree is believed to have fallen down in the 11th century from old age.
10. Trombelli, *Vita di S. Giuseppe,* par. i. cap. xxiv. n. 17.

expressed a desire to possess it. The Viceroy of Egypt complied with her wish, and made a present of the tree to France. Eugénie had it surrounded with a handsome iron fence for its protection, and two guardians were appointed to keep it, and to cultivate lilies and jessamine within the enclosure.

Chapter XXXVII

The Offices of Joseph.

WHY did not Joseph accept the offer of Aphrodisius? In his house Mary and Jesus would have found safety, comfort, ease, and repose. Joseph, however, as we have said, declined, though no doubt gratefully and graciously, the proffered hospitality, and preferred the seclusion of a poor cottage in an obscure village. And, in doing so, there can be no question that he was obeying the light from Heaven which guided his steps; but at the same time we may believe that he was illuminated in his understanding to realize the fitness of the command, grounded on the nature of the offices entrusted to him; and those offices were themselves the inseparable consequences of the state which our Divine Lord had assumed when He was born into the world.

First, then, He was pleased to appear in a state of poverty; secondly, He came as a child; thirdly, as an orphan, that is, without an earthly father. Now, these three states imposed on Joseph three corresponding obligations: first, that of laboring in order to supply His needs; secondly, that of rearing and instructing Him as He grew; thirdly, that of acting as His parent and guardian.

There is no denying that the Incarnate Word, His Blessed Mother, and her incomparable spouse professed through life the strictest poverty, yet we never hear, as the learned Cardinal of Cambrai observes, of the Son

of God having to beg His bread, either as a child or
during His hidden life. Who fed Him all that time?
Joseph, replies St. Jerome; for the Saviour chose to
share the poverty of His parents,[1] and contented Himself with the sustenance provided for Him in the house
of a poor carpenter. The Eternal Father did not will
that His Son should be fed in a miraculous manner,
as many great saints of both the Old and New
Covenants have been; neither did He deem it fitting
to preserve His temporal life by His own immediate
influx and action, as He communicates to Him His
Eternal Life in His own Bosom, where He is begotten
from all eternity. But He desired that Joseph should
have the glory of providing for Him who provides for
the necessities of all creatures. As the Eternal Father
engenders the Son of His own substance, it was meet
that Joseph, whom He had called to a participation of
His Paternity, should maintain the life of Jesus through
himself personally, not instrumentally through others,
and that he should employ all his diligence, devote all
his labors, and consume his whole strength in supply-
ing the Saviour's needs. The Mother of the Incarnate
Word was exempted from the pains of childbirth in
bringing her Son into the world, but Joseph was to
suffer much by his continual toil in preserving the
Divine Infant's life. The milk with which the Virgin
fed Him while a babe, she received, as the Church
sings, from Heaven;[2] it cost this sovereign maiden nothing; but Joseph was subjected to great fatigues for
many years in order to relieve the extreme poverty of
his Foster-Son. To increase His strength he weakened
his own; so that he might have said, like the holy Precursor, "He must increase, but I must decrease." Marvel of marvels! This great saint received into his arms
a poor and necessitous God, who deigned to be dependent on him for His corporeal food. Joseph shared with
his august spouse the glory of nourishing Him; she, of

1. *Epist.* xxii. *ad Eustochium.*
2. "Virgo lactabat ubere de coelo pleno."

her own substance, and he of his substantial strength.
Thus they combined in feeding and sustaining this Lamb
of God against the day of sacrifice, that He might be
able to bear that tremendous weight of suffering to
which the Eternal Father had sentenced Him for the
love of us. Thy laborious steps, O great saint, thy painful
journeyings, will—so God has decreed—be the means
of enabling this Divine Victim to walk, and, before long,
to tread the hills and valleys of Juda and the streets
of Jerusalem, there to publish the glad tidings of salvation. See this Adorable Infant stretching forth His
little Hands, the Hands that made and fashioned the
universe, to ask bread of Joseph! All creatures raise
their eyes to Heaven for sustenance: "All wait upon
Thee to give them food in season." (*Ps.* 103:27). But
this Sovereign Provider wills, O great saint, to seek
from thy hands His own aliment. When God, of old,
desired to manifest His supreme and majestic independence, He said, "If I were hungry, I would not tell
thee" (*Ps.* 49:12); but, O glorious Joseph, when the self-
existent God declared this, He made an exception in
regard to thee; for the eyes of the Incarnate Word were
to look to thee one day, and during many days, with
confidence for His daily bread. The royal prophet confessed that God needed not his goods (*Ps.* 15:1), and
for this very reason acknowledged Him as his God; but
thou, O incomparable Joseph, wilt know the Incarnate
God by the need He vouchsafes to have of thee, thou
wilt in this sign behold and acknowledge His incomprehensible goodness, His unfathomable love, His infinite perfections.

The second office which the Doctors of the Church
recognize in Joseph is that of the preceptor and teacher
of the Infant God.[3] The Saviour of the world, from an
excess of His infinite humility, willed in the first years
of His temporal life to manifest Himself with all the

3. "Joseph was nurse and preceptor to Christ the Lord in His infancy."—Peres, Epis-
cop. Urgellen, in *Matthaeum,* cap. xxxviii. St. Bonaventura calls Joseph "pater educa-
tivus," *in Lucam,* cap. i., and St. Cyril Hieros., "director Christi," *Catech.* vii.

feebleness and infirmities of childhood; for which reason, albeit He was the Eternal Word, He delayed speaking articulately, for, as the prophet Isaias, referring to
the future Messias, typically represented by the child
whom the prophetess bore, gives us to understand, there
would be a time in which the Divine Child should not
be able to pronounce the name of father or mother.[4] It
was needful, therefore, that Joseph should act as instructor to Him who knew everything. "Oh! with what sweet
delight did Joseph hear the stammerings of the Infant,"
says St. Bernard.[5] Preceptors and doctors explain the
truth to their disciples, but our saint was to teach the
very Truth to explain Itself. The Divine Saviour humbled Himself to ask light when deliberating on any
question, as if this had been necessary to the Incre-
ated Wisdom, and He was pleased to think it no disgrace to His Adorable Person to assume the appearance
of ignorance, seeing that He had taken upon Himself
the very likeness of a sinner. This humility moved Him,
as many learned writers have held, to ask counsel of
Joseph, follow his advice, and receive instructions from
him which to others would have been useful, but which
He could not need, and this with so much docility that
He was hereafter to be regarded as the apprentice of
a poor artificer. (*Matt.* 13:55; *Mark* 6:3). Only once did
Jesus do the scribes and doctors of the Law the honor
of appearing before them in the character of a disciple, but on Joseph He habitually bestowed it when He
willed that he should teach Him, as children are taught
by frequent repetitions, and should give Him His first
lessons in comportment and in virtue. Only once in His
life did the Saviour humble Himself to receive consolation from an angel (*Luke* 22:43), but never did He

---

4. Chap. viii. 4. "Before the child know to call his father and his mother, the strength
of Damascus and the spoils of Samaria shall be taken away before the King of the
Assyrians." If this passage be compared with verses 14-16 in the preceding chapter, it will be evident that this child represents, in parable, Him who is directly
spoken of as Emmanuel, whom a Virgin shall conceive and bring forth. In the figure there used: "before the child know to refuse the evil and choose the good," we
likewise see an allusion to the gradual manifestation of which we are speaking.
5. *Sermo de S. Joseph.*

receive instruction from any of these blessed spirits. To Joseph alone, in conjunction with His Blessed Mother, was this marvellous honor reserved. All the parental rights which she possessed were shared in their entirety by Joseph, and he had besides, as we have seen, those which specially belong to the father and head of the family; and the father is by right the teacher and instructor of his child.

Most true it is that our saint could teach the God-Man nothing which He did not already know, since He was full of knowledge from the first instant of His conception, but this Sun of Justice, infinitely luminous in Himself, did not choose to shine before men save in proportion as He grew in age and acquired knowledge in an experimental and practical manner like other children. It is a deeply mysterious subject which we can never fathom, but we must remember that St. Luke expressly says (2:52) that Jesus "advanced in wisdom and age," using the same word to denote both growths, the former of which was certainly a real growth. He does not say He advanced in age, and assumed the semblance of advance in wisdom, but He advanced in wisdom and age. Thus we have Scriptural authority for believing that Our Lord willed to learn from father and mother like other children in a true, though inscrutable sense.[6] Oh, the incomparable humility of the God-Man!

---

6. The following passage in an article on the "Sacrament of the Dying," communicated by the Rev. W. Humphrey, S.J., to the "Month" for August, 1887, is so much to the point, that the writer is glad to quote it in confirmation of the view which has been put forward in the text. After speaking of Our Lord's knowledge, both divine and human, Father Humphrey adds, "But besides His knowledge as He is Father in the human family of God's children by adoption, He has a knowledge which He acquired by becoming their Elder Brother, and by being in all things human, made like unto His brethren according to the flesh. This knowledge He gained for Himself. He gathered it gradually day by day. He earned it by experience. He would know what is in man, and know it, not only as perfectly as does any man, but in that way in which it is known to men. He would explore human nature for Himself throughout its length and breadth. For this cause did He will to be made of a woman, and to be made under that universal law under which He found mankind lying. To the law of sin He could not subject Himself; that is to say, He could not make the guilt of sin His own. But, short of this divine impossibility to the Divine Omnipotence, He would subject Himself to the law under which human sinners lay." The learned writer proceeds to apply this truth in a most consolatory manner to Our Lord's human compassion, but enough has been quoted for the purpose in view.

Oh, the adorable love by which He sought in all things possible to assimilate Himself to us, His brethren! But what an honor was awarded to Joseph to be the master and teacher of God manifest in the flesh! And, if this be true, how high a right to the title of father of Jesus did our saint thus acquire! Those who instruct others are held to acquire over them thereby paternal rights, because the communication of light and knowledge to a spirit is similar, in its order, to the communication of natural life to a body. A created spirit never created another spirit, but it can introduce its own thoughts and sentiments into one less highly gifted by an infusion of light and knowledge, which is a species of spiritual generation. The Angel of the Schools notes that St. Paul takes the name of father with regard to those Christians whom he has instructed. (*1 Cor.* 4:15). God, says the Apostle, is the origin of all paternity in Heaven as well as in earth. (*Ephes.* 3:15). Hence St. Thomas concludes that some of the angels are entitled to the appellation of father with respect to other angels, because they communicate their superior light to those who have less,[7] as a master may be called the father of his disciples. Jeremias was called the father of the people of Israel (*Jer.* 31:9) because he taught them the law of God; and Moses calls Jubal "the father of them that play upon the harp and the organs" (*Gen.* 4:21), because he was the first musician who taught men that art. We must acknowledge, then, that, since Joseph was externally the instructor of the Saviour, as if He had needed all the lessons which he imparted to Him, it would be unjust to deny to him the dignity of father of Jesus.

The third office which had been committed to Joseph was that of tutor or guardian of the Incarnate Word, who was always an orphan upon earth, and much more so than any ever were; for other orphans possessed, at least for a brief space, those of whom they were the natural offspring; not so Jesus, He was an orphan, not

7. *Summa*, p. i. q. xlv. a. 5.

by accident, or against His Will, as are those whom death has robbed of their fathers, but He was so by choice, having willed to be born on earth of a mother, with no father according to the flesh, even as He had eternally been begotten in Heaven from all eternity by a Father without mother. Nonetheless this Divine Pupil, who to show His love for us deprived Himself of a father, was pleased to provide Himself with a tutor or guardian, and clearly made known this His Will to the object of His choice. Every word of Scripture is, so to say, redolent of meaning, often of many meanings. We might almost have presumed that so it would be, but the quotations made by the Evangelists from the Books of the Old Testament, and the applications of them which in many instances we should scarcely have ventured on without their authority, place this beyond a doubt. We may, therefore, believe that St. Matthew insinuates this truth when recording the angel's words: "Take the Child," and may attribute a special meaning to them with reference to the charge laid upon Joseph. And as the Eternal Father confided to him the Incarnate Word, He gave him at the same time, along with the position of tutor or guardian, all the rights which appertained thereto. Joseph respectfully and lovingly accepted the office, and we find him always perfectly fulfilling its obligations. He speaks for Jesus, he negotiates all affairs in the name of the Saviour, and promotes all His interests with unflagging zeal. The appellation of tutor, guardian, or director of Jesus is constantly given by the Doctors of the Church and by other ecclesiastical writers of eminence to Joseph; and they see, moreover, in the peculiar connection thus divinely established between him and the God-Man one of the strongest grounds for awarding to him the title of father of Jesus. St. Cyril, for instance, says that our saint was called the father of Jesus because he was His guardian and director;[8] and the glorious Albert the

---

8. *Catech.* vii.

Great does not express himself less clearly when he says Joseph is the father of Jesus because he is His curator, that is, His guardian;[9] and we might quote many other high authorities who have seen reason to opine that the care and the labors of this charitable guardian elevated him to the dignity of a father. The Son of Sirach has declared that tutors take the place of fathers to those of whom they have the charge (*Ecclus.* 4:10); and the law even awards to guardians a portion of the rights of natural parents. St. Augustine said that Joseph merited the title of father of Jesus more than do other fathers in the natural order.[10] His line of reasoning deserves notice. It is notorious that a man to whom God gives a son born of a Christian marriage is esteemed to be more worthy of the title of father than those whose children have been the fruit of a union unsanctified by wedlock. Chastity, then, he argues, contributes to the honor of paternity and confirms the justice of its claims. Consequently (he continues), if anyone should have a son of his legitimate spouse, preserving at the same time inviolable virginity, as Joseph did in his union with the Mother of God, there would be a higher reason for calling such a one a father than any who have even lived in the bonds of matrimony. Such is the opinion of the great Bishop of Hippo. And, in effect, as God is the idea and model of all that is great and the very origin of all paternity, it is evident that anyone who should possess the quality and rights of a father in a manner which should most nearly assimilate him to the Eternal Father would in proportion have the highest claim to be himself called a father; and such was Joseph's case, he was the virgin-father of Mary's Son.

Joseph, then, was a supernatural father, and this consideration at once leads us to the solution of the question which heads this chapter, and enables us to perceive why it was impossible for him in any degree

9. *In Matthaeum*, cap. i.
10. *Sermo* xxxvi. *de Diversis.*

or form to share with another the obligation laid upon him in this character. A father, in the order of nature, is, it is true, bound to feed, instruct, and take care of his son; that is, he is bound, so far as in him lies, to provide for the support and education of his child, but he is not always or by any means bound to do this personally. He is not bound to toil for that purpose if in any other mode sufficient provision can be secured; and, as regards the education of his son, one of the strictest obligations of a parent, he may often prudently commit his instruction to substitutes, either because he has not the necessary time to bestow on it or because he is himself not capable of fulfilling this duty as well as it may be performed by others. But with Joseph all this was different. The charge laid upon him in virtue of his supernatural paternity was entirely personal. It was such a charge as never was laid on any other parent; and our saint knew this well, and estimated his duties accordingly. Jesus was to be fed by the labor of his hands, He was to be taught and trained by him exclusively. He and His Blessed Mother were to be cared for, protected, and guarded by Joseph alone. "Take the Child and His Mother": this was his commission, and he could not have satisfied its obligations under the hospitable roof of Aphrodisius. Jesus would there have been supported without his labor, He would have necessarily come in the way of other influences than those of His foster-father, and have learned in a measure through the medium of others. He would also have been independent, so to say, of the protecting arm of Joseph, to whose loving embrace and care He had been consigned.

Chapter XXXVIII

Abode in Egypt—Recall from Exile.

HAVING shortly noticed the different places in Egypt which tradition alleges to have been sanctified by the, at least, temporary residence of the Holy Family, we will cast a glance at the manner of their life in the village near Heliopolis where they finally settled. It need scarcely be said that the life of Mary and Joseph was, as everywhere else, a combination of the active and the contemplative. Fervent and constant prayer, with profound meditation on the divine mysteries, was their daily bread. Nor had they to go far to find God, seeing that they had Him with them really present and manifested to them in the Divine Infant, for whoever saw Jesus saw the Father, as Christ Himself afterwards taught. (*John* 14:9). Yet, notwithstanding their continual conversation with God, Mary and Joseph had to suffer much in Egypt; but to suffer for and with Jesus is the portion and the delight of the saints. They suffered the privations and sadness of exile. Great, indeed, we know, is the desolation experienced by those who find themselves completely isolated in foreign lands, never hearing the accents of their own native tongue, severed from all the familiar associations which are bound up with the habits of their life, and separated from every friend and relative whom they love.

Moreover, in the case of the chosen people, who, when banished from Palestine, found themselves not only among foreigners and strangers, but among the idolatrous heathen, strangers not to themselves alone but to the God whom they adored, and deprived of all participation in those rites and sacrifices which were the acceptable worship offered to Him in Judea, this desolation became even tenfold greater. It was a well-known fact that the Jews reckoned banishment from their country to be as great an evil as death itself; so that the Roman historian, Tacitus, observes that if the Jews were compelled to leave their beloved land, they feared not so much to die as to live. The 136th Psalm well represents the sorrow of the Jews in exile. "By the rivers of Babylon, there we sat and wept, when we remembered Sion. . . . If I forget thee, O Jerusalem, let my right hand be forgotten. Let my tongue cleave to my jaws, if I do not remember thee, if I make not Jerusalem the beginning of my joy." What must have been the feelings of Mary and Joseph, those devout observers of all the precepts and ceremonial of the Law, when the great and holy seasons recurred at which crowds were flocking to Jerusalem to pay homage to the God of Israel in His Temple! Mary had been brought up in the precincts of the Lord's House, and Joseph for years had exercised his trade in its immediate vicinity, and, although on their marriage they retired, by divine dispensation, to Nazareth, we know from their subsequent practice that the ninety miles which separated them from the Holy City would not have been allowed to hinder them from going up to keep the solemn feasts of the year.

To the sadness of this exile were added the straits of poverty, not such poverty or, rather, indigence as constrains its sufferers to go begging from door to door, but that simple and honorable poverty which renders daily labor needful for the earning of daily bread. Joseph resumed his carpenter's tools, and by his skillful work, for which, we are told, he always asked a very moderate price, procured for his holy spouse and for himself what was needful for their support. An ancient tradition asserts that Joseph never ate his bread for nothing. The Blessed Virgin also diligently plied her needle and her distaff, and the result of their united labor was that something always remained wherewith to succor the poor and the afflicted.

Meanwhile, all their care was centered in Jesus. Jesus was their overflowing consolation in exile, their infinite treasure in poverty, their sweet repose in fatigue. Of abstinence, gentleness, and docile obedience the Divine Infant was a perfect model; and His love of poverty was early displayed; for when He was a year old, and Mary, thinking it time to release Him from His swaddling-bands, that He might have free use of His limbs, was, with Joseph's acquiescence, about to prepare for Him a finely wrought vestment, He gave her interiorly to understand that He would wear nothing but a simple tunic of wool, woven entirely by her own hands; and this tunic was to last Him His whole life. The Virgin accordingly began to weave for Him that seamless garment which was to grow with His growth, and for which the soldiers were to cast lots on Calvary.[1]

It was a great joy to these holy spouses when they beheld Him begin to walk alone, and far greater still when, with His sweet infantine voice, He first called Mary by the tender name of mother and Joseph by the endearing name of father. Their hearts bounded with ineffable gladness at the sound, a gladness so great that, to temper its exuberance, it was needful for them to remember the prophecy of Simeon, and the persecution of Herod. Far removed as they were from the reach of the tyrant's fury, it did not cease to be a subject of deepest pain to them. Even in those days when news travelled very slowly, and when the cruelty of rulers caused but slight surprise, a massacre so barbarous as that of the little children of Bethlehem must have excited

---

1. Tradition relates that the soldier to whom the tunic fell by lot sold it, and, according to Sigebert, it was found in the year 593 at Zafat. The inhabitants of Paris and of Trèves have severally claimed its possession, but Cornelius à Lapide adjudges it to Trèves.

a very general horror, and the report can scarcely have failed to reach Egypt. Be this as it may, the Mother of God, we may believe, was sure to be divinely apprised of what had happened, and to have shed, along with her holy spouse, many tears of compassion over these innocent victims. Not but they knew that theirs was a glory and a gain unspeakable, since for one brief moment of pain they were to enjoy an eternity of bliss; still, the human heart naturally melts with pity at such cruel deeds, and sanctity, so far from extinguishing natural compassion, intensifies it; and then the thought of the bereaved and distracted parents and, above all, of the unhappy mothers, sprinkled with the blood of their babes butchered in their very arms, must have filled the tender hearts of Mary and Joseph with indescribable sorrow.

It is believed that the holy old man, Simeon, and Anna the Prophetess died about this time, not so much borne down by the weight of years as overcome with grief and horror at Herod's barbarities, and especially the slaughter of the babes of Bethlehem. Many saints have thought that Zachary was put to death by Herod because he had concealed his little son, the Baptist, concerning whose birth wonderful reports had been circulated in Jerusalem. St. Basil, St. Gregory Nazianzen, St. Epiphanius, St. Hypolitus Martyr, and others, whose opinion Baronius follows in his Annals, believed that it was to him Our Lord alluded when He spoke of the Zacharias who had been slain between the temple and the altar.[2] Tertullian says that for a long time the stains of his blood were visible on the stone floor of the Temple.[3] Elizabeth went and dwelt in the desert with her son John until her death, which, it is supposed, preceded the return from Egypt. How dear that sacerdotal family was to Mary and Joseph, bound as they were to it by the ties both of friendship and of consanguin-

---

2. Matthew 23:35; Luke 11:51. St. Jerome is of another opinion, but all he seeks to prove is that the Zacharias, son of Barachias, spoken of by Our Lord was not the father of St. John the Baptist.
3. *In Scorp.* c. viii.

ity, we well know. Their angels did not, we may believe, leave them in ignorance of events so deeply interesting to their hearts. Another source of grief must have been the thought that, having been compelled to leave Bethlehem suddenly without communication with any of their friends and relatives, these must have suffered much anxiety on their account, fearing possibly that the Child Jesus might have been included in the slaughter of the Innocents.

But, with all these causes for sadness, Mary and Joseph, we may be assured, never uttered a lamentation, still less a murmur. Nor did they ever invoke the divine justice and vengeance on the author of all these woes. But divine justice and vengeance, nonetheless, overtook the ferocious tyrant, who persevered to the last in his sanguinary deeds, even putting his own son, Antipater, to death shortly before finishing his own wretched life, struck with a torturing disease which preyed upon and consumed his very vitals. If the news of his death reached the ears of Joseph, we might, judging humanly, have supposed that he would see therein the removal of the one obstacle which stood in the way of the safe return of the Divine Infant to Judea. But Joseph would not have reasoned thus, or, rather, he would not have reasoned at all, but have waited for orders from on high. The angel had not said, "Remain in Egypt until Herod is dead, and then return," but, "Be thou there until I shall tell thee." (*Matt.* 2:13). The question here suggests itself, how long did the Holy Family abide in Egypt? Scripture is silent, and Doctors are not all agreed on the point. It would appear from history that Herod's miserable death occurred about a year and a half after the massacre of the Innocents. Hence Epiphanius concludes that the Holy Family's exile lasted two years. Nicephorus extends the term to three years. But it must be allowed that the general tradition of the Church—and such tradition is never to be lightly set aside even when probabilities seem to tell against it—allots seven years to their sojourn in

Egypt. St. Francis of Sales, indeed, is of opinion that it was five, while Baronius even prolongs their absence to the ninth year. Adopting, then, the common tradition, we are naturally disposed to ask why the summons of the angel was so long delayed. Not that we can expect to obtain any precise reply, but some possible reasons to account for it may be suggested in the way of surmise. Herod had divided his kingdom amongst his three remaining sons into four parts, under the name of Tetrarchies, allotting two portions in Judea to Archelaus—forbidding him, however, to assume the title of king until authorized by Rome—one to Herod Antipas in Galilee, and one in Ituria and Trachonitis to Philip. Now, Archelaus too closely resembled his father in pride and a capricious tyrannical temper to render the life of Jesus safe were He to return into Judea at once. The son of Herod must have been well acquainted with all that had so recently occurred, and, should it have reached his ears that the Child whom the Magi had adored as King of the Jews had escaped the slaughter of the babes in Bethlehem, he would have been seized with the same ferocious desire to destroy Him as had possessed his father. The angel's mission may, therefore, have been delayed until matters of serious importance as regarded his position should have diverted the thoughts of Archelaus into other channels and absorbed his attention, as the dissatisfaction which he gave his Roman masters and the complaints raised against him by his subjects must surely have done.

Time also in the divine decrees may have been deemed necessary for completing the high mission of the Holy Family in Egypt. Jesus, taking refuge among the idolatrous Gentiles, began to shadow forth even then what was to be manifested hereafter. He began, with Mary and Joseph, to do what He was afterwards to commission His Apostles to do. He had come first to the Jews, but, as they would not receive Him and would have persecuted Him even to death, He had passed over to the Gentiles, and fixed His abode with them, preach-

ing the doctrines of truth and opening to all the way
of salvation. Jesus, therefore, did not leave Egypt until
He had fulfilled His mission, that of commencing, even
while yet a child, to illuminate these unhappy idolaters
sitting in darkness and the shadow of death. He, the
Sun of Justice, came to the so-called City of the Sun
to give it the true light. Isaias, who had foretold the
coming of Christ into Egypt, had also said that there
should be "five cities in the land of Egypt speaking the
language of Canaan, and swearing by the Lord of Hosts,"
and that "one of them" should "be called the City of
the Sun." (*Is.* 19:18). Without this preparation to accept
the Gospel which the Holy Family was to effect, Egypt
might not have been so docile as it was hereafter to
the teaching of the Apostles. The blessing it had at that
time received was to be fruitful of good and to people
the immense solitudes along the Nile with holy
anchorites and hermits, such as the Pauls, the Macar-
iuses, the Anthonys, and countless others, so that St.
Augustine was fain to declare that Egypt through them
had become an image of Heaven, and the temple of the
whole world. Then were the glorious promises of the
prophet fulfilled: "In that day there shall be an altar
of the Lord in the midst of the land of Egypt, and a
monument of the Lord at the borders thereof. It shall
be for a sign and for a testimony to the Lord of Hosts
in the land of Egypt. For they shall cry to the Lord
because of the oppressor, and He shall send them a
Saviour and a Defender to deliver them. And the Lord
shall be known to Egypt, and the Egyptians shall know
the Lord in that day, and shall worship Him with sacrifices and offerings; and they shall make vows to the
Lord, and perform them." (*Is.* 19:19-21). This prophecy
of Isaias was, as we say, to receive a very remarkable,
though a partial, fulfillment, in the evangelization of
Egypt in the early centuries of the Church and its fruit-
fulness in saints, in followers after perfection, both men
and women, and in courageous champions of the Faith:
we say a partial fulfillment, for, like many other sim-

ilar predictions, it seems to have a wider scope, and to await a more complete accomplishment, a subject on which we need not here enter.

Jesus from His tenderest infancy displayed such divine beauty and grace in His countenance, in His every look, and in His whole behavior, that the mere sight of Him ravished all hearts. Meanwhile, His all-powerful prayer was ascending continually for them to the Eternal Father. He spoke but little, but those who heard His few simple words marvelled, as men afterwards were to do at the words of grace which proceeded from His lips, and were drawn to practice His counsels and cast away the vices of heathendom. The children and the women of Matarieh were the first to know this wonderful and heavenly Child; the report spread, and then both men and women came to see Him, not only from the immediate neighborhood, but from other towns and villages. Jesus had two Apostles to aid Him in His mission, Mary and Joseph; and who can calculate the power and the grace that accompanied their words and their every act? Whoever, indeed, beheld the Divine Infant and then lifted up their eyes to look at Mary and Joseph, said in their hearts, "These are truly angels of Paradise." Doctors have gathered from Oriental traditions that the Egyptian women, seeing Mary so beautiful, so gracious, so modest, and so discreet, conceived a great love for her, and numbers of them would come to visit her and bring her presents. They had such confidence in her, it is said, that in their bodily infirmities and other afflictions they had recourse to her assistance, and in their sorrows sought and found consolation from her lips. They would also bring their sick children to her, and she would gently lay her hand on their heads, or would place them near to her Divine Son, and they were healed. The Saracens, afterwards, were wont to say that no woman on whom Mary laid her hand ever died in childbirth.[4]

---

4. Jacobus à Valentia, *Tractat. in Magnificat;* Benedict XIII. *Sermo* xliv.

With respect to miracles ascribed by early tradition
to Jesus during His infancy, some critics have urged in
objection the assertion of St. John the Evangelist, that
the miracle of changing the water into wine at Cana
of Galilee was the first miracle which Our Lord performed. But there seems no reason for thus rigidly
interpreting this text, which, from its very wording,
may more readily be taken to mean that this was the
first public miracle which Jesus worked before His disciples to prove His divine mission and manifest His
glory. Nothing, therefore, says Maldonatus, need hinder us from believing that Jesus had privately performed miracles previously.[5]

It may well be imagined that the Blessed Virgin took
occasion of the resort to her of these simple heathen
women to instruct them in the knowledge of the true
God and in the practice of virtue, and bid them teach
the same to their children; and that she would also tell
them that the Kingdom of Heaven was at hand. As for
her holy spouse, Joseph, the great St. Hilary holds him
to be an Apostle, because he was commissioned to carry
the Word of God to the Gentiles, but not only was he
thus an Apostle in figure, but he himself (as already
noticed) was to take his part in the work of evangelization; nay, the learned Cardinal of Cambrai has
declared that he merited to be styled the first Evangelist, or preacher of the Gospel. "The angel," he says,
"evangelized the shepherds, holy Joseph publicly and
solemnly evangelized all";[6] and, doubtless, he had many
opportunities of gaining disciples to Jesus in the practice of his trade among the neighboring villages. In
Heliopolis he would be well known, and probably the
fame of his skill and his personal merit would cause
him to be sent for even from Memphis and other places.
Everywhere he would profit by the opportunity to speak
of the goodness of God, of the blindness of those who
adore idols, and to tell the Egyptians that soon a new

5. *Comment. in Joannem,* cap. ii.
6. *Tract. de S. Joseph.*

light would appear to show the world its error; that they must therefore turn themselves to the true God, and observe His holy laws: these and similar things he would say to them, and thus prepare the way of the Lord in those regions, and sow the seed which was to bear fruit hereafter a hundredfold.

But now the time was come when the Holy Family was to be recalled from exile. One night, as Joseph was taking repose after his labors, the Archangel Gabriel appeared to him once more, and bade him arise and take the Child and His Mother, and go into the land of Israel; for they were dead who had sought the Child's life. (*Matt.* 2:20). It will be observed that the angel does not say, "Herod is dead," but, "they are dead who sought the life of the Child"; giving to understand that others besides the tyrant had been implicated in the design to destroy Jesus. St. Jerome is of opinion that Herod had adherents among the priests and scribes who combined with him in plotting against the newborn King. Nor does this seem incredible, since we read, in the Gospel of St. Mark (*Mark* 3:6), that "the Pharisees going out immediately"—that is, after witnessing one of Our Lord's miracles—"made a consultation with the Herodians against Him, how they might destroy Him," one vile purpose thus uniting two most opposite sects. Herod, then, had his satellites, probably, even in the sanctuary, and, while they lived, the danger may still have been too great to allow of return. We have already alluded to other reasons which may have rendered delay desirable even after Herod's death, which, if it be true that the Holy Family abode seven or even five years in Egypt, must have occurred some considerable time before the angel's appearance to Joseph, and, in particular (as we have suggested), the sanguinary disposition of Archelaus, his successor.

This is the third time that we find an angel appearing to Joseph as the head of the Family to whose tutelage and direction the Mother of God and the Incarnate Word Himself were subjected. Jesus was now able to

speak, and might have signified that the time was come
for their return; for was He not God and the Lord of
all? But no, He says not a word, and interferes no more
than any ordinary child of His age would have done
with the plans and movements of its parents. As this
journey was not a flight, it was not needful that the
Holy Family should depart before the dawn. The Gospel,
as St. Jerome remarks, says nothing about night or
darkness, and he sees in this return, begun in the full
light of day, a type of what shall be at the end of this
age, when the Jews shall be illuminated by faith and
openly receive Christ the Lord. Joseph and Mary, always
full of benign courtesy and gratitude, would not, we
may be sure, set out without bidding adieu to their
kind neighbors. Such is the opinion of Benedict XIII,
and St. Bonaventura says that some Egyptian matrons,
greatly attached to our Blessed Lady and her Divine
Child, insisted on accompanying her a certain distance
on the road. The Holy Family, probably, returned by the
way that they had come, but Scripture is silent, and
even tradition has less to say on this subject than it
has regarding the flight. A pious belief, if no more, has,
however, been entertained by not a few as to a meeting with John, the future Precursor, in the desert, where,
as the Gospel tells us (*Luke* 1:80), he lived until the
time of his manifestation to Israel. P. Domenico Cav-
alca gives it a record in his *Life of St. John the Baptist,* but what amount of tradition may exist in support
of an incident on which the devout imagination loves
to dwell we have not been able to ascertain.

It is evident that Joseph's intention was to settle at
Bethlehem, an intention which, as we have seen reason to believe, he had entertained previous to the exile
into Egypt; but when he heard that Archelaus reigned
in Judea in the place of his father, Herod, he was afraid
to go thither. Hence we incidentally learn two things:
first, how little information concerning public affairs
had reached the Holy Family in their retirement; nor
need this be any matter of astonishment to us when

we reflect on the rareness of communication in those days, and on the widely different constitution of society, which caused its limitation in great measure to special classes. Joseph had heard nothing from the poor people with whom he conversed, and, we may rely upon it, he never made enquiries or went in search of news. His messengers were angels, not men; and he calmly awaited their orders and such information as it pleased God they should convey to him. In the second place, we learn that Joseph was aware of the character of Archelaus, and that he did not think that Jesus would be safe in his vicinity. Whether or not this would have been the case, it had been so ordained in the divine decrees that Jesus was not to be brought up at Bethlehem, but at Nazareth. While Joseph hesitated and, doubtless, prayed for guidance, the angel appeared to him for the fourth time to direct him how to act. "Being warned in sleep," we are told (*Matt.* 2:22, 23), "he retired into the quarters of Galilee. And, coming, he dwelt in a city called Nazareth: that it might be fulfilled which was said by the prophets, that He shall be called a Nazarite."

Chapter XXXIX

Abode at Nazareth—Education of Jesus.

HEROD ANTIPAS, Tetrarch of Galilee, was, equally with Archelaus, the son of Herod, the Ascalonite. But his mother was a Jewess, and he had not, like Archelaus, the son of a woman of Samaria, inherited the sanguinary temper of his father. True, we hear in the Gospel of his vicious and immoral life, and how, to keep his rash promise to a dancer, he cut off the head of John the Baptist, but we know also that he did it reluctantly; whereas to his father, Herod, and his cruel brother, Archelaus, the shedding of blood was a matter of supreme indifference; nay, rather one might say it was a ferocious propensity and passion. Moreover, he would not know that Jesus dwelling at Nazareth was the Child on whose account the Innocents had been massacred. The birth of the Messias was by the prophet Micheas associated with Bethlehem; and no one would have thought of seeking Him in Nazareth. Joseph might, therefore, by returning to his old domicile at that place, be entirely reassured as to the safety of the Divine Child. No doubt God could have protected His Son from all danger in Bethlehem, but so also He might have concealed Him from the rage of Herod without sending Him into Egypt. Archelaus, however, was not to be left long in possession of his power, being dethroned and exiled by the Roman Emperor; yet it did not please God on that account to bid Joseph leave Nazareth and take up his abode at

Bethlehem; for, as has been seen, it entered into the designs of Divine Providence that Jesus should be brought up at Nazareth, even as in the exile into Egypt a double purpose was fulfilled, as we have indicated.

It has been a question with commentators as to where in the Old Testament we are to seek for this prediction; indeed, the difficulty of identifying it has led to the supposition that the book in which it was contained was among those sacred writings which have been lost.[1] But undoubtedly the fact was as St. Matthew affirms; Jesus was to be called a Nazarite, and never to lose that name, which was to be inscribed on His Cross: "Jesus of Nazareth, King of the Jews." (*John* 19:19). He was not to be brought up and be known in the city of David His father, nor in the neighborhood of those who might have heard reports of the glories attending His birth. He was to be reared in obscure and despised Nazareth, so despised that Nathaniel, as we know, replied to Philip's invitation to come and see Jesus, the predicted Messias, the son of Joseph of Nazareth: "Can anything of good come from Nazareth?" (*John* 1:45, 46); and the Jews afterwards, reasoning with those who said He was the Christ, objected: "Doth the Christ come out of Galilee? Doth not the Scripture say that Christ cometh of the seed of David, and from Bethlehem, the town where David was?" (*John* 7:41, 42). So it pleased God, in His secret ways, that His Son might at once be hidden and manifested; manifested to those who were true of heart, hidden from those who would not see, and therefore took scandal at His supposed origin.

St. Jerome, however, has suggested a solution of the difficulty by showing that St. Matthew is referring, not to the precise words of the Sacred Text, but to their sense; and, in confirmation of this view, he notices that the Evangelist says, "That it might be fulfilled which

---

1. Other similar instances are the prophecy of Enoch, quoted by St. Jude (v. 14), who also alludes (v. 9) to the contention of St. Michael with Satan respecting the body of Moses, which is not mentioned elsewhere in Holy Writ; but both these may have been "originally known by revelation and transmitted by tradition." See notes to the Douay version *in loc.*

was said by the prophets," not naming any particular prophet, as he would otherwise have done; in which case the application of the prediction must, probably, be sought in the etymology of the name of the place itself. This has received various interpretations, and, prominently, that of Flowery. Now, Jesus was the Flower of the Field, and the Flower of the Rod of Jesse. Hence St. Jerome, writing to Marcella, says: "Let us go to Nazareth, and there, according to the interpretation of its name, we shall see the Flower of Galilee." The term Nazarite has also been considered to signify holy, separated, or set apart, and consecrated by God. Accordingly, we read of Samson, who was a figure of Jesus, that the angel declared he "was to be a Nazarite of God from his infancy and from his mother's womb; and begin to deliver Israel from the hands of the Philistines." (*Jgs.* 13:5). In this sense likewise the name would be supremely applicable to the Saviour of the world.

The two Evangelists, St. Matthew and St. Luke, both agree in stating that the Holy Family returned to Nazareth, and dwelt there, the latter omitting all mention of the Flight into Egypt, as the former had made no allusion to the Purification. Having, then, conducted the Holy Family back to Nazareth, St. Luke sums up his account of the boyhood of Jesus in these few words: "And the Child grew and waxed strong, full of wisdom, and the grace of God was in Him." (*Luke* 2:40). They are few words, but how much is contained in them! We have already commented on expressions used a few verses further on with reference to Jesus advancing in wisdom and age, when it was question of the mode in which our Divine Lord condescended to make progress like other children. Here, then, we shall only notice the remarkable words: "the grace of God was in Him." Some might think this was little to say of One who was Himself the very Source of all grace. And truly so He was, in virtue of His Divine Nature, but that Divine Nature was united to a perfect human nature, perfect, although having no human personality. He was "perfect God and

perfect man, of reasonable soul and human flesh subsisting," to use the words of the Athanasian Creed.
Jesus, then, had a human soul, the recipient of grace
as are other human souls, only the Spirit was not given
to Him by measure. St. Luke would seem to be especially the Evangelist of the Humanity of the Son of
God, which needed to be clearly proclaimed as well as
His Divinity. Heresies were to assail both. Accordingly,
he testifies to it emphatically in those words: "the grace
of God was in Him." St. Luke is not believed to have
personally known Our Lord, although Epiphanius seems
to consider that he was a disciple towards the close of
the life of Jesus. Be this as it may—and it is by no
means the common opinion—he himself does not pre-
tend to relate as an eyewitness, but only as "having
diligently attained to all things from the beginning."
(*Luke* 1:3). Yet we know that, although he had thus
carefully collected his information from eyewitnesses,
he, equally with the other Evangelists, wrote by the
inspiration of the Spirit of God; for inspiration, while
giving light to the mind of the writer, guiding him in
the selection of the materials he possesses and guarding him from error in his statements, does not preclude
the use of the natural faculties, as they might be
employed by other historians in the collection of facts,
and to secure accuracy. "He had diligently attained to
all things from the beginning"; that is, from the beginning of the life he relates, namely, that of Jesus; and
from what source could he have learned that beginning
save from the lips of Mary herself? The Annunciation,
the Adoration of the Shepherds, the Visitation, the Purification, and the Finding of Jesus in the Temple, are
related in detail by St. Luke, and by no other Evangelist; and who was there upon earth who could have
communicated these things to him but the Blessed
Mother of God herself, she of whom the Eternal Word
had taken human flesh?

It is not amiss to remind ourselves of this, for it
helps to throw a light on the manner in which Joseph

is spoken of in this Gospel. That manner must surely reflect Mary's wishes, and what were Mary's wishes at any time but to fulfill His Will of whom she was ever the handmaid as well as the mother? Now Joseph is always intimately associated with Mary by this Evangelist in their relationship to Jesus, and he stands alone in using the common term "parents," in speaking of them. This was the case in relating the Presentation of Jesus in the Temple, where he says that "His parents brought in the Child Jesus, to do for Him according to the custom of the Law"; and that Simeon blessed them both, as has been already noticed. And again, after Simeon's "Nunc dimittis," he says that "His father and mother were wondering at those things which were spoken concerning Him" (*Luke* 2:27, 33, 34), giving the first place, as usual in common parlance, to the father. We have already quoted these passages when relating the incidents of the Purification, but we recall them now as showing the light in which Mary desired her spouse to be regarded; and that light must undoubtedly have been the true one, designed by God Himself. St. Augustine—and he does not stand alone among the Doctors in this matter—observes that it is in order to demonstrate the sublime dignity of Joseph that St. Luke puts him on an equality with Mary in calling them both the parents of Jesus. That an Evangelist, who knew the mystery of the Incarnation, having himself previously narrated the Annunciation of the angel to Mary, should, speaking by inspiration, use this language, certainly shows that Joseph was—excluding always natural generation—a true father; not a mere putative father, or a father by adoption and by law. Since, then, he was not a father in the ordinary sense, that is, according to the flesh, he must have been so in a mystical sense, according to the spirit; and this is why St. Augustine frequently repeats that Joseph is so much the more truly a father in that he is so spiritually and virginally;[2] he is the true father of Jesus accord-

2. *De Concord. Evang. Serm.* li. cap. xx.

ing to the spirit, as Mary is His true mother according to the flesh. The Evangelist is, therefore, fully justified in calling this blessed couple conjointly the parents of Jesus.

Mary and Joseph, no doubt, resumed their old occupations in their humble abode at Nazareth; in addition to which they had now to provide for the care and the education of the Divine Child. He had been pleased to have Himself treated as other children of His nation, by subjecting Himself to all the rites and precepts of the Old Law; it is not surprising, therefore, if Mary and Joseph, who had fulfilled these obligations for Him, when, being an infant, He was unable to do so for Himself, should continue, in proportion as His age increased and permitted it, to direct and instruct Him in exercises of piety—He Himself manifesting such to be His desire—bringing Him up in accordance with the precepts of the Law given to Israel, and in all things which were conformable and suitable to their own condition in life. This would appear to us a very difficult and delicate duty for Mary and Joseph to perform towards their Son, so as at once worthily to correspond to the office with which they were charged, and duly to recognize the dignity of that Son.

Some observations on this subject which Vincenzo de Vit makes in his *Love of St. Joseph*[3] are worthy of being here quoted. Referring to this difficulty, he is of opinion that there exists in the very disposition of human nature itself a mode of conciliation. "It is an observation," he says, "which experience daily confirms, that among the various inclinations which it has pleased the Creator to implant in our human nature, there are two which strikingly manifest themselves in children from their earliest days: the tendency to imitation or to the reproduction of those acts which they see performed by those who surround them; and curiosity, or

---

3. Cap. xxvi. pp. 163-165.

the desire to know what these same acts signify. Now, there cannot be the smallest doubt but that the Child Jesus, by reason of His human nature, must have been endowed with all these natural qualities in their fullness and perfection, in virtue of which Mary and Joseph would, without in the least ignoring who He truly was, be drawn, as it were, without willing it and, I may even add, sweetly drawn and guided by Himself to the discharge of their parental office." That the Child Jesus had the first of these qualities, De Vit illustrates and proves from what He Himself said to the Jews with reference to His Divine Sonship. They had reproached Him with making Himself equal to God, and this was His reply: "Amen, amen, I say unto you, the Son cannot do anything of Himself, but what He seeth the Father doing; for what things soever He doth, these the Son also doth in like manner. For the Father loveth the Son, and showeth Him all things which Himself doth." (*John* 5:18-20). Now, this writer argues, if Jesus taught this of His Divine Nature, we may readily believe the like of Him in regard to His human nature, which in Him must have been most perfect. "Whence it may be concluded," he says, "that if it is the nature of the son to imitate his father, it is only necessary, in order to educate him, to set before him the example of his parents. Let these be perfect and the education will be perfect; and perfect, therefore, was the education of the Child Jesus. For His Heavenly Father had given Him in Mary such a mother as was a perfect vessel of election in the fullest sense of the term; nor was Joseph unlike her in the perfection which was her appanage; the same Eternal Father having chosen him to be her companion and co-operator in a ministry of so delicate a nature. . . . But example is not sufficient; the son needs something more. Scarcely has he learned from his parents the use of speech when immediately, from that innate desire which he has to know and understand, he besieges them with a thousand various questions, calling for an answer which cannot be evaded.

Not otherwise, I believe, did the Child Jesus act with regard to His mother and St. Joseph; and I feel it to be sufficient proof of this, that He behaved in a similar manner with the Doctors of the Law in the Temple, as we shall see, 'hearing them and asking them questions.'" (*Luke* 2:46).

An example of the solicitous care which the parents of Jesus took of His religious education is afforded in their yearly visits to Jerusalem to keep the Paschal solemnity, which was the occasion, when He was twelve years old, of the incident to which reference is here made, and which we are about to narrate more fully.

Chapter XL

The Finding of Jesus in the Temple.

ALL the males in Israel were bound by the Mosaic Law to appear three times yearly before the Lord, Lord, that is, at the Feast of the Pasch, at Pentecost, and at the Feast of Tabernacles. The place to which the Hebrews were thus obliged to resort was that in which the Ark of the Covenant was guarded by the priests, which, after being removed to different places, was by David brought to Mount Sion, and was afterwards lodged in the Temple which Solomon built for it at Jerusalem. (2 Kgs. 6; 3 Kgs. 8; 2 Par. 5). Women were not bound by this law, although they often observed it from devotion. We read, in fact, of Elcana, father of the prophet Samuel, and his whole family, including his wives, sons, and daughters, going every year to Silo, where the Ark then was, to join in the accustomed sacrifices. (1 Kgs. 1:3). Children also, as well as women, were exempted from this obligation, save that, by a custom which came to have the force of law, boys were obliged to keep all the Mosaic precepts, civil as well as religious, when they had completed thirteen years of age; and parents, we are told, were in the habit of initiating them in these observances during the previous year; these boys were consequently called "sons of the precept."[1] But, as has been just observed, fathers were often accustomed to take their children with them at a much earlier age to be present at the solemn feasts of the Law.

---

1. See Calmet's *Commentary on St. Luke,* ii. 42.

That the parents of Jesus observed this devotional practice, and always took Jesus with them whenever they went up together to Jerusalem, there can be no doubt. We cannot conceive them leaving the Divine Child behind at Nazareth, or even willingly separating themselves from His company. If the Evangelist makes no mention of any festival save that of the Pasch,[2] nor of the presence of Jesus at the Paschal solemnity until His twelfth year, it is on account of the incident which then took place, and which he relates. The Evangelists do not travel beyond their immediate scope and object;[3] we have frequent examples of this reticence on their part, of which heretics and unbelievers have not been slow to take advantage. St. Luke's expressions cannot be understood to imply that Jesus went up for the first time to Jerusalem when He was twelve years old, but only that on that occasion He remained behind. These are his words: "And His parents went every year to Jerusalem at the solemn day of the Pasch. And when He was twelve years old, they going up into Jerusalem according to the custom of the feast, and having fulfilled the days, when they returned, the Child Jesus remained in Jerusalem; and His parents knew it not." (*Luke* 2:41-43). The meaning is obvious. It was sufficient, in order to the fulfillment of the precept, to be present one day only in the Temple, but the Holy Family, mirror of all religious perfection, remained the whole week of the Azymes, or Unleavened Bread, in Jerusalem, as is implied in the phrase, "having fulfilled the days." After finishing their thanksgiving, Mary and Joseph prepared to return to Nazareth, in company, no doubt, for a portion of the way, until their respective roads would diverge, with not a few of their holy relatives. Various suggestions have been made as to how it was that Jesus remained in Jerusalem without the knowl-

---

2. Joseph would be under the obligation of attending all the three great feasts. Maria d'Agreda thinks that he attended two of them alone, but that at the Pasch Mary and Jesus always accompanied him.

3. On this subject and on the distinguishing characteristics of the four Gospels see F. Coleridge's Introduction to *The Life of our Life*, 2 vols.

edge of His parents. That by His divine power He could conceal Himself from them, and pass away unobserved, we can readily understand: herein does not lie the difficulty; but how was it that, careful as they were of Him, a whole day should elapse without their noticing His absence? The solution adopted by Canon Vitali, and the most usual, seems to be also the most satisfactory. It is as follows.

In order to avoid all confusion and disorder in that great mixture of persons of all classes gathered from every part of Palestine for the Paschal solemnity, and now returning to their homes, it had been arranged that, on leaving the Holy City, the men should assemble by themselves in bands, and the women in like manner. Thus they each set out separately, and remained separate until they all reached the halting-place for the night.[4] It was optional for children to accompany either of their parents. Jesus was in the Temple with Mary and Joseph until the close of their act of thanksgiving; but when this was concluded, and the Virgin was leaving on one side with the women, and Joseph on the other with the men, He by a marvellous act of His power withdrew Himself from their sight, Joseph being persuaded that He had remained with His Mother, and Mary, on her part, supposing that He had gone with Joseph. Maria d'Agreda says that they were both raised at that moment to an exalted state of contemplation, which diverted their thoughts from all external objects; and well might their attendance at the Paschal solemnities cast them into profound meditation, for they well knew that Jesus was the cause, the object, and the end of the great sacrifice then offered. They would never suspect that He had left them, and remained in the Temple, for this was an act on the part of the Divine Child quite unprecedented, an independent act, of which He had never before given an example. This hiding of Himself from the eyes of His parents

---

4. Epiphanius and, after him, St. Bernard are of opinion that the men and women travelled in distinct groups.

was an instance of the exercise of that divine power which He subsequently renewed in the case of the Scribes and Pharisees when they sought to stone Him (*John* 8:59), and again when His infuriated countrymen would have led Him to the brow of the hill whereon their city was built to precipitate Him thence. (*Luke* 4:29, 30). Without some such prodigy we could scarcely understand the loss of Jesus, considering the great love, care, and vigilance with which Mary and Joseph always watched over Him. And we know that it was through no fault of theirs that it occurred, but from the will of God, that the absence of Jesus might manifest the glory of His Father, the merit of His parents, and the deep counsels of Divine Providence.[5] Jesus, then, remained behind in the Temple, which was indeed His house, and which He made His chief abode during this ever-memorable *triduo.* Here, we may well believe, He prayed long and fervently for the salvation of men; and saints have told us that He asked alms in Jerusalem, to sanctify and bless by His example, not poverty alone, but extreme indigence.

Joseph having joined the men's caravan, where he would probably find his brother Cleophas and other relatives, while Mary was in the women's company, with Mary of Cleophas and others of their kindred, they journeyed as far as the city of Machmas (now El Bir). We can imagine that the pious pilgrims sang as they went the praises of God, or conversed about holy things, and especially the longed-for coming of the Messias; yet Mary must have been inwardly sad at the unaccustomed absence of her Son, who was the joy of her heart and the light of her eyes, but would console herself with the assurance that He was safe. He was with Joseph, and with Joseph He must needs be safe; neither, we may be sure, would she grudge her holy and beloved spouse the bliss of His company, because for the present she could not be the partner of it. And now

---

5. Isolano, tom. i. par. ii. cap. xiv.

the sun was sinking, and they were all nearing the
walls of Machmas, the first station of those who were
returning from Jerusalem into Galilee. Soon the terrible truth disclosed itself—Jesus was not with Joseph
and He was not with Mary! Tradition supports the
assertion here made, that it was at Machmas[6] the
Blessed Virgin discovered that the Child Jesus was not
in their company, and Martorelli, in his book on the
Holy Land, which he visited, says that a beautiful church
was anciently dedicated to her there, in memory of the
poignant grief of this most tender of mothers, and that
at the time of the Crusades, having been found in a
dilapidated state, it was rebuilt by the soldiers of the
Cross. The walls, he adds, occupy a space of thirty-two
metres in length, but they were in ruins in his time,
seeming in their desolation to participate in Mary's sorrow.[7] Was ever sorrow, indeed, like unto her sorrow?
Yet Joseph's might well bear some comparison there-
with, since his soul was, according to its measure, filled
to overflowing with unutterable grief. Next to Jesus,
who was pre-eminently the Man of Sorrows, must, without question, rank the Queen of Dolors, His Mother,
for, after the Human Soul of the Word Incarnate, with
Its immeasurable capacities for sorrow and suffering,
must follow, at whatever distance, that of His most holy
Mother, which was a very ocean of sorrow; and next to
hers, and closely resembling it in the same marvellous
capacity, was, surely, the soul of the incomparable
Joseph, divinely chosen to be her spouse, and made so
like to her. These two stand by themselves in a proxi-
mate pre-eminence of sorrow, as Mary herself may be
said to have recognized in those remarkable words
addressed to her Son: "Thy father and I have sought
Thee sorrowing." (*Luke* 2:48). Their grief must have
admitted of comparison, or she would not have uttered
them, and uttered them, too, to Him who was the Truth

---

6. Adricomius, *in Ephraim,* n. 66. See also P. Quaresmio, *Elucidazione della Terra
   Santa,* tom. ii.
7. *Terra Santa,* cap. xvii. p. 394.

Itself, and knew what was in the hearts of all men. "Why," says Cartagena, "were both sorrowing but that both loved; and why were both so sorrowful but that together they loved so much? Mary sorrowed because she was a mother; Joseph because he was a father. The sorrow of Mary was the sorrow of Joseph; both alike sorrowed. The love of Mary was the love of Joseph. Their sorrow and their love for the Child Jesus were alike, according to their respective capacities; immeasurable and illimitable. Mary is all sorrow and love; Joseph is all sorrow and love."[8] The love and tenderness of Joseph for the Divine Child were, indeed, inexpressible; his sorrow, too, was therefore like to that of Mary, a very ocean, unfathomable to us, whose shallow hearts are, in comparison with his, so cold and insensible. He had, besides, a poignant sense of grief peculiarly his own, in that he had received from above the special charge of Jesus; and what account could he now give of that precious deposit?

But to return to the Gospel narrative. St. Luke's words are: "Thinking He was in the company, they came a day's journey." Each of them, as is evident, believed Him to be so until they met at the close of the day. The Evangelist continues: "and sought Him among their kinsfolk and acquaintance"—this, as we understand it, would be naturally their first step, however hopeless, before retracing their way—"and, not finding Him, they returned into Jerusalem seeking Him." The explanation we have given, which is the one most usually adopted, and which is easily reconcilable with the words of St. Luke, would seem to approve itself to the mind more than that which De Vit, in his Life of our Saint, prefers. According to him, there was no separation between Joseph and Mary, they travelled all day together, and, not seeing Jesus with them, were satisfied that He was in the company of some of their kindred and friends; and, in order to exonerate the Blessed Virgin and her holy spouse from any imputation of neg-

8. *Encom. S. Joseph,* Orat. i.

ligence in this journeying a whole day without ascer-
taining where Jesus was, he says that a reason may
be found for their conduct in the custom of their nation,
to which some allusion has been made, namely, that
boys who had completed thirteen years of age were held
to be bound by all the Mosaic laws, and hence became
personally responsible for their actions. It was a kind
of emancipation from paternal control, for which parents (as we have said) were in the habit of preparing
their sons the previous year, by a certain relaxation in
their exercise of superintendence and authority, according them a reasonable liberty. Now, though (he says)
all this was not needed in the case of the Child Jesus,
he seems to think that His parents would conform themselves to the common practice, that nothing might tran-
spire to those around them of the secret committed to
their keeping. But such a reason can hardly be judged
sufficient to account for this apparent want of solicitude. Solicitude, considering the youth of Jesus and the
mixed crowd of persons who composed the caravan,
would be natural in the most ordinary parents, and it
would have implied no peculiar exercise of authority if
that solicitude had sought relief in enquiry and search.
How much more might we anticipate that Joseph and
Mary, cognizant also, as they were, of the perils which
had beset His infancy, would not acquiesce tranquilly
for a whole day in the absence of Jesus without ascer-
taining, at least, that He was in safe keeping. No doubt
this loss was a mystery from beginning to end, but in
whatever way it may have pleased God thus to hide it
in the first instance from the knowledge of Mary and
Joseph, and silence anxiety in their hearts, the method
suggested does not seem to be the most probable, for
the reasons we have given.

If, however, we cannot accept De Vit's views on this
confessedly difficult question, we entirely agree with
him in believing that the three days' loss ought to count
inclusively from the day when Jesus withdrew Himself
and remained behind in Jerusalem, and not that Mary

and Joseph sought Him for three whole days in Jerusalem. There seems to be a kind of parallel between this loss and the three days during which Jesus remained in the grave, which was, in fact, only one whole day and a portion of two others. Of the third, indeed, it was the veriest fraction of a day, for He rose from the grave very early in the morning and before the sun was above the horizon. Yet St. Mark's words are: "and after three days rise again." (*Mark* 8:31). This was the Hebrew mode of computing days, a portion of the day counting for a day. So also, in the loss and finding of Jesus, the three days probably include the day on which Joseph and Mary journeyed unconscious of their loss until near its close; the second, during which they were wholly engaged in their weary and agonizing search for Him; and the third, on which they joyfully found Him in the Temple, but how early in the day that might be we do not know.

Tradition tells us little or nothing of the particulars of the previous search, but saints and favored souls have had visions on the subject, which furnish matter for pious meditation and assist our devotion in its consideration, especially those of Maria d'Agreda. She dwells particularly on the calmness and equanimity which Our Lady preserved notwithstanding her inward martyrdom, which could only be compared to what she was afterwards to endure at the foot of the Cross; many, indeed, have been led to believe that for several reasons the three days' loss was the most severe of Mary's dolors. Yet she never for one moment lost her interior peace of mind; and this was the more wonderful and meritorious because, as the same contemplative tells us, God left her during those three days in an ordinary state of grace, deprived of all the special favors with which her soul was enriched at other times. Of the glorious Patriarch, St. Joseph, she also says that he suffered incomparable affliction and grief, going from one place to another, sometimes with his holy spouse, sometimes alone, while she made search in another direction. His life, she adds, would have been in grievous peril if the hand of the Lord had not fortified and supported him, and if the Virgin most prudent had not herself in the midst of her own sorrow consoled her spouse and entreated him to take some brief repose. For the love he bore the Divine Child was so intense that it urged him to seek for his lost Treasure with an anxiety and a vehemence which made him forget either to eat or to sleep. Our Lord revealed to Jeanne Bénigne Gojos, a nun of the Order of the Visitation, who lived in the 17th century and had a great devotion to the Sacred Humanity, that the pain which both Mary and Joseph suffered was so great that without His secret assistance they could not have survived. Their sorrow, He said, was simply incomprehensible, and that He alone could understand it. From His revelations to this holy soul we also gather that this third dolor of Our Lady was one of the chief sufferings of our Blessed Lord Himself.[9]

At last, both of them having received an angelic suggestion to repair to the Temple, they hastened thither, and there they beheld Jesus seated in the midst of the Doctors, "hearing them and asking them questions." The hall where the Doctors held their conferences and also admitted disciples who sought instruction from them, was, it appears, not in the body of the Temple; Mary and Joseph might, therefore, have entered the sacred building, and missed the object of their search, but the time was come for the close of their trial. All eyes were fixed upon Jesus, for the Doctors, whom He had first interrogated, had now themselves become the questioners, and were listening with admiration to the words of wisdom which came from the lips of the Boy-God. "All that heard Him," says St. Luke, "were astonished at His wisdom and His answers." (*Luke* 2:47). And truly His divine loveliness was in itself sufficient to entrance them. A kingly majesty was on His youthful brow. His beau-

9. See F. Faber, *The Foot of the Cross,* chap. iv. pp. 214, 215.

tiful hair rested on His shoulders; and we are told that it never grew beyond the length suitable for man, and, moreover, that not one hair of His adorable Head ever fell from it until plucked out by the cruel Roman soldiers. His eyes were radiant with the light of truth and the fire of charity. What was He saying, and what had they asked? No doubt, it had reference to the promised Messias, the expectation of whose advent was general in Israel at that day. The same favored soul whom we have already quoted says that He was rectifying their erroneous notions concerning a glorious and warlike Deliverer, who was to restore political independence to their nation and give them sovereignty over their enemies and oppressors. He was pointing out the prophecies, by them overlooked, which spoke of the humiliation and sufferings of the Messias; and, had the hearts of the listeners been as open to grace as were their eyes and ears to the charm of what they saw and heard, they must have recognized the predicted Liberator in the marvellous Boy whose wisdom so astonished them. Nevertheless we may hope that some good seed may have been sown in the hearts of more than one among them, which was later to bear fruit. We are reluctant to think that He who accorded to His Apostle Peter a miraculous draught of no less than three thousand souls at his first sermon should Himself on this occasion, when He mysteriously forestalled His own future public ministry by occupying Himself thus early about His Eternal Father's interests, have drawn no single one into His net, and that bare admiration and wonder were all that He succeeded in eliciting. Be this as it may, we cannot penetrate the secret counsels of God, nor expect always to see what we call the reasons of things. Even in the natural world we are constantly at fault in this respect; how much more should it be so in the higher region of grace, in the invisible things of God, and the secret dispensations of His Providence!

Even Mary and Joseph are said to have wondered on seeing Him. (*Luke* 2:48). There was something new to them in His voice, manner, attitude, and bearing. Never had they seen Him like to that before. Doubtless they stood for a moment looking on, silent for very joy and awe. Joseph, indeed, continued silent. Though, as the father and head, he had the first right to question the Boy concerning His absence, he spoke not a word, leaving it to the Mother to make that touching remonstrance to her Son and her God which we so well know: "Son, why hast Thou done so to us? Behold, Thy father and I have sought Thee sorrowing." We have already made several comments on her mention of Joseph's sorrow along with and indeed, as it were, before her own, and have pointed to all which such mention implies with reference to the rights, dignity, and position of her incomparable spouse, and will only here subjoin two further observations: first, that great and immeasurable as had been Mary's grief, it had not only not made her forget that of Joseph, but had not prevented her from sorrowing deeply for the anguish of soul which she knew he was enduring—this may give us some slight idea of its intensity; secondly, that she knew how dear he was to Jesus, since in her pathetic remonstrance and appeal she alludes to this sorrow of His father as sure to move His filial heart as much as would the thought of her own. Jesus replied: "How is it that you sought Me? Did you not know that I must be about My Father's business?" or, as some have rendered the last words, "in My Father's house?" Whichever rendering be adopted, the meaning is substantially the same; but it was a meaning hidden for the time both from Mary and from Joseph, for the Evangelist says: "They understood not the word that He spoke unto them." In whatever sense we are to understand this temporary ignorance on the part of His parents, we cannot, at any rate, suppose that they did not comprehend that He was speaking of His Eternal Father and of the mission which He had come upon earth to fulfill. Mary and Joseph well knew that their Jesus was the true Son of God, and they knew also the end for which He had come. The angel had clearly announced it to them. Independently, therefore, of all the heavenly illuminations which they, and especially the Mother of God herself, must have since received from the Divine Child, no obscurity could exist in their minds on this matter. That which for the present had been withheld from them was, it would seem, the full knowledge of the order, mode, and time in which this divine mission was to be accomplished, and, in particular, the place in that order which the present unexpected act of Jesus held, or what was its full significance. The reply of Jesus to His mother did not as yet raise the veil, but light, no doubt, came to her, and to Joseph also, when they had once more with them Him who is "the true light of men." For, even as hereafter at the marriage-feast of Cana of Galilee He publicly manifested His power at His mother's request, before the hour was yet come,[10] so, when now displaying the first rays of His glory before the Doctors of Israel, and in the very midst of His divine instructions, a word from Mary made Him leave all, and meekly return with her and Joseph to Nazareth. It is a mystery quite beyond our comprehension—though a fitting subject for meditation and reverent conjecture—this assertion by Our Lord of His sovereign independence even in His boyhood; to be immediately followed, as it was, by His voluntary and complete subjection to His parents for so many subsequent years. "And He went down with them, and came to Nazareth, and was subject to them." (*Luke* 2:51).

---

10. It is scarcely necessary to observe that when Our Lord says His hour was not come, we are to understand that it would not have come but for His mother's intercession. What a light is here shown on the wonderful potency of prayer and, above all, on Mary's influence with her Son!

Chapter XLI

The Subjection of Jesus.

THE Evangelist sums up in these few words, "He was subject to them," the history of eighteen years of the life of the Saviour. Of what He did or what He said during that long space of time we have no record save this—that He upon whose bidding the angels wait received and obeyed the commands of Mary and Joseph. St. Luke has devoted a large portion of his Gospel to relating details of the early Infancy of Jesus, and of the last hours which He spent on earth, but in regard to His occupation during eighteen entire years of His adorable life he has only this brief sentence. Is it because the Son of God did nothing either mysterious or marvellous during that time? It would be impious to entertain such a thought. Is it because the Evangelist knew no more than he told? This is scarcely credible in the case of one who must have learned from the lips of the Blessed Virgin herself all the particulars which he gives of the Annunciation, the Nativity, and the Adoration of the Shepherds, and who has not omitted one word of the "Magnificat," or of the "Canticle of Zachary," or of that of the ancient Simeon. How is it, then, that he has no more to tell us? It must be because the whole employment of Jesus during those eighteen years was to obey in everything the most holy Virgin and St. Joseph; so that, although He performed innumerable heroic acts of piety, humility, patience, zeal, and all other virtues, nevertheless, to all appearance,

His sole occupation during that whole period was the doing the will of His parents. St. John, the beloved disciple and the last of the Evangelists, who treats of those portions of the life of Jesus which the rest had omitted or only lightly touched upon, has added nothing to these few words of St. Luke concerning the hidden life of Jesus, the Man-God, although his intimate association with Mary during many years after Our Lord's Ascension furnished him with the opportunity of knowing as much or even more than may have been communicated to the other. We may, therefore, conclude that Jesus applied Himself in such wise to the practice of obedience during those years that His life is fully described in the short words of the Evangelist—that He was subject to Joseph and Mary. But how much is contained in these words! They well deserve that we should bestow some deep consideration upon them, and specially as regards the obedience paid to Joseph; for Jesus was subject, not only to the mother who had borne Him, but to the father whom He had Himself elected and endowed with the authority which appertains to the paternal relationship; and such authority in the family is supreme. That of the two parents is joint as respects the child, but it is the father's which is necessarily absolute, since the wife also is subject to him; nor was it otherwise in the Holy Family.

Two truths, then, present themselves for our acceptance. First, that Joseph was invested with the right of commanding Jesus Christ; secondly, that he in effect used that right, the right of being obeyed by Him whom all things obey. We may notice in the Gospels that the Saviour subjected Himself in different modes to three different classes of persons: to His Heavenly Father, to the Blessed Virgin and St. Joseph, and to ecclesiastical and secular rulers. When He obeyed His Eternal Father, He did so as matter of obligation, because, considered in His human nature, He depended upon God, and naturally owed Him homage and submission. When He executed the orders of secular and ecclesiastical rulers, it was without any obligation whatsoever on His part, for no king, emperor, or pontiff possessed jurisdiction over the Sacred Humanity of Jesus, united to the Word, infinitely raised above them, and incapable of inferiority in their regard. But when He submitted Himself to the rule of the Blessed Virgin and St. Joseph, He recognized in them a certain authority to command Him, and a certain superiority which no one else possessed; although (as St. Ambrose points out) this authority was not communicated to them independently of His Will, but only because He was pleased thus to subject Himself to their rule and take them for His superiors of His own free choice.

Cardinal Toledo teaches that we must judge of the Saviour in His submission to the Blessed Virgin and Joseph in the same manner as we regard His obedience to the Law of Moses. The Incarnate Word was in no way subject to that Law; yet, from an excessive love of humiliation and of obedience, He willed to submit to the necessity of keeping it when He abased Himself to receive the rite of circumcision, by which, according to St. Paul, the recipient publicly contracted the debt or obligation to fulfill all the precepts of the Law. (*Gal.* 5:3). Thus Jesus, according to the rigor of justice, was in no way subject to Mary and Joseph, who, so far from being His natural superiors, were themselves His legitimate subjects. And well He manifested this when He separated Himself from them to remain behind in Jerusalem without asking their permission, nay, without even apprising them of His intention. Nevertheless, even as He abased Himself from the height of His throne in Heaven to the lowliness of the crib, so also, when He became man, He humbled Himself from the elevation to which the supreme dignity of His Sacred Humanity raised Him, to place Himself in the quality of an inferior at the feet of Mary and Joseph. Sons are not bound to follow the guidance of their parents and to obey them precisely because they are their sons; for, if this were so, a son would never be emancipated, but so long as his father lived would remain under his control and dominion. But this is not the case, since a son may even become his father's superior, or be raised to the position of his prelate. Respect he would always continue to owe him as his father, but not obedience. Children are bound to obey their parents as well as to hold them in all respect, chiefly on account of the dependent state in which they are born. Nature thus places them in subjection to their parents, from whom they receive nurture and instruction in all that is necessary for attaining and developing the perfection of man's estate; which perfection is only, as it were, in germ and potentiality within them. Jesus, then, on coming into the world, did not place Himself under the guidance of the Blessed Virgin solely because she had contributed a portion of her pure blood to form a body for Him; neither did He subject Himself to Joseph solely because he was Mary's spouse; but because in His birth He willed to be weak and helpless like other children who need their parents' care and assistance.

It was not without design that the Incarnation was announced to the Blessed Virgin before the coming of the Word, and to Joseph after the accomplishment of the mystery. This design was not solely that we might be given to understand that Joseph had no part in it, but (as St. Ambrose[1] says) because the Word would not become incarnate without the free consent of Mary, nor be born as a poor and abject child, almost forsaken of the whole world, before our saint had accepted the care of Him and the charge of bringing Him up as his son, and had thus been invested with the right, bestowed on him by Heaven, of exercising authority over Him. Joseph, thy wife shall bear a Son, who shall feel all the rigors of cold, the sufferings of hunger and thirst, and all the infirmities of this life; He will thus be obliged to have recourse to thee. In this wise the Holy Spirit declares (as St. Thomas shows when

1. *Hom.* ii. *in Natali Domini.*

expounding this passage of the Gospel) the power of St. Joseph, manifesting to us the necessity Jesus was pleased to have of him for His nurture, and the offices which he was to render to Him. This was also the teaching of the Angelic Doctor's master, Albert the Great, who addresses St. Joseph in like manner, telling him that, although he had in no wise contributed to the conception of the Saviour, nevertheless it must be confessed that he had been in a certain way necessary for His bringing up, in consequence of the condition in which He willed to come into the world.[2] So that this Divine Infant seems to place Himself in the arms of Joseph and implore his aid, as though He was incapable of defending or supporting Himself, and thereby puts him in possession of all the authority which other fathers have over their children, an authority which we may say comes of natural right as well as by divine institution.

It implies no derogation from the dignity and supereminence of the holy Mother of God to affirm that, as regards the authority to command Jesus and rule His actions exteriorly, Joseph had received higher powers than even Mary herself; for this is only according to the order appointed by God, to which the Holy Family entirely conformed. The Gospel clearly proves that such was the case, by relating how the angels did not bear the orders of Heaven to Mary, but to Joseph. And wherefore save that he was the lord of this Sacred Family, who was in everything to be the prime mover of its actions, and to whom it appertained to determine in particular all that was necessary for the care and preservation of Jesus, his Son? A learned interpreter of Scripture[3] observes that, although the Virgin was the first to know that her Son should be named Jesus, nevertheless the angel did not send St. Joseph to learn it from this sovereign lady, but informed him of it in a special apparition, and explained to him the signifi-

---

2. *In Matthaeum,* cap. i. St. Anselm says the same.
3. Laurentius Aponte *in Matthaeum,* cap. i.

cation of this Name, even as if he alone had been concerned in the matter. For (as this same Doctor continues to show) Joseph, in the capacity of father of the family, ought not to receive his orders from his spouse, nor was it meet that the lord of a house should not dispose things except by the expressed will of those who were dependent on him. The angels made the same declaration in favor of Joseph's authority by revealing to him the necessity of the flight into Egypt, leaving the Blessed Virgin to be informed of the will of Heaven from the lips of her spouse; and, again, it was to him that the message was addressed when the term of exile had arrived. Moreover, when Joseph was apprehensive of going into Judea for fear of Archelaus, it was from the angel that he sought and received light, although at his side was the Queen of angels, and even the Creator of the angels. The Mother of God and the Incarnate Word Himself honored his authority by their silence, as being the head of the Family, to whom perfect obedience was due.

Joseph, then, accepted and used the authority given to him over Jesus, but with fear and trepidation, to use Origen's expression.[4] He never gave Him a command in anything except in humble obedience to the command which he had himself received; and he did so with the same reverence as that with which the angels serve Him in Heaven; and with good reason, for it was, indeed, a fearful thing to be charged with directing the conduct of a God, and to be placed as superior over Him in whose presence the highest of creatures, the most exalted of the angelic hierarchies, the Seraphim and the Cherubim, prostrate and annihilate themselves, casting their crowns at His feet. Moses was raised to a high dignity when he was appointed ruler and legislator of the people of God, but here we have one who was exalted to be ruler and governor of the God of that people. Nay, as Scripture tells us that the Lord said to Moses, "Behold I have appointed thee the God of Pharao"

4. *Hom.* xx. *in Lucam.*

(*Exod.* 7:1), we may also be allowed to say that Joseph was, in a manner, set to be the God of God Himself. Words which, taken literally, are exaggerations or paradoxes become needful, so to say, in order to enable our minds to grasp a fact which, from its very magnificence and startling nature, is liable to evade our full apprehension—namely, the obedience of God to a man. It is said in the Book of Josue, when "the sun stood still in the midst of heaven, and hasted not to go down the space of one day" (*Josue* 10:13, 14) at the voice of the leader of Israel, "there was not before nor after so long a day, the Lord obeying the voice of a man"; but not for twenty-four hours alone did the Lord obey the voice of Joseph, but for well-nigh thirty years. Moreover, it must be noted that Josue prayed first to the Lord, and then commanded the sun, which was only a material creature of His hand, but Joseph commanded the Sun of Justice Himself, who had called all things out of nothing.

Next to the unapproachable dignity of the great Mother of God there is none that can be compared to that of Joseph. The great Chancellor of the University of Paris, Gerson, says that, as the obedience of Jesus to Joseph was an inestimable act of humility, it implies, correspondingly, in Joseph an incomparable dignity.[5] This authority of Joseph is, in fact, so singular that, not only has no man, however favored and exalted, whether by miraculous or prophetical or apostolic powers, but no angel has ever shared it even for a moment, nor ever will during the eternal ages; and, if this be so, we may well hold, with Gerson, that the having received the obedience of the Supreme Lord of all things belongs to Joseph as an exclusive and unexampled honor. In this glory he stands alone with Mary. God said to St. Bridget: "My Son was so obedient that when Joseph said do this or that immediately He did it."[6] The blessed spirits of Heaven must have contemplated such a spec-

---

5. *Sermo de Nativ.* vi.
6. *Revelations*, b. vi. c. lviii.

tacle with inconceivable amazement and admiration: the Very Son of God neither moving a step, nor speaking a word, nor taking food or repose, save under Joseph's direction. They must have marvelled to behold Him—and that at an age when other sons are emancipated—willingly prolonging for eighteen years the period of submission, making Himself a humble apprentice in Joseph's workshop and laboring with him at his trade; for it was in this character, as the Gospel tells us, He was familiarly known to His countrymen, who, scandalized afterwards at the wisdom and power with which He spoke, querulously asked, "Is not this the carpenter's son? Is not this the carpenter?" (*Matt.* 13:55; *Mark* 6:3). Sight more admirable to the angelic hosts was this self-humiliation of the Eternal Word than the creation of the visible world, when God laid the corner-stone thereof, and the morning stars together praised Him, and all the sons of God burst forth in joyful melody. (*Job* 38:6, 7).

The Son of God once declared that He came, "not to be ministered unto but to minister"; at another time He said, "I am in the midst of you as he that serveth" (*Matt.* 20:28; *Mark* 10:45; *Luke* 22:27); and of this He gave a striking example before the Last Supper which He ate with His Apostles, when He took a towel, and girded Himself, and washed their feet (*John* 13:4, 5); but for eighteen years He had performed the lowliest offices in the House of Nazareth. St. Basil, in the 4th chapter of his "Monastic Constitutions," says that the Saviour worked indefatigably all the day to serve and obey Mary and Joseph, who thus received the continual ministrations of their God. St. Justin, in his "Dialogue with Tryphon," affirms that the Incarnate Word helped St. Joseph in his workshop, relieving him in his toils as far as human strength permitted; for this beloved Son had the greatest respect for His foster-father, and, according to St. Jerome, could not fail in this obligation. Necessitous persons look for no help in their domestic work but such as their children can give them; and (as St. Laurence Justinian observes) the Son of God, desiring in nothing to distinguish Himself from common people, was as a servant in the house of Mary and Joseph, that He might one day say with truth that He came, not to be ministered unto, but to minister. Again, St. Bonaventura says that Mary and Joseph were too poor to have servants, but the Lord of the World by His ministrations stood in the place of servant to them.

Let us, then, with the learned and devout Gerson, contemplate this King of Glory, this God of Majesty, this Sovereign Lord of men and of angels, demeaning Himself in such wise as regards His parents that He might well be believed to be their servant rather than their son; often (he says) lighting the fire, preparing the meals, washing the dishes, or carrying water from the fountain.[7] This adorable Saviour passed the last three years of His life in His public ministry and in marvellous acts of charity towards all who needed help; but the time was short which He devoted to this display of His goodness to His people in comparison with that which He had devoted to Joseph, never leaving his side for so large a portion of the life He spent on earth, occupied with the one abiding solicitude to obey him and render him filial duty and submission. "We are not to suppose," says St. Bernard, "that the Mother of God and her spouse bade Him only do such things as were agreeable, and never what was difficult or would have been contrary to His natural inclination. We may believe, for instance, that Jesus would not so soon have left the assembly of Doctors in the Temple, where He was occupying Himself about the interests of His Eternal Father, had Joseph and Mary, who had been seeking Him for three days, been willing that He should remain longer. But, as He knew they desired to take Him with them, docile to His mother's voice, He arose and returned with them to Nazareth."[8] But all this was in accordance with His divine purpose and will, which

7. *Josephina,* dist. iii.
8. *Sermo in Cantic.* xix.

was that, while inwardly reverencing and adoring Him, His parents should outwardly treat Him as other children are treated, using their own discretion and prudence in His guidance.

As it is impossible to fathom or duly comprehend the humility of the Son of God, who was pleased to occupy for so many years the position of an inferior in a poor carpenter's house, placing Himself entirely under his orders and at his disposal, so also is it beyond our power adequately to realize the grandeur of Joseph's exaltation. But the power given to him over the Saviour and His most holy Mother was united in him to a proportionate fund of prudence and rectitude to enable him to sustain such a charge with all the decorum and perfection that was needed. Above all, let us consider what must have been the rectitude of his will, which was so exact that a God was pleased to accept it as the rule of His exterior actions. Holy Scripture and all theology, nay, even natural reason, teaches us that the Supreme Will of God must be the regulator of all the movements of our will. And yet Jesus Christ, who had the Law of His Father deeply graven in the midst of His heart, and who Himself was the Living Law, had imparted such equity and rectitude to the will of our saint that He subjected His own will to his. Hence we may infer, with the learned Chancellor, that, since the Saviour of the world was infinitely exalted above all men and angels, and all things created or possible to be created, and one moment of His divine life was more precious in the sight of God than a million of ages of the life of all creation, it is a legitimate consequence of this truth to hold that it was a greater glory for Joseph to command Jesus, not for thirty years, as in fact he did, but for a single moment, than to have had absolute power unto the end of time over the whole creation of God. God, after the creation of the world, was not richer than He was before, neither did He become more powerful after the Incarnation of the Word than He had been for all eternity. Nevertheless, had it been possible that the authority of God should receive any increment, the creation and government of all the spheres would have added far less to it than the Incarnation of His Son, because, having hitherto governed only creatures, He then began to command His Divine Word. Now, it was this power which He was pleased to share with Joseph; so that the authority of this great saint may be said to have been magnified to such a degree as in some wise to bear a resemblance to that of God Himself. Oh, the incomparable greatness and glory of Joseph! What have we as yet done for the honor of him whom the Eternal King so much desireth to honor?

The following beautiful passage from the Pastoral Letter of the Bishop of Nottingham, Advent, 1887, which fell under our notice after the above was written, will serve to illustrate much of what has gone before, and to quicken and deepen our perception, in detail, of the life which the Holy Family led at Nazareth, and of the obedience which, in His divine condescendence, Jesus paid His parents.

"In the Holy House of Nazareth the Child was the teacher of His parents, not taught by them.[9] The Eternal Wisdom of God could learn nothing from any creature, even in His human nature. Divine light, and teaching, and grace poured forth from His every act and word into the souls of His father and mother. Yet, while He thus enlightened them—the two most perfect of His creatures—His every look and word were those of a docile and obedient child. He followed their directions and obeyed their commands, and also the commands of His Heavenly Father, sent, not to Him directly, but to them for Him. He sat at their feet, hearing them and asking them questions, as He did with the priests in the Temple, while they always hung upon His words, and pondered them in their hearts, and wondered at

---

9. It is hardly necessary to observe that this assertion, that the Child Jesus was not taught by His parents, in no wise excludes the mysterious condescension by which He was pleased to learn from them in a secondary and experimental sense; to which, indeed, the Bishop himself immediately afterwards alludes, where he speaks of Jesus sitting at their feet, hearing them, and asking them questions.

His wisdom and at His answers. How marvellous must have been that school of Heavenly Wisdom, in which Mary and Joseph were but pupils, where even the Virgin of Good Counsel, the Seat of Wisdom herself, and her dear Spouse Joseph, the just man, the Son of David, did not always comprehend the Word that was said, but had to ponder divine mysteries in their hearts, waiting for further illuminations of the Holy Spirit! What perfect and consummate wisdom was there breathed forth! What inconceivable perfection and holiness of life was there displayed! The angels who looked on in adoring admiration might have reversed the words of our prayer, and have besought God that His Will might be done by them in Heaven, as it was done by Jesus, Mary, and Joseph upon earth. For thirty years was Jesus subject to His parents, and for thirty years did that Paradise of Delights, the Holy House of Nazareth, continue to offer to us a model of every Christian virtue, a type and pattern of what our homes should be, or which, at least according to their measure, they should imitate.

"Dear children in Christ, visit in spirit that Holy House. Consider its poverty, and the rudeness and simplicity of its furniture. Behold also the exquisite cleanliness, order, and neatness which is manifested in every detail. Though poor, it is bright and cheerful, made so by the looks and words of loving hearts, and the labors of loving hands. The Eternal God, and the Queen of Heaven and her Spouse, chose not to have earthly magnificence around them. Had they possessed it, they, being perfect, would have sold what they had, and given to the poor. They chose the better part of voluntary poverty, working with their hands that even so they might have wherewith to give to those who were in need. They knew how many of the houses of their children must be poor and destitute. Therefore they took their part in poverty and destitution, to show that the deepest poverty can be enriched and made happy by the love of God and man.

"How can we sufficiently admire the unremitting, uncomplaining, self-sacrificing toil of Joseph, who was honored by the Eternal Father with the office of governing and working for His Eternal Son and the Ever-Blessed Virgin Mother! How shall we wonder at the sweet, gentle, assiduous labors of Mary, watching over the comfort of her husband and her Child, never forgetting nor omitting anything which might cheer or alleviate their earthly lot, and brightening their home with her beautiful and loving smiles! How shall we adore the gracious Child, advancing daily in wisdom, and age, and grace with God and man, manifesting ever more and more to His parents' wondering eyes the hidden perfections of His Godhead, and captivating their love by His reverent obedience, and sweet attentions, and gentle loving ways! What a school of love was there! Jesus the Ocean of created love and charity; Mary full of grace and love as much as was possible to a pure creature; Joseph, the Guardian-Father of Jesus, the Virgin-Husband of Mary, the Companion and Disciple of both, and filled by God with that supreme love which such offices required. Every kind of created tenderness was there, following upon charity, and unspeakably dear to the God of charity, who has known how to create so many varieties and sweetnesses of love in the heart of man. There was the ineffable mutual love of husband for wife and of wife for husband, intensified as well as purified by the virginity of both. There was the love of father and the love of mother for their Child; for He was the Child of both, pre-ordained to be the recompense and bond of their virginal union. There was the love of the Child for His parents, intense and perfect, as must have been every kind of love in the Sacred Heart of God. . . . There was the pattern of charity, piety, and mutual service and kindness, which should be imitated in every Catholic home. There was also a pattern of religious observance and of the worship of God. We read in the Holy Scriptures how perfectly Our Lord and His parents observed the law of Moses, even when they might have justly claimed to be dispensed from it. We know He and His Blessed Mother and St. Joseph were ever engaged in unceasing love and contemplation of the Divinity. We can imagine, then, something of the assiduity, reverence, and devotion of the spiritual exercises of the Holy Family in their humble home. Prayer of the heart without ceasing, prayer in common many times a day, prayer undistracted, prayer made with adoring reverence in the visible presence of God, prayer enriched with the divine blessing of Him who prayed. There also was the virtue of temperance in its perfection. In Jesus and Mary it found no evil passion to restrain, and in Joseph a Saint already made perfect in self-denial. Yet it lost nothing of its perfection or of the fullness of its practice. Obedience, self-sacrifice, humility, mortification of the appetites, meekness, chastity, modesty, sobriety—all concurred to the holiness and happiness of that home."

Chapter XLII

Joseph's Interior Life of Prayer and Contemplation.

THE inner life is the true life of a man, and all the splendor and merit exhibited in the visible and sensible actions of the saints have their principle within and their source in the heart, hidden from men and patent to God only. The Royal Prophet was well persuaded of this truth, for, after his panegyric of the surpassing beauty of the Spouse who had won the heart of the Eternal King, he confesses that it is needful to look within, for it is thence that all her glory proceeds: "All the glory of the King's daughter is from within." (*Ps.* 44:14).

We may safely affirm that never was there a saint whose life was so interior as was that of Joseph. Duly to honor him, then, it behooves us, with the aid of light from above, to endeavor to penetrate into his soul, there to admire the priceless treasures of grace and the virtues with which God replenished it, especially while his life was "hid with Christ in God." (*Col.* 3:3). In considering this interior life of Joseph we may securely take as our guide the pronouncement of Holy Church, and adopt her language concerning him in those hymns composed in his honor which have been admitted into her divine offices. Now, what does she say? "Others after a pious death attain to perfect bliss, but thou, O Joseph, while yet living on earth art in the enjoyment of God, like to the saints in Heaven."[1]

The Holy See has authorized these words, and the voices of countless priests have consecrated them in all the sanctuaries of our holy religion in which they have been sung. May we not add that they have been in a manner canonized by the general veneration with which they have been received and reechoed in the hearts of the great body of the faithful? If, then, we desire to know what was the life which Joseph led while on earth, that secret life, that life of the Spirit, that life which passes between God and the soul, we are taught by the Church that it was like that of the Blessed in Heaven. And that we may not suppose that there is any exaggeration in such an estimate, the Church reiterates, or rather reinforces, her first utterances, assuring us that in the hidden life of Joseph privileges may be discerned which none of the saints in Paradise enjoy. His lot on earth surpassed even that of the saints in Heaven.[2] This suffices us; we need no further description of the interior of Joseph than that with which Holy Church has herself supplied us.

Now, we know that the saints in Heaven are full of light, burning with love, and plunged in delights inexpressible. Full of light, because penetrated with the resplendent rays and receiving the powerful impression of the Uncreated Light in their understandings;[3] burning with divine love, because in Heaven they behold nothing but what is lovable, and because they participate in their measure, according to the prayer of the Son, in that love which unites Him and His Eternal Father;[4] immersed in ineffable joys, because in Heaven all is perfectly conformable to our feelings and inclinations, and to the spiritual faculties of our souls. With truth is the bliss of Heaven called "the joy of the Lord" (*Matt.* 25:21, 23), since it is union with Him who is

---

1. "Post mortem reliquos mors pia consecrat: tu vivens, superis par, frueris Deo."
—*Hymnus in Festo S. Joseph,* die xix. Martii.
2. "Mira sorte beatior."—*Ibid.*
3. "In Thy light shall we see light."—*Ps* 35:10.
4. "That the love wherewith Thou hast loved Me may be in them, and I in them."
—*John* 17:26.

essential Joy, as He is also Light and Love. Such also was Joseph's life on earth; full of light, burning with love, and plunged in ineffable delight. Nor let it be supposed that any contradiction is implied between what is here said and the assertion that he led a life of inward martyrdom, a martyrdom of love. We shall have occasion to return to this subject hereafter; it may be sufficient meanwhile to remark that the highest joy and the greatest suffering and sorrow are not incompatible, since we know that Our Lord's human soul possessed the Beatific Vision while He was leading a life of suffering on earth, and even during His Passion, though He did not permit His inferior nature to derive any consolation therefrom. In this state He stands alone, since it resulted from the union in Him of two natures—the Divine and the human—in virtue of which His human soul enjoyed the vision of God. Still, saints, in their degree, and after His pattern, have been enabled to rejoice and sorrow at the same time, and even to exult in the midst of the keenest anguish, through the grace communicated to the superior region of their souls.

Scripture teaches us that there are two principal ways in which God communicates supernatural light to His dearest friends on earth. The first is through prayer; and the second is by a ray of divine wisdom, with which He graciously enlightens the understanding. Joseph, then, during his whole life had his soul raised in God, "the Father of Lights" (*Jas.* 1:17), by the highest contemplation; and, in the next place, this great God united him to Himself by infusing into his understanding the purest rays of His infinite wisdom. Hence his soul was full of light. If little, comparatively, is said by the Evangelists respecting Joseph, we may be sure that that little has always a special meaning, which we should do well to study and examine. We are often surprised by what saints and Doctors of the Church have extracted out of certain passages of Scripture which to our denser spiritual senses would not have been discernible. When St. Luke mentions Joseph and Mary wondering at what they beheld and heard on finding Jesus in the Temple, many holy writers have believed that this was no ordinary wonder. The Evangelist, so parsimonious of his words, would scarcely have recorded so particularly what might have been readily supposed of any ordinary parents. It has, then, been believed by saints and Doctors that the two holy spouses were rapt in a species of ecstasy, that highest form of ecstasy of which the most perfect souls are alone capable, and which leaves the mind in the full exercise of its faculties. For the suspension of the senses is no measure of the sublimity of the rapture, as all who have the slightest acquaintance with mystical theology are aware. Far from this, it is a well-known fact that a soul new to such divine favors, and but moderately advanced in the spiritual life, will swoon away or become outwardly insensible at the slightest supernatural communication, although graces of a much higher order would fail so to affect one who was more familiar with these divine operations, and who had made greater progress in the life of perfection. That Our Lady's life was one of almost abiding ecstasy we may well believe, an ecstasy indefinitely heightened by every fresh manifestation of the glory of her Divine Son; and her ecstatic state must have surpassed all to which saints have been raised. Nevertheless, we cannot imagine that she was ever deprived of the use of her external senses; and of holy Joseph we may believe the same.[5] How do we suppose he was interiorly engaged when in his workshop with Jesus at his side? Doubtless he was in silent rapture, but at the same time giving full exterior attention to the work in which his hands were occupied. And how was his mind employed during his journeys? It was contemplating the infinite perfections of God-made-Man, whom he held in his arms or led by his hand. How,

---

5. See concerning St. Joseph's ecstasies, Eduardus Vastorius, *In Enar. Coruscationum;* Damianus, *Sermo de Natali Domini; Enar.* xix.; and Joannes Bourgehesius, *in Harmon. Evang.* p. 75, who says that St. Joseph was in almost continual ecstasy.

also, during his exile, apart from converse with men? His life, in short, was a continual communication with God by means of never-ceasing prayer, not only while waking, but even while sleeping, as several Doctors opine.

It is worthy of notice that whenever the angel brought to Joseph any command from God, he always spoke to him when sleeping. This singular mode of apparition, we have good authority for believing, was more glorious than that which has been customary with other saints, and was a mark of the eminent virtue of Joseph. Such was the view of a learned interpreter who flourished more than eight centuries ago.[6] We may fairly conclude that Gerson had the same thought when he tells us that the slumber of this great saint was not an effect of nature but of grace, which never ceased to operate in his soul at those times when he gave some repose to his body.[7] Or rather, did not Gerson, with many other Doctors, mean to teach us thereby that Joseph was raised to that state of spiritual silence and plunged in that mystic sleep during which contemplatives discourse with God after having attained to the most perfect union with Him? The learned Simon de Cassia, indeed, held that this sleep of our saint was a rapture, one of those ecstasies which were continual during almost his whole life.[8] St. John Chrysostom compares the sleep of Joseph with the trance into which God plunged Adam when He formed Eve;[9] and, since many Doctors judge that this deep sleep or trance of the first man was an ecstatic slumber, we may readily admit that the sleep of Mary's spouse was akin to ecstasy, and that his slumber was mysterious in its character. The sleep of Peter in his dungeon and that of Joseph differed widely. The angel caused a great splendor to fill the prison, in order to make the Apostle open his eyes; and this did not suffice, until the blessed spirit touched him, to rouse him out of his deep slumber. But

---

6. Christianus Druthmaurs, *Exposit. in Matthaeum,* cap. iv.
7. *Josephina, et Opusculum de Conjugio Joseph et Mariae.*
8. Lib. ii. cap xvi. *in Evangelia.*
9. *Hom.* i. *in Matthaeum.*

each time that the angel came to speak to Joseph when sleeping, he had only to present himself and speak one word in order to be recognized, heard, and obeyed; because this great Saint, in whom the exercises of nature scarcely suspended the operations of grace, slept a sleep more resembling an ecstasy than a common slumber; and it was easy for him to perceive and hearken to an angel at the same time that he was familiarly conversing with the God who sent him.

In order to taste the sweetness of contemplation, it was necessary for Arsenius, that solitary so famous in ecclesiastical history, to retire into the desert. "Fly, Arsenius; leave the world, and keep silence," were the words by which the angel called him from the imperial court into solitude. But Joseph, toiling in his workshop, making laborious journeys, and daily treating for the purposes of his trade with persons of various classes, had his spirit always perfectly united to God and hidden in a mysterious solitude. The spouse in the Canticles says that her spirit watched during her bodily repose: "I sleep, but my heart watcheth." (*Cant.* 5:2). Joseph, on the contrary, might have said that his body watched while his spirit slept, for, according to the Father of the Church just quoted, while his exterior senses were occupied in those important affairs with which Heaven had charged him for the government of the noblest family which ever existed on earth, his spirit was always in a mystic sleep conversing with God, having been raised by contemplation above all created things, and separated from all the importunate ideas which sensible objects suggest;[10] almost after the manner in which angels perform their offices on earth without losing either the memory or the savor of heavenly things. The Archangel Gabriel, when treating with the Blessed Virgin of the mystery of the Incarnation of the Word, was not distracted from the contemplation of the Supreme Good; nor did Raphael cease to fix his eyes on God

---

10. *Hom.* iv. *in Matthaeum.*

while acting as guide and companion to the young Tobias.
Our Lord, indeed, expressly tells us that the angel-
guardian of every little child beholds the face of His
Father in Heaven. St. Athanasius lays it down as almost
an impossibility that Joseph could for a moment turn
away his mind from the contemplation of heavenly
things.[11] The young Tobias, says St. Augustine, led his
blind father by the hand to guide him on his way while
that ancient saint taught his son the road to Heaven
by his salutary counsels; but we may say, on the contrary, that, while Joseph guided Jesus on His journeys,
his own soul was rapt into the empyrean by profound
contemplation, to which the Divine Infant drew him.

How much we should love to know the nature of this
high contemplation of our saint while he held Jesus in
his arms! He does not tell us; he speaks not, either
because his tongue is unable to describe the greatness
of those things which God manifests to him, or because
words must cease in the mouth of one whose spirit no
longer discourses, since it has found its joy and perfect
repose in one idea which occupies and fills it. If fervor
of heart should unloose the tongue in contemplation,
it will only be, says St. John Climacus, to form one
word. "Master!" exclaimed Magdalen, in the ecstasy
which the sight of the risen Saviour caused her. (*John*
20:16). "My Lord and my God!" were the sole words
which the Apostle Thomas could utter when called to
touch the wounds of Jesus. (*John* 20:28). "O Goodness!"
was St. Bruno's ejaculation when in prayer. "My God
and my all!" were the sole words which the tongue of the
great St. Francis of Assisi could pronounce during his
long and delicious contemplations. St. Louis, Bishop of
Toulouse, spent his time of prayer in saying these three
words: "God suffices me." It needed only the exclamation, "O Charity!" to send St. Francis of Paula into an
ecstasy; scarcely had he uttered it when his spirit was
raised above all created things into closest union with

---

11. *Sermo de Descriptione Dominae Nostrae Mariae.*

God. Thus we may believe that during his continual prayer Joseph could only say, "O Jesus, my Son!" and that in pronouncing these words his spirit would enter into the profoundest contemplation of the infinite perfections of the God-made-Man. If the prayer of the contemplative is, as we may say, only one word addressed to God, so also it is but one word that God on His part causes the contemplative soul to hear. Witness what the Evangelist relates of Jesus, who said only "Mary" when making Himself known to her who in her rapture could say only "Master." In the same way we may imagine the Infant Saviour saying only to our contemplative saint, "Joseph, My father," but in these words, accompanied with tender embraces, He says all things to him. As we know that the Eternal Father and His Only Son have for the everlasting ages uttered but one single word, Each to Other, a word which exceeds all discourse, for it comprehends all things, and will continue to utter it forever, a word which never ceases, but is repeated through eternity;[12] so also the earthly father of Jesus and this beloved Son-made-Man spoke few words during the long period of their association, but undoubtedly they treated each other as father and son; and, in saying this, we say what furnishes abundant matter for contemplation, and, indeed, it contains more than we are able to grasp or comprehend; for it would be necessary to penetrate into the very depths of the interior of Joseph's soul as well as that of our Divine Lord to understand its full signification.

St. John the Evangelist enjoyed for a brief hour a blissful ecstasy while reclining on the bosom of the Saviour, but how many times did not the Saviour Himself take His repose on that of Joseph, and sleep sweetly in his arms! Every kind of divine and human light enclosed in the Heart of the Saviour must, in a sense, have been infused into the soul of Joseph, when He thus lovingly reposed in his embrace. "Come ye to Him

---

12. "God hath spoken once" (*Ps.* 61:12). St. Augustine thus expounds this passage.

and be enlightened," says the Royal Prophet. (*Ps.* 33:6). But how could Joseph approach nearer to Him? He has Him in his arms, resting on his bosom. Jesus, then, does not treat Joseph merely as a friend, to which privilege He admitted His Apostles, communicating to them some of His secrets (*John* 15:15), but as a father, raising his spirit to understand the highest mysteries; so that, if we are to credit St. Bernardine,[13] we must place the incomparable Joseph at the head of all the greatest contemplatives, since he lived in a continual state of contemplation, in its most exalted form. His life was, therefore, a life of divine illumination; and, if the Israelites could not endure to look on the face of Moses when he came down from converse with God on the Mount by reason of its dazzling brightness, so we may conceive that the very angels themselves beheld with astonishment the radiance of Joseph's countenance, when, raising his spirit to God by contemplation, God came to him in resplendent beams of light, imparting to him a thousand extraordinary gifts for the perfect illumination of his soul.

---

13. *Sermo de S. Joseph.*

Chapter XLIII

Joseph's Singular Faith and Supernatural Wisdom.

THERE are two perfections which we are called upon specially to admire in Joseph: his most singular faith and his eminent supernatural wisdom. These were two rays, as it were, of the Divine understanding descending into the mind of Joseph.

God endowed him with the most lively faith which any saint ever received—always excepting the great Mother of God—and this alone merited for him the title of "just," as a great Cardinal has observed.[1] Again, what light must he have possessed to believe, simply on hearing the few words which the angel spoke, more mysteries than had been proposed in the course of many centuries to all the ancient Patriarchs and Prophets of the Old Testament! We are so accustomed to the Gospel narrative that, perhaps, we have never sufficiently realized St. Joseph's merit in this matter. Yet, as we have observed, what the Evangelists do not say is as full of meaning as what they do say. St. Matthew tells us how the angel said to Joseph, "Joseph, son of David, fear not to take unto thee Mary thy wife, for that which is conceived in her is of the Holy Ghost; and she shall bring forth a son, and thou shalt call His name Jesus, for He shall save His people from their sins" (*Matt.* 1:20, 21); but what he does not tell us is that Joseph

---

1. Jacob Card. de Vitriaco, *Sermo in Vigil, Nativ. Domini.*

uttered a word in reply or asked a single question. Yet in this sleep of his there were revealed to our saint the mysteries of the Trinity, the Incarnation, the Redemption, and reconciliation of man to God. He was called to believe that a Virgin should become a mother, and that the son she had conceived was God Himself; that this child was to deliver his people, not, as his countrymen all expected, from the dominion of the Romans, but from the slavery of sin and the tyranny of the devil; in fine, he was required to believe all these mysteries as contained in the angel's message to him, and on his testimony alone, without any miraculous guarantee that he spoke on the part of God. Oh, the sublime faith of Joseph! "O holy and just Joseph," exclaims an illustrious Cardinal,[2] "who didst believe at once, and most firmly, so many, so new, and so unheard-of things!" Thou didst despoil thyself of thy own lights, to submit thy spirit to the word of an angel, penetrating, in an instant, and at their first announcement to thee, so many and such deep truths. Thou neededst not the stimulus of miracles, which have been so necessary in order to lead other men to humble their souls and take upon them the yoke of the Faith; neither wast thou won thereto by the knowledge which we now possess, that for ages since the coming of the Messias so many nations and countless souls have embraced it. All this weight of evidence thou didst lack, but for the assurance of thy faith thou didst ask no greater pledge or proof than Heaven was pleased to grant thee.

We have in Holy Scripture no instance of faith equal to that of Joseph. Compare Gedeon's behavior when an angel came to tell him, in the name of the Lord, that he should deliver Israel out of the hand of Madian. That "most valiant of men" required more than one miraculous sign (*Jgs.* 6:17, 36-40), and those of his own selection, both to ascertain who it was that spoke to him, and also to encourage him to lead the people forth

---

2. Cardinal de Cambrai, *Tract. de S. Josepho.*

to battle. And this defect of perfect faith we meet with, not only in the Old Testament, but also in the New. Some great saints who lived in the times of Jesus and of His Apostles exhibited weakness of this character. Zachary has the testimony of the Evangelist that he "walked in all the commandments and justifications of the Lord without blame" (*Luke* 1:6), still he required something more than an angel's word to believe that his wife should bear a son in her old age. Yet he might have called to mind that such a miracle was not without precedent, since God had vouchsafed a similar boon to Abraham, the father of the faithful, and to his wife, Sara. What comparison, therefore, could there be between the demand made upon Zachary's faith and that which was required of Joseph? Moreover, the angel spoke to Joseph only in his sleep, while to Zachary he solemnly appeared while engaged in the holy functions of his office, standing on the right side of the altar of incense. (*Luke* 1:11). Yet he doubted, and said, " Whereby shall I know this?" (*Luke* 1:18). Ananias was bidden, not by an angel, but by the Lord Himself, in a vision, to go and restore his sight to Saul of Tarsus; yet so alarmed was he at the very sound of the fierce persecutor's name that he ventured on a remonstrance, telling the Lord—almost, one might say, as if He who knoweth all things was not fully acquainted with the circumstances or hardly appreciated the danger of the commission He was giving him—how much evil this man had done to His saints at Jerusalem, and how he had received authority at Damascus to bind all who should invoke His Name; and it was necessary for the Lord to reiterate His command and assure His faltering servant how Saul was a vessel of election before he did His bidding. (*Acts* 9:10-15).

Scripture, often sparing of details, is always particular in giving us word for word the objections and difficulties made by servants of God to divine intimations and commands, whether through slowness of faith or lack of courage. The absence, therefore, in the case of

Joseph, upon every such occasion, of all reply or even request for explanation is full of significance; a significance which we are bound to notice, because it is meant that we should do so. Joseph always believed without hesitation; and this, not because what was proposed to his belief was easy, or that this great saint did not possess a mind capable of perceiving the profundity and the difficulties of the mysteries declared to him; far from it. Joseph was gifted with a mind of large capacities, which he had cultivated and fortified during his whole life by meditation on heavenly things. He also obeyed without remonstrance or delay; and this, not because the commands laid upon him involved nothing arduous in their execution: witness his rising in the middle of the night to flee into Egypt, and asking none of those questions which human prudence would have suggested before encountering the many privations, sufferings, and dangers of such a journey, not for himself alone, but for the two persons whom he loved incomparably more than he loved himself. And how are we to account for all this? How is it that on the angel proposing to him things so hard to believe and difficult to execute, and Joseph being fully competent to perceive all that was apparently incredible in the promises of Heaven and startling in the orders conveyed to him, nevertheless he behaved as if the fullest demonstration had convinced his understanding, and the most complete experience or acquired knowledge had smoothed all the seeming obstacles which stood in the way of obedience? It is because this admirable saint had received from God the most excellent gift of faith, and because his mind was penetrated with the rays of that supernatural light which causes us to adhere to all that God has revealed to us. It was because he lived a life of light on earth, so that in him faith, in itself obscure, was associated with an illumination so brilliant that it resembled that light of glory which fills the understandings of the Blessed in Heaven. The Fathers of the Church are frequent in their admiration of Joseph's undoubting faith. St. Irenaeus,[3] St. John Chrysostom, St. Jerome, and St. Augustine, as well as others, might all be quoted to this effect. St. Anselm (or the author who goes by his name) has a pleasing and ingenious remark as to why, when the angel bade Joseph return into the land of Israel, he did not give him fuller directions. It was, he says, because he desired to have to return to speak to him again.[4] It was a pleasure to this exalted spirit to witness the greatness of Joseph's faith and the submission of his spirit to all the revelations of Heaven. St. Augustine, perhaps above all, gives the highest commendation to the faith of Joseph when he compares it to that of our Lady herself,[5] whom her cousin, St. Elizabeth, filled with the Holy Ghost, addressed as "blessed art thou who hast believed." (*Luke* 1:45).

The supernatural light which Joseph received along with this eminent faith endowed his soul with the most singular prudence and wisdom, gifts which in the natural order he had already possessed in a remarkable degree; for this exalted prudence and wisdom was, indeed, requisite in one to whom was entrusted a higher office than was ever confided to the very angels themselves. Sufficient proof is afforded to us of the eminent supernatural wisdom possessed by Joseph, in Our Lady's behavior when he communicated to her the orders he had received from Heaven to flee into Egypt. Did not Mary know that this journey must be full of hardships and perils, and was not the safety and preservation of her Divine Son the dearest object of her heart? Was she ignorant of the additional danger involved in this sudden departure in the darkness and cold of a winter's night, unprepared and unprovided as they were? Yet she asked not a question to assure herself of the certainty of Joseph's vision in slumber. She, so enlightened in heavenly mysteries, must have known how dif-

---

3. *Adversus Haereses,* cap. xl.
4. *In Matthaeum,* cap. ii.
5. *De Nupt. et Concep.* cap. xi.

ficult and delicate a thing it is to pronounce upon the truth of a revelation, since bad angels as well as good not only can manifest themselves to our exterior senses, but may have access to our imaginations. Nay, even in the case of purely intellectual visions, of which God alone can be the author, since He alone can penetrate into the spirit of man, it is very difficult and needs a high gift of discernment to distinguish them with certainty from those which are formed by the ideas residing in the imagination. All this, as being deeply conversant with the secrets of the inner and mystical life, Mary well knew. Was it not natural, then—would it not seem to have been her duty—under the supposition of any, the slightest, doubt, to ask her spouse to explain the circumstances of this vision in sleep, in order to be sure that it was a supernatural operation, not an illusion? St. Epiphanius[6] asks where is the caution and the prudence which Mary had evinced when heretofore she addressed that question to the angel: "How shall this be done?" (*Luke* 1:34). And yet it seemed as incredible that a God should be forced to take refuge amongst idolaters to save His life, as that a maiden should become a mother without losing her virginity. No one could have blamed Mary if she had asked for some explanation, nor would our saint, we may rest assured, have made the least difficulty in satisfying her anxiety, had she expressed any on the subject. But the Holy Virgin, without replying a word or spending a moment on examining the revelation with which he acquainted her, arose without delay; in which she not only gave a proof of perfect submission, but observed the rules of a prudence altogether divine; for she was so entirely convinced of the wisdom of Joseph and of his supernatural penetration, enabling him to comprehend the most exalted mysteries, that she venerated his words as oracles, knowing that one to whom God had accorded so much light could never hold what was false to be true.

---

6. *Adversus Haereses,* cap. li.

This testimony which the Blessed Virgin gave on this occasion to the wisdom of Joseph is the highest conceivable, when we consider the surpassing light which illuminated her own spirit. Her unquestioning obedience to his directions in a matter of such inappreciable importance, and the estimation in which she clearly held his guidance, are more glorious to him than if all living creatures, the angels included, had united in praising him. God had, in fact, bestowed on Joseph so excellent a gift of wisdom that it enabled him at once to distinguish mysterious from natural slumbers, the voice of angels from that of bad spirits in their disguise, and the revelations of God from the workings of the imagination. And Mary knew it.

Chapter XLIV

Joseph's Love and Life of Bliss.

HEAVEN is the birth-place and home of love. Its blessed inhabitants love much, love forever, and love only what is worthy of love. Joseph, however, was blessed by anticipation, for he passed all his days in the exercise of divine love, and lived a life of love upon earth. The Evangelists do not record a single word of this great saint; he observed, indeed, a marvellous silence. Not, however, an ungracious silence. The silence of ordinary men, as well as their irrepressible flow of words, is often merely selfish. But Joseph's silence and his speech were alike prompted and regulated by the law of charity, a law which excludes both garrulity, on the one hand, and, on the other, a reserve which might offend. We may, therefore, say with truth that Joseph never uttered a superfluous word without thereby attributing to him a taciturnity which would have rendered him unwelcome and distasteful to his neighbors. His words, indeed, were never superfluous, for they had their source in love, but they were also ruled by his will, not forced from him as the expression of his feelings. Hence, we repeat, Joseph's silence was marvellous. How, indeed, would he whose heart was burning with the sacred love of Jesus pour itself forth in converse with men? But even as regards that one absorbing occupation of his heart, his words were few. True love is not talkative; even in the interior of his holy home Joseph spoke little; and it was the same with Mary, his spouse. Their hearts met and were united in this one love, and few words were needed to express mutually what they inwardly felt and lived upon. But we shall have more to say later on of Joseph's silence as well as of his habitual state of contemplation.

When God elects anyone to fill a high office or undertake a great work, He gives him, not only a corresponding elevation of mind, but, above all, much largeness of heart. We see how He dealt with Solomon to fit him to rule a great kingdom: "God gave to Solomon wisdom and understanding exceeding much, and largeness of heart as the sand that is on the sea-shore." (*3 Kgs.* 4:29). So, when He prepared Joseph to hold the place of father to the Saviour, He must have bestowed on him a heart larger beyond measure than what He gave to the King of Israel, that he might be able to love as a father the Son of God Himself; and this, according to the Abbot Rupert,[1] is what the Eternal Father did when He called Joseph to a participation, not only of His dignity, but of His love as a father. He either formed in him an entirely new heart or infused an exceeding increase of tenderness into the heart which he already possessed. Certain it is that He filled him with a love surpassing in generosity and fervor that of any other father; for it was needful that Joseph's paternal love should be in a measure proportioned to the perfections of this Adorable Son. Natural love is sufficient for earthly parents, but the love which our saint bore to Jesus, as His appointed father, was not a mere human love, it was also a supereminently divine love; for, in loving his Son he was exercising the most perfect love of God; since He whom he called his Son was at the same time his God.

As in creatures all is finite, so all is capable of increase. What, then, may we imagine, must have been the growth of this ardent love in the heart of our saint during the long period which he spent with Jesus! Those things which tend naturally to add to human love, in him min-

1. *In Matthaeum,* cap. i.

istered fresh fuel to the divine flame within him. The constant association with the Son of God made Man and given to him as his own Son, the serving Him and being served by Him for thirty years, and, we must add, their marvellous resemblance created a bond between them which was unequalled of its kind. This resemblance, we are told, by that devout client of St. Joseph, the Chancellor Gerson, in his magnificent panegyric of the Saint before the Council of Constance, was most remarkable in his countenance and even in all his outward demeanor. This likeness would be to a certain extent natural, inasmuch as Joseph was nearly related to Mary, but it was, moreover, the expression and result of that extraordinary similarity of temperament and disposition which bound together Jesus and Joseph by a greater natural sympathy than had ever existed between two individuals. And, as nature thus tends through consanguinity to produce a resemblance which fosters love, and as its power in their case had been peculiarly enhanced, so may it also be piously believed (as has been already suggested) that the Holy Ghost in forming the Body of the Incarnate Word heightened this similarity and conformity in such a manner as to add a supernatural character to the relationship which was to unite Jesus with Joseph by a closer bond than ever united a son to his human father.

Another powerful source of love is mutual knowledge. Without some kind of knowledge there can, properly, be no love; and, generally speaking, those love Our Lord best who have the greatest knowledge of His perfections. But to whom were those adorable perfections made known so fully as to Joseph; to whom first—with the exception of Mary—was revealed His Name of Saviour, which contains them all in compendium? How exalted must have been Joseph's perception of the majesty of the Incarnate Word, enclosed in the sacred womb of the Virgin, even previously to this revelation, since it was needful for an angel to descend from Heaven to prevent his withdrawing from his august spouse, as

in his humility he was about to do! Such is the opinion, at least, of many holy Doctors, as being the most
probable, and, at the same time, the most honorable to
Joseph and to Our Blessed Lady. It was given to Joseph
to be the first to know and become enamored of the
riches of the Saviour in the poverty of the crib, and
lovingly to adore the splendor of His glory in the obscurity of the stable. The familiarity to which he was admitted with the Divine Babe, and all the mysteries of the
Infancy, must have inundated his soul with ineffable
sweetness. Mary pondered them in her heart, and so
did Joseph likewise; and all were food for love. And
what shall we say of the thirty years? Who, save the
Blessed Mother herself, ever enjoyed so close and prolonged an intimacy with Jesus as did Joseph? Who,
then, can have equalled him in love? Holy souls have
dwelt on the thought that for many long miles during
the flight into Egypt Joseph carried Him in his arms,
partly to shield Him from the wintry blast in the folds
of his cloak, and partly—especially during the early
part of the journey—to conceal Him; and all that time
he felt the beatings of the Sacred Heart against his
own, and learned secrets which had never been confided even to the blessed spirits in Heaven.

Again, how much does suffering nourish love, and
endear the beloved one for whom the suffering is undergone! We see this constantly in the case of fond parents. But what parent ever suffered so much for his
son as did Joseph for Jesus? All his sufferings were
on His account, and were brought upon him because
he was father to the Messias. He was the first to suffer persecution for Him. The martyrs suffered because
they were disciples of the Son of God, but Joseph paid
the penalty of having been made father to the Incarnate Word. All, however, that he endured was joy
unutterable to his soul, because it was for Jesus, and
gladly would he have welcomed tenfold more cruel
sufferings, that he might give the Saviour fresh proofs
of the tender love of his heart. And what father ever

toiled for his son as did Joseph for Jesus? Other fathers, it is true, concern themselves much for their children's interests, still those children are not their exclusive thought or occupation. But Joseph was so entirely occupied with the interests of Jesus that everything else may be said to have had no place in his thoughts, or to have been perceived and valued only as subservient to that one object.

And not his external actions alone were given to this dear Son, whatever labor, trouble, fatigue, or privation might thus be involved; but, as the Incarnate Word, like His Eternal Father, desires to be served in spirit (*John* 4:24), thus also did Joseph serve Him, never permitting his mind to form a thought, or his heart to entertain an affection, which did not tend to the service of Jesus. The inordinate fondness which not a few parents feel for their children is the unhappy source of many of the sins into which they are themselves betrayed; but Joseph's love for his Son could be only a source of sanctity to him, and the zeal which he evinced to consecrate his whole being to His service is an incontestable proof of that sanctity, as well as the fruit of the love which he bore Him. For this love and this sanctity were, in fact, one and the same thing. Jesus was his God, and, in loving Him, he was loving the Supreme Good as the blessed love Him in Heaven. We must ever bear in mind that there was this singular character in all the acts of Joseph, whether external or internal, which gave them (as Suarez observes) an eminent value. They were performed immediately towards the person of Christ, so that, just as the sin of those who crucified Our Lord was increased in magnitude by the dignity of His person, so with much fuller reason were Joseph's acts of piety and love towards the Person of Jesus beyond measure enhanced, since he performed them with perfect knowledge and love of Him who was their object; a knowledge and a love surpassing that of the very angels themselves and of beatified spirits.

Joseph's life on earth was, indeed (as we have said),

an anticipation of the bliss of those glorified spirits. Bliss implies the full satisfaction of all the desires of the soul, which, having obtained what it sought, and possessing what it longed for, without possibility of losing it, has ceased from all solicitude and is in perfect peace. The soul in a state of bliss is like a body which has found the centre which attracted it, and where it remains undisturbed. Men are continually hoping to find this repose in such earthly objects as allure them, but, when they have obtained them, their hearts are still restless and dissatisfied, because man was made for God, the Supreme and Infinite Good, and without Him cannot know true bliss. But in Jesus Joseph possessed his God, he possessed Him who forms the joy of the Blessed in Heaven; and hence he enjoyed that perfect peace which results from the fulfillment of all the heart's desires. Jesus and Mary were his; what else could he desire? If anxiety for his precious charge troubled at times the surface, so to say, of his soul, it never ruffled the depths below—the inner man. All was tranquillity there. His heart was always replete with satisfaction. No man (says a learned writer) was ever so blessed on earth as Joseph.[2]

Perfect bliss implies, besides the possession of the desired object, the soul's full appreciation and taste of it. In order that this spiritual taste should be intense and penetrating, the soul must be very pure and joined in closest union with God; for, even as food most agreeable to the taste can impart no sweetness to the palate if not in contact with it, so, in order that the soul may taste God, it must be united to Him perfectly. Both these conditions were found, in a supereminent degree, in Joseph. He had ever led a most pure and innocent life, and had merited (as we have seen) the title of "just." His obedience to God was so entire that (according to St. John Damascene[3]) he never failed during his whole life to observe all the precepts of the Law with

---

2. Gaspar à Melo Augustinianus, iu *Matthaeum,* cap. i.
3. *Orat.* i. *de Dormitione; Orat.* iii. *de Nativitate.*

an exactness worthy of the father of Him who came, not to destroy the Law, but to fulfill it. This, however, would have been little had he not also embraced all the truths of the Christian Faith; nay, before the Gospel was published he observed all the Evangelical counsels with an unequalled perfection, so that an illustrious Doctor of these later times describes him as uniting in one an excellent disciple of Moses, an incomparable Christian, and a spiritual man of the highest perfection.[4] The ancient Joseph, who in his purity, as in other things, was a type of our saint, spoke, when tempted to evil, as if he enjoyed a holy impossibility of sinning: "How *can* I do this wicked thing, and sin against my God?" (*Gen.* 39:9). In how much higher a degree must this have been true of our Joseph, penetrated as he was by such great lights of faith, revealing to him the claims of God upon our fidelity and love with far greater clearness than the Joseph of Genesis could have possessed. And, in effect, how could he have been judged worthy of the honor of ruling and guiding two persons who were impeccable, the one by nature, the other by grace, unless he, too, had been in a certain sense incapable of sinning? For it would have been neither reasonable nor becoming that a wandering star should direct the movement of those heavenly lights, in which there was nothing either defective or irregular. St. John Chrysostom invites us to witness the purity of his soul, never stained by the corruption of sin;[5] and the learned Nicetas ascribes to him "a soul irreprehensible in all things."[6] The united Greeks also honor him in their hymns and prayers as a man altogether holy. Such a one, as exempt from sin as it was possible for a creature to be, was marvelously disposed and fitted to taste of heavenly sweetness. We have already alluded more than once to the close union of the soul of Joseph with Jesus, a union so close that it may be characterized as

---

4. Simon de Cassia, *in Evangelia,* lib. ii. cap. i.
5. *Hom.* iv. *in Matthaeum.*
6. Quoted in *Catenae Patrum Graecorum: in Matthaeum,* cap. i.

a complete transformation; that to which the highest contemplatives aspire in this life, and in which, in proportion as it is attained, the soul loses itself blissfully in God, to lead henceforth a life altogether heavenly.

It would be superfluous to add more; particularly as no accumulation of words or of comparisons could adequately explain or illustrate a state so singular and exceptional as that to which Joseph was exalted. Sufficient has been said to prove that the soul of our saint must have been immersed in a bliss which was, in a way, similar to that of the Saints in Heaven. St. Irenaeus affirms that he served Jesus with a continual joy;[7] and a Doctor of later times has declared his belief that Joseph died because unable any longer to sustain the excess of joy caused him by the presence of the Saviour.[8]

But one main difference, a difference to his advantage, existed between the bliss of Joseph and that of the Saints in Heaven. Great as is their joy it bears no fruit. Nothing can add to the measure of their essential beatitude, because nothing can now increase their sanctity. Peter, the Prince of the Apostles, is no holier now than when first he was admitted centuries ago to behold the Face of God in Heaven, and receive his everlasting reward. But Joseph, plunged in an ocean of joy while yet on earth, was meriting every moment its further increase, even by his very joys themselves, which were the fruit of love; and that love, while he was still "in the way," was a merit as well as a reward. The measure of the Saints' merits who have arrived at the goal was closed at the instant of their death, and their recompense was determined, which could henceforth receive no addition save what was accidental. Joseph, while he lived on earth, merited its increase continually by his practice of the most excellent virtues; we cannot wonder, then, if his joy increased to such a degree as to consume his mortal life, as the Doctor just quoted maintains. Another source of the growth of his joys may be

---

7. *Adversus Haereses,* lib. iv. cap. xl.
8. Joannes Bourghesius, *in Harmon. Evang.* lxxvi.

found in the progressive display of the glory of the God-made-Man. For the Saviour, accommodating during His Infancy the manifestation of His person to the order of nature, discovered to this beloved father fresh rays of His divine perfections, as He advanced in age. (*Luke* 1:52). One day he would give proof of His infinite wisdom, another, of His absolute power over creatures; on another occasion it was His prudence or His mercy which He would exhibit. This Divine Flower of the Field, budding and blossoming on the Rod of Jesse, day by day unfolding Its lovely flowers and giving forth a fragrance of Paradise, must have filled the heart of the virgin-father in whose garden It flourished with an ever-increasing delight.

The joys of Joseph on earth had also more extension than those of the Saints in Heaven, because, with the exception of the favored band whose bodies were raised after the Resurrection of Jesus, and who accompanied Him in His glorious Ascension, only the souls of the saints enjoy beatitude, their bodies awaiting the second coming of Our Lord. But the soul of Joseph, replete with spiritual delights even while on earth, could not but communicate to his body a special felicity; for, if the unborn Baptist leaped for joy at the near presence of Jesus still enclosed in His mother's womb, what must have been Joseph's sensible joy who lived ever in His company! The sight of Jesus will be one of the joys of our bodily eyes after the resurrection, but the eyes of Joseph had this joy while he was on earth. Abraham saw His day from afar, and was glad (*John* 8:56); but what must have been the gladness of Joseph who was close to Him for nigh upon thirty years! To His three favored Apostles He showed Himself only once in His glory, when He was transfigured before them on Mount Thabor; but we can have no hesitation in believing, with a holy and great preacher,[9] that to Joseph He thus manifested Himself not once only but very often; not to strengthen his faith, but to reward it. It was St.

9. Bernardine de Bustis, *Sermo* xii. *de Desponsatione Beatae Mariae.*

Hilary's[10] opinion that our saint recognized the mystery of the Incarnation and the majesty of the hidden Word in the womb of the Virgin by the resplendent rays which invested her and issued from her sacred bosom. This splendor (continues the same Father), although imperceptible to the dull eyes of other men, was so dazzling to Joseph that he forbore to look on her face until after her delivery. The Master of Theologians, who examined the subject with scholastic rigor, did not disapprove of the opinion held on this subject by certain Fathers of the Church,[11] who thus interpreted a passage in St. Matthew upon which the impugners of Our Blessed Lady's virginity have endeavored to fix an impious and revolting meaning. If this Sun of Justice shone with so brilliant a light while yet in Mary's womb, it seems, to say the least, highly probable that when He had come forth He would often allow Joseph to behold Him enveloped with glory. This view is confirmed by St. Bridget's revelations, who assures us that the Blessed Virgin told her that she and Joseph often saw Jesus surrounded with light.[12] And what was true of one of Joseph's senses, his eyes, was true of all the rest, which shared, no doubt, in the joy of his soul. No music could equal that of one single word from the mouth of Him whose voice could give sight to the blind, hearing to the deaf, and raise the dead to life. But what could have been comparable to the delight of the Saint when receiving the caresses of his Adorable Son, and even the kisses of His divine lips! For Jesus did not wait for Joseph to ask this favor of Him, as does the spouse in the Canticles—his humility would have restrained him—but, as St. Bernard[13] and the learned Gerson[14] both teach, anticipated his desire by clinging lovingly to his neck and fondly kissing him after the manner of little children. These tender embraces of the Divine

10. Quoted by St. Thomas, in *Matthaeum,* cap. i.
11. See Origen, *in Matthaeum,* cap. i.
12. Chap. lviii.
13. *Sermo* xliii. *in Canticum.*
14. *Super Magnificat.*

Infant must have filled the senses as well as the soul
of Joseph with joy and delight unspeakable.

May we not, then, with the fullest reason accede to
the Church declaring that the interior life of Joseph on
earth was similar, nay, in some respects superior, to
that of the Blessed Saints in Heaven?

Before leaving this subject of Joseph's interior life,
which, exalted as it was, above all that any of his devout
clients can attempt to equal, is nevertheless the model
and pattern of all interior souls, it may be well to say
a few words more concerning his abiding state of contemplation and his silence, if only for the sake of obviat-
ing misconstruction. This is the more necessary because
the devil is not slow to perceive what inappreciable
advantages are to be derived from love and devotion
to St. Joseph, and uses his wiliest arts to keep us at
a distance from him. Unable to persuade us that Joseph
did not enjoy a pre-eminence in sanctity, as he does
now in glory, through his association with the Ever-
Blessed Virgin and the office he fulfilled towards the
Eternal Son of God, the evil one, under the pretext of
exalting him, would at least endeavor, by obscuring the
human side of his character, with all its winning graces,
to diminish what we may call our familiar affection for
him; for familiarity is not in itself derogatory to genuine respect and veneration, as every page in the Gospel
history relating the intercourse of Jesus with His Apostles amply proves. This, we believe, is to many a very
hurtful idea, leading also, as it does, to the persuasion
that heroic sanctity cannot accommodate itself to
nature.

When, therefore, it is asserted, as we have seen it is
by several holy Doctors, that Joseph's life was one of
unceasing contemplation, or ecstasy, as it may be called,
it must never be supposed that this inward attention
to God produced a state of absorption which unfitted
him for the charities and amenities of life. We have
said already that it was of that kind which left the
fullest exercise to all the lower faculties of the mind

as well as to the senses, and, as such, it never obtruded itself on the notice of others, being far removed from that rigidity or abstraction which creates a separation from friends and fellow-creatures. This would appear from the Gospel narrative itself. Joseph was evidently a well-known character in Nazareth. All sorts of persons were familiar with him. They had often greeted and conversed with him. They knew, as we may say, what manner of man he was. They had had dealings with him in his trade; he had worked for them, and, we may be sure, had done his work well, and at a generously moderate price. "Is not this the son of the carpenter?" they said, speaking of Jesus; the carpenter with whom they were all well acquainted. Had there been anything stiff and repellent in the father's demeanor or strange and forbidding in his silence, something probably would have been alleged in disparagement of the Son. But there was nothing in Our Lord's beautiful ways, His ease of speech and winning kindness, which surprised them. All this, we may conceive, was natural and to be expected in the son of a man who had been so trusted, so loved, and so admired in Nazareth and its surroundings. What surprised and irritated them in Jesus were the divine claims and assumptions of one who was, as they thought, the son of the carpenter, their fellow-townsman, with whom they had held familiar intercourse. Joseph, then, we cannot doubt, was all that is human, acceptable, sympathetic, and attractive; known no less for his geniality and kindness than for his integrity and conscientious work, perhaps also for its singular excellence; and it is observable that he is spoken of, not simply as *a* carpenter, but as "*the* carpenter," as though to mention his trade was to name the man.

Again, as to his silence in particular: although we can never be persuaded that Joseph was not sparing of his words, it nowise follows (as we have already suggested) that he was any the less loved on that account. People are not loved for their much speaking, but for speech in season—"a word in season is most excellent,"[15]—and often all the better loved because they know how to be silent and to listen to others rather than indulge their own loquacity. There is a silence which says much, and much that is far more pleasing and engaging than speech would be; a charitable, sympathetic, and expressive silence; and such, we may be sure, was Joseph's. It was a silence which inspired a loving reverence and confidence, which never made him difficult of access, or which hung around him a heavy and unpleasant garb of mystery.

The life of bliss, therefore, all interior, which Joseph led on earth no more hindered his sweet companionship with friends than the vision of God interfered with that of the gracious angel, Raphael, when journeying with Tobias, towards whom he conducted himself during their association, not with the estrangement and reserve of some superior being, but with a marvellous kindness and brotherly affection, so that, until he revealed himself, the young man had no suspicion that he was not what he seemed. Or, to use a still higher, but in some respects a more appropriate comparison, that life of exalted bliss which Joseph inwardly led took away none of the exterior charms of his human intercourse, any more—with reverence we say it—than the Divine Nature in Jesus, his Foster-Son, whom he so closely resembled, detracted from the loveliness and lovableness of His perfect human nature. Nay, rather, the supernatural and the divine would indefinitely enhance the beauty and attractiveness of the natural and the human.

---

15. "Sermo opportunus est optimus." Prov. xv. 23.

Chapter XLV

The Death of Joseph.

HOLY Scripture does not record the death of Joseph. It simply ceases to mention him. That he died before Jesus entered, at thirty years of age, on His public ministry, has certainly been by far the most general opinion, and there appear to be strong reasons to render it the most probable. Yet there are persons—and persons of erudition too—who entertain the opinion that he may even have lived until after the marriage-feast of Cana. We must own to perceiving no valid reason that can be advanced in support of this view, while there seem to be many against it. First and foremost, we should be inclined to place the general belief or, at the least, persuasion of the great body of the faithful, never to be lightly regarded, who certainly hold that Jesus did not begin His public life until His dear foster-father had died the death of the just, died "in the arms of Jesus and Mary," as the Litany of St. Joseph expresses it. A second strong reason for sharing this passive traditional view, as it may be called, is that when the time for the close of the hidden life had arrived, during which Jesus had been subject to His parents, Joseph's work would appear to have been finished and his mission ended. Mary had still a work to do on earth, but Joseph had not; the office for which he was chosen seems now to have been completed. Moreover, we cannot imagine Jesus permanently leaving the house at Nazareth while Joseph lived; for, evidently,

He removed thence when His public life began, and, so far as He had henceforth any fixed abode, dwelt at Capharnaum, His mother accompanying Him thither. She is mentioned from time to time, and is an especially prominent figure at the marriage-feast at Cana in Galilee, where her Divine Son worked His first public miracle at her request. Is it conceivable that, if Joseph had still been living, he should have been passed over in marked silence? Marked, we say, because the invitation given to the disciples of Jesus is mentioned as well as His own, and the presence of His mother. If Joseph's death had not been previously recorded, no more is it recorded at any subsequent time; any argument founded on the omission is, therefore, worthless. No; Joseph, we believe, had gone, and his unnoticed departure is quite in accordance with all that had preceded concerning him. He passes out of sight when he had accomplished the office with which he had been entrusted.[1]

During the years that followed the return to Nazareth Joseph had beheld and, like Mary, must have inwardly pondered the increasing glory of the God-Man. "Jesus," says the Evangelist, "advanced in age and wisdom, and in grace with God and men." (*Luke* 2:52). "Grace with men" can only mean "favor." What wonder if Jesus found favor with men in those days? The human heart is not so corrupt that it cannot admire and value what is lovely and lovable. And truly lovely and lovable was the "Son of the Carpenter." He set before His neighbors an example, always sure to captivate and win approval, of reverence and duty to His parents; He was kind, compassionate, mild, gentle; as yet He did and said nothing to wound their pride or offend their self-love. He had not begun to reprove, or rebuke, or speak with authority, and so He found grace in their eyes. It was not to last. The expression of advancing in grace

---

1. It is only just to state that St. Bonaventura certainly seems to hold that Joseph's life was prolonged until after the beginning of the public ministry, an opinion which Isolano must have shared, since he believed that Jesus baptized Joseph as well as His Blessed Mother.

with God, whether the word be understood here also as signifying favor, or be taken in the sense of an advance in grace in the usual acceptance of the term, presents the same mystery as do some other few passages of a similar character. The mystery and difficulty spring from the assumption of a human nature by the Eternal Son, a nature henceforth as completely His own as was His Divine Nature. In the favor of the Eternal Father it was not possible that this Divine Son, made Man, could advance. From the first He was His Beloved Son in whom He was well pleased, and He had also the plenitude of grace from the first moment of His conception. As, however, it pleased Our Lord not to become incarnate at the full age of man, but to pass through the stages of infancy, childhood, and adolescence, so also He willed to accommodate the manifestation of His grace, wisdom, and power to the natural development to which He had subjected Himself. They underwent no real increase; but the proportion in which it behooved Him to manifest them in connection with His natural growth was capable of increase; and it is in this sense that it was true to say that He advanced in wisdom and in grace. And the same must be understood of the grace, or favor, of His Eternal Father, which was openly manifested at its appointed times and seasons, and in proportion to the exterior manifestation of grace in Jesus. The first special instance recorded is when He was baptized by John. "Heaven was opened, and the Holy Ghost descended in a bodily shape as a dove upon Him, and a voice came from Heaven: Thou art My Beloved Son, in Thee I am well pleased." (*Luke* 3:21, 22). The Evangelist then, after giving His age and genealogy, proceeds: "And Jesus, being full of the Holy Ghost, returned from the Jordan, and was led by the Spirit into the desert." (*Luke* 4:1). St. Matthew, in like manner, after recounting the baptism of Jesus, says: "Then Jesus was led by the Spirit into the desert" (*Matt.* 4:1); and St. Mark, in his parallel account, uses these remarkable words: "And immediately the Spirit drove Him out into the desert." (*Mark* 1:12). But was not Jesus full of the Holy Ghost before His baptism; and had He not always been led by the Spirit of God? Most true, indeed; but it would appear that He now received for manifestation the grace of His mission, which was about to begin, and the public sanction, so to say, and declaration of the favor with which His Eternal Father regarded Him.

But that which Jesus could not Himself receive, a real increase of grace and wisdom, was imparted in abundance to Mary and Joseph, who for so many years drew from the Fountain of all grace and sweetness, and drank of that water which He was afterwards to promise to the Samaritan woman, of which whoso drinks he shall never thirst again. (*John* 4:13). That Mary, from the companionship of her Son, and through her faithful co-operation, was continually receiving an increase in grace and in all spiritual gifts is the general teaching of the Fathers of the Church; and that, next to her, Joseph derived similar fruit we cannot doubt. God had predestined him to partake of these blessings, and had therefore given him the name of Joseph, which signifies increase, a name most appropriate to him (as Albert the Great holds), who in virtue, as regarded himself, his neighbor, and God, received such sublime augmentation.[2] And, if Joseph profited much in the School of Uncreated Wisdom—that is, Jesus—he also must have derived much light from the Seat of Wisdom—that is, Mary. If Mary, like a brilliant lamp, illuminated the whole Church (as the same Doctor affirms),[3] how much more must she have enlightened her most beloved spouse, Joseph! The learned Cartagena[4] says that Joseph penetrated with clearest cognition the most hidden secrets of the heart of Mary, which was the depository of the secrets of God. And, along with his increase in wisdom, his increase in grace proceeded. If, as the Scrip-

---

2. Lib. *Super Missus est.*
3. Lib. *Super Missus est.*
4. Lib. iv. Hom. ix.

ture says, "the path of the just, as a shining light, goeth forwards, and increaseth even to perfect day" (*Prov.* 4:18), what must have been the meridian splendor of this pre-eminently just man, who received in such abundance the light of grace from the Author of grace Himself, and from her who is the treasury and channel of all graces! "What merits and what copious graces adorned his holy soul during his whole life!" says an excellent Doctor, Matthias Navaeus; and, seeing (as he adds) that after his virginal marriage he, next to Mary, was nearest to the Principle and Source of all grace, it is to be believed (according to the doctrine of St. Thomas) that, next to her, he had a larger participation thereof than all other saints.[5]

But Joseph was also advancing in age, and it is generally supposed that towards the close of his days he suffered much from the infirmities of declining years and from enfeebled strength. That he suffered we need not doubt, but there seems reason to question the opinion that he sank under the natural effects of old age, and with a frame worn out by constant labor. A tradition has been preserved in the Eastern Churches, which always cherished much devotion to our saint, that Joseph never underwent any natural decay of strength. This tradition was committed to writing in an ancient legend, as Isolano asserts, and was translated from Hebrew into Latin in the year 1340. It states that, although Joseph grew old in years, the strength of his body never diminished, nor was his eyesight weakened; not a tooth in his mouth had decayed, nor had his memory failed him in the least, but he retained all his powers, and the unimpaired vigor of his limbs, even as in the days of his youth.[6] Nor does this seem incredible; nay, we might make bold to say that it is highly probable. Moses, who brought the children of Israel out of the land of Egypt, died at the age of a hundred and twenty years, and he would not have died even then except that God

5. *Encom. in S. Joseph,* Orat. i.
6. Isolano, tom. ii. par. iv. cap. ix.

would not permit him to bring the people into the promised land on account of his one act of disobedience when he struck the rock (*Num.* 20:11, 12): "And Moses, the servant of the Lord died there, in the land of Moab, by the command of the Lord; and He buried him in the valley of the land of Moab over against Phogor; and no man hath known of his sepulchre until this present day." Moses died, not of natural decay, but by the command of the Lord; for we are expressly told, "his eye was not dim, neither were his teeth moved."[7] Is it, therefore, surprising to learn that he who brought, not Israel, but the Lord of Israel, out of the land of Egypt should have enjoyed the same immunity? It does not follow that Joseph had not felt the fatigues and sufferings of his laborious life, fatigues and sufferings all endured for Jesus. For his greater merit he was not exempted from their natural results, but God sustained him under them, and secretly restored his exhausted strength, that he might be able to begin afresh with "youth renewed like the eagle's." (*Ps.* 102:5). Still less does it ensue from this continual bodily renovation that he did not suffer intensely from what has already received a passing allusion, a martyrdom of love. Saints have at times felt the torrents of this love poured into the frail vessels of their earthly bodies as surpassing their powers to support, and have cried out, "Too much, O Lord, too much!" We may well conceive, then, that without miraculous aid the heart of Joseph could never have borne the excess of the love which continually

---

7. Deut. 34:5-7. We entertain a strong persuasion that nothing is particularly recorded in Scripture without an object. Wherefore, then, this special mention of the perfect state of Moses's body when he died, not from any natural cause, but by the command of the Lord, and was buried by Him? There must be some mystery underlying this obscurely related event, especially as in St. Jude's Epistle (v. 9) allusion is made to that contention between the devil and the Archangel Michael about the body of Moses which we have had occasion to mention. His body, we may well believe, remained entire and untouched by corruption, as have the bodies of many saints; and God, willing thus to preserve it, kept it in concealment under angelic guardianship, almost, we might say, as if He designed to make some further use of the mortal frame of the great lawgiver. Would it be rash to suppose that this design was connected with his appearance on Mount Thabor at our Lord's Transfiguration, in company with Elias, who certainly was still in the body: "And behold two men were talking with Him. And they were Moses and Elias" (St. Luke 9:30)? Both are described, in similar terms, as "men."

flooded it. Moreover, he is believed to have undergone the martyrdom of dolor in the spirit akin to that which Mary was to sustain at the foot of the Cross, when the sword pierced her soul, as Simeon had foretold (*Luke* 2:35); indeed it has been thought that he was allowed to witness interiorly, by anticipation, all the successive stages of the Passion; and in this there is nothing improbable, since it has pleased God to admit many of His saints to a similar participation of His sufferings, by retrospection, in the contemplative state to which He has exalted them; some of them even receiving in their persons the impress of the Sacred Stigmata. Less favor and opportunity of merit could not well be shown to Joseph. Once, on the day of his feast, the Saint appeared to the Venerable Marina de Escobar, and said to her, "The Lord gave me great knowledge of the Holy Scriptures and of prophecy, and I knew all that the Redeemer would have to suffer. The Cross which He had ever before Him from the first moment of His conception, I, too, had present to my mind, which was pierced with it; and thus, while holding this Most Holy Lord in my arms, and often reflecting on all He would have to endure, my tears would pour down upon His sacred garments; at other times, while keeping Him folded in my arms when it was cold, I would warm His Sacred Hands by breathing on them." What a sweet picture we have here of the compassion of Joseph, so that we may say of him what we say of Mary, that he was a martyr, and more than a martyr, because he suffered in the spirit the torments which Christ suffered in His Sacred Body; for, although Joseph was not present at the Passion of Our Lord, being already dead, nevertheless he had been tormented beforehand by His stripes and His thorns, by the buffets, contempt, and ignominy He was to endure, by His cruel nails and agonizing Cross. His love was the measure of his grief, and, since the love which he bore to the Redeemer was, next to that of Mary, the greatest—for no natural father ever loved an only son as Joseph loved Jesus—so also, next to her sorrows, must rank those of her holy spouse. Well, therefore, may we believe that it required no less than a continual miracle to support him under this inward martyrdom.

Towards the close of his days, when God was about to call his holy soul from earth, He may have first diminished and then entirely withdrawn the miraculous support He had so long secretly supplied to enable the Saint to endure his fatigues and, still more, his consuming charity; and God having thus ceased to allow this elixir of life, as we may term it, to repair the inroads made on Joseph's strength, the result would be a state of languor and of drooping powers which, though different in its cause, would be sufficiently similar in some of its effects to what a natural and internal fever might have produced; and this would account for the belief already alluded to, that Joseph suffered much from growing infirmities before his death. But this holy man did not really die either of natural infirmities or from natural fever. His fever was that of divine love, and his weakness was that of a frame unable to bear the excess of that love. That Joseph died of the love of God was the opinion of St. Francis de Sales. "A saint," he says, "who had loved so much during his life could not die save of love; and, having completed the office for which he had been destined, it only remained for him to say to the Eternal Father, 'I have finished the work which Thou gavest me to do'; and to the Son, 'O my Child, as Thy Heavenly Father placed Thy Body in my hands on the day when Thou camest into the world, so now, in this day of my departure from the world, I place my soul in Thine.' Such, I conceive, was the death of this great Patriarch."[8] We may add that the holy Doctor, Alfonso Maria de' Liguori, considered this belief of St. Francis de Sales, that Joseph died of the pure love of God, as most reasonable.[9] Here we have the decided opinion of two holy Doctors of the Church, and

8. *Treatise on the Love of God*, b. vii. chap. xiii.
9. *Meditation* vi. *On the Death of St. Joseph.*

we may therefore safely adopt it as our own.

That Jesus and Mary lovingly tended and comforted Joseph on his bed of death, there never has been doubt. Hence holy Joseph is considered by all Catholics as the tutelary saint of the dying, and is constantly invoked to obtain for them a happy death. St. Bernardine of Siena says that it is certainly to be piously believed that at the death of Joseph both Jesus and Mary were present. What consolations, illuminations, and revelations of eternal good things must not the dying Saint have then received from his holy spouse and from the most loving and compassionate Son of God, Christ Jesus![10] "To know," says the seraphic St. Leonard of Port Maurice, "that Joseph was truly great, as he was just, greater still as a spouse, and, above all, great as a father, it suffices to behold him in the arms of Jesus and Mary rendering up his soul to his Creator. See Joseph lying upon a poor pallet, Jesus on one side, Mary on the other, and, above, countless bands of Angels, Archangels, Seraphim, all in readiness devoutly to receive this holy soul. O my God, who can ever tell the outpouring of affection at that last parting of Joseph from his sweet Jesus and Mary! What thanks, what protestations, what supplications, what excuses, does this holy old man offer in his extremity! His eyes speak, his heart speaks, his tongue only is silent; but his very silence speaks."[11] Well, therefore, may Holy Church, contemplating Joseph dying, thus sing: "O happy beyond measure, O blessed beyond measure, art thou, at whose side in thy last hour watched Jesus and Mary with aspect serene."[12] But the Lord willed to give to His dear father a signal favor for his consolation before the hour of his departure. While Joseph, supported by the tender hands of Jesus and Mary, lay on his poor

---

10. *Sermo de S. Joseph,* cap. ii.
11. *Panegir. di S. Giuseppe,* n. x.
12. "O nimis felix, nimis O beatus,
    Cujus extremam vigiles ad horam
    Christus et Virgo simul adstiterunt
        Ore sereno."
    —*In fest. S. Joseph; hymn. ad Laud.*

couch in an ecstasy of love, lo! he was raised to so sublime a rapture as to taste by anticipation the joys of
the Blessed in Heaven, and beheld the Divine Essence,
the Face of God, His glory, which Moses in vain requested to see. (*Ex.* 33:18). Maria d'Agreda says that
this rapture lasted twenty-four hours.[13] That he should
have had this marvellous favor conceded to him, which
holy Doctors have believed was more than once, if not
often, bestowed on Mary, is far from incredible. If we
are to accept the revelations of saints, Joseph had frequently (as already noticed) seen Jesus transfigured
and invested with a glorious light, as the three Apostles afterwards beheld Him on Thabor. In thus manifesting Himself to them, one, at least, of our Saviour's
reasons seems to have been to prepare them to endure
the sight of the ignominy and sufferings of His Passion. May not, then, this surpassing vision of the Face
of God have been accorded to Joseph, not only as a
reward for his parental care and love, but to soften to
him the pains of the last passage?

The Blessed Trinity appointed Joseph to be their
ambassador to the Fathers in Limbo, to announce to
them the Incarnation and coming of the Son of God, of
which mystery he had been the ocular witness and in
which he had taken so large a part. If, then, John the
Baptist was the Precursor of Jesus on earth, Joseph
was to be His Precursor to the souls detained in Limbo
and anxiously looking out for their release. Joseph,
returning to himself, said to Jesus, "Now I die happy,
hoping that Thou wilt soon come to deliver us."[14] It was
his *Nunc Dimittis.* Isidoro de Isolanis, the devout col-
lector of so many Oriental traditions and legends,[15] says
that Jesus held the hand of Joseph in His for long

---

13. She does not mean that his vision of the Divine Essence lasted as long, but that
such was the duration of the rapture wherein he was admitted to this vision.
14. Bernardine de Bustis, *Mariale,* Sermo xii.
15. It need hardly be said that these traditions have no actual authority, but many,
we cannot but think, are founded on fact. It is impossible, indeed, to separate the
ore from the dross, but it seems allowable to cull what has probability in its favor,
as several Doctors and saints have done, to aid our pious meditations. The particulars of Joseph's death were, according to Oriental tradition, related by Jesus
Himself to His disciples one day, when seated on Mount Olivet.

hours, and blessed his body, that it might not see corruption, a pledge of the glory which He reserved for it.
No evil spirit dared to disturb his peace. And so this
great saint patiently and happily expired, Michael and
Gabriel bearing his pure and holy soul to the bosom of
Abraham. Jesus closed his eyes with His own hand.
The friends and near relations of the saint washed and
anointed his body with precious ointments, according
to the Jewish custom, and from amongst the multitude
of angels in attendance the Lord commanded two to
clothe him in a white robe. They remained reverently
watching the body. Isolano says that he died at Nazareth.
If so, it would be likely that the whole city (as he
relates) would follow their holy townsman to his grave.
Calmet also believes that he died at Nazareth, but tradition points to Jerusalem as, at any rate, the place of
his sepulture. He may probably have gone up with Jesus
and Mary to celebrate the feast of unleavened bread,
the Pasch, which was always kept at the full moon following the 14th, and died on the 19th of March, as the
Roman Church appears to hold.[16] The Venerable Bede,
quoted by the Continuators of the Bollandists, consid-
ers that it was probably by divine disposition that his
death occurred at that season of the year, in order that,
according to his desire, he might be buried with his
ancestors. He adds that two sepulchres, devoid of all
ornament, were pointed out in the Valley of Josaphat,
the one being that of the holy old man, Simeon, who
took the Infant Jesus in his arms, and prophesied concerning Him, the other that of the just Joseph. Some
critics, however, have disputed its vicinity to that of
Simeon, and Bollandus believes that the other tomb
alluded to might be that of Joseph surnamed the Just,
proposed with Matthias for the Apostolate. But any way
we may rely on the tradition, attested by Bede and

16. "Hac die Joseph meruit perennis gaudia vitae.—On this day Joseph merited the
joys of eternal life."—*Hymn. ad Laud.* The Roman Martyrology confirms this view,
as to the place of his demise: "In Judea was the birthday" (that is, the transit)
"of St. Joseph, spouse of the Blessed Virgin." Had he died at Nazareth, it would
have said "in Galilee," not "in Judea."

adopted by the Bollandists, that the now empty tomb
of Joseph was in the Valley of Josaphat, a tradition
which still prevails at the present day. St. Jerome,
indeed, was of opinion that his sepulchre was included
within the limits of the garden of Gethsemani, and that
it was not without a mystery that Jesus made choice
of that spot for prayer, especially on the night of His
agony. Possibly He desired to engage us to seek to have
Joseph near us when we are in our last agony, and
hence to enjoy the consolation of his patronage at that
dread hour.

Chapter XLVI

The Glory of Joseph in Heaven.

GOD proportions His graces to the office with which He entrusts a man, and his glory in Heaven will be proportioned to the fidelity with which he has discharged it. If this be true, and it is undoubtedly true, what must be the glory of Joseph! To whom was ever committed an office which for its sublimity could be compared to that for which our saint was chosen? And who can question his faithful correspondence with the high graces which he must have received in order to its due discharge? Well, therefore, may we address him, as do the United Greeks in one of their hymns, by the singular epithet of "more than a saint," or, rather, as "pre-eminently a saint," by the superexcellence of the graces he received from Heaven and his perfect correspondence with those graces. So far, then, from its being rash to hold that Joseph surpasses all the Saints in glory, even as he exceeded them in grace, the learned Suarez is of opinion that it is a belief both full of piety and in itself most highly probable. Many other eminent ecclesiastical authorities might be quoted in support of the same view, but the name of Suarez may suffice to warrant our conviction of what recommends itself even to our natural reason. Moreover, if it be once conceded that Joseph, being specially associated with the mystery of the Incarnation, was constituted in a higher order than any other, however exalted, in the hierarchy of the Church, namely, that of the Hypostatic Union, it follows that no comparison can be attempted between him and other saints, because he possessed a different and more eminent kind of sanctity.

And this is no new opinion in the Church. We need not wonder, then, if the Blessed Veronica of Milan,[1] when rapt in ecstasy and raised in spirit to behold the glories of the empyrean, distinguished the incomparable Joseph exalted above all the Blessed; nor if a celebrated Doctor of these later centuries[2] should have written that Jesus Christ denied the first seats in His Kingdom to the ambitious pretensions of His disciples, James and John (*Mark* 10:35-40), because these places were reserved for Mary and Joseph; and was it not meet, indeed, that the Son of God should keep those nearest to Him in Heaven who had been nearest to Him on earth? We cannot well conceive that it could be otherwise. "Was there ever any pure creature," says St. Francis de Sales, "so beloved of God or who better deserved that love than Our Lady or St. Joseph?"[3] All the Fathers of the Church are agreed that the Joseph of Genesis was a type of the most pure spouse of Mary, and that his brilliant exaltation over his brethren was a shadow of the glory of the second Joseph, and a kind of prophecy of what was to occur in his case. Is not this implicitly to concur in the doctrine of Suarez and of those other eminent authorities who expressly affirm the elevation of Joseph above all the Saints in Paradise? Finally, the Church herself in her offices appears to favor and accredit this truth, by calling Joseph the honor and glory of the Blessed;[4] words which imply his superiority.

But this superlative glory of Joseph's soul, although constituting his substantial and essential beatitude, is by no means all that appertains to that beatitude. Man being composed of a united soul and body, the

1. Declared Blessed by Leo X. Her life was written by Isidoro Isolano.
2. Cartagena, Lib. iv. Hom. viii.
3. *Entretien*, iii.
4. "Coelitum Joseph decus."

happiness and glory of Heaven are promised to the body as well as to the soul, and form no inconsiderable portion of it. Now, we have every reason to be persuaded that Joseph truly rose from the grave, and, if so, that his body also shines with a luster and enjoys a bliss surpassing that which the bodies of other saints shall ever enjoy. It is of faith that many bodies of the saints arose with the Incarnate Word, and that they appeared to numbers of persons in Jerusalem (*Matt.* 27:51, 52), giving them undoubted proofs that they were truly risen. Moreover, it is the opinion of St. Thomas and of well-nigh all the Doctors that these saints were not subject to death anymore, but, after having for some time communicated on earth with the disciples of the Son of God, they, when the forty days were expired, followed Him in His Ascension to render His entrance into Heaven still more brilliant and glorious. It seems scarcely necessary to allude to the idea entertained by some as possible, that these saints returned into their tombs after rendering their testimony. With all respect to those who have favored this notion, among whom are some honored names, not only is it to our mind in every way repulsive, but it seems to destroy the value of the testimony itself, seeing that their bodies were to return to dust. Dismissing, then, a conjecture unworthy, as it appears to us, of the goodness of God and of the great work which Jesus had achieved when He rose triumphant from the grave and, ascending into Heaven, led captivity captive (*Ps.* 67:19), and displayed the trophies of His victory in these first children of the Resurrection, let us ask ourselves who of all the ancient saints were likely to form a portion of this chosen band. St. Matthew, wholly occupied in relating what immediately regards our Lord Himself and in establishing our faith in the principal mysteries which concern Him, has neither specified the number of those who were called to share the Redeemer's triumph over death, nor given the name of anyone among them; he simply says that they were "many."

We, therefore, naturally conclude that certain great patriarchs and prophets of the Old Law must have been thus chosen. But which of these patriarchs or prophets, however magnificent the promises made to them or declared by them, however high in the favor of God they may have stood, could be compared for greatness and dignity with Joseph, to whom it was given to be a father to Him who is the God of all the patriarchs and prophets, and to feed, support, and protect Him who created and sustains all things? Could these ancient saints be selected for the glory of the Resurrection and Joseph left in the tomb? But, more than all, how can we believe that this loving Saviour, who gives life to whom He will (*John* 5:21), and therefore had the power to choose whom He would to share His glory in body as well as soul, can have called from their graves this multitude of His servants and friends and omitted His dearly-loved father? Impossible! No proof seems required to establish a fact which, so to say, proves itself by its simple statement.

Isolano, among the Oriental traditions which he collected, gives a touching instance of the love with which Jesus spoke of Joseph while on earth, saying to His disciples, to whom the knowledge of His divine origin had already been revealed: "I conversed with Joseph in all things as if I had been His child. He called Me son, and I called him father; and I loved him as the apple of My eye." These and similar legends represent, if they do no more, the current opinion in the East in days near to the Gospel times. We gather from them more or less of evidence confirmatory of our conviction that Jesus did not regard His apparently close relationship to Joseph as a mere shield or mask, but recognized a real relationship therein, which, though not of the natural order, was nonetheless endearing. And, if we are to credit the revelations of saints, in Heaven this relationship still endures, and He still calls Joseph father. Appearing one day to Marina de Escobar, accompanied by the saint, He said to her: "See, here is My father, and whom I regarded as such upon earth; what think you of him?" It was, we might almost say—if it be permitted to do so without irreverence—as if He were proud of him, proud of having had him for a father on earth, and desirous to show this holy soul his glory. The Bollandists also relate how Jesus appeared one day to St. Margaret of Cortona, and told her He took great pleasure in her devotion to His foster-father, Joseph, who was most dear to Him, and expressed His wish that she should every day pay him some special act of homage.[5] The heart melts with tenderness at such thoughts, even as it recoils from the idea that the close bond between Jesus and Joseph was only temporary, and merely ordained for a passing object. If, then, that bond still exists, assuredly Joseph is with Him in body as well as soul as truly as he was in the workshop of Nazareth, where they worked by each other's side for so many years. St. Bernardine of Siena, that glory of the Seraphic Order and great lover of Joseph, in the admirable sermon which he delivered in honor of the Saint, after declaring his conviction that Joseph enjoyed the same privilege as Mary in the resurrection of his body, concludes with saying that, as this Holy Family—that is, Christ, the Virgin, and Joseph—had been united in a laborious life and in loving grace while on earth, so also their bodies and souls reign together in Heaven in loving glory, according to that Apostolic rule: "As you are partakers of the sufferings, so shall you be also of the consolation." (*2 Cor.* 1:7). Gerson, after saying that words fail him worthily to extol that admirable Trinity—Jesus, Mary, and Joseph—adds that, after Mary, Joseph is nearest to Jesus in Heaven, even as, after her, he was nearest on earth. P. Giovanni Osorio will not hear of Jesus, Mary, and Joseph being divided in Heaven, or of anyone being nearer to Mary in glory than her most sweet spouse, nor nearer to Jesus, after Mary, than His reputed father, since on

---

5. Apud Bolland. die 22 Februarii.

earth there were none so closely united as Jesus, Mary, and Joseph. Isidoro de Isolano, whom we have just quoted, also says that Joseph, spouse of Mary, arrayed in two robes like the ancient Joseph—that is, with the blessedness of his soul and body—accompanied Jesus in His Ascension into Heaven, and sat down next to the King of Glory,[6] that place being, according to Cartagena, on His left hand, the right being reserved for Mary.

It would be long to quote all the concurrent opinions of the learned and the holy, but we cannot omit that of Suarez. After saying much in praise of St. Joseph, he adds that, according to the sufficiently received belief, it was probable that he was reigning gloriously with Christ in Heaven, both in body and in soul.[7] If Suarez could call this a sufficiently received belief more than two hundred years ago, what would he have styled it at the present time, when it is held well-nigh universally? Finally, we must content ourselves with citing the opinions of two saints of these later ages, St. Francis de Sales and St. Leonard of Port Maurice. The former, after speaking at some length of the resurrection of Joseph, thus concludes: "St. Joseph is, therefore, in Heaven in body and in soul; of that there is no doubt."[8] And St. Leonard, in pronouncing his eulogium, exclaims that Joseph was transported in body and in soul to the empyrean by a particular privilege, which appears to be indicated in the Proverbs, where it is said that all of her (Mary's) household are "clothed with double garments,"[9] which interpreters have understood as signifying the twofold glorification of soul and body.

But let us look at the subject from another point of view. Our Divine Lord in calling from the grave this multitude of saints intended them, as the Master of

---

6. In speaking of two robes, he alludes to the robe of silk with which Pharao invested the viceroy of Egypt, in addition to his own, when he placed him in his second chariot (*Gen.* 41:42).
7. Tom. ii. in p. iii. S. Thomae, disp. viii. sec. ii. a. 2.
8. *Entretien,* xix. n. 22.
9. Prov. 31:22. *Panegir. di S. Giuseppe,* n. 4.

Theologians teaches,[10] to serve as witnesses to the reality of His own Resurrection, in order that the disciples and the rest of the faithful should not imagine that it was a phantom who had appeared to them, but should firmly believe that it was truly He Himself, Jesus of Nazareth, whom they beheld. We know how hard of belief they were, and how, when they saw Him walking on the Sea of Galilee, notwithstanding all the wonders they had witnessed, they had cried out for fear, imagining it was an apparition.[11] And, although He had repeatedly told them He should rise from the grave, they refused at first to credit the testimony of Mary Magdalen and the other women; nay, Thomas refused to believe the word of the other ten Apostles, declaring that unless he had ocular and tangible proof he would not believe. Now, the Resurrection of Christ was, we may say, the very cornerstone of Christianity. It was that which the Apostles were to be sent forth preeminently to teach. "If Christ be not risen again," says St. Paul writing to the Corinthians, "then is our preaching vain, and your faith is also vain." (*1 Cor.* 15:14). As, then, the Apostles were to preach this truth to the world, Jesus made use of these risen saints to confirm their faith in His Resurrection; they were to be to the Apostles what the Apostles were afterwards to be to all the nations of the earth. Angels were employed by Him for the same purpose, declaring it to the women on that first Easter morn, and showing them His open sepulchre. (*Matt.* 28:5, 6; *Mark* 16:6; *Luke* 24:5-7). But the Son of God desired also to have the testimony of men, and that, not only to His own Resurrection, but to His power to raise from the dead whomsoever He would. He, therefore, by His divine omnipotence and the virtue of His victory over the grave, raised to life the bodies of His dearest friends to overcome the incredulity of His followers. But was there any among

---

10. "They rose, to die no more, because they rose to manifest the Resurrection of Christ."—St. Thomas, *in Matthaeum,* cap. xxvii.
11. *Matt.* 14:25-27; *Mark* 6:48-50; 16:11, 14; *Luke* 24:11; *John* 20:25.

them whose testimony would have been more credible than that of Joseph? What patriarch or prophet of the Old Testament could have given the witness to Jesus that the spouse of Mary could give? Abraham beheld Him in spirit from afar, but Joseph saw Him with his bodily eyes in his own house for many years. David prophesied the coming of the Incarnate Word, and described His principal actions, but Joseph had received Him into his arms when He came into the world, and took part in almost all the mysteries of His life. If Joseph, then, who, according to this pious belief, was certainly among the risen saints, could have said to the Apostles, "This is the true Son of Mary, Jesus of Nazareth, the only Saviour of men; this is truly He whom I saw born in a stable, the same whom I circumcised, whom I carried into Egypt, whom for a long time I sustained by my labor, and who labored with me in my workshop at Nazareth, He is the same, doubt it not, disciples of Jesus," must not this testimony, given by one who was also personally known to them, have been a more convincing proof of the Saviour's Resurrection than what all the Fathers of the Old Testament could furnish? The Spirit of God had taught us by the mouth of prophets the eternal generation of the Son of God, angels proclaimed His temporal generation when He was born in Bethlehem, but to Joseph was given the honor of declaring to the nascent Church what may be called the immortal generation of Jesus, that is, His Resurrection from the dead by the power of the Spirit. (*Rom.* 8:11; *Eph.* 1:19). All that the other resuscitated saints might say could not have had such persuasive efficacy as would have had the testimony of Joseph risen from the dead. May we not be permitted to apply to him the words of Ecclesiasticus respecting the ancient Patriarch: "His bones were visited, and after death they prophesied" (*Eccles.* 49:18), or preached? Whatever may be their meaning as regards the elder Joseph—for no tradition has reached us of any wonder or miracle wrought by his precious relics—they were amply verified in the great saint, his prototype, if, indeed, it were given to him to publish to the Apostles the Resurrection of the Saviour, and, through them, as we may say, to preach to the whole Church.

Jesus is the Bread of Life, of which whosoever partakes shall have eternal life. Hence the Fathers often call the Flesh of Jesus Life-giving Flesh. Contact with It in the Holy Eucharist pours graces into our souls and deposits the germ of our future glorified bodies. If this be so, we may consider, with St. Francis de Sales, that Joseph, having enjoyed the honor of being so closely united to Jesus, of kissing Him devoutly, embracing Him tenderly, and bearing Him so often folded in his arms, must have had a sufficient title to an anticipated resurrection. The Flesh of Jesus is like a heavenly magnet to draw to Itself the bodies of those who have been honored and sanctified by Its touch. Were they as dry and heavy as the clods of earth which cover them, the Son of God promises them the agility of eagles to fly to Him when, at His second coming, His voice shall be heard by them in their graves: "Wheresoever the Body is, there shall the eagles be gathered together." (*Matt.* 24:28). But can earth have detained the body of holy Joseph until the consummation of ages, whose union with the Saviour had been so close and so endearing? St. Augustine—or whoever may be the author of the *Treatise on the Assumption of the Blessed Virgin*—and other Fathers of the Church give as a reason for believing in the resurrection of Mary that it would have been indecorous that the body of one who was so closely united to Jesus, of whose flesh He had taken flesh, and who had rendered Him so many services, should have remained the slave of death until the end of the world. Now, what is pre-eminently true of the Mother of God applies in large measure to him whom Jesus called His father on earth, and who served Him with such matchless devotion; so that we may readily believe or, rather, we are irresistibly led to believe that he who was more intimately united to Him than was any other saint must thence have derived a right superior to that of all others to share the bliss and glory of His risen Body.

The ancient Joseph, when about to die, besought his brethren not to leave his remains in Egypt, but to bear them to the promised land; and Moses faithfully fulfilled the last will of the Patriarch, and carried the relics of this holy man into Palestine. (*Gen.* 50:24; *Exod.* 13:19). We see here a figure of Joseph, the spouse of Mary, who, when at the point of death, full of confidence in the Saviour's love, recommended, not his soul only, but his body, to that dear Son, who gave it His blessing; and that blessing was a promise. Jesus, who had so often sweetly reposed upon the bosom of Joseph, who had nurtured, defended, and toiled for Him during thirty years, would not leave Him in the Egypt of this world, but, when he passed to the promised land, took him with Him into Heaven, there to enjoy without delay the fullness of eternal bliss. Thus may we say with the Prophet that Joseph had "a double portion" (*Ezech.* 47:13) in that true land of promise, the blessedness of the body as well as of the soul.

Many other reasons might be alleged in support of this belief, and in particular the desire of Mary. When the Blessed Virgin rose from the sepulchre on the day of her glorious Assumption, would she, so to say, have been satisfied had she not seen her chaste spouse, Joseph, similarly glorified? The most pure and holy marriage of Joseph with Mary was, like his paternity, to endure forever. It was ordained in connection with the Incarnation of the Word, and, as that mystery was still subsisting, and would subsist throughout eternity, so was it also with this alliance. The Word espoused human nature to Himself forever, and Joseph was united forever with the Most Blessed Virgin; and, as death did not sever the tie which united the Word to the Body and Soul which He had taken, so neither did it sever the tie which bound together the hearts of Mary and Joseph. She loved him, and will love him as her spouse for all eternity, and must therefore have ardently desired the full completion of his bliss. Even if the loving heart of Jesus had not shared that desire, He must have yielded to the solicitations of her at whose request, for a motive immeasurably less pressing, He had changed the water into wine at the marriage-feast of Cana. St. Peter Damian has left on record his opinion, that St. John the Evangelist is risen and glorified both in body and soul in Heaven, because he was like to Mary in virginal purity, and so intimately associated with her that we cannot conceive the one being raised without the other.[12] But how incomparably more weight such reasons have in favor of her virgin spouse!

Further, we may confidently hold that, had this venerable body been left on earth, God would never have allowed it to remain concealed, and thus to be deprived of the honor given to the relics of saints much inferior to him. Ecclesiastical history frequently alludes to miracles which it pleased the Lord to work in order to the discovery of the precious remains of many of His servants, that men might render them due veneration, transport them to their churches, place them under their altars, and honor them with religious cultus. But of Joseph nothing remains save the ring he placed on Mary's finger on the day of their espousals, for the possession of which two cities have contended, and a few fragments of his garments, to which pious homage is still paid. Angels were charged to bear the Holy House of Nazareth into Catholic lands, that it might not be left in the possession of infidels; and, if God thus willed that this material tenement should be preserved and honored, is it conceivable that He should have abandoned the body of him who was the owner of that house and the pure spouse of His Blessed Mother, and left it all these centuries in the cold grasp of death? We have every reason, then, to conclude from such facts as these that earth no longer possesses the body of our saint. Indeed, a latent, if not a positive and declared convic-

---

12. *Sermo* ii. *de S. Joseph.*

tion, seems to have dwelt in the hearts of the great body of the faithful, when visiting his sepulchre in the Valley of Josaphat nigh to that of his most holy spouse,[13] that, like her, he is not there, but is glorified in body as well as soul.

Many learned Doctors, and among them (as we have said) St. Francis de Sales, consider that several of the alleged reasons for his anticipated resurrection amount to demonstration. Nay, God Himself seems to have authorized the belief by a striking miracle; for when St. Bernardine of Siena, preaching in Padua, declared that the body and soul of Joseph were both glorified in Heaven, a rich cross of gold was seen to shine over the head of the preacher, proving to the very eyes of those who surrounded him the truth which he was conveying to their ears. The pious Bernardine de Bustis, who was himself a witness of this marvel, also most firmly held that Joseph rose from the grave with Christ and, along with the risen Saviour, went to visit his holy spouse, and is now enjoying eternal life and glory ineffable, soul and body, in their company.[14]

How great the glory of the beatified body of Joseph may be, it is beyond the power of our feeble imaginations to conceive. We only know that it must be proportioned to the glory of his soul. It is certain that the Body of the Lord, when He rose victorious from the grave, possessed such marvellous endowments and was adorned with such matchless splendor that all earthly magnificence and beauty is but a shadow of its glory. The living palace of the Incarnate Word, in which, as the Apostle says, "dwelleth all the fullness of the Godhead corporally" (*Col.* 2:9), must needs thus be gifted and enriched. But Jesus was not only rich in Himself, but rich in order to impart His riches. His followers are to be partakers of it, each in his measure, and that measure, be it small or great, will include and, indeed, will consist in likeness to Himself. The beloved disci-

13. Bede, *De Locis Sanctis,* cap. lx.
14. *Mariale,* p. iv. Serm. xii.

ple, unable to describe the future blessedness of the sons of God, says, "It hath not yet appeared what we shall be," and then he adds, "We know that when He shall appear we shall be like to Him." (*1 Jn.* 3:2). That is all he could say; and it was the highest thing he could have said. That adorable Body being, indeed, the first and most perfect of all corporeal beauties, we cannot estimate the riches and glory of other bodies save by comparing them with this divine exemplar. When the Son of God, then, was willed to raise His father Joseph with Him from the grave, we feel that He had what we might almost call a special obligation to grant him a singular likeness to Himself. Joseph had been very like to Him on earth, and it was fitting that he should be so in order to confirm the opinion that he was truly His father; and now, in the resurrection, Jesus enhances that likeness, not to establish, but to recompense the paternity of Joseph, and to preserve that just conformity in Heaven which was befitting the relationship subsisting between them, a relationship which, next to that which united Him to His immaculate Mother, was the most intimate and the most glorious. When Joseph, therefore, entered Heaven on the Ascension Day, he presented to the eyes of the angels the most magnificent object, next to the Sacred Humanity of the Eternal Son, which they had ever beheld. Mary, their Queen, was, it is true, to shine with still more resplendent lustre, but never for a moment must we imagine that her arrival on the day of her Assumption caused the glory of her spouse to pale; on the contrary, it increased and intensified it through that celestial law of reflection of which we have the type and similitude in nature on this earth of ours. The bodies of all the Saints will be invested with light, a light which emanates from the Lamb, who is the lamp and the sun of the New Jerusalem (*Apoc.* 22:5), but the Saviour and His most holy Mother will delight in causing the brightest beams of their glory to irradiate through all eternity the beatified body of Joseph, who, abiding ever in close proximity to the central splendors of the empyrean—the Sacred Humanity of the Incarnate Word and His most holy Mother—will be even penetrated with their light—as a precious metal glows with the same intenseness as the furnace in which it is plunged, or, like some pure mirror, which, confronted with the sun, faithfully repeats its image—a light too dazzling for mortal eyes to gaze upon. What more can we say? Jesus, Mary, and Joseph, the earthly Trinity, now together enthroned in the blaze of supernal glory, shine in that light eternal which by communication becomes, as it were, common to all three.

Chapter XLVII

The Patronage of Joseph.

GOD never caused the virtues and singular merit of Joseph to shine with greater splendor than when He said to him by the mouth of the angel, "Take the Child and His mother" (*Matt.* 2:13, 20); for in them He committed to him His most precious treasures, giving him thus the preference over all the blessed spirits of Heaven; and Joseph received these two sacred persons into his care, to be their protector, their guardian, and defender. If, then, Heaven made Joseph the protector of Jesus and Mary, we may rest assured that he was at the same time made the protector and patron of all men. When Jesus Christ hanging on the Cross said to the Blessed Virgin, indicating St. John, "Woman, behold thy son" (*John* 19:27), we believe that we were all entrusted to His Mother in the person of the beloved disciple. So also when the Eternal Father confided the Incarnate Word and His Mother to Joseph, He confided us all to this great saint; for the Incarnate Word had us all in His adorable Heart, and the Blessed Virgin, the new Eve, was to conceive us all in her heart of sorrows when she stood beneath the Cross on Calvary. We were to be the children of her pain, as was to Rachel her second-born son, Benoni. (*Gen.* 35:18). To be devout to Joseph, therefore, is not merely our interest in the highest sense, neither is it to be considered, on the other hand, as a mere pious practice to be cultivated or not at pleasure, but it is our duty; since that which is the desire of Jesus and Mary comes to us with the force of an obligation, which we cannot disregard without irreverence to them as well as great spiritual detriment to ourselves. Add to which, that the Church's example powerfully attracts us to this devotion, and the example of this loving mother is meant as a guidance to us, which no faithful child of hers can refuse to follow. But first we will speak only of the desire of Jesus and Mary that we should honor Joseph very greatly.

What is the Saviour's most ardent desire? Is it not that all should imitate Him perfectly? By this imitation we magnify God, and efficaciously promote our own salvation. Now, let us attend to the example He set before us with respect to St. Joseph. He was the first who had recourse to this great saint. Never did son belong so absolutely and entirely to his father as did Jesus to Joseph; and, indeed, it was conformable to reason that He who had written in our hearts that beautiful precept—for it belonged to the natural law before it was proclaimed and enforced from Sinai—"Honor thy father," should Himself keep it most exactly. Never, also, did son serve his father with such assiduity and love as the Incarnate Word served our saint. Wherefore, when the Saviour testifies His earnest desire that we should imitate Him, He at the same time manifests (as the devout Bernardine de Bustis[1] has pointed out) His wish that we should love and reverence St. Joseph. And, indeed, it would be a monstrous thing if the members of His Body did not honor him to whom their Head paid such profound submission.

This desire of Our Lord is grounded on His adorable perfections; on His justice as well as on His gratitude. It is certain that the Saviour wills that His saints should be venerated on earth in recompense of their merits. We find Him eulogizing them both before and after their death, giving them power to

---

1. *Mariale,* p. iv. Serm. xii.

work miracles like His own, undertaking their defense when unjustly accused, and promising to those who for His sake despised worldly goods a reward a hundred-fold greater even in this present time as well as eternal life in the world to come. (*Matt.* 19:29; *Mark* 10:30; *Luke* 18:29, 30). Clearly, then, the Son of God desires that the devotion and love which men pay to His saints should constitute part of the accidental glory which shall crown their merits. His justice also would have regard to the proportion and degree of those merits; and He would have those most highly honored who merited the most. But, amongst the friends of God in Heaven, who has equal merit with Joseph? Having, then, excelled all in sanctity, the Son of God, in order to do him justice, requires that men should acknowledge it by their most profound respect and fervent love.

There is, however, another sublime office which Joseph faithfully discharged as well as that of a tender father and guardian of Jesus, which the Lord will not have forgotten in Heaven or be willing to leave without corresponding exaltation on earth. St. Bernard considered that Joseph was united with the Saviour in the quality of a coadjutor, whom God gave to His Son as His associate in the most magnificent of all His works, the redemption of men.[2] According to the Abbot Rupert, it was not without mystery that Christ was promised to Abraham as man, to David as his successor in his kingdom, but to Joseph under the name of Saviour (*Matt.* 1:21); in order that we may be persuaded that, although Joseph had no share in the formation of the Body of Jesus, neither did he place the crown upon His head, he nevertheless contributed to making Him the Saviour of all men, journeying and laboring and toiling along with Him, and supporting Him by the fruit of his toils for so many years. And thus (he says) he was the last of the Patriarchs to whom

---

2. *Super missus est,* Hom. ii. 16.

the Messias was promised, but in a more excellent manner than all.[3] Albert the Great held that in this respect
he could call Joseph the support of the whole human
race, because, in taking the charge of the bringing up
of Jesus Christ, he contributed much to the salvation
of men. To Him he devoted the best years of his life;
for Him he renounced every personal satisfaction, and
even every personal thought, in order to aid in bringing about this one affair, the reparation of lost man,
and the opening to sinners the way of eternal life.[4] No
wonder, then, that the Church should now give him the
title of co-operator with the Saviour in the redemption
of the human race;[5] for, indeed, the Greeks had anciently
called him, by the mouth of St. Chrysostom, the partner and mediator of the mystery of the Incarnation.[6]
The justice of Jesus, then, requires that Joseph should
receive upon earth the honor which he merited by having thus assisted Him in the great work which He came
down from Heaven to accomplish.

But the Saviour desires that Joseph should be honored by us, not from justice only, but from gratitude.
It belongs to noble and generous hearts to feel gratitude, and the more noble and generous they are the
more lively is that gratitude. Great souls are tenderly
thankful even for small services, while little and mean
souls overlook the greatest. But what heart can compare with the Heart of Jesus, that fathomless well of
love? The Gospel teems with proofs of His generous
appreciation of any affectionate act of homage shown
Him, and His magnificent requital of the least services;
nay, He makes charity, as done to Himself in the person of the poor and suffering, the rule by which He will
judge the nations when He comes to sit on the throne
of His majesty: "As long as you did it to one of these
My least brethren, you did it to Me." (*Matt.* 25:40). And

---

3. *De Divinis Officiis,* cap. xix.
4. *In Lucam,* cap. i.
5. "Te Sator rerum statuit pudicae virginis sponsum, dedit et ministrum esse salutis."
    —*Hymn.* "Coelitum Joseph," etc.
6. "Consortem, et mysterii hujus mediatorem."—*Hom. de Ove et Pastore.*

what is the recompense? The inheritance of a kingdom! See, too, His treatment of the penitent Magdalen, when she came behind Him silently as He sat at meat in the Pharisee's house, and anointed His feet with ointment and washed them with her tears, kissed them, and wiped them with the hairs of her head. Answering the censorious thoughts of the Pharisee with a parable, the Lord then said, "Dost thou see this woman? I entered into thy house, thou gavest Me no water for My feet; but she with tears hath washed My feet, and with her hairs hath wiped them. Thou gavest Me no kiss; but she, since she came in, hath not ceased to kiss My feet." Thou gavest me no kiss! Wonderful complaint of injured love! The Lord of all things would, then, have valued a kiss, that token of affection, from His host! Are any words in the Gospel more astounding or more sweetly touching? "My head with oil thou didst not anoint; but she with ointment hath anointed My feet. Wherefore I say to thee, Many sins are forgiven her, because she hath loved much." (*Luke* 7:36-47). Some tears, some kisses, a little ointment, the offering of a penitent's love, and the payment—forgiveness of her many sins! Again, when He sat at meat in Bethania, at the supper prepared for Him six days before the Pasch at which He was to suffer, and this same woman, Mary Magdalen, broke an alabaster box of precious spikenard, pouring it over His head, and a murmuring arose among some of the disciples, suggested by the hypocritical traitor, Judas, at this waste of what might have been sold for much and given to the poor, Jesus with holy vehemence defended her, and said, "Amen I say to you wheresoever this Gospel shall be preached in the whole world, that also which she hath done shall be told for a memorial of her." (*Matt.* 26:6-13; *Mark* 14:3-9). Worldwide glory for this one act of love and honor! The Redeemer desires that it be published and spoken of even as were His birth, His circumcision, His journeys and labors, His miracles, His Passion and death! Her name was to be known as extensively as the Church was to be

known; and preachers, evangelizing the world, were at
the same time to exalt this holy action by which she
had honored Him. But compare for a moment what this
loving penitent did for Jesus with Joseph's thirty years'
service, his paternal care, his journeyings, his fatigues,
his exile, his daily unceasing toil, all, in short, which
in body and soul he suffered for the God-Man. Can He
have forgotten that Joseph was, along with His holy
Mother, His first adorer on earth, and for long years
His only adorer? Can He have forgotten how He lay in
his bosom, and how that tender father shed tears over
Him when, as a Babe, He wailed in the crib or wept
in his arms; for Jesus gave Himself to Joseph in all
the helpless dependence of infancy, and willed to make
Himself indebted to him for His earthly sustenance?
Can He have forgotten or neglected to pay that debt
of gratitude? Is it possible that He should have so magnificently recompensed Magdalen's testimony of love to
the extent of ordaining that the whole earth should
esteem her for it, and should not have shown His gratitude to Joseph by holding him up to the veneration of
all men, a veneration, too, commensurate with his life-
long devotion to Himself? No, we cannot doubt that,
alike from justice and from gratitude, the Saviour of
the world ardently desires that we should honor Joseph
in a very special manner. This adorable Son of Mary,
as He labored while on earth that all men should know,
love, and serve His invisible Father in Heaven, so now
that He is in Heaven, He disposes all things by His
Providence to exalt the glory of His visible father on
earth, and moves all hearts by His Spirit, which dwells
in His Church, to an ever-increasing love and veneration of him. The very quality of father of Jesus in itself
gives St. Joseph an incontestable title to be called the
father of all the faithful. The Saviour of the world made
no difficulty in recognizing Joseph as His father, and,
in so doing, He gave him power to receive us all as his
children. And, if Joseph is truly the father of all
Christians, so may we be assured that God has given

him the heart of a father for us all. The Venerable
Mother Magdalen of St. Joseph, one of the first of the
Carmelites of St. Teresa's Reform who passed into
France, said, "As it pleased God that Joseph should
take the place of father to His Only Son, He gave him
in consequence a grace of paternity towards all men,
made him incline all his thoughts and all his affections
towards them, and moves him to procure for them as
much good as could the tenderest of fathers for his children."[7] Joseph, then, is our patron and more than our
patron; he is our father, even as he was the protector
and father of Jesus, who in assuming our nature made
us His brethren, and in adopting Joseph as His father
made him necessarily our father also, and desires with
all the love of His adorable Heart that we should consider him as such.

We will now speak of Mary's desire that her spouse
should be honored, which must be with all Catholics a
most potent motive and incentive to render him due
reverence. The lives of the Saints abound in proofs of
this her ardent desire. Many a time has the most holy
Virgin undertaken the panegyric of her spouse, in order
to incite them to be devout to him. We have frequent
instances of this in the works of St. Bridget, which are
held in high esteem by the Church, and, in particular,
in her *Revelations.*[8] Here she relates how the Mother
of God called St. Joseph her dear spouse, and made to
her such a magnificent eulogy of him, that the Saint's
admiration and love for the father of Jesus were greatly
increased thereby for the rest of her days. The Queen
of Angels manifested also to St. Gertrude the glory of
her spouse, as she tells us in her *Revelations.*[9] It was
on the festival of the Annunciation, when, being rapt
in ecstasy, Heaven was opened to her, and she beheld
the great St. Joseph seated on his throne; and, each
time his name was pronounced, she saw all the other

7. See her Life, lib. ii. cap. iv.
8. B. vi. chap. lxix.
9. B. iv. chap. xii.

saints reverently bend their heads in token of their profound respect. Mary has also shown herself very desirous that her servants should have recourse to Joseph in all their necessities. The holy director of St. Teresa, P. Balthazar Alvarez, when visiting Loreto, remained for hours in fervent prayer in the chapel where the Angel Gabriel announced to Mary that she was to be the Mother of the Messias. The humility of this holy man bade him conceal what had passed between him and the Blessed Virgin on that occasion; but it transpired subsequently on his deathbed; when, on one of the religious exhorting him to recommend himself to Joseph, and presenting to him a picture of the Saint, P. Balthazar replied: "You are right; that is what the Mother of God once said to me." The astonished religious enquired of the Infirmarian, Brother Sancio, the same who had accompanied the Father to Loreto, whether he knew anything of this circumstance, who replied: "I remember, on leaving the House of Loreto, he said to me, 'I have just conceived a great devotion to St. Joseph.'" [10] And, indeed, it was most fitting that the Blessed Virgin should specially interest herself in the glory of her spouse in the very place where she received so many services from him, and that she should wish him to be devoutly venerated in that holy dwelling where she was herself exalted to the honor of conceiving the Incarnate Word, who willed to be committed to the paternal care of Joseph, and to be regarded as his son.

Mary rejoices exceedingly when she can associate her pure spouse with herself in the glory and honor paid to her. Hence, to manifest her own love, and procure him a greater number of clients, as well as to testify her gratitude to those who were devout to him, she has frequently appeared in company with him. Alexis of Vigevano, a devout Capuchin lay-brother, had always been most devout to St. Joseph, and, after honoring

---

10. *Vie du P. Balthazar Alvarez*, t. ii. chap. xxvi.

him in life, enjoyed the consolation of a visit from him on his deathbed, together with the Queen of Heaven. It was on the 19th of March, 1581, the anniversary of Joseph's transit from earth, when, feeling death to be approaching, Brother Alexis collected what little remaining strength he possessed, to beg the religious, his brethren, who were assisting him, to light some candles, for that St. Joseph was coming to him. They did so, and very soon the dying man exclaimed: "Here is the Queen of Heaven, here is St. Joseph! Kneel down, O fathers, and give them a worthy reception." So saying he expired. St. Philip of Cantalice had the same grace in death of a visit from Joseph and Mary.

Another proof may be alleged of Mary's desire that those whom she singularly loved and favored should have a tender devotion to her spouse, in her having more than once bidden them change their name for that of Joseph. It is related, for instance, by Surius in his history of the Premonstratensian Order, and by many other authors who have written the life of the Blessed Joseph de Stinuald, how the Mother of God bade him take the name of her spouse in the place of Hermann, as he was previously called, in order to oblige him to feel increased love and devotion for his new patron. God never changed the names of the ancient patriarchs save for grave reasons, and in order tacitly to reveal to them the great designs which He had with regard to them; and when Jesus Christ gave a new appellation to some of His Apostles, it was also for the purpose of signifying to them the illustrious employments and charges for which He had elected them. Thus, in like manner, we may infer that our Sovereign Lady deemed the promotion of the honor of her spouse a matter of so much importance, that she has even bidden some of her children resign their own names and take that of Joseph, in order that they might never be forgetful of him, even as men never forget their own proper selves.

Our Blessed Lady appeared to St. Teresa, when in

an ecstasy, and, after bestowing on her the most loving caresses, clothed her in a robe of beautiful whiteness, and with her own hands put a golden collar and cross round her neck, in recompense (she told her) of the honor which she had procured for St. Joseph.[11] Upon several other occasions also she magnificently rewarded the Saint for her devotion to her spouse. It is because Joseph is still her spouse that Mary is thus tender of his honor. What loving wife is there that does not glory in the exaltation of her husband as in her own? She identifies herself with him, and reckons his good name as hers. But what wife ever loved so tenderly as did Mary? And no greater proof can we have that this most holy, most pure, and most perfect union still subsists in Heaven, than her ardent zeal for Joseph's honor.

But Mary wishes it, not from love only, but, as her Divine Son also does, from gratitude. Joseph was her protector as well as her spouse. Joseph (says St. Chrysostom) was espoused to the Mother of God that he might be to her a tutor and guardian, and an aid near to her in every vicissitude of life. He was to be as a father to her, as well as a spouse, to protect and defend her from all injury. From the very first he began to be her shield and her protection, guarding her reputation from all slanderous attacks. Albert the Great, accordingly, calls him the advocate and patron of the Blessed Virgin,[12] because he sheltered her from the penalties which her divine delivery would have brought upon her. He was the protector at once of her virginity and of her honor. She remembers his affectionate care of her, his fatigues, his sufferings, his anxieties, and the perils to which he exposed himself to save the Child and His Mother, for the two were never separated. Both were confided to him, and Mary has not forgotten his self-sacrificing discharge of the stupendous responsibility thus laid upon him. Common gratitude would not have been unmindful of such services as Joseph's, and

---

11. Ribera, *Vita S. Teresae*, lib. i. cap. xv.
12. *In Lucam*, cap. ii.

Mary's gratitude is not common. It is worthy of herself. See how she repaid the mere social kindness of an invitation to a marriage-feast, and besought her Son to work a miracle to save the giver of the feast from being humbled and mortified in the eyes of his guests. Now, if the Blessed Virgin had recourse to the power of her Divine Son to reward the slight honor which had been shown her on this occasion, can anyone doubt the surpassing desire which she now feels in Heaven that all men should love and honor him who so loved and honored her for the thirty years they dwelt together on earth?

What has been already said of Our Lord's desire that we should copy the example He gave us of reverence and submission to His foster-father, applies equally to Mary; for never did any wife reverence and honor her husband as did the Queen of Heaven and Mother of God the humble carpenter of Nazareth. That carpenter was her husband, her head, her guardian, her pure and spotless companion, and that sufficed to make her honor him as she did. Gerson, carried away with his enthusiasm, does not know which to admire most, the humility of Mary or the sublimity of Joseph, who was thus exalted. But, after giving us this splendid example on earth, and this marvellous testimony of the respect with which she regarded him, could it be possible to believe that Mary, too, as well as her Divine Son, does not ardently long to see us honor Joseph with a special cultus above that which we pay to any other saint?

Both Jesus and Mary, then, desire that we should regard Joseph as our father and our patron. Such is the doctrine of Albert the Great, who, when examining the reasons which rendered the marriage of St. Joseph with the Blessed Virgin, not only most profitable, but in a certain sense necessary, gives as the twelfth of these reasons, that this marriage was ordained in order to make men regard Joseph as their father, even as they recognize Mary as their mother. Not one of us but desires to be a child of Mary during life, and to experience her accustomed merciful aid at the hour of death. But can we be children of Mary without being children of Joseph? If Jesus would not be called her son without, at the same time, calling Joseph His father, how can a Christian reckon her as his mother without looking upon Joseph as his father? If the Saviour would have deemed it an offense to the most chaste marriage of the Queen of Angels not to have reverenced Joseph as His father, even as He obeyed Mary as His mother, shall not a Christian fear to offer, in some sort, an insult to those sacred espousals, if he should treat with indifference the spouse of Our Lady, whom he owns as his mother, and thus separate those whom it has pleased God so closely to unite? And, as the Fathers of the Church have drawn from the passage in Holy Scripture which says that Joseph was "the husband of Mary, of whom was born Jesus," his right to the title of father of Jesus, so may we also say that Joseph, being the spouse of Mary, who has conceived all Christians in her heart, and will bring them forth to the supernal light of Heaven, is therefore likewise the father of those same Christians. But if these things be true, as they assuredly are, what are we to think of the power of Joseph's intercession for us, and of its fervor? Their measure is the love of Jesus and Mary for Joseph, and his love for us, and these are beyond our ken, or even our capabilities of comprehension. A great servant of God has said that Joseph holds in his hands, not only a key of Paradise to open the door of Heaven to all his friends, but a certain kind of power over all the riches of Heaven.[13] Our Joseph, of whom the ancient patriarch was only the figure, merited to be made on earth the steward of the house of God, and of the first family in the world, and now, in glory, the distributer of the heavenly graces conceded to mankind. All the graces which we have received from Heaven, or hope for in the course of our

---

13. Bernardine de Bustis, p. iv., *Mariale,* Sermo. xii.

lives, or which all men have ever received or shall receive, are, beyond imagination, inferior in worth to the Sacred Persons of the Saviour and His holy Mother; and, as the Eternal Father willed that Joseph should, in a peculiar manner, have them in his keeping and possession, does it not seem more than probable that He should have confided to him the administration of His other treasures, even such as are supernatural, all which are of infinitely less value, and were, indeed, contained in Jesus and Mary? The viceroy of Egypt, as the Abbot Rupert says, possessed all the power of Pharao,[14] but our Joseph is far more powerful, for he may be said to hold, after a manner, in his hands all the graces of the Saviour, which are the admirable instruments of the supreme power which God exercises over our hearts and wills, without infringing their rights or depriving them of their liberty. Moreover, death, as we have said, did not interrupt the society and community of goods which subsisted between the Blessed Virgin and St. Joseph when on earth. A heavenly marriage, such as was that of Joseph and Mary, was to last forever. Our Sovereign Lady, as St. Bridget tells us in her *Revelations,* still calls St. Joseph her beloved spouse, and it is indubitable that she never thought of separating herself from him. Now, since the Blessed Virgin is, as it were, the general depositary of all the riches of Heaven, we cannot but infer that St. Joseph shares in the glory of distributing them amongst us. The Spirit of God seems to assure us by the mouth of the Wise Man, that in his chaste spouse Joseph possesses everything and needs no external goods, for such is the interpretation which has been put upon that passage in Proverbs where the valiant woman, the type of Mary, is described: "The heart of her husband trusteth in her, and he shall have no need of spoils." (*Prov.* 31:11). We should do a kind of injury to St. Joseph if we were contented with calling him the spouse of the Queen of <u>Angels</u>, and to Mary also, if we were not persuaded

14. Lib. iii. *in Canticum.*

that through her favor and by her desire he has the glory, not only of sharing her riches, but enjoying the privilege of opening the treasures of Heaven and dispensing them to all who devoutly invoke him; that is, that she wills that he should be associated with her in her patronage of men, and that they should be his children, even as they are hers.

But, to form a judgment of what Joseph can do for us in Heaven, we need not dwell only on the thought of the treasures of graces which we believe God has placed in his hands, but still more must we regard the victorious efficacy of his intercession. Mary's petitions cannot be refused. Solomon said to his mother, Bethsabee, after placing her on a throne at his right hand when she came to him with a petition, "My mother, ask; for I must not turn away thy face." (*3 Kgs.* 2:20). But Jesus will never disappoint His mother, as that great king did, for Mary knows what she asks, and cannot ask anything amiss; and, if Mary's requests cannot be turned away by her Son, neither can she turn away those of her spouse when he addresses them to her. Ill would he know her who should believe her capable of denying anything to him to whom she has bound herself, and whom she loves more than any creature ever loved another. The intercession of Joseph is not less powerful when he turns to Jesus. He goes to Him with the confidence of a father to a son, for this relation still exists between them in Heaven, as we have shown. If the supplications of other saints are so efficacious with the Lord, founded as they are on the claims which their merits have conferred upon them, what must we think of the all-prevailing efficacy of those of Joseph? If the reciprocal love which subsists between Jesus and His saints gives them the well-grounded hope of obtaining what they ask for their clients, what must not be the sure expectation of Joseph, the hearts of this adorable Son and of this virgin father being knit together by so many ties of singular and especial love! We may figure to ourselves that when Joseph presents a request in favor of those who have invoked him, the Son of God would reply, after the manner of the king of Egypt to his type, the ancient Joseph, "The extent of My heavenly kingdom is before thee, give to those thou lovest what thou pleasest."[15] What, again, cannot Joseph do in favor of sinners since we find Moses, when wielding the power of prayer, so mighty to disarm the wrath of God against His rebellious people that this "King of tremendous majesty" speaks as if His suppliant held Him deprived of liberty to chastise the guilty. "Let Me alone," He says, "that My wrath may be kindled against them, and that I may destroy them." (*Exod.* 32:10). And Moses gained his suit. But how much more irresistible the gentle violence—if we may use the expression—which Joseph exercises over Jesus, the Supreme Judge of the living and the dead! The loving sighs of that great saint, his sweet words, and the looks of mingled tenderness and respect which he turns on Him whose countenance unites in itself every beauty, Divine and human, so enthral Him as to leave Him, as it were, no freedom to pour forth His just anger on the guilty. Joseph will take no denial, and the indignation of Jesus must yield to the request of a father whom He loves so much. Oh, the infinite compassion of the Sacred Heart which has provided sinners with such a patron, who ever has near access to the throne of mercy, and has a right to obtain for them graces and favors which they have long themselves demerited! And, if such be the power of Joseph to impetrate favors for us when we have greatly offended, what may he not obtain for us when the face of the Lord is not averted from us! And how great and overflowing is the testimony to his love for us his children and his power with Jesus, as displayed in the results of his intercession! It would need a volume by itself to treat that subject adequately. Countless as the stars of Heaven revealed by the modern telescope are these proofs of his loving patronage, which have been experienced and are being experienced

15. *Conf.* Gen. xlvii. 6.

every day. Such are the fruits of devotion to Joseph;
and the tree is known by its fruits. Is not this marvellous—might we not say miraculous?—abundance sufficient alone to demonstrate that Joseph has been divinely
given to us for our patron in a singular and incomparable manner?

If Joseph, then, is our patron and the most powerful of patrons on every conceivable ground, and on many
more which enter not into our limited powers of comprehension, so also is he the patron of all and every
class, not generally only, but for special reasons in each
case. He is the patron of families, since he was the head
of the Holy Family. He is the patron of the poor, since
he voluntarily embraced and followed for all his days
a life of poverty. He is the patron of the artisan, as the
workshop of Nazareth testified for so many years. He
is the patron of the rich who seek a better inheritance,
since he held in his possession for nigh upon thirty
years the true riches, and, now that he is in Heaven,
possesses the key of God's treasury; he is the patron
of the suffering, of travellers, of exiles, of the afflicted;
he is the patron of the married, and he is the patron
of virgins; he is the patron of the dying, but, above all,
we might say, he is the patron of priests. The priest is
another Joseph. His whole office repeats and reflects
him, not in figure only, but in many ways even literally, since it is given to the priest to be obeyed by Our
Lord as Joseph was. He comes at his calling and remains
in his custody to be carried where he wills and to whom
he wills. The priest is privileged to touch and reverently handle Him who was born of Mary, the Incarnate
Word, and even to convey Him, concealed in his bosom,
to the sick, when due honor would not attend Him on
the road if held visibly in his hands, or danger would
menace Him, as when Joseph fled with the Divine Child
into Egypt. Could the resemblance be more perfect and
complete? A priest without devotion to St. Joseph would
be a kind of anomaly. Truly it would seem that such a
one—if such there be—could not realize the superem-

inent dignity for which he has been chosen and anointed. And here, in preference to any words of our own on a subject so transcending our capacity, we willingly quote the words of a writer to whom we are so much indebted in these pages:

"To you I now turn, venerable Ministers of the Altar, Priests of the Most High, wise dispensers of the Blood of Jesus Christ, and entreat you to execute the command which God has given to you, by the mouth of a great king: 'Go to Joseph, and do all that he shall say to you.' (*Gen.* 41:55). And, since one of the most illustrious Doctors who have flourished in the schools assures us that St. Joseph must be regarded as the exemplar of all those who held any considerable position in the Church,[16] you cannot excuse yourselves from choosing him as the object of your particular devotion. You, then, I conjure who so often touch the Body of Jesus Christ, love this saint, who was the first of all men who had the honor to receive the Saviour into his hands. You, who sacrifice Jesus on the altar during the Divine Mysteries, venerate this saint, who may glory in having offered to the Eternal Father the first-fruits of the Adorable Blood of the Incarnate Word in His Circumcision. Consider Jesus on the altar lying on the sacred corporal, as Joseph contemplated Him in the Crib wrapped in His poor swaddling-bands; bear this Man-God through the streets of our cities, and to the houses of the sick, but let it ever be with the same sentiments of piety with which St. Joseph was animated when he held Him in his arms during the journeys he made. Finally, distribute to the faithful this Divine Saviour hidden under the appearance of bread, but endeavor at the same time to do this with all the reverence wherewith St. Joseph presented Him to the shepherds who came to adore Him."[17]

But, if Joseph is the special patron and model of priests, still more—may we not say?—is he the protec-

---

16. Albert the Great, *in Lucam*, cap. i.
17. P. Joséf Moreno, *Discurso* viii.

tor, guardian, guide, and leader of those who to their
sacerdotal character have added that of missionary, to
bear the Gospel to the heathen, traverse the desolate
places of the earth, forego every comfort, and brave
every danger for this glorious work. Joseph is the first
missionary; first in point of dignity and first in point
of time. He carried the Word of God Himself but a few
days after His birth to a heathen people. The kingdom
of God came nigh to them in Joseph's arms, and, as we
have seen, he himself did the work of an Apostle and
an Evangelist among the Egyptian idolaters. It was
through the ministry of Joseph that Jesus entered into
Egypt, and it has been in like manner that the Faith
of the Saviour has been established in infidel lands.
Few, perhaps, are aware, for instance, of the extraordinary devotion to St. Joseph which prevails throughout
the continent of America. It came there with the Faith.
"On the conquest of this New World," says P. Antonio
Parades, or the unknown author of a work entitled
Devotion to St. Joseph in New Spain, generally attributed to him, "the first Fathers planted devotion to St.
Joseph with the true Faith."[18] And what was true of
the whole of Spanish America was true also of the
French Canadian missions, and wherever the Gospel
was preached to the Indians of the northern continent.
Everywhere the missionaries brought with them St.
Joseph, and propagated his devotion, seeking from him
the graces needed for themselves or for those confided
to their ministry; and everywhere was devotion to this
gracious saint received and adopted with fervor by their
neophytes. What we say of America we say equally of
every other land trod by the feet of those who bring
the glad tidings of salvation to the heathen. Anyone
who would convince himself how intimately associated
is St. Joseph with the life of the missionary of our day,
and how dear he is to his heart, has only to glance at
the pages of the *Annals of the Propagation of the Faith.*
St. Joseph, indeed, would seem to be the inseparable

18. Quoted by P. Vallejo in his *Life of St. Joseph* (English Translation), b. iii. c. iv.

companion—nay, we might say, the necessary property—
of the missionary. That which first contributed to the
propagation of our holy religion is still as powerful as
ever to produce the same effects. It was under the lead-
ership of St. Joseph and by his instrumentality that it
was first promulgated. He was the first preacher of
Jesus, the first confessor of the Faith, the first Apostle
to make Him known in the lands where he journeyed;
and we may therefore well believe that God desires and
wills to cause His Church to flourish and spread, and
receive an abundant outpouring of graces, through the
all-prevailing intercession, and under the patronage of
this Enos of the New Covenant, who first began to
invoke the Name of the Lord (*Gen.* 4:26), and who merited (according to St. Bernardine) to be called the key
of the Old Testament, because he opened to it the door
of Christianity.[19]

It is a great satisfaction to know that the English
Missionary College, at Mill Hill, near London, is dedicated to St. Joseph, whose statue crowns the lofty edifice. Nor are testimonies wanting to the singular favor
and protection which our glorious Patriarch extended
to an institution so dear to his paternal heart, the marvellous answers which he accorded to prayer, and the
extraordinary assistance which he afforded in meeting
and overcoming the difficulties of its establishment; to
which may be added the conspicuous successes with
which its operations have already been blessed.[20]

19. *Sermo di S. Giuseppe.*
20. We may here take occasion to recommend to all clients of St. Joseph the *Illus-trated Catholic Missions,* published monthly; of which we have been reminded by the fact that one of the embellishments of the cover represents the Saint's flight into Egypt with the Child and His Mother, having above it the inscription: "First Foreign Missionary."

Chapter XLVIII

The Cultus of St. Joseph in the Early Church.

THE third motive urging us to devotion to St. Joseph is, as has been said, the example of Holy Church inciting us to practice it; albeit this third motive is but an iteration of the former two. For Jesus speaks to us in the Church through the Holy Spirit, who dwells in her; and Mary, whose spouse is that same Spirit, by whose operation she became the Mother of God, may also be said to speak to us by the Church's voice. The prophecies which are applicable to Holy Church, and are actually so applied, are often, if not always, equally applicable to the Queen of Heaven, the Immaculate Mother, who appeared in vision to the angels ere earth's ages began, clothed with the sun, with the moon under her feet, and crowned with twelve stars. She and the Church are so intimately identified, and the voice of the Church is so truly known and acknowledged to be the voice of the Holy Ghost, whom Jesus sent to take His place when He ascended to the Father, that to say the Church wills anything is all one with saying that Jesus and Mary will it.

We will now proceed briefly to consider what was the devotion to St. Joseph in primitive ages and the public cultus paid to him. In the next chapter some account will be given of the extension of that devotion in later times, and the great increase of honor awarded to our glorious Patron, an extension and an increase which have in them something truly marvellous. But

God does not work as with an enchanter's wand. He works by His general government or Providence, as we term it, in the Church as in the world, silently, and, for the most part, though not always, slowly; acts, in short, so far as externals go, so far as things are patent to our eyes, by what we call secondary causes. Yet, in the kingdom of His grace, how inefficient without the afflatus of His Spirit would these secondary causes seem when scrutinized by the eye of faith! The world does not look below the surface.

The devotion of the early ages to our great patriarch and saint is what first concerns us; and here we are met at the outset by a fact somewhat surprising, if not startling, at the first glance, particularly when we confront this devotion in its beginnings with that decision of the immortal Pius IX, which rejoiced the hearts of the faithful of our times, declaring St. Joseph the Patron of the Universal Church. For it cannot be denied that the Christians of the first ages did not display the same ardor in rendering public honor to St. Joseph as they did to many other saints. The Church from the beginning greatly venerated St. Peter and St. Paul, and the glorious Precursor, St. John the Baptist; it paid particular honor to St. Stephen, the Protomartyr, and to the other heroes who shed their blood for Christ. The Fathers abound in eloquent praises of these saints, while they seem to pass over St. Joseph in comparative silence. Not but that from their works we can gather a whole *catena* of testimony to Joseph's prerogatives and claims. The sublime position which he holds among all the Saints of the calendar may be abundantly proved from the pages of St. John Chrysostom, St. John Damascene, St. Epiphanius, St. Augustine, St. Jerome, St. Ambrose, and many more lights of the early Church. Still it remains true that the ancient Fathers enlarge more fully and, generally speaking, descant with more animation upon other saints, and especially upon the martyrs. It might, indeed, be fitting that his cultus should retrace in a measure the life led by the Saint at

Nazareth, which was hidden and unnoticed; and thus the devotion to him would have no prominence in the first ages of the Church. But it is one thing for that devotion not to exhibit itself in any striking manner before the world, and another for it not to exist in the hearts of the faithful. We are about to notice some irrefragable evidence that such was far from being the case; but, first, we may ask how was it that, if belief in Joseph's high prerogatives and exceptionally exalted position really existed, it did not find stronger utterance in the first centuries, and that Joseph did not begin until later to receive the public homage due to him. St. Gregory Nazienzen believed that it was not fitting that the Church should in the beginning explain itself so clearly regarding the adorable perfections of the Holy Ghost, the invisible and uncreated Spouse of the Blessed Virgin, before the Divinity of the Saviour had been solidly established.[1] In like manner, it might be necessary that the faithful should not publicly manifest their devotion to the visible spouse of Mary in any high degree until the virginity of that Sovereign Lady had been acknowledged by the whole world. Let us hear P. Segneri on this subject. He proposes to himself the same difficulty: why did the Church allow so long a period to elapse before awarding to Joseph those honors which it paid, not to the Baptist alone, but to saints inferior to him? "I will give you the reason," says the sacred orator, "in few words. It was precisely because Joseph was so noble, so exalted, and so sublime a saint, and, it may be, so superior to all other saints. I know that this sounds strange to you, but listen, and I will make it clear. In those early times of the Church there were malignant men, of whom the heresiarch Cerinthus was head, who, in their malice, desiring to detract from the glory of an Incarnate God, asserted that, even as He was the true son of Mary, so also was He the true son of Joseph. This, you see, was a horrible blasphemy,

---

1. *Orat.* xxxvii.

and it was necessary for the Church to adopt every means to confute it. Seeing, therefore, that if she held up Joseph to high honor among the people, she might be giving the perverse a greater handle whereby to accredit their error with the simple, what did she in her wisdom do? She preferred to go into the opposite extreme, and only manifest a moderate esteem for Joseph, setting before him many who, without doubt, in merit could not take rank as his equals. Such was the rare prudence which it behooved the Church to exercise in order to preserve unstained the glory of Christ. Wherefore, I will not imitate a modern writer, illustrious though he be, who, turning to Joseph, besought his pardon in the name of the whole world for the little account made of him during so many centuries. The Church of God is guided by special lights in all her acts. And, therefore, I am fain to believe that, if Joseph was not always honored publicly as he is now, it was through prevision, circumspection, and a certain dissimulation, not through any neglect for which his forgiveness ought to be publicly implored."[2]

But is it quite true that the Church left the Saint for so long a time in oblivion, and gave no public testimony of the high esteem which was due to him? This would be an exaggerated, if not a false view. In the East especially we meet with proofs that devotion to St. Joseph was cherished from the earliest, that is, from Apostolic times, and many traditions of him were current in these regions. Papebrock, one of the continuators of the Bollandists, says that St. Joseph was honored among the Copts, or Egyptians, and his feast kept in the primitive ages of Christianity, even before the time of St. Athanasius, that is, in the beginning of the fourth century; so that Trombelli, following Papebrock, concludes that, from the traditional recollection of the Saint's sojourn in those countries, he was venerated there long before St. Athanasius sent mission-

---

2. *Paneg. di S. Giuseppe,* p. ii. n. 12.

aries to instruct the inhabitants in the rites and discipline of the Church of Alexandria.[3] In Syria[4] and Persia also we find traces of early honor paid to St. Joseph; and in the Greek Church his cultus is confessedly very ancient, for we have monuments of it from the time of Constantine the Great, and even earlier still. Martorelli says, "The site of an ancient oratory dedicated to St. Joseph is still pointed out on the slope of the hill between the Grotto of Milk and the Great Church of the Holy Crib, afterwards built by St. Helen, mother of Constantine."[5] In that sumptuous basilica, as Nicephorus Callistus testifies in his *Ecclesiastical History*[6] (quoted by Martorelli), was a magnificent chapel, or oratory, sacred to St. Joseph. In several of the Eastern menologies we find mention of St. Joseph. Thus in the menology of the Greeks, published by Cardinal Sirleto, we find these words on the 26th of December: "The celebrity, or solemn memory, of Our Holy Lady Mother of God, the Ever-Virgin Mary, and of the holy and just Joseph, her spouse."[7] According to Assemani, also, St. Joseph is mentioned in the menology of the Emperor Basil and other Greek menologies on the 25th and 26th of December, and on the Sundays before and after the Nativity of Our Lord. The ancient hymns of the Greek Church likewise bear witness to the honor paid to St. Joseph. In the time of St. Ignatius, Patriarch of Constantinople, lived that St. Joseph who, from his composition of sacred hymns, had the surname of the Hymnographer. He states that the feast of St. Joseph was celebrated on the Sunday after the Nativity, and he gives for that Sunday a canon which concludes thus: "Thou, O God-bearing Joseph, wast the guardian of the Virgin who preserved

---

3. *Vita e Culto di S. Giuseppe*, p. i. c. xxii.
4. "In the calendar of the Syrians the seventh Sunday before Christmas was the feast of the Revelation to Joseph, Spouse of the Blessed Virgin." —Florentinus, *Notes on the Martyrology*, March 20. See *Life of St. Joseph* by P. Vallejo, book iii. chap. i. p. 313.
5. *Terra Santa*, cap. vii. p. 166.
6. Lib. viii. cap. xxx.
7. Tom. iii. par. i. p. 499.

virginity intact. Be thou, with her, mindful of us, O Joseph."[8]

Testimonies to St. Joseph's public cultus in primitive ages are more scarce, as might be expected, in the West. The most ancient church dedicated to him in Italy, so far as we know, was a parish church in Bologna existing in the year 1129; but in all probability it was considerably older, for the suburb where it stood had acquired from it the name of St. Joseph. It must not, however, be inferred that St. Joseph was not honored in other ways, or that devotion to him did not exist in the hearts of the faithful in the Latin Church as well as in the Greek. It could not be that Rome, the centre and mistress of all Catholic doctrine, should have allowed the sacred fire of devotion to this great saint to be extinguished in her bosom. Rather, may we say, was it laid up in her bosom, as subterranean Rome attests. One thing we must bear in mind, that most of the churches in those days were built as shrines to honor the relics of the martyrs to whom the sacred edifices which contained them were dedicated. Now, of St. Joseph no actual relic existed, only some portions of his garments sanctified by contact with his holy and now, as we believe, glorified body. Rome possesses a splendid relic in the pallium or mantle of the saint, so much the more to be venerated as it must so often have enveloped the Divine Infant when clasped in Joseph's arms. This precious relic was kept in the ancient collegiate church of St. Anastasia, built about the year 300 by Apollonia, a noble Roman matron, in order there to deposit the body of St. Anastasia, Virgin and Martyr. It is believed that St. Jerome, when called to Rome by St. Damasus for the affairs of his Pontificate, celebrated Mass, during the three years of his abode, at the altar where this relic is preserved. The chalice of which he made use is still shown. In this ancient church, on the altar of St. Jerome privileged by Gregory the

---

8. *Preface to the hymns of St. Joseph the Hymnographer,* published in Rome by P. Ippolito Maracci, 1661.

Great, is a rich tabernacle containing a portion of the wood of the Cross, of the veil of the Blessed Virgin, and of the cloak of St. Joseph, venerated there ever since the days of St. Jerome. An inscription upon a stone on the right hand attests the antiquity of these relics, and the fact of St. Jerome having offered the Sacrifice of the Mass at this altar.

Allowing, then, as it must be allowed, that in the matter of public cultus there was a preponderance in the first ages of that which was paid to Apostles and martyrs, it does not follow that the piety of the faithful did not largely supply for this deficiency; and we have good reason to believe that it did. As De Vit points out, one thing is the public cultus which may have been conceded to any saint in the Church of Christ, and another, the estimate held of the degree of his sanctity independently of that homage. If the cultus assigned to any individual be, as it undoubtedly is, a proof of his sanctity, it must not be taken as arguing comparative deficiency of sanctity in other holy persons, who for one reason or another have not received similar or equal public marks of honor. If Joseph, however, did not in early times possess splendid basilicas dedicated to him in Italy, the pictures and basso-relievos of the Catacombs and of private oratories contain abundant memorials of him. The labors of Cavedoni, De Rossi, Bortolotti, Garucci, have gone far to vindicate the honor of the primitive Church, reproached by some with having well-nigh forgotten the glorious Spouse of Mary. What matter if the early martyrologies do not commemorate him?[9] His name was engraved in the hearts of the faithful and sculptured in marble and bronze in the underground cradle of the Roman Church. The Greek epigraph inscribed on a gem of the fourth or fifth century, brought to light by Cavedoni, speaks volumes for the loving confidence reposed in him by the early Christians. Thus it

---

9. Benedict XIV shows that St. Joseph's name was inscribed in the Roman martyrology before the eighth century. He also notes that his name was invoked publicly in the Litanies at Bologna.—*De Servorum Dei Beatificatione, etc.*, app. ii. par. ii. lib. v.

runs: "O Joseph, assist me in my labors and give me grace." Neither can we say that the Church overlooked St. Joseph in her festivals; for whenever she celebrated a mystery with which he was associated, such as the Annunciation, Nativity, Circumcision, Epiphany, Presentation, we invariably find that Joseph was commemorated, lauded, and honored, and often, in the Divine Offices throughout the year, is there glorious mention of Joseph in the Liturgies of the first centuries.

But it will be said, and has been said, that the Church from the beginning seemed to pay greater honor to the Baptist than to Joseph, for it celebrated, not only the feast of his Decollation, but even of his Nativity long before that of St. Joseph was established. St. John the Baptist's name was inserted in the Canon of the Mass, St. Joseph's is not yet there[10]; again, in the Litanies of the Saints, which form part of the public worship of the Church, the name of the Baptist precedes that of St. Joseph; from all which it might be argued that it would be theologically erroneous to attribute to Joseph, after Mary, superiority in dignity, glory, and sanctity above all the saints and angels.

The difficulty, taken collectively, seems considerable; but, examined in detail, it no longer assumes the same importance. As to the first objection, that the Church instituted the feasts of St. John the Baptist before that of St. Joseph, it would prove too much; for it would prove that the Baptist was superior to the Blessed Virgin herself, inasmuch as the Nativity of Our Lady was not kept before the 6th or 7th century, when the Nativity of St. John the Baptist had long been solemnly observed. St. Augustine, who lived in the 4th century, says, "The Church celebrates only two Nativities, that of John the Baptist and that of Christ";[11] and Gerson, in his famous sermon on the Nativity of Mary, clearly says that the feast of her Nativity was instituted by the

---

10. St. Joseph has since been added to the Roman Canon per the Sacred Congregation of Rites, Decree Novis hisce temporibus (November 13, 1962): AAS 54 (1962), p. 873.

11. *Sermones* cclxxxvii. et ccxcii. *de Sanctis.*

Church later than that of the Baptist, and in consequence of a miracle; angels having been heard on the
8th of September singing melodious canticles to the
Queen of Heaven. Any argument, therefore, grounded
on such priority of observance is valueless. The Church
had good reason for celebrating early the Nativity of
the Baptist. It was particularly described in the Gospel,
he was sanctified while yet unborn, his birth was honored by the presence of Jesus and Mary, glorified by
miracles, and it pre-announced the Birth of the Redeemer
Himself. Concerning Joseph's birth there is not a word
to be found in Scripture; it only states that he was the
son of Jacob. Again, the Church had good reason for sol-
emnizing the feasts of John the Baptist, because he was
the great Precursor of Christ, and demonstrated His
Divinity. As regards Joseph, on the contrary, it had reason for keeping him in the background and almost, we
might say, hidden, in view of the vile heresies of the
Cerinthians, fearing (as St. Bernardine of Siena observes)
lest the amplification of his cultus might furnish a pretext to the heretics to assert that he was not the reputed
but the natural father of our Divine Lord; and it is for
this reason also (as the saint notices) that care was
taken in those days to add "putative" to his title of
father,[12] a precaution which (as we have seen) the Evangelist St. Luke did not take, neither did Our Lady herself. The reason is obvious. It was the same as that
which acted as a kind of drawback on the public honor
given to Joseph by the Church in those early times.

The argument drawn from the insertion of St. John
the Baptist's name in the Canon of the Mass, and
Joseph's absence from it to this day, is found in like
manner worthless when we come to examine it; for it
would imply that Joseph is inferior, not only to the
Baptist, but to St. Chrysogonus, SS. Cosmas and
Damian, St. Agatha, and St. Lucy, because the names
of these saints were from the beginning in the Canon
of the Mass, while St. Joseph's is not there yet. But

12. *Sermo de S. Joseph.*

what Catholic would venture on such a conclusion? It has been already observed that it was the martyrs who were chiefly the objects of public cultus in the early times. The Bollandists[13] are of opinion that the Church of those days thought that it was most profitable to hold them up to be honored by the faithful in order to excite them thereby to imitate their courage under persecution. Accordingly, all the Saints whose names are in the Canon were martyrs. Now, St. Joseph is not honored as a martyr but as a confessor; and indeed, strictly speaking, he was not a martyr, although his whole life was an interior martyrdom, second in intensity only to that of Mary, the Queen of Martyrs.

But St. Joseph's name is placed in the Litanies of the Saints after that of St. John the Baptist, even in these later days, when the same reasons for reserve no longer exist. Does not this imply that in the judgment of the Church he is his inferior in sanctity? By no means. When at the instance of kings, prelates, heads of religious orders, and the devout laity—indeed we may say of all Christendom—the name of Joseph was, in the year 1726, inserted in the Litanies of the Saints by Benedict XIII, it was placed before all the Apostles, confessors, and even all the martyrs with the one exception of St. John the Baptist. It had been previously matter of debate in the Congregation of Rites as to which of the two precedence should be given; and, if it was ruled that it would not be convenient to remove the Baptist from his original position, this was because he was a martyr of such special and singular eminence, and belonged, besides, to the order of patriarchs and prophets; and, moreover, he had retained the first place in the Litanies used by the Dominicans, Discalced Carmelites, and other religious orders. Further, Benedict XIV,[14] after descanting on the eminent sanctity and

---

13. *In Vita S. Joseph,* 19 Martii.
14. This Pontiff, as Cardinal Lambertini, had been Promoter of the Faith when the subject was discussed under his predecessors, and had given his vote for retaining the Baptist in his position. His statement, therefore, may be regarded as conclusive in respect to the motives of the retention.

high dignity both of Joseph and of John the Baptist,
declares expressly that in placing the Baptist before
Joseph in the Litanies no regard was paid to the greater
or less sanctity or superiority of the one in regard to
the other. Otherwise it would seem to be implied that
the Church placed the saints in the Litanies in the
order of their merit. But who, he asks, without a special revelation from God could assert that St. Anthony
excelled St. Benedict in sanctity, or that St. Agatha was
greater than St. Lucy? We have, then, the best authority for knowing that the Church in allowing the Baptist to retain his position in the Litanies of the Saints,
and in placing Joseph after him, has passed no judgment as to their respective degrees of sanctity. That
was a point which never entered as an element into
the discussion. And what is here said of the Baptist
and St. Joseph may be applied also to the angels who
are placed before both of them, because such had been
their place in the ancient Litanies, and because of their
angelic nature, which is superior to that of men, not
because of their superior excellence or dignity.

It must be borne in mind that, although all who are
accounted most devout and learned in the Church hold,
and have long held, that Joseph ranks next to his august
spouse in sanctity and dignity, and above all other saints
and even the angels themselves, and, moreover, we may
venture to add, held it by implication from the beginning, as the statements and admissions of so many of
the holy Fathers abundantly demonstrate, nevertheless
it has never been doctrinally ruled, and could not therefore have been made the basis of the Church's action
in the matter in question. This was decided on other
grounds. No doctrine has been more devoutly held among
Catholics than that of Mary's immaculate conception,
and yet, until defined in the year 1854, her festival on
the 8th of December was called only the "Conception
of the Blessed Virgin" in the public offices of the Church;
neither was she addressed in her Litany as "Queen conceived without original sin" until the doctrine was

declared to be of faith. Such is the Church's mode of procedure. We have said that in the Litanies which had been in private use among the religious orders St. Joseph was placed after St. John the Baptist, but we ought to add that there was an exception. The Theatines, who were Regular Clerics living under monastic rule, and to whom P. Alessandro Salaroli, Postulator of St. Joseph's cause in the matter of the Litanies, belonged, invoked St. Joseph in their Litanies and private devotions immediately after the Blessed Virgin, considering that such was the place befitting her holy spouse; and such, indeed, is the place which it may piously be believed the Church is in process of assigning to him. If in her wisdom she should ever do so, it will imply no derogation of the honor and dignity of St. John the Baptist, any more (if the comparison may be permitted) than his honor was diminished when the Divinity of the Son of God was proclaimed by a voice from Heaven and all men began to flock to Christ. "He must increase, but I must decrease" (*John* 3:30); and this the glorious Baptist said without repining, or, rather, he said it rejoicing at the success of the mission committed to him of pointing out the Lamb of God, and declaring that it fulfilled his joy. And now that he is reigning gloriously in Heaven, he would rejoice to see the father of Jesus and spouse of Mary receiving all the honor so justly his due, and occupying the position in the public worship of the Church which would seem naturally and essentially to belong to him.

Chapter XLIX

The Cultus of Joseph in Later Times.

"JOSEPH is a growing son, a growing son." (*Gen.* 49:22). Such was the prophetic benediction pronounced upon the ancient Joseph, the type of the second, by his father Jacob. This prediction, fulfilled in the temporal order in the case of the patriarch Joseph, has been spiritually accomplished, after a striking manner, in his prototype, our great Patron. The process of growth is sometimes slow and imperceptible, sometimes more rapid, and in that of plants is preceded by a season when the germination is occult and vitality seems to be suspended, and, to outward appearance, even extinct. And so we have seen it, in a measure, as respects devotion to our Joseph. It had its hidden and inactive season and its slow expansion. Some of the secondary causes which, under the superintending Providence of God and the guidance of His Spirit in the Church, operated in producing this retardment, have been briefly noticed. They offer an intelligible and, to a great degree, a satisfactory explanation of it, but it becomes more difficult to account for the subsequent rapid and extraordinary development and extension of this devotion in the same manner, namely, by the consideration of secondary causes. True it is that it pleased God to raise up holy and eloquent champions of St. Joseph's claims, yet they would have been like voices crying in the wilderness, or would have produced only a partial and temporary effect, but for the

Spirit of God breathing in the hearts of the faithful, and preparing them, like touchwood, to take fire and kindle into flame.

The voice of the Holy Ghost makes itself heard in the Church in divers ways. First and foremost, He speaks by the infallible voice of Peter, defining and proclaiming a doctrine *ex cathedra,* either singly or with the concurrence of the Bishops assembled in Council. Again, He often makes His voice heard through these same Princes of the Church, though not with infallible authority until confirmed by the Sovereign Pontiff. And, again, He speaks through the body of the faithful, lay as well as clerical. How often we have seen the first movement making itself felt from below, welling up, growing in volume, and increasing in extent, and so ascending to the highest ranks, both of laity and clergy, until the final decision of Rome came to put the seal on what was thus plainly shown to be the will of the Holy Ghost. A comparison, or illustration on a smaller scale, may be drawn from what has occurred occasionally in past times in the election of bishops and other superiors in the Church. There would seem to have been no deliberation concerning the persons most eligible for such office among those on whose suffrage the choice rested, but, without being able to say whence the impulse came, or under what impression they concurrently acted, and without regard to prescribed forms, all with one united voice have combined in the same election. "The Spirit breatheth where He will, and thou hearest His voice, but thou knowest not whence He cometh." (*John* 3:8).

Something analogous may be observed in the wonderful movement and development of devotion to St. Joseph during the last centuries, a movement and a development which have gone on increasing in intensity, and are continuing to increase from day to day. Truly the growth is now like that of tropical vegetation in its rapidity, or, rather, it is much more marvellous, fed by an occult power, as was Jonas' ivy, which sprang up in a night to shelter his head from the burning Asiatic sun. Joseph is become, indeed, our acknowledged shield and protector, as he was the shield and protector of Jesus and Mary when on earth. He hides us under the shadow of his patronage, tempering and guarding us from the scorching rays of adversity and the fire of temptation. And this protecting tree, which has so marvelously grown and flourished in these latter days, has no worm at its root to destroy it as had Jonas', but will prosper and extend its branches more and more; for it is the tree "planted by the running waters." (*Jonas* 4:6; *Ps.* 1:3). "Joseph is a growing son, a growing son by the fountain."[1]

It is to the honor of their Order that "the Fathers of Carmel, according to the general opinion of the learned," as Benedict XIV observes, "were the first to import from the East into the West the laudable practice of giving the fullest cultus to St. Joseph";[2] which words must, certainly, be taken in the mouth of this great Pontiff to imply a more than ordinary honor, an honor superior to that which was given to other saints. For Benedict XIV lived in the first half of the 18th century, when the veil which had obscured the resplendent glories of Joseph had been drawn aside; the reasons which had accounted for his quasi-obscurity no longer existed and, indeed, had long ceased to exist. That such there had been Benedict XIV appears to admit, when he says that it is evident that there was now nothing to form an obstacle to the amplification of the cultus of St. Joseph, particularly after the large concessions made by the Roman Pontiffs in favor of its amplification.[3] The Carmelites, then, were the first to honor St. Joseph by a special office in Europe. If they possessed a more ancient one while they were in Syria, it seems to have subsequently fallen into disuse and been forgotten. Nevertheless, devotion to this great saint, to the revival

---

1. Hebrew Version.
2. *De Servorum Dei Beatificatione, etc.*, lib. iv. par. ii. cap. xx. n. 17.
3. *Ibid.* n. 16.

and increase of which their illustrious reformatrix, St. Teresa, was in after centuries to contribute so largely, and which the sons of Elias originally transplanted from Carmel, although it may have languished for a time, cannot have died out; for from them it would seem the Franciscans acquired it, and also the Dominicans. The Seraphic Order of St. Francis of Assisi was among the first to fix eyes of affectionate homage on Joseph. Every sympathy of their holy founder's heart, who so loved Jesus and Mary, and was so great a worshipper of poverty and humility, must have drawn him to cherish and promote that devotion, and to place the most unbounded filial confidence in the great exemplar of these virtues. The Franciscan legends, indeed, are full of marvellous instances of the Saint's miraculous protection extended to the brethren of their Order.

These two religious families, then, the Franciscans and the Dominicans, began even as early as the 14th century to cultivate devotion to Joseph. They were both of them soon to furnish splendid champions of the Saint's high claims and prerogatives; but the first to raise aloft his standard and proclaim him as the most powerful Patron to guard and to save the Church from the perils into which the great schism had plunged it, was a son of Catholic France, the celebrated Gerson. His name was Jean Chartier, but he was called Gerson from the village where he was born, in the diocese of Rheims, A.D. 1363. At the age of thirty-two he had already attained the distinction of Canon and Doctor of Sorbonne and of Chancellor of the Church and University of Paris.[4] In 1414 he was sent as ambassador of Charles VI, King of France, to the Council of Constance, where he used all his endeavors to bring about the extinction of the schism; for there were at that time no less than three claimants to the chair of Peter. Gerson, for this end, had a weapon in his quiver of the potency of which

---

4. A claim was set up at one time on behalf of Gerson for the authorship of the *Imitation of Christ*. Although this idea is now generally discarded, yet its mere entertainment may be taken as an evidence of his reputed sanctity and spiritual discernment.

he had no doubt. This eminent man had imbibed sentiments of the deepest devotion for St. Joseph from his master, Pierre d'Ailly, Cardinal of Cambrai, who, writing on the prerogatives of the Saint, had said that he esteemed him worthy of the greatest veneration among men and as deserving to have his festivals celebrated with the utmost solemnity, seeing that the King of kings Himself had been pleased to honor him so highly.[5] His disciple, the famous Chancellor, had taken up the same cause with all the fervor of his heart and all the vigor of his powerful intellect. He employed the great influence which his learning and high position gave him in many quarters for its promotion; he appealed to Doctors, to ecclesiastics, and even kings and princes, to engage them to join with him in procuring the establishment of this devotion; he even wrote a poem in honor of the Saint. But all this was surpassed by what he was moved to do, as we may well believe, by a special impulse of the Spirit of God, when preaching before the Council. To proffer advice on so high a matter to all the Bishops of Holy Church assembled in council required, indeed, no ordinary boldness. The sermon, moreover, which he was appointed to preach and to which such frequent allusion has been made, did not directly embrace the subject on which he was led to enlarge. His sermon was on the Nativity of Our Blessed Lady. Yet, leaving his immediate topic, he devoted three parts of his discourse to a splendid laudation of St. Joseph and an exposition of his supereminent prerogatives. Of the Saint's power of intercession Gerson uses these striking words: "He does not entreat, he commands—*Non impetrat, sed imperat.*" And these very words were addressed to the assembled Princes of the Church, who heard and approved. Such, then, being the position and power of Joseph, Gerson believed that, in order to put an end to the schism and restore peace to the Church, solemn honors ought to be decreed to him. "If for such an end," he said, "that is, to obtain peace

5. *Tractat. de S. Joseph.*

for the Catholic Church, it may seem good to this most holy Synod to institute something to the praise and honor of the virgin spouse of Mary, which honor shall redound to her and to Him who was born of her, Christ Jesus, let your enlightened devotion, blessed Fathers, consider."[6]

The Franciscans and Dominicans, as we have said, were soon to furnish ardent promoters of St. Joseph's honor. St. Bernardine of Siena, one of the glories of the Seraphic Order, was born, in 1383, at Massa Carrara. This great lover of Jesus could not but be most devout to Mary and Joseph. Upon the latter he composed a discourse, to which frequent reference has been made, and delivered it, not only at Padua and Bologna where he chiefly made his abode, but in many other cities of Italy which he visited, striving to calm the dissensions between the Guelphs and Ghibellines. Here we find him employing Gerson's weapon. It was by magnifying Joseph that peace was to be sought. Everywhere he exalted the glory of the Saint, maintaining that he was sanctified in his mother's womb, setting forth his dignity as the virgin spouse of Mary and foster-father of Jesus, and asserting that he had been assumed into Heaven in body as well as soul. It was while declaring this prerogative of Joseph from the pulpit at Padua, that a golden cross (as has been related) was seen to shine over his head; of which we possess the sure testimony of the pious Bernardine de Bustis, his brother Franciscan, who was also a fervent advocate of St. Joseph's honor and of devotion to the Holy Name, of

---

6. It is gratifying to learn, from the preacher's own testimony in one of his letters of exhortation on this subject, that our country was not behind in devotion to the Saint; for he says that in parts beyond the sea, meaning, no doubt, England, the feast of St. Joseph was celebrated with solemnity on the octave of the Purification of Our Lady, if not hindered by Septuagesima. The Carmelites, in fact, were in England as early as 1240, whereas their first convent was not established at Paris until 1259; which was the parent house of all those in France and Germany. St. Louis had imported them from the Holy Land in 1254. England, therefore, took the lead, which Scotland seems to have followed, for the Breviary of the Church of Old Aberdeen (St. Machar's Cathedral), printed at Edinburgh in 1509, contains the feast of St. Joseph for March 19th. The Nave of the Old Cathedral is now used as the Protestant Parish Church. The Chancel was destroyed at the so-called Reformation.

which St. Bernardine of Siena was the great apostle.[7]

To St. Bernardine succeeded, in the commencement of the sixteenth century, Isidoro Isolano, a native of Milan and a highly distinguished member of the Dominican Order. His work on the gifts of St. Joseph, to which frequent allusion has been made, contains almost prophetic announcements of the future glorification of our saint, one of which has been already noticed. The Dominicans, in fact, vied with the Franciscans in striving to establish the glory of St. Joseph. Albert the Great had even in the thirteenth century composed an office in his honor, which was not, however, generally adopted. Later on P. Gaetan, General of the Friars Preachers, commissioned P. Isidoro Isolano to compose a new office, which contributed powerfully to promote the cultus of the Saint in the Order. Isolano must, indeed, be reckoned among the foremost who labored to lay open to the world the heart of Joseph, so full of graces and merits, but as yet so little known, save to a restricted number of persons, chiefly belonging to the religious Orders, which all more or less distinguished themselves by their devotion to the holy Patriarch.

Meanwhile in Spain she who merits to be called, not a star only, but the sun of Carmel, had already risen on the horizon of the Church. Teresa of Jesus, born at Avila in Old Castile in 1515, had from her youth up conceived a tender devotion to St. Joseph, greatly strengthened by her recovery through his intercession from a protracted illness, which had baffled the skill of the physicians. She took him as her special patron and protector, and, when she joined the Carmelite Order, she seemed altogether imbued with this devotion, which may be said to be its inheritance, however much neglected and forgotten it had been; and so ardently

---

7. St. Bernardine of Siena, in expressing his wonder that the early ages of the Church did not promote the public cultus of St. Joseph, gives two reasons in explanation, one of which we have already noticed as probably true, viz., to avoid affording a pretext to heretics, and the other, that it was not customary with the Church to celebrate the saints of the Old Testament; but this reason does not hold good, for St. Joseph belongs to the New Testament as well as to the Old, or, as Suarez says, he belongs to both, a statement afterwards approved by Benedict XIV.

did she exert herself for its propagation, that many who have not given much attention to the efforts made in the previous century, and particularly to those of the learned and devout Chancellor, Gerson, have attributed its revival solely to her influence. It is true, indeed, to say that none contributed so effectually as did St. Teresa to make the love of St. Joseph take possession of the hearts of the great body of the faithful, and in this we may, possibly, see a special divine dispensation. Jesus Christ did not will that His Gospel should be published by crowned heads, or by Doctors of deep erudition, in order that the foundation of the Church might be attributed to Divine Omnipotence alone. For the same reason He would not propagate the glory of His foster-father and move the whole world to love and honor him by means of the credit and reputation of one of the greatest and most learned of men. No doubt, he and others who labored with him and after him have been richly rewarded in Heaven, but they were not to reap the full fruit on earth which might have been expected. Our Lord chose for this end a simple virgin, in order to manifest more clearly that this was the work of His own hand, and that devotion to Joseph was the inspiration of His Spirit. Such, at least, was the opinion of P. Patrignani.[8] As it was the Queen of Virgins who manifested to the Jews of old the high and excellent qualities of the Saint by taking him as her spouse, it was also, seemingly, well fitting that one of the most eminent and marvellous virgins who was ever seen upon earth, the seraphic St. Teresa, should take this same saint for her special protector and move all the children of the Church to venerate and love him. Or, rather, we might say, by making use of a simple maiden to stir up the piety of the faithful, the Lord desired the world to be persuaded that it was He Himself who had enlightened the eyes and touched the hearts of Christians in an extraordinary and altogether divine manner to gain them to St. Joseph.

8. *Divoto di S. Joseph,* lib. i. cap. xii.

This devotion has established itself among Christians very much after the manner in which some new points of faith have been ruled by the Church, or some changes in discipline have been brought about and practices of piety have been authorized by her. The Faith of the Church has always been the same substantially and in principle, although, with the progress of time, it has been more clearly formulated by explanation and expansion of its articles. The faithful were not in the beginning acquainted in detail with all the truths contained in the Canonical Books, but as time went on it pleased the Spirit of God to enlighten their minds to discern the inner meanings of His word, and thus to acquire a perception of dogmas of which they had previously possessed only a scant and imperfect knowledge. Such also has been the commencement of the extraordinary love which the Church now manifests to St. Joseph. From its very foundation it undoubtedly held that he was perfectly just, the true spouse of Mary, and the worthy father of Jesus, and esteemed him to be a great saint, neither has it ever failed in the essential of the devotion due to him. But it is true also that sentiments of piety towards him and veneration for his dignity have very much increased in later times; for, meditating on what Revelation teaches concerning Joseph, and on what the Fathers in all ages have written of him, men have discovered in him a fund of merit which they had hitherto only dimly perceived, and have examined with more attention the great obligations we owe to him, in which they had not been fully instructed, or by which their hearts had not previously been so vividly touched. It was the work of the Holy Ghost, and in the sixteenth century St. Teresa was His most powerful instrument for its furtherance. That century saw the rise and progress of the Protestant (so called) Reformation. Joseph was needed, for the days were "dark and calamitous," when God (as F. Faber says) is wont to bestow His gifts; devotion to Joseph was needed, and the religious instincts of the faithful were drawn to embrace, and, as it were, seize upon it as soon as it was presented to them. Of the seventeen monasteries, both of men and women, which St. Teresa founded, twelve were dedicated to St. Joseph, and every inmate of those houses was an ardent lover of the Saint, every religious a preacher of his glories, every nun a zealous promoter of his honor. Throughout every province of Spain and Portugal the fire which St. Teresa had kindled spread rapidly. Each Carmelite convent was a centre whence it radiated, and it was not long before her daughters had crossed the Pyrenees and were accomplishing the same work in France and Belgium. Teresa's personal influence, her sanctity, and her writings gave a wonderful impetus to the devotion, which manifested itself in the number of books which now appeared—Lives of the Saint, sermons, panegyrics, manuals of devotion, poems in his honor—all magnifying his virtues, prerogatives, and singular glories, the assured advantages of his protection, and the marvellous power of his intercession. To this St. Teresa had already given a testimony familiar to most Catholics, but which we must not omit to quote. "I cannot," she says, "call to mind that I have ever asked him at any time for anything which he has not granted; and I am filled with amazement when I consider the great favors which God hath given me through this blessed saint; the dangers from which he hath delivered me, both of body and soul. To other saints Our Lord seems to have given grace to succor men in some special necessity; but to this glorious saint grace, as I know by experience, to help us in all. And Our Lord would have us to understand that, as He was Himself subject to him upon earth—for, having the title of father and being His guardian, Joseph could command Him—so now in Heaven He does whatever he asks. Many persons whom I have recommended to have recourse to him have known this by experience; and many already devout to him have had fresh evidence of this truth."[9]

---

9. *Life of St. Teresa*, chap. vi. sect. x.

The learned Echius had already recorded his conviction that whatever Joseph might ask for us of Jesus or Mary, it was impossible that he could meet with a refusal; and Bernardine de Bustis expresses the same sentiment. Giovanni Cartagena maintains that Joseph has a quasi-right to obtain what he asks, a right founded on the position he occupied in the Holy Family upon earth, and the services he rendered to the Divine Infant and His Blessed Mother. Many similar testimonies to the claims of Joseph and the power of his intercession, of which St. Teresa has bequeathed to us her personal experience, might be cited. But enough, perhaps, have been given. God's time had come for "this dear devotion," as F. Faber calls it. An electric current seemed to circulate through the hearts of the faithful in the 16th, 17th, and 18th centuries, and not through Europe only, but wherever Christians were to be found. The following passage from F. Faber's work on the Blessed Sacrament gives a concise summary of the extension of this devotion to every country and clime and its diffusion through every class. "Gerson was raised up to be its Doctor and theologian, and St. Teresa to be its saint, and St. Francis of Sales to be its popular leader and missioner. The houses of Carmel were like the Holy House of Nazareth to it, and the colleges of the Jesuits its peaceful sojourns in dark Egypt. The contemplative took it up, and fed upon it; the active laid hold of it, and nursed the sick and fed the hungry in its name. The working people fastened on it, for both the Saint and his devotion were of them. The young were drawn to it and it made them pure, the aged rested on it, for it made them peaceful. St. Sulpice took it and it became the spirit of the Secular Clergy.[10] And when the great Society of Jesus had taken refuge in the Sacred Heart, and the Fathers of the Sacred Heart were keeping their lamps burning ready for the resurrection of the Soci-

---

10. "The Venerable Olier says, 'The Blessed Virgin gave this great saint to me to be my patron, telling me that he was the patron of hidden souls, and adding these words: Nothing, after my Son, is dearer to me in Heaven or on earth.'"—Herbert, Bishop of Salford, *A Letter on the Patronage of Joseph,* 1876.

ety, devotion to St. Joseph was their stay and their consolation, and they cast the seeds of a new devotion, to the Heart of Joseph, which will some day flourish and abound. So it gathered into itself Orders and congregations, high and low, young and old, ecclesiastical and lay, schools and confraternities, hospitals, orphanages, and penitentiaries, everywhere holding up Jesus, everywhere hand in hand with Mary, everywhere the refreshing shadow of the Eternal Father. Then, when it had filled Europe with its odor, it went over the Atlantic, plunged into the damp umbrage of the backwoods, embraced all Canada, became a mighty missionary power, and tens of thousands of savages filled the forests and the rolling prairies at sundown with hymns to St. Joseph, the praises of the foster-father of Our Lord."[11]

The Sovereign Pontiffs responded to the united supplications of the faithful, and proceeded to decree solemn public honors to St. Joseph. We shall not attempt to enumerate these concessions, the most important of which have been recorded by Benedict XIV as having been made up to the time of his Pontificate in the middle of the 18th century, and must content ourselves with a very brief notice of the principal. The feast of his transit on the 19th of March takes the precedence. We have seen that in Gerson's time it was only locally and partially observed. In 1481 Sixtus IV appointed it to be kept by the whole Church, and in 1621 Gregory XV raised it to the dignity of a festival of obligation, with abstention from servile work. The next remarkable concession was the extension of the Office of St. Joseph to the whole Church, and its elevation to a double of the second class, having the addition of proper hymns in Vespers, Matins, and Lauds, with its antiphons, versicles, and lessons taken from the 39th and 41st Chapters of Genesis, commemorating the wisdom and felicity of the ancient patriarch, who typified the foster-father of Jesus. This elevation to a double of the second class, with the addition of the hymns, etc., was due

11. Book ii. sect. v.

to the instances of a venerable servant of God, Sister
Clara Maria of the Passion, one of the noble house of
Colonna, who, having joined the Carmelites of St.
Teresa, was filled with the zeal of her holy mother and
labored energetically to obtain an increase of honor to
St. Joseph. The lessons of the first Nocturn, the chap-
ters, antiphons, and responsories, taken for the most
part out of the New Testament, were composed by Pope
Clement XI, and by his authority added, on the 3rd of
February, 1714, to the Office, which had already been
extended to the whole Church. The beautiful hymn, *Te
Joseph celebrent,* with the other two at Matins and
Lauds, is attributed to Pope Clement X, who was also
most devout to St. Joseph.

The next important addition to the public honor of
our saint is the Proper Office for the feasts of the
Espousals of the Blessed Virgin and St. Joseph, accorded
first to various religious Orders, dioceses, and provinces,
and ultimately extended to the whole Church. Gerson,
who had been very urgent for the establishment of this
feast, composed an office for it, which seems to have
been only partially used. Permission, however, after his
time was granted by Paul III to the Franciscans, and
also subsequently to other religious Orders, to celebrate
the feast, using the Office of the Nativity, but substi-
tuting the word Espousals for Nativity. They kept it on
various days. The same Pope commissioned an eminent
Dominican, Pietro Aurato, to compose a proper office
for the feast, which was adopted; and, finally, on the
22nd of August, 1725, Benedict XIII conceded this office
to the States of the Church and to the kingdoms which
had solicited it, fixing its celebration universally for
the 23rd of January. The last concession recorded by
Benedict XIV was the insertion of St. Joseph in the
Litanies, which has been already noticed.

But this was not to close the series. "Joseph is a
growing son." The conviction of his power and will to
succor the afflicted and the desire for his aid and patronage had been springing up and increasing in the Church,

and the more so as the calamities of the times thickened and threatened around her. A voice seemed to make itself heard saying, "Go to Joseph." It was that same Order of St. Teresa, ever singularly devout to the Saint, which took the lead in placing itself under his patronage. In the General Chapter held in 1621, the glorious St. Joseph was unanimously chosen as the patron or father of the whole Reformed Order of the Carmelites. An office was afterwards composed for him, and, with the Church's approbation, in 1689, the feast began to be celebrated under the title of the Patronage of St. Joseph on the third Sunday after Easter. It was generally observed throughout Spain in 1735. Every religious community, every Order, every diocese, not to say well-nigh every kingdom, was now seized with a desire to enjoy a like privilege, and place itself under the special patronage of the Saint. The Venetian State was the first that received an indult to this effect from the Holy See, which favor was successively granted to other States as well as Churches at their request. These requests were by no means limited to Europe. Allusion has already been made to the great devotion to St. Joseph which had been propagated in the New World. Mexico took a leading part in promoting it, and a Provincial Synod of New Spain had already, in 1555, chosen St. Joseph as the general patron of that Archiepiscopate and province, and ordered his feast to be observed; but, earlier still, P. Antonio Parades says the first provincial council had chosen the Saint as patron of the then rising Church. Nowhere, therefore, was the Apostolic indult welcomed with greater joy, and nowhere was the feast observed with greater solemnity.[12] Finally, the immortal Pontiff Pius IX had scarcely ascended the Pon-

---

12. See *Life of St. Joseph* by P. Joseph Ignatius Vallejo, S.J., himself a Mexican priest, who tells us that the custom of keeping the 19th day of each month in honor of the Saint began in the city of Mexico, but afterwards spread throughout New Spain, where, in many of the churches, its celebration might have been mistaken for a general jubilee, so great was the approach to the Sacraments. As a remarkable proof of the devotion of Spanish America to the Saint he mentions the custom of people giving or adding his name in Baptism or Confirmation so frequently that, when ignorant of a person's name, a stranger would always address him as Joseph.

tifical throne when, moved, as he declared, both by the example of his predecessors and by the special devotion which from his youth he had ever entertained for this great Patriarch, on the 10th of September, 1847, he joyfully[13] extended to the whole Church the feast of the Patronage of St. Joseph as a double of the first class. St. Joseph was now universally honored by three great feasts, and, with regard to the last, the Patronage, it is evident that the Church desired to mark the lofty opinion she entertained of the efficacy of his intercession, since of two only does she universally celebrate the Patronage, and that also with their own proper Mass and Office, those of Mary and Joseph. Pius IX did not cease in his frequent Allocutions to recommend to all the most tender devotion to St. Joseph next to Mary; and on the 9th of June, 1862, in his Allocution on the Canonization of the Japanese Martyrs, after having urged all the Bishops to encourage in their respective dioceses devotion to the Saint, on proceeding to implore the divine aid, immediately after the invocation of the Ever-Blessed Virgin he invoked St. Joseph before SS. Peter and Paul. This was the first time that the change was made, and it was significant, as differing from the practice of his predecessors.

But this was not all. It is very remarkable how in all her pressing needs and calamities, the eyes of the Church have ever turned to this great saint, and a desire has been enkindled in the hearts of many to do him honor as a means of obtaining peace. It was the plea urged, as we have seen, by the Chancellor Gerson at the time of the great schism; and again, a century later, when Europe was menaced from without by the increasing Ottoman power and inwardly torn by the Lutheran heresy, the learned and pious Dominican, Isidoro Isolano, was moved to lay his work on the gifts of St. Joseph at the feet of Adrian VI in 1522. Believing, as he said, on no light grounds that the most holy prayers of Joseph would restore peace, he besought the

---

13. "Magno animi Nostri gaudio" is the expression used by the Holy Father.

Vicar of Christ to institute feasts in his honor, to be observed with much veneration throughout the Church. And elsewhere, in his work, he had said, with a kind of inspired prescience, "The Lord for Himself and for the glory of His Name raised St. Joseph to be the head and special patron of the kingdom of the Church Militant."[14] In the same century, that fervent advocate of the power of Joseph, Teresa of Jesus, never ceased to the day of her death to hold him forth as our most powerful protector, especially in the great necessities of the Church. Such were the feelings and such was the language of the learned and the holy in all the latter ages of the Church with regard to Joseph, but the time had not yet come for his glorification as its Universal Patron. It was reserved for the days of tribulation which marked the Pontificate of Pius IX; and may we not believe that Mary hastened the day? Pius IX had defined her Immaculate Conception as an article of the faith on the ever-memorable 8th of December in the year 1854, and Catholics had hoped that now peace was at hand, and the days foretold by the Blessed Grignon de Montfort, and called by F. Faber "the age of Mary," were about to dawn; a season of triumph and a happy breathing-time to the Church before the last terrible persecution and the coming of Antichrist. But it was not to be so yet; and Canon Vitali entertains the pleasing and pious belief that Mary wished to share her glory with her spouse, and that to the mediation of Joseph, as well as her own, should the restored peace of the Church be attributed, and so she stirred the hearts of the faithful to turn to their Bishops, and the hearts of the Bishops to turn to the Vicar of Christ, and warmly entreat him to deign solemnly to declare the Patriarch St. Joseph Patron of the whole Catholic Church. Many of them now addressed petitions to the Holy Father, submitting for his consideration most learned and solid reasons; and fully did the Pontiff's heart respond to their desire.

---

14. *Summa de donis S. Joseph,* par. iii. cap. viii.

Accordingly, when the whole body, gathered round him in the great Vatican Council, unanimously renewed their request, Pius IX, who to his fervent zeal for the glories of Mary had ever united a most tender and affectionate regard for the glories of Joseph, moved by the Spirit of God, made no delay in satisfying the ardent aspirations of the whole Episcopate.[15] Thus, in the calamitous year, 1870, he declared the glorious St. Joseph Patron of the Universal Church, and caused the decree to be promulgated by the Congregation of Rites on the 8th of December, a day sacred to the Immaculate Virgin. By this decree Joseph's feast of March the 19th was raised to a double of the first class.

We are constrained, as heretofore, to omit many other concessions to the Saint's honor, as well as to forego the slightest attempt to notice the ever-increasing love and veneration with which he has continued to be regarded, and its exhibition in a thousand ways. It would require a volume by itself to undertake a history of that kind. By the Church's authority the cultus of St. Joseph has now been so increased and exalted as to exceed very much all that is paid to any other saint, excepting only Mary. The Holy See has now also—not dogmatically, it is true, but virtually, we may say—declared the authority and dignity of Joseph to surpass that of any angel or saint; since, although many have been chosen as patrons of some city, diocese, or kingdom, none has been recognized as Universal Patron, save only Joseph. Nor let it be objected that the Archangel Michael was already the Patron and Guardian of the Church, for it is easy to see that he is not so in the comprehensive sense attributed to St. Joseph. St. Michael, as the vanquisher of Lucifer, is appointed to protect the Church against her fierce invisible foes, like

---

15. From England alone were sent to Rome during the Vatican Council two enormous rolls heavier than a single man could carry, containing the signatures of nearly 200,000 people, petitioning that St. Joseph might be declared Patron of the Catholic Church. This was the result of an appeal sent from St. Joseph's Missionary College. The Archbishop of Westminster and the Bishop of Beverley presented it to the Pope.

some valiant general who, sword in hand, defends the frontier of the kingdom. He is not, like Joseph, a patron in the sense of having a paternal jurisdiction committed to him by God, who has made Joseph the minister of His court, both in the heavenly and the earthly Jerusalem. That St. Michael is not recognized by the Church as Universal Patron, in the full sense of the term, is proved, moreover, by the fact that his feast was never made one of general precept, or raised to be a double of the first class. The same may be said of the relative positions of St. Joseph and St. Michael as patrons of the suffering souls in Purgatory. The Church, then, has now by implication clearly declared the true position due to Joseph, namely, that next to Mary, his Immaculate Spouse.

After devotion to him had seemed to slumber for thirteen centuries, he began his ascent, and this delay and subsequent glorious development has been, as we have seen, in accordance with the designs of God in His Church. But it is impossible to find any parallel to this in the Church's annals, and, in spite of all that can be said, it defies explanation by any mere natural causes. Devotion to other saints has arisen in the ordinary way, and has either diminished or increased as time went on from various concurrent circumstances. But not of one, after remaining in the shade for ages, can a similar marvel be recorded, even in the most reduced and limited proportions. The course followed by devotion to our great Patriarch has been in itself a miracle, yet a miracle such as is easy to Him who is described in Scripture as *ludens in orbe terrarum* (*Prov.* 8:31), "disporting Himself on the globe of the earth." Truly the divinely ordered process by which it has been brought about is worthy of our profoundest admiration. "The harmony of the Church's devotions," says a writer in the *Dublin Review*,[16] "springs from and is dependent upon the higher harmony of her doctrine, which in its turn is interpenetrated and influenced by the former;

16. April, 1871, p. 413.

for, just as dogmatic definitions are the expressions of the Church's mind, so devotions are the expressions of the Church's heart; and, although the heart is guided and ruled by the mind, yet the mind is ever influenced by the heart. This is why (to use the words of F. Faber) 'the devotions of one age become the dogmas of another, as in the case of the Immaculate Conception; and the dogmas of one age become devotions in others, as it was with the mysteries of the Sacred Humanity and the Maternity of Mary. Thus time goes on, commuting dogma into doctrine and devotion into dogma by a double process continually. There is no safety in devotion if it be separated from dogma, though it may sometimes go before, and sometimes follow after.'"[17] There is nothing parallel to this outside the living body of the Church, as the writer proceeds to point out. "This mutual harmony of doctrine and of devotion, which may very well be said to correspond with what St. Paul calls the 'unity of the faith and of the knowledge of the Son of God' (*Ephes.* 4:13), is the exclusive prerogative of the Catholic Church, and therefore a marvellous confirmation to every believer of her divine mission to mankind; for no mere human system could ever have succeeded in weaving together so many countless threads into one harmonious design, as are to be found in the perfect unity of the elaborate lacework of the Church's definitions and devotions—we might even add, of her Ritual and Office. There is no harmony in false doctrine. The fragmentary Christianity which exists outside the unity of God's Catholic Church has no beauty of proportion, no slow and sure growth or development, no variety of devotions springing out of and interlacing one another, yet always exactly corresponding with the wants of every age. It is but an orderless succession of distorted and unconnected doctrines, abortive efforts, and stunted growths."

It does not enter into the necessarily limited scope

---

17. *The Blessed Sacrament,* b. iii. s. vi.

of this work to describe the joy and exultation with which this definition of the Holy See was received, or its fruitful and splendid effects. There was joy also, doubtless, in Heaven at beholding the spouse of Mary beginning to receive the full honors which are his due. Now, if the Church, ruling and ruled, teaching and taught, combined in a movement so general, and with such a transport of fervor, which may truly be called the work of the Most High, in rendering these great honors to St. Joseph, who can any longer doubt—we are quoting Canon Vitali—the primacy of Joseph over all the Saints and angels? Who can henceforth separate him from Mary's side? Who can deny him a cultus, of *dulia* it is true, but superior to that which is paid to any of the Blessed?[18] Gerson's celebrated master, Pierre d'Ailly, Cardinal of Cambrai, had written in his *Treatise on St. Joseph* that this saint must be highly glorified, for he had greatly humbled himself. Long years had our holy Patriarch been hidden in his profound humility, like a candle under a bushel, and had loved to remain so, but the time was come when he who humbled himself was to be exalted, and to be exalted in proportion to his humility. He was now to become the light set upon its candlestick to illuminate the whole Church with its beneficent rays. But if so, why has not the longed-for peace been granted? Of the power of Joseph's intercession and of his good-will who can doubt? If the Queen of Heaven and her spouse are both raising their pure hands together in our behalf, why is the Church still left in so much tribulation, and her foes allowed to revile and trample on her? This may be—we again adopt Canon Vitali's sentiments in preference to hazarding any surmise of our own—this may be either because great graces are only to be obtained by much and prolonged prayer; or, possibly, because the august Virgin, so solicitous for the honor of her holy spouse, desires to see him still more highly exalted in our hearts and minds, occupying his true post on earth as he does

18. Cornel. à Lapide, *in Matthaeum*, i. 16.

in Heaven. She desires that in our public, as in our private, devotions we should honor him inseparably united to herself. God joined him to her by an indissoluble virginal tie, and neither saint nor angel ought to separate them; that is, that throughout the world he should be placed next to her and be exalted above all without exception. Such was the prophetic anticipation of Isidoro Isolano, who, as early as 1522, wrote: "The hidden merits of Joseph shall be by degrees unveiled and made manifest to the whole world; and an inexhaustible treasure be revealed. The Vicar of Christ upon earth will command the feasts of the reputed father of Jesus and spouse of the Queen of the world to be celebrated to the utmost boundaries of the Kingdom of the Church Militant. In the calendar of the Saints the name of Joseph shall be sung at the head, not in the rear. Even as in Heaven he was ever above, so on earth he shall not be below."[19] This prediction of the pious Dominican is already virtually fulfilled; it remains that it be literally so, and this great truth be declared matter of dogma.

All that in process of time has been formally defined by the Church was, as we know, already included in the Deposit of Faith. Joseph, as we noted at the time, became patron of the whole Mystical Body of Christ from the moment that he was made patron and protector of Jesus and Mary. The less is included in the greater. The Eternal Father made him ruler over all His possessions when He committed these precious treasures to him. He gave him, it is true, a delegated, but by grace a real, jurisdiction and participation of his power, as Pharao gave to his ancient type; and these prerogatives he has not lost in Heaven, but (as St. Bernardine of Siena observes) the familiarity which subsisted between him and the Son of God on earth and the reverence He showed to him as His father are only perfected and consummated in glory. And the same must be said of Mary. No wonder, then, that his inter-

---

19. *Summa de Donis S. Joseph,* par iii. cap. viii.

cession should be more powerful than that of all the Saints, Mary only excepted; and she shares all she has with him. He has access to all, and, if she is the channel of graces, Joseph is their steward. "Neither power nor goodness," says Canon Vitali, "are wanting in Joseph; not power, for, being comprised in the order of the Hypostatic Union, being near to Jesus, and most near to Mary, he shares in some way the infinite goods of the one, and the quasi-infinite power of the other. Being, indeed, the most fortunate head of this Sacred Family, he can, in a certain manner, by the provision of the eternal counsel of God, generously dispose of the goods of both; and Jesus and Mary alike rejoice to place at his option and in his trust the dispensation of those heavenly graces which, for the infinite merits of Jesus and by the all-powerful intercession of Mary, are poured down in such abundance upon men."

Let us join, then, in the pious Canon's prayer, that the day may not be far distant when Joseph's surpassing dignity shall be declared matter of faith, and that the Virgin's wish that, after Jesus and herself, the primacy of St. Joseph over all the Blessed shall be proclaimed, even as his universal patronage has been proclaimed, may be speedily accomplished. It is impossible, when this honor is paid to Joseph and he is invoked by us with faith, that he should not save the Church from the emissaries of Satan, as he saved the Redeemer from the satellites of Herod.

The celebrated theologian, Matthias Navaeus, wrote in 1630 thirty-one encomiums of St. Joseph, which he called a crown of thirty-one gems for the spouse of the Virgin. In his fifth prayer he exclaims, in the fervor of his zeal, that it appears quite unbefitting that the blessed Joseph should be invoked after St. John the Baptist or other later saints in the public offices and prayers. Nor let it be imagined that to give Joseph his post of honor next to Mary would be to depose the angels and St. John the Baptist. They would remain in their eminent glory precisely where they were. Honor in Heaven, being bestowed by God, is associated with the place He has chosen for the Blessed one, be he angel or saint. There alone is his honorable post exclusively and inalienably his own. It is not as on earth, where honor is given conventionally and relatively, often by a false standard and as often withdrawn. It is real, essential honor. Therefore St. John the Baptist and the angels are not exalted by having Joseph placed beneath them, neither are they lowered by his occupying his proper post. His superior glory is no detriment in Heaven to their own; rather does it add to their radiance, even as the lower ranks of angelic spirits are illuminated by those above them. And if so, neither therefore does it detract from their honor in the Church upon earth, whose worship figures that of the Jerusalem above.

Joseph is a growing son. He will grow until he has attained his full measure and stature, and until the earthly Trinity, the shadow of the Ever-Blessed Trinity in Heaven, shall receive in all its members its adequate and predestined glory. All that remains owing to Joseph will be paid. The Holy Ghost will teach us what that may be, even as Our Lord promised His disciples, when speaking of the Paraclete: "He shall receive of Mine and show it unto you." (*John* 16:15). But in order that Joseph may thus grow to his perfect stature on earth, he must grow in us. We must learn to know him intimately in order to unlock the treasures of merit and greatness laid up in him. That we may realize fully the transcendent dignity of Joseph, we must draw on the inexhaustible storehouse of Holy Scripture, and reflect on its hidden meanings, hidden to those who pass over its oracles without scrutiny but open to all, unlearned as well as learned, who ponder them in their hearts, while to this fruitful meditation, most fruitful for both wise as well as simple, those who are competent can add the study of ecclesiastical traditions and the writings of the Fathers and Doctors of the Church, which, as well as the monuments which research is ever bringing to light, combine, when examined and compared, in manifesting what is so precious but has so long remained, in a manner, hidden in this great saint. All will thus, in their measure, be forwarding a work most dear to Jesus and Mary and most profitable to themselves.

"In order," says Canon Vitali, "that Joseph, our most powerful patron, should interpose for us, for our families, for the Catholic Church, for the whole world, what remains for us to do? One thing for us, and one thing for our Holy Mother the Church. We, by true love to Jesus, by sincere devotion to Mary, by the practice of Christian virtues, by filial tenderness and frequent exercises of piety towards St. Joseph, must render ourselves worthy of his special protection. All, of whatever state or condition, must recognize him as their mirror, master, and leader—princes, ecclesiastics, seculars, monarchs and subjects, pastors of souls and cloistered religious, priests and laymen, lettered men and artisans, virgins and married, young and old, men and women, rich and poor—all must hold him as their particular advocate, for he has to protect all in life, in death, and after death, that is, in Purgatory. . . . Then our Holy Mother the Church will certainly be neither reluctant nor slow to declare that Joseph is in glory and dignity superior, next to Mary, to all the angels and all the Saints, thus placing Joseph in his true position, always and immediately close to his spouse, without any exception, in the public prayers, sacred rites, and the Most Holy Sacrifice; and thus on the feasts of Mary her dear spouse, Joseph, will ever be commemorated, and on the feasts of Joseph there will be a sweet memorial of Mary, even as fitly takes place on the feasts of the holy princes of the Apostles, Peter and Paul." Many writers have put forth compendiums of the life of Joseph and devotional exercises in his honor, but how can enough be ever said or written of him? It was to add his testimony of the filial affection which he bears to this good and loving Father that the same devout priest tells us he took up his pen.

The writer, who has borrowed so largely from his pages, may humbly join in expressing a similar sentiment. The love of Joseph, and the desire to lend ever so small a help to the rendering him more fully known and glorified, have been his incentives to undertake this work. Should it, with God's blessing, have the slightest share in obtaining this result, it will ever be to him a consolation and a joy.

Decree of Pius IX Declaring St. Joseph Patron of the Universal Church.

Quemadmodum Deus Josephum ilium a Jacob patriarca progenitum constituerat universæ terræ Ægypti, ut populo frumenta servaret, ita temporum plenitudine adventante, cum Filium suum Unigenitum, mundi Salvatorem, in terram missurus esset, alium selegit Josephum, cujus ille primus typum gesserat, quemque fecit Dominum et Principem domus ac possessionis suæ, principaliumque thesaurorum suorum Custodem elegit. Siquidem desponsatam sibi habuit Immaculatam Virginem Mariam, ex qua de Spiritu Sancto natus est Dominus Noster Jesus Christus, qui apud homines putari dignatus est Filius Joseph, illique subditus fuit. Et quem tot reges ac prophetæ videre exoptaverunt, iste Joseph non tantum vidit, sed cum eo conversatus, eumque paterno affectu complexus deosculatusque est: nec non solertissime enutrivit, quem populus fidelis uti panem de coelo descensum sumeret ad vitam aeternam consequendam. Ob sublimem hanc dignitatem quam Deus fidelissimo huic Servo suo contulit, semper Beatissimum Josephum post Deiparam Virginem ejus sponsam Ecclesia summo honore ac laudibus prosequuta est, ejusdemque interventum in rebus anxiis imploravit. Verum cum tristissimis hisce temporibus Ecclesia ipsa ab hostibus undique insectata adeo gravioribus opprimatur calamitatibus, ut impii homines portas inferi adversus eam tandem prævalere autumarent, ideo Venerabiles universi Orbis Catholici Sacrorum Antistites suas ac Christi fidelium eorum curæ concreditorum pre-

ces Summo Pontifici porrexerunt, quibus petebant ut
Sanctum Josephum Catholicæ Ecclesiae Patronum con-
stituere dignaretur. Deinde cum in Sacra Œcumenica
Synodo Vaticana easdem postulationes et vota enixius
renovassent, Sanctissimus Dominus Noster Pius Papa
IX nuperrima ac luctuosa rerum conditione commotus,
ut potentissimo Sancti Patriarchæ Josephi patrocinio
se ac Fideles omnes committeret, Sacrorum Antistitum
votis satisfacere voluit, eumque Catholicæ Ecclesiæ
Patronum solemniter declaravit; illiusque Festum die
decima-nona Martii occurrens, in posterum sub ritu
duplici primae classis, attamen sine octava, ratione
Quadragesimæ, celebrari mandavit. Disposuit insuper
ut hac die Deiparæ Virgini Immaculatæ ac castissimi
Josephi Sponsae sacra, hujusmodi declaratio per præsens
Sacrorum Rituum Congregationis Decretum publici
juris fieret. Contrariis non obstantibus quibuscunque.

Die 8 Decembris, anni 1870.

C. EPISCOPUS OSTIEN ET VELITERNEN.
CARD. PATRIZI, *S.R.C. Præf.*
D. BARTOLINI, *S.R.C. Secretarius.*

Loco ✠ Signi.

Translation

As God appointed Joseph, son of the Patriarch Jacob,
over all the land of Egypt, to store up corn for the people, so, when the fullness of time was come, and He
was about to send on earth His Only-Begotten Son, the
Saviour of the world, He chose another Joseph, of whom
the first Joseph had been the type, and made him Lord
and Ruler of His household and possession and Guardian
of His greatest treasures. And Joseph espoused the
Immaculate Virgin Mary, of whom was born by the Holy
Ghost Jesus Christ Our Lord, who deigned to be reputed
before men the Son of Joseph, and was subject to him.
And Him whom so many kings and prophets desired
to see, Joseph not only saw, but abode with, and

embraced with paternal affection, and kissed, yea, and most sedulously nourished, even Him whom the faithful should receive as the Bread come down from Heaven, that they might obtain eternal life. On account of this sublime dignity which God conferred on His most faithful Servant, the Church has always most highly honored and lauded the Most Blessed Joseph next after his Spouse, the Virgin Mother of God, and has implored his intercession in all her great necessities. And now that at this most sorrowful time the Church herself is beset by enemies on every side and oppressed by heavy calamities, so that impious men imagine that the gates of Hell are at length prevailing against her, therefore the Venerable Prelates of the whole Catholic world have presented to the Sovereign Pontiff their own petitions and those of the faithful of Christ confided to their care, praying that he would vouchsafe to constitute Saint Joseph Patron of the Catholic Church. Moreover, when at the Sacred Œcumenical Council of the Vatican they renewed still more fervently this their petition and prayer, Our Most Holy Lord, Pius IX Pope, moved thereto by the recent deplorable events, was pleased to comply with the desires of the Prelates, and to commit to the most powerful patronage of the Holy Patriarch, Joseph, both himself and all the faithful, and solemnly declared him Patron of the Catholic Church, and commanded his festival, occurring on the 19th day of March, to be celebrated for the future as a double of the first-class, but without an octave, on account of Lent. Further, he ordained that on this day, sacred to the Immaculate Virgin Mother of God and Spouse of the most chaste Joseph, a declaration to that effect should by this present Decree of the Sacred Congregation of Rites be published. All things to the contrary notwithstanding.

On the 8th day of December 1870.

CONSTANTINE, BISHOP OF OSTIA AND VELLETRI.
CARDINAL PATRIZI, *Prefect of the Sacred Congregation of Rites.*
D. BARTOLINI, *Secretary of the said Congregation.*

Place ✠ of Seal.

Prayer to St. Joseph

O GREAT and good St. Joseph, chaste spouse of the Immaculate Mary, and guardian of the Word Incarnate, we place ourselves with confidence under thy protection, and beg of thee to teach us to practice the virtues of the Child Jesus. We thank God for the singular favors He was pleased to bestow upon thee, and we earnestly desire to become pure, and humble, and patient, like unto thee. Pray, then, for us, St. Joseph, and through that love which thou hast for Jesus and Mary, and which they have for thee, obtain for us the invaluable blessing of living and dying in the love of Jesus, Mary, and thee. Amen.

Holy Joseph, patron of a happy death, pray for us.

✠ Saint Benedict✝Press

Saint Benedict Press, founded in 2006, is the parent company for a variety of imprints including TAN Books, Catholic Courses, Benedict Bibles, Benedict Books, and Labora Books. The company's name pays homage to the guiding influence of the Rule of Saint Benedict and the Benedictine monks of Belmont Abbey, North Carolina, just a short distance from the company's headquarters in Charlotte, NC.

Saint Benedict Press is now a multi-media company. Its mission is to publish and distribute products reflective of the Catholic intellectual tradition and to present these products in an attractive **and accessible** manner.

 TAN · BOOKS

TAN Books was founded in 1967, in response to the rapid decline of faith and morals in society and the Church. Since its founding, TAN Books has been committed to the preservation and promotion of the spiritual, theological and liturgical traditions of the Catholic Church. In 2008, TAN Books was acquired by Saint Benedict Press. Since then, TAN has experienced positive growth and diversification while fulfilling its mission to a new generation of readers.

TAN Books publishes over 500 titles on Thomistic theology, traditional devotions, Church doctrine, history, lives of the saints, educational resources, and booklets.

For a free catalog from Saint Benedict Press
or TAN Books, visit us online at
saintbenedictpress.com • tanbooks.com
or call us toll-free at
(800) 437-5876